HEIDE HATRY
ICONS IN ASH

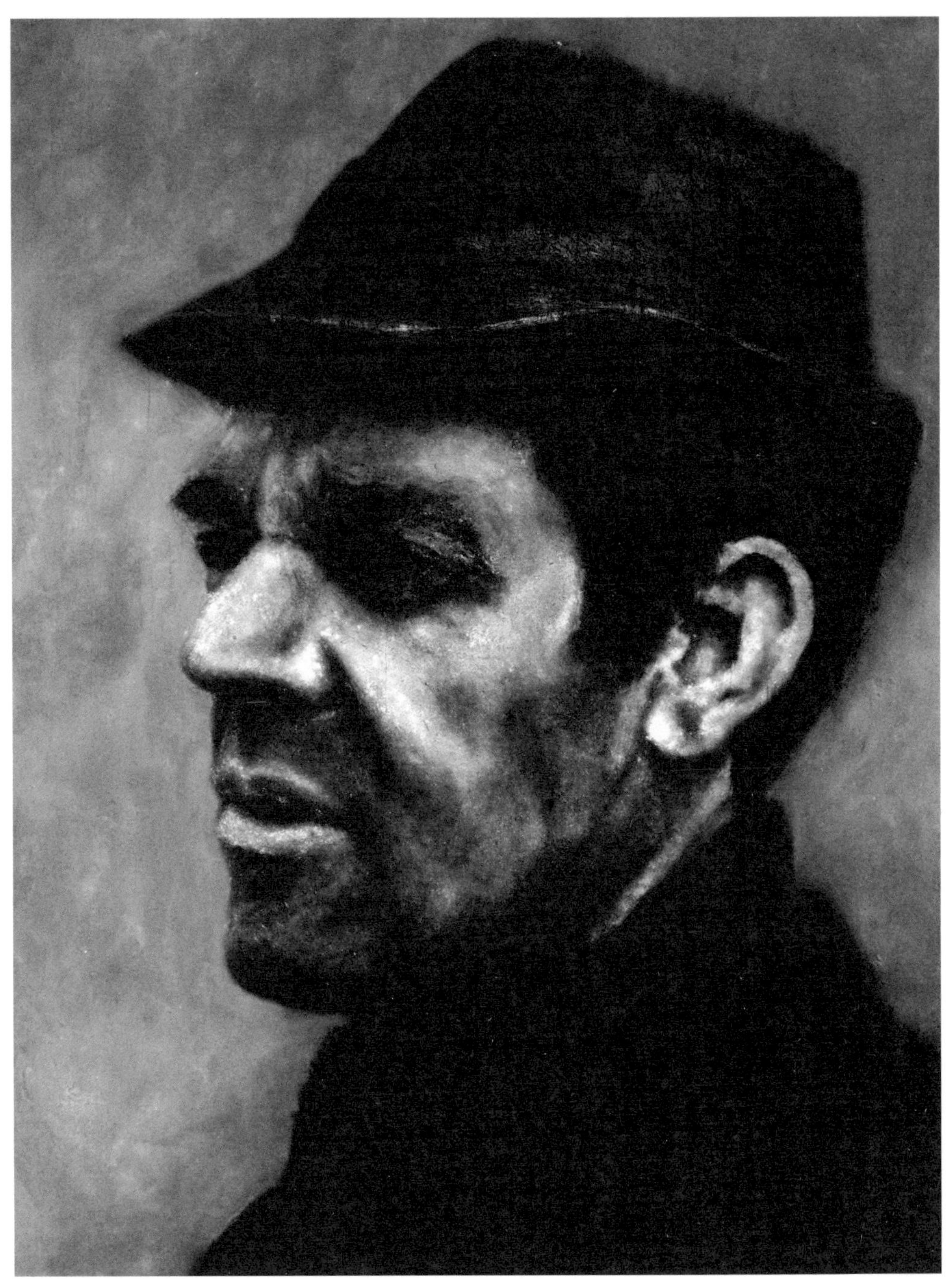

HEIDE HATRY
ICONS IN ASH

a collaborative conceptual artist's book

Station Hill of Barrytown

in association with
Ubu Gallery New York

For Paul Schmid
and Stefan Huber

Contents

APPENDICES

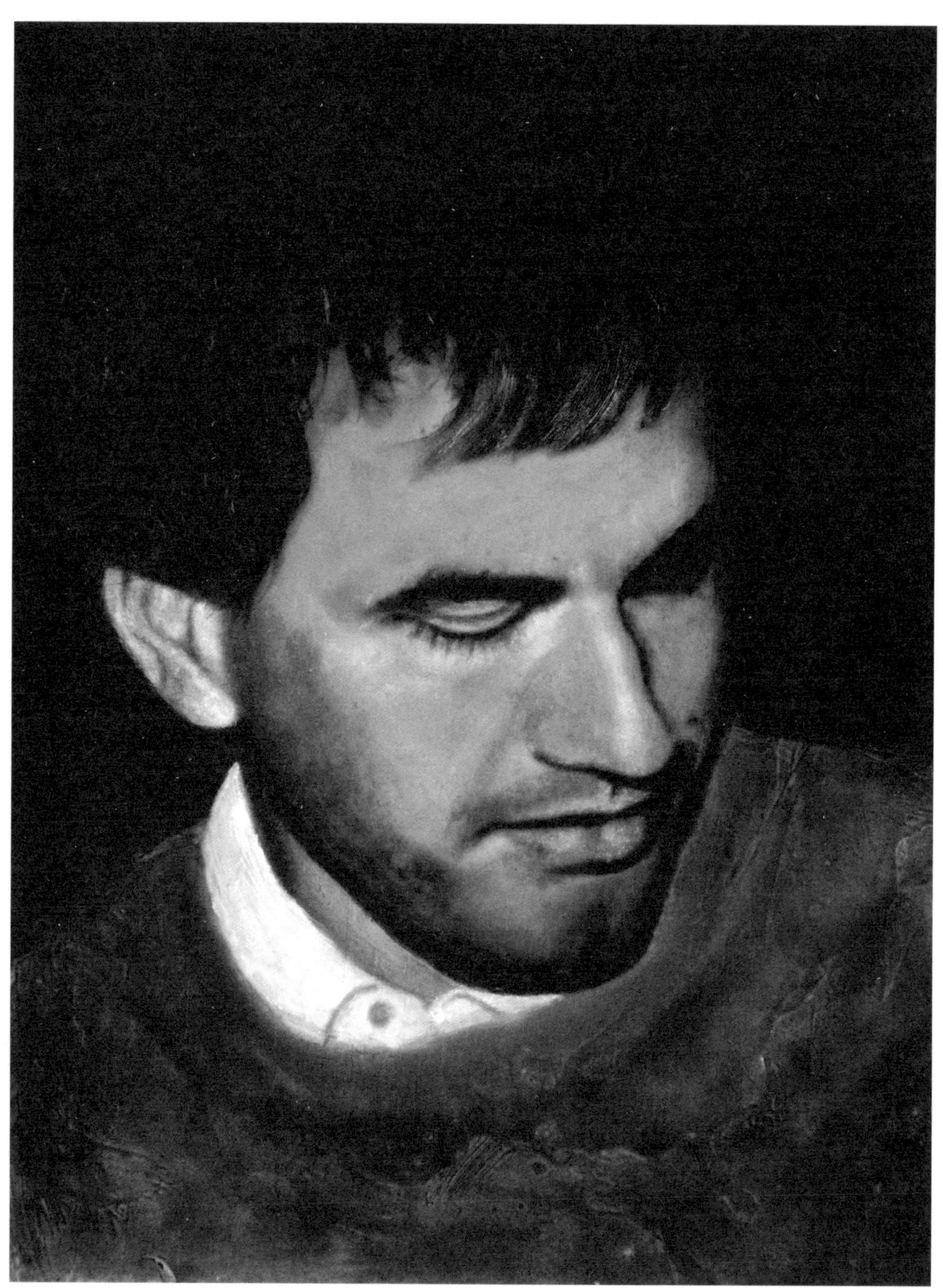

Icons in Ash: From Art Object to Art Subject
Heide Hatry

The idea that art is, or should be, subversive is so widely accepted, so weary and so reflexively invoked, as to be almost meaningless. And this subversive, or worse, "transgressive," art is patently ineffectual in the world. The art that I love doesn't just hint that life could be different, doesn't just hold out a desperate resistance against the irresistible or subtly insinuate criticism of a seemingly insuperable and basically unalterable "totality," but actually changes it *now*. It speaks to me, confronts and questions me. It is not merely subversive, but actually revolutionary. Standing before it, I can feel it working upon me in the shiver that runs down my spine, the heart pounding with confusion or racing with exhilaration, the involuntary tension in my throat, as if I have been seized and throttled by the work. No doubt someone observing me will think that something is wrong. And it is. Art is criticizing my life: telling me that I have not been paying attention, or making the effort that it demands, that I have abdicated something of my humanity, that I have been negligent. I see possibilities where there had been only things and situations. What had been rigidly silent is talking to me. What had been set in stone is suddenly in flux. We expect to see things a certain way, and so they cooperate: they let themselves be seen that way. But that is not what they are.

For a long time the materials that I use have been fundamental to what is happening in the art I make, and there's a reason for this. During much of the history of art, the aesthetic object dissembled reality, first to mimic it using materials that had been extracted and refined from it (minerals, plant fibers, animal reductions, etc.), and more subtly and pertinently, to make things appear as they are not or to distract us from what they are: to falsify history, propagate myths, support systems of oppression, reinforce artificial hierarchies as if they were the will of God, and in general, to imply that the way things are is the way things must be; that we live in a realm of facts; that possibility is dead. But there are other facts, which simple materials, evidence of the world, can bring to light, and with them other possibilities.

In the several large-scale projects in which I used offal from the animal-slaughter industry to create objects and representations of objects, my intention has been to exploit the disparity between image and material, between expectation and knowledge and, ultimately, between appearance and truth, to compel my viewer to acknowledge some of the unpleasant realities on which our pleasant, smooth-functioning world is built: the ubiquitous deceit, methodical injustice, willing ignorance, and, in the end, the great mass of death in which we quietly acquiesce just in living the way we do.

On the one hand, by building in layers of distance between the viewer and the art-object, and on the other, by using "real-world" material that we generally deem problematic and which we are at pains to keep out of view, I have been working with a different kind of aesthetic object, one that first retreats from the viewer who experiences it, and then aggressively returns once her guard is down, insisting on its truth. I think of this work as thematizing a potential of the artwork that is buried in the normal perceptual and social practices of receiving it. I am trying to make art *subjects* instead of art *objects*, things that *are* in themselves and which demand from us something that doesn't already exist: the response to something real. I am creating the conditions for an encounter with this reality.

When my father died, now many years ago, I was distraught. There was no one to whom I felt so connected at the very core of myself. Though we hadn't been able to spend much time together for quite a while, and certain misunderstandings had colored our relationship, I always expected to fix that when time and circumstances would permit. I couldn't believe that now I would never have the chance to make that happen. It took years before I could even think about him without collapsing inside. And then I was again taken unawares by death: one of my closest friends killed himself. In my devastation, the still unresolved pain over my father's death angrily returned to reinforce my grief.

My art ideas usually come to me in a sudden jolt, like a revelation – the solution to a problem I didn't quite understand *was* a problem. They arrive as if they had been gestating in secret and only now were emerging fully formed. I can remember that I already felt a strange calm the moment I thought: *I have to make portraits out of my father's and out of Stefan's ashes.* Of course I didn't have their actual ashes – in Germany ashes must be buried – so I was forced to use a substitute. Nevertheless, making the portraits was both comforting and energizing in itself – I felt that it was in some way a shamanic act – and once they existed, I lived with them as if my father and Stefan themselves were there with me. I cried and I screamed at them and explained myself and talked to them and listened, and soon their ethereal presence melded into my life: my connection to the people I loved was no longer broken by death.

Since then, I have made quite a few portraits for others out of the real ashes of the deceased, for people who were suffering much as I had been or in any number of other ways, and they, too, have experienced a deep solace in communion with these potent images of their loved ones. They often tell me that having them in their lives in this way has been transformative. Some say it was not the "closure" that they had imagined they wanted, but a re-opening, or a sense of continuity that has been extremely important to them; others describe their relation to the portraits as what they imagine holy relics must have meant to the ancient Christians, a powerful, ineffable, and irreducible *presence*.

In *Icons in Ash* I want to reintegrate life and death: to touch death, work with death, to be an artist of and for death, to let it speak in its mundanity, its grandeur, its familiarity and its mystery, its uniqueness and its universality, to redeem it from oblivion, to give it its own life again. For me, this is a fundamental act of reconciliation. Though it may be commonplace to say that in the modern era we have isolated or banished death from our lives, that we cannot bear to look it in the face, as if we are embarrassed by it, the simple fact of grief makes it obvious that a different relationship is not only possible, but that it is necessary. Judith Butler observes that the phenomenon of mourning tells us that death is inherently social. If we want to be able to understand and to live with it, we have to reintegrate it into our social being. We have to remain connected to the dead and with what they have meant and still mean to us.

Banal and unworldly at the same time, let's say tenuous, or maybe ghostly, the power of these deceptively ordinary images comes from something beyond their appearance, though that is still quite relevant to their effect, and they look the way they do for profound internal reasons. I would like to say that it comes from their *substance*, in a quasi-scholastic sense of the word, a notion that late modernist painting acknowledged in its own way in insisting that its images were in fact "just paint." My images, instead, undermine this always somehow artificial-seeming and folksy ethic in *being* the thing they represent. The fact that you are actually *looking at that person*, that person who no longer exists in our usual way of thinking, achieves something that portraiture has never succeeded in doing, though this was always its impossible ideal, supplanted by the notion that "art" somehow shows the "true" person in a way that he or she could never appear in life. Our feeling that the portrait has always held a secret is embedded in the quasi-Platonic truth that the greatest of them transcends by an ineffable sorcery not only the moment, but every moment, that they *are* their subject: We say, "It's you," when the portraitist succeeds in conveying the essence of the person. But even with the advent of the pure image, with the development of the photograph, which much more so than the painted portrait is always a relic from the past and hence in a profound sense a *memento mori*, the image is no more than a shade, for the person depicted has already ceased to exist before the image even comes to be. In looking at vast numbers of photographic portraits, we see what is common more than what is individual. They blend into a sort of typical human being, and show us the consanguinity of the race, its common legacy and its common fate rather than its incalculable specificity. We see emptiness; we see death. If they hold a secret, it is this absence, this loss.

My portraits, by contrast genuinely embody a secret: the secret truth of life. Not that we die, not that life is merely the unfolding of death, or that in death nothing remains, but that death is the relationship in which we stand or will stand to everything that is important to us, a relationship of memory, of transformation, of reintegration, and of art, which are in fact the only modes of immortality that we know. Death is our secret, and the way we keep it, the way we are true to it, is art. Art is always created from ashes, from the ashes of our experience, of who we once were, which becomes lifeless, forgotten, anonymous, or futile, only if we fail to make something of it, to tend it, to care about it, to remember. It reminds us that death is a very particular relationship among us, that it is ours, that we are the keepers of life for the dead and of the dead for life. We each have our particular responsibility to it, and only by abdicating that responsibility does death become the sullen and intractable force as which we tend to see it today.

In these small, modest images, with which I have now lived for years, images that do not merely represent but which *are* their subjects, I have experienced an effect similar to what I have sometimes felt in small, dim Russian churches in the presence of subtly radiant icons, the uncanny experience that we are not alone, that our truth is a simplicity that we rarely encounter. The icon is a peculiar object. Although it does not subscribe to what we normally think of as an aesthetic, it nevertheless projects a power that even the greatest artworks seldom achieve. And I think in this respect it is similar to these portraits in ash: It does not so much try to imitate something or to point beyond what it is; as to actually *be* something, not merely to represent it, and that means to be essentially particular. The "veronica," the "true image" – of course the fusion already shows that this is a paradox that will not be resolved – on the Shroud of Turin, to give an extreme and obviously problematic example, bears the trace of the actual presence of its subject. The contact that it embodies mysteriously persists. We remain within the charged field of a lost presence. In these *Icons in Ash*, our relationship, the profound, ineffable contact we have had with the dead, persists: and their life persists in us. This is the mystery that I wish to share.

Negation and Return

Gavin Keeney

I.

Everything we know to be true we have either experienced or must take on faith. This represents the fundamental, yet irreducible existential foundation for judgment and knowledge, whether of the Kantian type or the Husserlian type. If Edmund Husserl famously, and to the annoyance of many at the time, disappeared into subjectivity in his process of reduction that eliminated everything we cannot know for sure, he did not quite disappear into mysticism as Schopenhauer did at the end of *The World as Will and Representation*. In many ways Husserl's so-called crime was that he returned to the Cartesian subject. For Arthur Schopenhauer, the Germanic arch-pessimist, "representation" held no real promise for true knowledge, its claims to truth at least half mired in what can only be called ideological claims, or instrumentalized versions of the existential foundation noted above, averaged over millions of people perhaps, such that consensus via representation means very little to anyone seeking truth.[1] Instead, revelation calls to subjects, transfixed like deer in the headlights of Allen Ginsberg's drunken taxi cabs of absolute reality, and an escape route is essential.

Heide Hatry's project, unnamed at the time of its inception, eventually took on the name of *Icons in Ash* via the original suggestion of "Icons in Ashes."[2] The latter would have retained the powerful double entendre of a reduction of religious orthodoxy to ashes; albeit to substitute a very different order of religiosity freed of conventional justifications by way of a transcendental function that brings what is distant or remote (e.g., in classical iconology the saint or archangel) into a charged relationship with the here-and-now.[3] The holy icons of, for example, the Byzantine tradition have agency insofar as they are doorways to a form of sublimity in the world that is generally only understood in its being embedded in religious ritual. "Icons in Ashes" would have, therefore, freed the icon by way of a

---

1 To paraphrase Joyce Cary and his Abstract Expressionist protagonist in the novel *The Horse's Mouth*: "Half a moment of revelation is worth a million years of know nothing." Asked who lives a million years, the ne'er-do-well painter replies, "A million people every twelve months."

2 The artist in correspondence with the editor.

3 In current exegesis of the Event, such as in the works of Alain Badiou (and traceable to Husserl by way of Jacques Derrida), transcendentals are higher-order schema that escape capture in everyday experience but end up being encoded in the works sponsored by the Event through the fidelity of the author/witness. This is also irreducibly Kantian though it favors the outside (impersonal agency) versus the inside (artistic autonomy).

rhetorical iconoclasm, to speak of other things. In the case of the portraits made with the ashes of family and friends, Hatry's work touches on all of the above problems and all of the implied justifications for bringing the departed closer to those who remain in or of this world – but with the attendant question of whether the ashes contain any trace of the departed soul bracketed in classic phenomenological fashion due to the unspeakable mystery of transcendence and the ineffable nature of mortal remains.

There is nothing macabre in any of this, nor anything Victorian "goth" – though the faux-duplicitous title "Icons in Ashes" would, indeed, have been misunderstood as incendiary.[4] In expecting criticism of working in this way with ashes (human remains after all), criticism that is nonetheless legitimate but also of a personal versus objective tenor, an artist may undertake classic proleptic maneuvers to confound or divert, in advance, any controversy. It is called a preemptive strike – and it is fully justified in the Arts and Letters. Or they may openly court controversy, which is generally a waste of time. Yet the icons included in the project *Icons in Ash* have, arguably, a built-in immunity to criticism – for, they are holy in their own right or rite, and they partake of the mysteries of faith beyond any canon or doctrine. They are statements of universal sublimity – negation and return. Only those terrified of the same could object.

II.

In India there are charitable organizations that undertake the transport of ashes of deceased Hindus to holy sites for final rites and deposition in rivers.[5] Not all Hindus can be cremated on the banks of Ganges and ceremonially dispatched directly into the immense sweep of the holy river, slowly drifting toward present-day Bangladesh (formerly East Pakistan, formerly East Bengal).[6] This practice, tied so intently to holy sites and shrines, is partially and historically animist at the symbolic level. Shrines, devotions, exhortations multiply in India as elsewhere in South Asia. If, as projected, India has six hundred million people living in cities by 2030 (as opposed to China's hoped-for one billion by 2020), the deposition of

---

4 While several of the essays here invoke Victorian "goth," the purpose is to de-sensationalize what might otherwise be misunderstood as mere artistic provocation on the part of *Icons in Ash*.
5 "The local unit of the Sadvichar Parivar Charitable Trust . . . is a multi-faceted operation accommodating within its fold the running of a hospital, several eye clinics and the performing of philanthropic activities such as feeding *shira*, a sweet semolina dish, to pregnant women in hospitals and the transporting of the ashes of dead Hindus to holy sites." Amrita Shah, *Ahmedabad: A City in the World* (London: Bloomsbury, 2015), p. 129; with reference to developments on the outskirts of Ahmedabad, previously noted for ashrams amidst green space; i.e., the sudden appearance of anodyne high-rise office and residential towers, huge shopping malls, combined with low-rise middle class housing estates and theme park like temples, all representing the "materialization of the Hindu Rashtra – an actualization of the fantasies that drive the idea of a Hindu state . . . a socialized religiosity" rooted in neo-liberal economic expansion. Ibid., p. 126.
6 The tragic partition of India after independence has led to the slow consolidation of Hindu nationalism and the demonization of the Other (primarily Muslims, though the Hindu caste system might be seen as the basis for this hyperbolic privileging of faith plus station). Similar to the fiction of secular Israel, India is currently held in thrall to the dual enchantments of imported neo-liberalist capitalism and renascent, nativist Hindu fundamentalism.

ashes will no doubt take on a peculiar urgency through sheer volume, the animist aspects of deposition tied to managing a burgeoning population of both the living and the dead.[7] For neo-liberal India, there may be a business model awaiting discovery – the elegant and ancient animist practice corrupted by Capital. The peculiar late-modernist transformation of India now underway is marked by the preservation of the sacred rites and sites in concert with the application of imported neo-liberal values. Far from producing a secular state, the opposite is the case. The practices associated with the deposition of ashes is a type of mirror that reflects practices ancient and practices modern. And far from there being a modernization of these rites, the modernization of India is instead undergoing acculturation to ancient Hindu conventions of privilege and vacuous exceptionalism associated with the caste system. The intention of the deposition of ashes in rivers, while linked to the idea that once one's ashes have reached the sea it is possible to reincarnate anywhere in the world, carries a peculiar, yet apposite projection that the sea connotes universality, and that immersion in that universality is the best possible option. Yet the neo-liberalized aspects of caste suggest otherwise, and the possible neo-Calvinist expectations of the living for a favorable return to Earth is countered only by a reverse, non-self-serving exception – such as that exercised by Nehru, when he stipulated that half of his ashes be spread over India, by air, as if to confirm that he intends to return to India to continue his modernization efforts when/if Atma finds a new body. Nehru's bequest is an exceptionally graceful bow to universality in contingency (and vice versa), or a transcendental-contingent gesture to the symbolic logic of the holy rites associated with ashes in India.

What *Icons in Ash* mirrors, as project, is the sublime purpose of the project. It is not an innocent venture, strictly delimited by a personal agenda on the part of the artist or on the part of those donating the ashes of friends and family. It is larger than the sum of its parts – ashes, wax, coal and white marble, and the history of portraiture (plus history of funerary rites). Many of the essays in this book circle and inscribe the merit of the project in the personal – first-person anecdotes prevailing where the history of art or the anthropology of death give way. The range of responses by the authors is subtle. There is a consilience of sorts, however, around the theme of what remains and what has departed – or, what has been negated and what returns. It appears in the essays that eschew orthodoxy and bear witness to those existential rites noted above that signal a rapport with what one chooses to call truth (via anguish or via celebration, but all situated in the register of sublimity as universal, transpersonal agency).

III.

If neo-liberal India is quietly animist, neo-liberal America is quietly neo-Calvinist. Both currents run like an underground river through the socio-economic and socio-political landscape of their respective homelands. In the case of America, this underground river

---

7 These figures are cited in Shah, *Ahmedabad: A City in the World*, p. 153.

is also what makes *Icons in Ash* a quietly subversive project, as all such projects have an unconscious content (as history itself has an unconscious aspect) that the author or artist only half understands – willingly.[8] The work of Joseph Beuys is of this order, as is the work of Marcel Broodthaers. The production of irreligious-religious icons from ash signals a type of phoenix (mythic and imaginary), a pseudo-gothic conceptualism plus a subtle resurrection of faith in the most simple of material gestures – i.e., ashes as medium for portraiture. The return (resurrection through flames) is through the highly proscribed formal operation of the works. There is cheap formalism and there is sublime formalism. The difference is known only to those who favor the latter. From Kazimir Malevich to Agnes Martin to James Turrell the key is phenomenological-artistic reduction. And if, incidentally or half intentionally, Hatry's icons index a greater problem, the crass and avaricious landscape of neo-liberal America with its neo-Calvinist penchant to reduce everything to privilege and demonize the poor, the subversive side of *Icons in Ash* jumps forth from this crisis through its powerful torsion expressed through Nietzschean negation combined with affirmation – of ash to image (and of image to ash), of icon to portrait (and of portrait to icon), of transcendence to liberality (and of liberality to transcendence), of iconicity to critique (and of critique to iconicity). In essence it is all very personal – as death is the last thing that should be instrumentalized. There is madness in genius…

The agency of the icon proceeds in *Icons in Ash* by way of an elective poverty of signifiers (a progressive-artistic nihilism in the highest sense, versus in the abject sense) – i.e., holy poverty as principal and principled representational tactic. That they are almost photo-realistic is part of the conundrum of their artistic values (how they operate versus what or who they depict).[9] They are two-way mirrors that reflect what is before and behind the picture plane. As representations, what they broadly portray is the existential condition of their origin (mourning), plus the sensibilities and values of their principal spectator/ addressee – the donor of the ashes. Value is doubled. This series of reductions (as noted above) embedded in the image, ironically or otherwise, makes *Icons in Ash* fully an "American" project; and whether the artist concedes such hardly matters.[10] The threshold for the unconscious is, after all, the image as mirage. The reality of the image is the image

---

8 The poet Rainer Maria Rilke refused psychoanalysis for this reason. He was not interested in knowing precisely his sublations, repressions, or sublimations. He feared it would destroy his muse. For the same reason Gaston Bachelard, by way of Novalis, speaks of "dialectical sublimation" (in *The Psychoanalysis of Fire*) and "continual sublimation." The latter is effectively co-equal to Freudian repression. At some point or another the rational subject has enough information and prefers to go "extraterritorial" – i.e., off the map.

9 Hatry discusses this in her conversation with Marc Pachter included here. She does so in relation to the work of Gerhard Richter, which swerves between photo-realism and high abstraction, with his blurred works or over-painted photographs residing somewhere in-between as philosophical-artistic compensation for the confused.

10 Since leaving antiquarian bookselling in Heidelberg, Germany, and moving to New York to subsequently pursue performance and installation art, Hatry's various projects have taken on a quiet urgency that places them at odds with the *commercium* of the New York art world. The projects actually have no obvious monetary concern, and the icons clearly are "sacred" in this regard versus "profane." That alone justifies the reading that New York needs Heide Hatry far more than Heide Hatry needs New York.

itself. It does and does not exist in time and space. To paraphrase and expand upon St. John the Evangelist, "In the beginning was the image of the word, or the word as image…"[11] So also at the end. And to paraphrase and expand upon Jean-Jacques Rousseau, "When the social contract is broken or corrupted, leave it (for the immemorial origins of liberty)…"

The project *Icons in Ash* departs company with the sensationalist aspects of much of contemporary art, the apparent mash-up of genres and gestures that has followed the collapse of modernism and post-modernism, for a terrain that crosses both conceptualism and figuration, but without resort to inhabitation of either.[12] Perhaps Hatry's icons stop briefly in each sub-territory to consider the prospects on offer (to take the view), shifting then upward toward a "transmontane" or magical-realist region that holds no allegiance to any one territorial and artistic worldview. In many respects, and in terms of iconicity, the images are much closer to Malevich's late works of Russian peasants than the severity of his more famous Suprematist icons, the latter, which were indeed based on, or influenced by, Russian Orthodox icons. The difference would seem to reside in the austere humanism invoked in both Malevich's paintings of peasants and in Hatry's portraits of the dead – again, a refusal by the image (here a depiction of human fragility as it exists between the living and the dead) to succumb to external conditions, or a refusal by the artist on behalf of the image to facilitate the instrumentalization of the event of the works in the series. Each icon is destined for a private viewing by the donor of the ashes; perhaps to reside in a secret shrine or altar, hidden in a cupboard or wardrobe. At its best, the series *Icons in Ash* is process and performance – an extension, however delayed or deferred, of funerary rites and mourning, if you wish. But it is also much, much more. The double reduction (human to ash, plus mourning to portrait "painted" with ash) leads to affirmation of life. That it also negates ethically, artistically, and socio-politically "dead" forms of instrumentalism is its transcendentalist offering to the history of art and portraiture.

September 21, 2016
Ahmedabad, India

---

11 This is the beginning and the end (the rhetorical and visual foundation stone) of Andrei Tarkovsky's great last film, *Sacrifice*. Regarding Russian icons, see Tarkovsky's *Andrei Rublev*.
12 Here we must bracket the term *super-contemporary* because of its overriding concern with the living artist and the spectacle of the *commercium* of the art world, plus its general disregard of history and tradition. In other words, its immense self-regard.

THE GOOD DEATH: SOME REFLECTIONS ON THE PHILOSOPHICAL APPREHENSION OF DEATH IN THE WEST

John Wronoski

Death is the muse of philosophy. – Arthur Schopenhauer

There's no dead man that's better than any living man, and all living men are more or less the same. – John Merrick Eisenlohr, who graciously attributed it to William Faulkner

Metaphysical categories are not merely an ideology concealing the social system; at the same time they express its nature, the truth about it, and in their changes are precipitated those in its most central experiences. Thus death comes within the scope of history, and the latter in turn can only be understood through it. – Theodor W. Adorno

The thought of suicide is a great consolation; by means of it one gets through many a dark night. – Friedrich Nietzsche

The real event of death is imaginary. – Jean Baudrillard

Regarding death in itself, even the philosophers who have been most voluble on the subject, for whom it is at the heart of ethics, metaphysics, epistemology, politics, poetics, psychology, aesthetics, linguistics, even logic – and ponder for a moment what that means in each of these realms – have concurred that there is actually nothing to say. It is a cipher, the utterly intimate and uniquely personal experience that we (can) never actually have – as Wittgenstein said, "Death is not something that we experience." It is (beyond) the limit of our language (though for many it is the very essence of language: The word is the death of the thing), whose inherent ambiguity admits the possibility that it is also everything, or at any rate, just about anything, and of course, nothing. Statements of the form "death is ____" or "____ is death," with a special inclination toward the provocative, paradoxical, or unexpected, are abundant in the annals of human letters, as they are in ordinary speech, and for almost every one of them, its opposite has been compellingly turned out as well.[1] As Levinas writes, "There is no determinate being, everything can count for everything else." How much more so for "something" that is not being at all.

---

1 For example; Death is God; To look upon God is death; Death is immortal; Death has been vanquished; Death is the immutable; Death is nothing; Death is life; Life is death; Death is knowledge; Knowledge is death; Death is peace; Peace is death; Reproduction is the beginning of death; The truth is death; Death is truth; Death is illusory; Death is the refuge of illusion; Death is reality; Death is a metaphor; Death is hope; Hope is death; The past is death; The future is death; Death is cruel; Death is kind; Death is other; Death is my own; Love is the death of the self; Creation is death;

Although Socrates famously described philosophy as practice for death (or preparation or rehearsal for death, or, in some translations, and more piquantly, the practice *of* death), he nevertheless dismisses the mortal fretting over it that must have been commonplace even among the noble Greeks as time wasted pondering the imponderable,[2] in which he was eloquently, or flippantly, followed by Diogenes, Epicurus,[3] and Cicero, among others. And difficult though it is to gainsay their insight, it is perhaps even more so to submit to the early Wittgenstein's dour injunction, that "of that about which we cannot speak, we must remain silent," for the thing we cannot talk about is at the center of our concerns. And indeed impervious and still persistent mythologies have been formed and systems or anti-systems or potent fragments of thought still crystalize around it. It is the nothing on the basis of which, in relationship to which, everything human *is*, by which our existence is articulated and made meaningful. We might well wonder whether philosophy, or for that matter, poetry, or maybe even society plain and simple, would exist at all in a world without death. Immortality might invoke Eden, or perhaps a desperate longing even surpassing the thirst for life (or flight from death) that would seem to have animated our actual history.

The mere fact of the generational continuity of human society dictates that our lives are permeated with death, nurtured by it. We live among the creations of the dead, we are dominated and even oppressed by them, with little chance of much altering the ways of life they have established, at least in their deepest existential core, as they confront us during our own. We live amid death, in fact death and the legacy of the dead is really the most stable, the most reliable, and in some sense the most beautiful aspect of our world. Our words are the words of others, our ideas the ideas of others, of the dead; they flow from sources we cannot locate, from memory, the realm in which the dead live, in which dead moments, people, ideas, practices, and beliefs live on. Thoughts, ideas, are ghosts, which speak to us from a past or a no-where (utopia); memory is bringing things back from the dead; knowledge, for Plato, is memory with which we have returned from the beyond.

Even in an era of blinding technological change, the crucial determinants of human behavior are far more likely to stretch back into dead antiquity (and collaterally, into irrecoverable childhood) than to respond essentially to the cutting edge of the present. We walk among the dead, learn from them, hear, read, and respect their words as we rarely do those of the living (and theirs, too, arise from among those of the dead). Death is under

---

Language is death; Literature is death; Philosophy is death; Change is death; Stasis is death; Dialectics is death; Every death is different; Death is always the same; Death is but an instant; Death is forever; Death is impossible; Death is all (there is); All is death; Death kills the world; Death is constant; Death never takes place; The past is death; Death is always in the future; Death is eternal; Death *is*, etc.

2 In Adorno's analysis, Heidegger, too, disdained what he called "brooding over death." "[He] sought to use reflection on death to discourage, precisely, reflection on death." Theodor W. Adorno, *Metaphysics: Concept and Problems* (Stanford, CA: Stanford University Press, 2001), p. 131.

3 Epicurus's well-known and elegant argument runs: Why should I fear death? If I am, then death is not. If death is, then I am not. Why should I fear that which can only exist when I do not?

our feet, mingled in the waters of Earth, it is the sustenance of fire; we breathe it, feed upon it, move our engines and our economies with it; we live through it, we live on it, upon it: all life is founded on death, coexists with it, and even subsists on it. We require death in order to live, we kill, or which secretly amounts to the same thing, allow others to die, in order to live and, almost universally, obliviously to what we, or some of the best of us at least, might have learned or come to believe over many centuries,[4] for we have elaborated vast systems of thought and all-encompassing structures of culture and social practice devoted to understanding, managing, and containing death, including deciding, if mostly tacitly, or by delegation, who shall die that we might live. Some will say that the strict purpose and inspiration of human culture has been to address the fact of our death, to come to terms with or to resist it, even to distract ourselves from it or to defer thinking about it at all, Scheherazade-like, or, to deny it altogether. It would not be too much to say that culture is the work of death. Though we know that our ideas of freedom, of responsibility, of decision, with which our ideas of death are mingled, are historical, that they have come into existence, that they are not "ontological," there is still a sense, after all this time, in which we actually do not know whether we have moved beyond the most primitive relationship to death, or whether our developed relationship to it is really progress rather than self-delusion, mere words and obfuscation rather than actual understanding. It is not very difficult to get even the most rarified philosopher to admit that she does not really know what happens to us after death nor what our appropriate relationship to it must be, never mind all the rest.

The history of Western philosophy might well be seen as a politics of death. From the very outset, death has both oriented its agenda and served as the test of its seriousness, or more pointedly, of its worth; it has provided the perspective from which the relative nullity of opposing ways of thinking, or *a fortiori*, of not thinking, has been argued. And the millennia-long debate over, or struggle to control the terms under which we understand the meaning of death has had profound consequences for how we have envisioned both our political lives and our ethical responsibilities. We might go so far as to say that what is at stake in the politics of death is precisely the content of ethics.

What it means to die has always been understood to address, if perhaps not to answer, the fundamental questions of who we are, of why we exist, and the philosophical enterprise has, accordingly, always extrapolated from what or who it has concluded we are at the various stages of its transit to how we should be: We are beings for whom self-understanding is self-determination. Unlike the literary "understanding" of death exemplified in the epic or in tragic drama, in which it remains essentially incomprehensible – as didactic as its presentation might be, death is a matter of fate, or the province of the gods, its ways opaque to men, and any insight we are afforded by the spectacle of the deaths of our heroes can

---

4 We still, after millennia, accept the "truth" that war is a "separate" province in which murder may be justly and justifi-ably perpetrated.

be only that of the helpless spectator – philosophy began with the proposition that death is meaningful, that to ignore death means precisely never to become human, that we can conjure with its meaning, and in fact, that we can take a hand in making it meaningful.[5] The notion of the good life, of the meaningful life, has always been intimately entwined with a teaching of the meaning of death.[6] As Jacques Derrida said in his final interview, "We learn to live from death [and the other]."

To the ordinary person, the non-philosopher, as Socrates observes in the *Phaedo*, the practice of philosophy is, in itself, more or less the equivalent of death in its rejection of, disdain for, or simple neglect of the things that make life bearable, perhaps even pleasant or positively exciting for most of its inhabitants, its progressive effort to do without them for the sake of thought, which can thrive, it would seem, only in their absence, a notion in which we might already locate a little potential quibble with the philosophical project in general. And Socrates agrees, but with the qualification that the philosopher's death-in-life is evidence of his abiding passion for truth and far from a privation or a punishment – rather, if anything, a divine charge – and his death *to* his body means the death of his thralldom to worldly concerns, as he projects will be, in heightened form, the death *of* his body. Since the philosopher "is always pursuing death and dying," since he sees it (yes, death and dying) as the proper occupation of a lifetime, why would he not be gratified when it finally arrives?[7]

For Socrates, in a way that parallels his constant pursuit and always deferred attainment of wisdom, though the philosopher is the votary of death, he nevertheless lives within and necessarily relates to a community that holds unrestricted sway over the lives (and deaths) of its citizens (a phenomenon described by Hegel, under far different social conditions, as the pure prerogative of the state) without being able to question, since his relation to it is essential, the power it wields. For him, philosophy is not an asceticism, or a standing outside of the enveloping social structure, but a specifically political calling, while it is Plato's political motive to apply stress to just this aspect of state power, and communal life, in advancing his own meritocratic (or perhaps literally "aristocratic") conception of the state. He has Socrates take pains throughout the death dialogues to make reference to the "heroes" whose lives have been exacted in the vagaries of state-sanctioned, or even state-initiated warfare, even, or rather, especially, under the shadow of his own impending "sacrifice." He therefore stands at a historical and philosophical crossroads at which he – the philosopher – seizes the reins of death, appears both to undermine the hypocrisy of the state and to sublate the reigning understanding of death, insisting that at its highest pitch

---

5 In fact, the meaning of the death of Socrates, the first philosopher, is precisely that he dislodges the trajectory of fate; he overpowers it through the assertion of his (rational) will, infusing it with human as opposed to otherworldly meaning.

6 Even a soul as profound as Tolstoy's was collapsed by the possibility that death was meaningless, i.e. (in his case), that it spelled the end of existence, and he was briefly on the verge of suicide on that account.

7 At the risk of getting slightly ahead of ourselves, is not Plato/Socrates saying that the philosopher's "own thing" (his essential, true, and just being) is *to die*?

– that to which the self-aware human being must aspire – death modeled on the example of Socrates is also an act of heroism, but of true heroism, chosen in full understanding of its social and ethical if perhaps not its (possibly chimerical) metaphysical meaning, and not merely the more or less blind loyalty or cleverly extorted conformism of the commonly acknowledged hero. Socrates certainly saw the human relationship to death as an ethical matter, as a matter of virtue in the same sense that a hero's death for his *polis* was considered a matter of virtue, and he unhesitatingly exemplified his view in his own dying.

Henceforth, and the prerogative has been purchased by Socrates, the philosopher is the one who speaks of death, who controls the discourse around it, who establishes the conditions for the good death,[8] which are scarcely distinguishable from the conditions for the good life, though with the obvious and crucial proviso that the former has a determining effect on the latter, whereas the disposition of the latter might well be considered to be in abeyance pending resolution of the former. Although it would be too much to say that the philosopher is the master of death, that is indeed the image that both Platonism and, later, Christianity are keen to portray, a (notionally salubrious) falsehood to which the extraordinary valor of this Socrates or the selflessness of that Jesus lends credence among the more fearful, oblivious, or unreflective, and establishes an impossible or nearly impossible model for their disciples as the standard of ethical action, initially perhaps in relationship only to the matter of death, but inevitably to ethical action *tout court*.

That the deaths of two obscure and distinctly humble teachers, or more improbably, philosophers – not soldiers, kings, heroes, rebels, or even selfless parents, mind you – more than two millennia ago remain the most remembered, contemplated, discussed, and perhaps even the most remarkable instances of individual human death in Western history, its benchmark, if you will, and this in spite of the fact that neither of them left a written legacy, though at least one could surely write and the other, whose acolytes did not set about formulating his posterity until several generations after his death, quite possibly could as well, would appear to say much about the nature, quality, and standing of our ideas of death over the centuries. First, perhaps, that there didn't seem to be a lot more that could be said for quite a long time, at least in part because the inaugural philosophical relationship to death was so definitive, so powerful and so extraordinary, and second, that the embodiment of such standards as theirs implied would become all but inconceivable *vis-à-vis* the vastly more complicated, if not necessarily deeper, understandings of our responsibility to death in modernity. In fact, while both of their deaths might reasonably be seen as sophisticated forms of suicide,[9] or, conversely, as acts of philosophical terrorism, the way that they died, and the reasons for which they chose to accept, or really, to actualize

---

8 The very term, "good death" sounds like an effort to domesticate it.

9 The "greatest" deaths almost require that choice be fundamentally involved, otherwise they must appear, like all our deaths, to be something to which we are subjected, and hence over which we have, in the end, no control. Our heroes stride inexorably *toward* their fates.

their "fates," established a precedent of thinking about death and about how that should be done in its relationship to life, to meaning, and to social structure, that has by and large persisted, its many curious twists and turns notwithstanding, into the present, insuring that a fundamental self-doubt remains a crucial aspect of that endeavor for almost everyone (else), and hence at least some measure of philosophical engagement as well.

In a time, such as our own, in which mere existence is widely considered to be a good in itself, when life is commonly viewed as essentially precious, an unquestionable "gift," it might be problematic, at least in the West, to understand how such intelligent men with "such rich futures still ahead of them"[10] could have accepted, nay, chosen, deaths that a few simple words, or a conciliatory gesture on their part, or even mere retreat, would have been sufficient to forestall. Of course, even the slightest consideration of the inveterate practice of questioning the way things are, which was the principal fault of both of them, is quite enough to suggest that they were already less sanguine about existence as it is than the common run of men; and "the many," "*hoi polloi*," could understand that and grasp that they were dissatisfied and headed for a bad end based solely on their disturbing propensity for thinking (too much) – that, and talking quite a lot.

Socrates famously declared – at least it strikes us as a declaration as it has echoed down through the ages – that "the unexamined life is not worth living." He himself continued to examine his own rather peculiar one right up to the moment of his death, surrounded by fellow seekers, having dispatched his disconsolate young wife to the company of their offspring, regarding whom history is chiefly silent.[11] Investigating the nature of "the good life" that he espoused, the teaching of which Adorno offhandedly remarks in the preface to his masterpiece of wistful hopelessness (or secretly hopeful despair), *Minima Moralia*, is the aboriginal, if sadly forgotten, purpose of philosophy, as opposed to propounding a positive doctrine, would seem to place Socrates in a unique position among his fellow philosophers.[12] The latter effort would be left to his (very) wealthy acolyte, Plato, though he himself (or his literary character) did certainly insinuate doctrine in the inconspicuous breaths between bouts of the treacherous dialectic, his interlocutors already reeling in the heady ether of reason as they assented to just about anything the master, or his creator, might care to say.

Like them, we are thrall to a good story or a spellbinding argument. And we tend, though trained, still eager readers, to overlook the "absurdities" that occasionally arise in texts produced in cultures and times remote from ours – we're attuned to the functioning of

---

10 We have, after all, come to think of Socrates's seventy as the new sixty.

11 With the exception of Aristotle's comment that they turned out "silly and dull," evidence perhaps of Socrates's conviction that virtue cannot be taught, or maybe that he did not choose to make the experiment in their cases. And the structure and role of the family in society was not something that Socrates (or Plato) viewed as terribly wisely conceived anyway.

12 At least up until the appearance of Jacques Derrida, and even then, with plenty of qualifications.

genre after all and to the analogic imperative of the imagination – and even to search for inoffensive, if meaningful correspondences within the more enlightened fabric of our own. Well, something like that is what we once thought, anyway. So, when Socrates tells us that death is the realm of truth, immutable truth, while our corporeal existence is but that of appearance and deceit, we've more or less heard it before in Christian or other folkloric form and hardly raise an eyebrow. When he further remarks, however, that only "there" (in death, mind you), do "ideas," or "forms" exist in their purity, perhaps we tend to wake up a bit, or wonder how that might be. That the key to the central notion of Platonism is hidden in a rather touching and under the circumstances astonishingly casual discussion, in a dialogue whose apparent pretensions to philosophical truth are modest at best – it is, after the report of his deathbed conversation with some of Socrates's closest friends and disciples as opposed to one of the many abstruse doctrinal disputes to which the majority of the dialogues are devoted – makes us wonder what other sleight of hand might be afoot here? That the foundation, mind you, of his ontology, cosmology… ethics! relies upon an utterly undecidable, undiscoverable, undemonstrable – if we may be so crude – recourse to myth, or fairy-tale, that precisely in the moment of his death he leaves his trusting friends with a fable,[13] makes us want to say, "Wait a minute, Socrates, you can't just say that and move on." But on top of that, he's claiming that *death* is the most desirable state of human affairs, or "being," if you please, his obvious (but as always, double-edged) effort to defuse its power over the imagination notwithstanding, here, right at the dawn of philosophy; for make no mistake this is the moment of its dawning. Though we've heard tell the grim proclamation of Silenus, this still has to come as a shock. Well, what could he say to that, after all? He's announcing a perspective, the philosophical perspective, or really, the philosophical *story*, although it sort of sounds like an argument. And just a few seconds ago he was ranting on about the poets again. That, presumably, was his famous irony. And aside from the metaphysical issues, this is where he's demonstrating the moral priority of the philosopher over all other men. And what was that he was saying about suicide?[14] Wasn't he about to say that for those who really understand death (or did he mean who really

---

13 That the dialogue begins with the report that this putative antagonist of poetry has been versifying Aesop should be a clue that many of "Socrates's views," as of course we are well aware, are less self-evident than they seem.

14 Although suicide naturally crops up in the consideration of death, and far more often than not in a mode of at least implicit non-judgment if not crypto-approval, the modern history of Western philosophy has been notably timid in expressing what it knows perfectly well to be the obvious right of any human being to dispense with his or her own life, taking of course certain particular conditions into account. We are even tempted to see the position of a philosophy on the question of suicide as evidence of its seriousness, or of its honesty, or lack of it – Goethe's disclaimer in later editions of *Werther* strikes us almost as damning, though it's also not difficult to understand the distress of an artist whose work has suddenly taken on a life in the world, in his particular case. We are also sensitive to the fact that it is inherently a deeply personal, and a family, matter and that therefore to generalize might not serve it honorably. In any case, though suicidal literature has not had a prominent place in philosophical history, it is worth considering that suicides have likely spent more time cogitating at death's doorstep than anyone among us – they have invariably died a thousand and one deaths – and there is certainly something to which we would do well to pay attention in their reflections. Between the magnificent poles of Stefan Huber and Mitchell Heisman, there is an ocean of tortured and terrifyingly attuned thinking.

understand life?), it's perfectly ok, in fact it's (almost) imperative? I suppose maybe it's not necessary to spell out every little thing. But how did that relate to slavery, again?[15] There is so much packed into this one "minor" dialogue, and all in the hours before Socrates will die and never again be there to qualify his remarks, or to answer for them.

Socrates's death, this death that a small concession or two would, presumably, have been enough to avert, was a heuristic one, the literary and the real. As his every other recorded act, it serves to support or to instantiate a world-view, to ratify it at the highest level of seriousness, to make a point, and to teach a lesson, and, most strategically, to plant seeds of doubt or dissatisfaction, to create the next generation of philosophers. If his life was not worth saving at the cost of (continuing) living among his fellow citizens, in their polity (or, alternatively, and perhaps more tellingly in some respects, outside of it) and under their laws, the laws in accordance with which they had sentenced him to death, and which he would refuse to flout although his death definitively condemns them as corrupt, then what of their lives, their implicitly unexamined lives, and of the society they had created?

What is the lesson of his death? That the status quo, the way life is lived, is wrong? That it is impossible (and yet for that very reason utterly necessary) to be a philosopher (here at the very dawn of philosophy) under such circumstances; that society is broken when the highest function of man has no place in it (which was, of course, what had made that function come into being in the first place, "disappointment [being] the beginning of philosophy," as Simon Critchley views it)? Naturally, no society wants questions to be raised, its practices to be reflected upon, received opinions to be examined; society moves forward, inexorably. Reflection is not a normal or perhaps even a possible social function, Socrates's efforts

---

15 Socrates raises and then quickly lets drop an apparently current "mystic" analogy for the relationship of the soul to the body, namely, the body as "guardhouse" to or "guard-post" of the soul, which, he comments has "difficult implications," by which, I think we can surmise, he means that this understanding of things would suggest that the lower realm of the body would be responsible for the higher faculty of soul, or conversely, that the latter would be beholden to the former. And of course this might also seem to imply the mortality of the soul, which doesn't advance Socrates's present agenda. In fact, he raises it merely to move on to a related analogy which replaces the wooden or impersonal aspect of the previous with a problematic but still more comprehensible and "organic" relationship, remarking, "This much I think we can agree is true, however, the gods are our keepers, and we men are their possessions," an implicit analogy to slavery that he then makes overt: "If one of your possessions were to destroy itself without intimation from you that you wanted it to die, wouldn't you be angry with it and punish it, if you had any means of doing so?" Although he is speaking of the natural attraction of the philosopher to death and of the relationship of that attraction to suicide, which he clearly condones, if he is at pains to dissemble his position for the sake of the non-philosophers, or less developed philosophers around him, the implicit comparison of the proper relationship of the soul to the body as of master to slave – it is only when the body has in fact been mastered that the soul may exert its prerogative – is telling as to Plato/ Socrates's view of the relationship of the philosopher to the many, as of philosophy to ordinary life. And it implies that the "slave" (or the non-philosopher) has no genuine relationship to death: His life is the prerogative of someone, or something else; to the extent that it is mere analogy, to the state, or to the gods, for example, but in hard reality as well. Since death, for Socrates, is freedom, as we shall see, the prerogative of death must be protected against the slave. At the same time, it is obvious that Socrates recognizes, if he perhaps cannot say it in those words, the patent truth that slavery is a reasonable inducement to suicide, opening a gap within the history of philosophy that will remain an unspoken, unspeakable, fault within it for millennia.

notwithstanding, or rather particularly revealingly. And what of the fear of death, which is the (putative) basis for community, the city, politics, for civilization, in the face of which Socrates's own calm and processional exit is a slap and a cold, harsh assessment? Is that not a deeper critique of human nature, or behavior, or habit at least, and which Socrates intends to expound in his own attitude toward it? That it is not so much childish or undeveloped as simply corrupt? This is death as critique of life, but far more interestingly, life as critique of death. Or, does he want to say above all that questioning is the essence and the calling of humanity and that to fail to question, ever to halt in self-satisfaction, is abdication of the human, is death itself, by comparison with which that other death is as nothing?

If the point of Socrates's death, then, was to preserve the possibility of a philosophy of justice, of doing what is one's own (and necessary) thing, it insists that death must be within one's control in some sense, not merely the potentially arbitrary effect of other (social) commitments. Socrates's model would undermine many centuries in advance Hegel's analysis of the overriding power of society and its prerogative relationship to individual death:[16] "The individuals who, absorbed in their own way of life, break loose from the whole and strive after the inviolable independence and security of the person are made to feel in the task laid on them their lord and master, death."[17] And at the same time, in another sense, it would ratify it.

It fulfills, including the debt to society, as it transcends the function of death, adumbrating, or at least imagining a society that respects the individual and which is respected in turn, pointedly proposing a better way, even as it pointedly exemplifies the corruption of its current form. The Christ, too, showed that the willingness to die is the mark of a real, a serious life, and, like Socrates, he knew that this could not be a (realistic) model for everyone, that death should be a continuous and not a cataclysmic event regardless of the determining circumstances... with occasional, and crucial exceptions, that society by necessity (almost by definition) cannot brook the kind of seriousness that diminishes the power of death, perhaps because it requires its power in support of its own distinctly mundane purposes. On the other hand, it may not be necessary (or even possible) for all to have or be able to have a good death, but the good death itself must be possible for the whole to survive uncompromised, exactly as with the good life as it exists in the practical sphere: it is not guaranteed by a social order, but its possibility must be assured. Already in Plato, the suggestion that any individual could do the same, could emulate Socrates, is problematic, and yet this is the model on the basis of which any meaningful social existence is to be established, the almost impossible possibility that it requires. Although, like Christ's, it does so at the cost of (ironically inexpiable) guilt, Socrates's death is sacrifice for the good of the whole, for only thus is its own potential revealed to it.

---

16 It was Hegel, after all, who would refute the "philosopher's death," the suicide by which he would demonstrate his power over, or even complicity with, that greatest of human adversaries.

17 G.F.W. Hegel, *Phenomenology of Spirit* (Oxford: Oxford University Press, 1977), pp. 272-273.

When, in Book II of *The Republic*, Socrates casually remarks that of course the ideal society consists of perhaps fifty people, but since the development of the race has outrun that desideratum, he will address the matter of the modern large-scale city-state and its appropriate mode of governance instead, he both recognizes the "natural" tribal heritage of humanity and accepts the fact that structural complications are going to dictate that post-tribal statecraft is more of an art than a science, and undoubtedly far from straight-forward. Implicit, however, might well be the notion that in the tribal state of nature, if you will, the role of the philosopher will not yet have come into being, and the tortured questions over which he presides will not (yet) have arisen, or might be adjudicated without discussion. Such lives seem to require no examination: one accepts one's part in the social whole with natural grace, while one's individual nature is molded uniformly, and uniformly well, by the group, whose interests are univocal, unquestioned, and more or less unchanging over time, if, quite understandably, riven by inescapable internal psycho-dynamics, as Bataille (after Nietzsche and Freud) and Baudrillard (against Freud and Marx) will delineate. And life and death both sustain and are sustained by the interests and practices of the group, without the intrusion of doubt as to their value, justification, or *raison d'être*. Life is almost invariably good life, as is death, if we may apply concepts here that really post-date the sphere of activity, or inquiry, at hand.

To emulate the natural ways of the tribe on a much larger scale, a division of labor and a relatively adventitious structural hierarchy become necessary, an imposition of roles (if one predicated on the acknowledged wisdom of the rulers) as opposed to naturally or conventionally arising leadership and obedience. The "noble lie," however much it reflects a significant if partial truth about the differences among human beings – what we call by a single name is actually a diversity of more or less un-reconcilable types united by participation in an array of faculties, distributed in unequal share among them – comes into being, is created, in order to manage the impulse toward social mobility, differential degrees of natural desire or energy, the resentment of preference, or the inequitable distribution of the most tedious, dangerous, or unpleasant work. Again, it is on the assumption of the wisdom, beneficence, and un-self-interested objectivity of the leader(s) that such a system coheres, and to that end, Plato proposes the rule of the dispassionate "philosopher-king."

The philosopher, whose advent, as we have insinuated, is predicated on the rise of social disparity, internal disagreement, the decline of a unitary world-view, the demise of a univocal social order – we might note that the role of the philosopher enters history with democracy, with the emergence of a plurality of opinions and their public debate – and even the institutionalization of (economically) salutary hypocrisy, is, as we have all heard in high school, a "lover of wisdom." As Socrates never tires of noting, a "lover of wis-dom," in tireless pursuit of it, but actually wise only in the limited sense of being aware of his own ignorance, as against the vast wash of others who are not. The good life, the virtuous life, the just life, which perhaps slightly disingenuously, or, for that matter question-beggingly, means doing what is appropriate to one (in other Platonic words, "one's own thing") consists, for the philosopher, in examining life, an example of which he sets for others, for whom, he insinuates, it is, if unbeknownst to them, their calling as well, in his monomaniacal quest(ioning).

When Socrates felt compelled to subject the proclamation of the Oracle of Delphi to the effect that he was the wisest of men, or at least that there was no man wiser, to examination, already implying that nothing was sacred to him (save, perhaps, the truth which revelation is obviously inadequate to establish), his not so infrequent protestations of piety, or at least pragmatic recourse to the divine when he was in a philosophical tough-spot notwithstanding, he interrogated politicians, poets, and the most skilled of artisans, (and, I think we might admit, other teachers, famous teachers who charged money for their instruction, if only in the course of the conversations recorded in Plato's works),[18] and he found that all of them professed to wisdom that they did not in fact possess, leading him to conclude that the oracle had been correct, if only in the ironic sense that it was merely in his recognition of his own ignorance that he was wiser than they, who were even more pointedly ignorant in not being aware that they were ignorant at all. The pride of such ignoramuses is, of course, a dangerous thing with which to trifle.

Human differences notwithstanding, the basic structure of the person is, in principle, consistent across their variety. In the Platonic schema, reason (naturally) stands above perception and emotion, orienting them in their effort to come to terms with reality, judging among the good and bad, right and wrong, beautiful and not, and deciding upon objects of desire. Everyone may be able to live his own life, to be just, or good, according to the prevailing social standards, but only through self-understanding, through the examination (and, as the Socratic example makes clear, the relentless examination) of his life (and of course, acting accordingly) is his existence in fact genuinely human, one in which value even has meaning. Ostensibly the examination alone is sufficient at least to justify it (to make it worthwhile), if that does not of course necessarily mean that it is good, but from the Socratic perspective, to know and not to do is really tantamount to not knowing at all. In any event, regardless of one's natural disposition or philosophical endowment, Socrates sees it as a necessary criterion of good living that one examine one's life, that one seek wisdom, whether one find it or not, that is, in effect, indeed, that one be a philosopher.[19]

Whether or not everyone *can* be a philosopher, it is quite evident that very few actually take that burden, that responsibility, upon themselves. For most, not only is the pursuit a

---

18 It is perhaps noteworthy that he did not speak with businessmen, common working men, soldiers, sailors, religious figures, women, slaves, etc.

19 Like everyone, Socrates well knew, as his ontological schema indicates, that we are appetitive and emotional as well as rational beings; in attempting to subordinate, not just subordinate but eradicate, the "lower" faculties, he certainly understood that he was (more or less) arbitrarily advocating reconfiguring the human soul, or at least effectively disavowing its most ordinary, prevalent, and in some sense most human aspects. The more "rational" construction, namely, that we are thinking (and feeling) throughout our bodies, entirely dissolves such hierarchies from the outset.

waste of (valuable) time, but they are at least dimly, secretly, aware that the whole tenability of their actual way of life relies precisely upon its remaining unexamined.[20] And the very notion of the Platonic philosopher-king would seem to acknowledge this. With its forcible wrenching of the philosopher out of his preferred way of living to attend to the political well-being of the community,[21] the quite reasonable denial of ascendency to those who actually crave power, and the natural dismissal of the individual concerns or possible (political) role of the many, it is clear that his existential status is unique. The philosopher is, perhaps in spite of himself, the only one who inhabits his society fully, as he simultaneously inhabits, and self-consciously so, its contradictions and hypocrisies, which ironically also makes him its perfect outsider. He is the exception in which the rule may be viewed, as in a perverse mirror.[22] In other words, excellent king material.

When Alfred North Whitehead said that all of Western philosophy is a footnote to Plato, he spoke precisely, as there would be no possibility of a footnote to Socrates, who, we might reasonably assert, inaugurated it, though he famously did not actually write any philosophical works, and who would scarcely exist in the minds of posterity had Plato, a dramatist *manqué* prior to his invention of the dialogue form, not created the character Socrates – he is portrayed as having abominated at least philosophical writing[23] – representing what we can only surmise is an indissociable *mélange* of the thinking and philosophical methods of the both of them, but (or hence) with a built-in distance that insures an intrinsic self-reflexivity, a self-questioning, that, quite reasonably, leaves "answers" or resolution perpetually in the future even while expressing more or less definite views for the now. Like the art of which Plato is so famously skeptical, its understanding relies upon the interpretation of his audience (any given member of which becomes something akin to a judge hearing divergent claims, if not a participant in the dialogue itself, a structure certainly invoked and sustained by the death dialogues), and is necessarily diverse and variable.

Plato's use of Socrates enabled him to prevail upon the voice of a martyr for truth (without having to sacrifice himself on the same altar) to express positions that take advantage of the fact of his teacher's extreme level of sincerity, one might say mania but for his disconcerting equanimity, to legitimize them, even if Socrates might well in fact not have

---

20 On the other hand, one might well argue that the examined life is in itself impossible, or that only some imperfect approximation of it is possible, and that this has intimately to do with both the structure of life in relation to death and of the inherent limitation of our perspective as an individual.

21 That we know that Plato did in fact seek political power, or at least influence, regardless of his undoubtedly unimpugnable motives, casts the notion of the impressment of the philosopher into political service in a rather peculiar light.

22 The trope of the solitary philosopher, separated from "the rest" even while among them reveals the philosophical position on death: it is not a burden that can be shared. Death is solitude, the solitary life of the philosopher and the exceptional life of the king. For Levinas, "solipsism is the very structure of reason." There can be no "other"; it is always brought into the kingdom of death, an inherently monarchical (or totalitarian) tendency.

23 In some sense, just what philosophy is is in question right here in the writings of the acolyte about the rejection of writing by the master.

espoused or even supported them much beyond their use as suggestions for thought: Here is a man of undisputed wisdom (his own disavowals notwithstanding, or precisely on account thereof), and these are his (actual) words. Plato's political views, or his conception of the "forms" (or "ideas") seem rather unlikely to have coincided exactly with those of Socrates, yet they implicitly partake of the purity of his motives, his philosophical disinterestedness, and his indifference to danger, or actual suffering, in pursuit of the truth, even as they prosecute interests of their own.

Though Plato comments but little on the matter of death outside of the four dialogues explicitly devoted to the circumstances surrounding the death of Socrates, these are particularly important in establishing the pervasive subtext to the effect that the valor, the insistence, against all reason, of Socrates's way of life as a thinker also informs his own, and his ideas as well. If philosophy is in fact a matter of life and death, as it is dramatically portrayed in Plato's works, who is better equipped both to teach the nature of the good life, and to steer a polity that, left to itself (in this case, to "the people"), is bound to fail to recognize and perhaps to abandon exactly what is most precious to it – both the circumstances of the recent Persian Wars and the very disposition of the case of Socrates tend to undergird that position – than one for whom the (pure, un-self-interested) truth (which, recall was justice, was beauty, all of which, miraculously in the view of Levinas, derive from the Good, that is, the ethical realm, and constitute one of the profoundly humane "exceptions" in Western philosophical history) was of greater importance than his own existence? And on top of that, a valiant soldier, even a war hero, who had proven his deep commitment to the city-state of Athens, again as against the value of his own life.

Socrates's leisurely drift toward death as portrayed in the Platonic death dialogues perhaps suggests that we are all under sentence of death, though we don't know the exact moment when it will be carried out. And his implacable focus on the "things that matter most," even in the face of his demise, virtually defines the "philosophical attitude" that may well represent the one realm of human existence in which philosophy is still commonly held in esteem. Although Plato's time was a transitional one in the ancient world, when new notions of human life, the soul, morality, knowledge, thinking, writing, etc., were emerging if still far from fully articulated, it is clear that an over-arching and long-standing commitment to virtue, to honor, and to the common good informed the values, and in general, the actions of even the ordinary Athenian. The idea of a moral act outside the aegis of the polity, of human meaning at all outside of it, wasn't really a tenable concept, with the possible if only nascent exception of Socrates's own peculiar hyper-individualism, which could and did of course co-exist with and within the social whole, if in far different ways than it might in modernity, and which never impinged upon his profound respect for the sanctity of the *polis*. Though it was far from the sort of integral and self-contained, perhaps animistic, society eulogized, or longed-for, or imagined by the Baudrillard of *Symbolic Exchange and Death* (1976), it was social in ways that, at our remove, we can scarcely comprehend, such that Aristotle could define human beings as the *zöon politikon* (social, or even political animal), and the valence of every act, including death, referred fundamentally to the social amalgam; it cast its shadow, or equally its light, into the future of the group and did not mark a terminus in itself of the sort as which we tend to conceive it nowadays. Death, even the anomalous death of Socrates, was a part of that, as he clearly understood, and through which act he could therefore communicate his dispute with the powers-that-be well beyond its moment, as philosophy or politics rather than as a mere personal or legal difference of opinion.

How different the death of Christ! Already by the heyday of the Roman Empire, though it took its culture from the Greeks, a brutality and a social distance, perhaps in part due to the us/them mentality of a conquering civilization, was commonplace, and death as spectacle thematized a truism about life: Kill or be killed. Though gladiatorial and other spectacle forms of death still partook of the noble indifference of the warrior, they were also infused with the terror of the trapped or hunted animal, a death that was not one's choice but which was visited upon one by a greater, and a ruthless, power. In Christ's compacted, excruciating torment, itself an example of one *modus* of the death-spectacle, and his submission throughout to a greater will and purpose – though certainly not that of his tormentors – we can only foresee a figure of (what we would come to think of as) the Christian view of life, aspects of which include the world as a place of misery, deceit, callousness, brutality, cowardice, and greed through the pious or defiant endurance of which one wins immortality (an *agon*-model in itself), expiation by fire for the sins of distant fathers (which is yet a form of social continuity), a dire sense of (one's) responsibility (to the extent of projecting it, if you will, over the entire human race), love of one's neighbor even beyond oneself, forgiveness of one's enemies, ignorance as an excuse ("forgive them for they know not what they do"), disdain for our sublunary interlude and its woes, the vision of ecstatic transcendence, etc.

If for the ancients, equanimity in the face of death, a value certainly not pioneered by Socrates even if the character of his particular example brought a new thing into the world, was deemed a virtue, a mark of honor, and, thenceforth, of wisdom, perhaps even an *examen crucis* of wisdom, the early Church took the model of Christ's death, the model of martyrdom for the truth, deeply to heart, frequently "volunteering" their lives in emulation of it and so constituting a model of the good death.[24] Certainly many more Christians went to their deaths with equanimity than philosophers, and far more ordinary (and even extraordinary) people became followers of Christ than ever became philosophers, though it meant not just equanimity before, but a sort of love-relationship to death, which would be joined by enthusiastic persecution from without. For the early Christian, we are all called to save the world, to be the Messiah, if you will, and each in his small way could do that, in emulation of the Christ.

---

24 As Nietzsche comments in *The Gay Science*, "When Christianity came into existence, the inclination to suicide was very strong – Christianity turned it into a lever of its power."

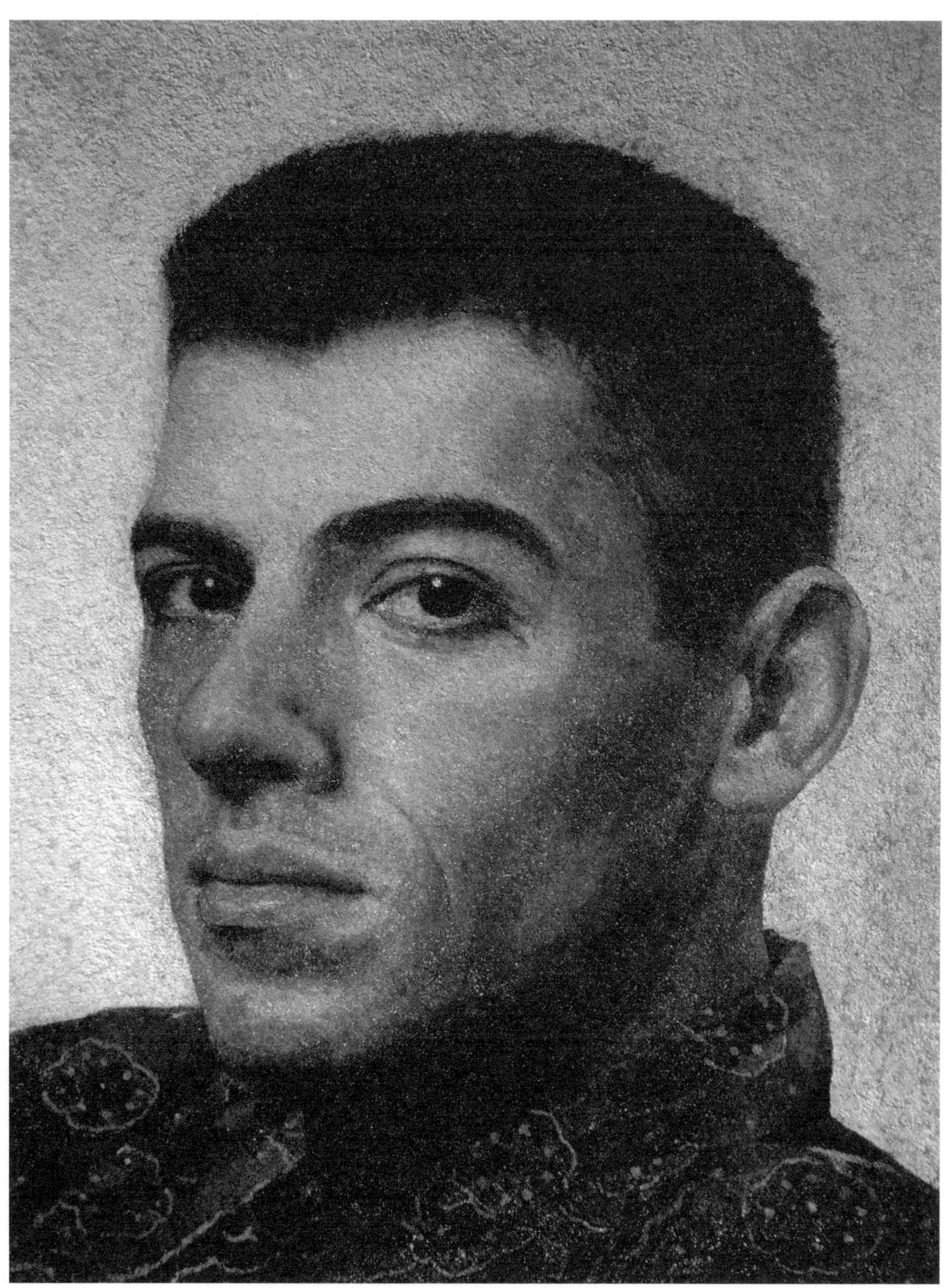

For all their similarities, one of the two great ancient (Western) models of the relationship of death to life implies a (socially-based) continuity of life and death – its very method elides any abrupt transition, Socrates talking right up to the end, and instead likens itself to that sleep with which he often identified it – while the other establishes a historical fissure involving a bitter struggle and identifies death as the dividing-line between earthly life and the hereafter, the fissure from which the great abyss, betokening an all but insupportable burden of responsibility, will eventually open up. For the Greeks, as for most early cultures, the afterlife, to which Socrates generally gave rather tepid credence, was merely a way of saying that things (and who people had been) persist even in the absence of that which, or those who, brought them into being, that future history is our post-death existence, in memory, in children, the relict, unresolved events, the consequences of actions taken, and in things created, where the very notion of the "shade" implied ever-diminishing strands of real-world agency. Both of them died, in a stronger or weaker sense, on behalf of those who remain, but the inherent urgency (and agency) that Christ's death invoked determined a radically different posterity. Where Socrates was the model of unconcern with the passing of time – of wasting time, as almost every other Athenian would have seen it – so long as it was devoted to the examination of the most important things, Christ's death demanded that time not be spent idly, for eternity is at stake,[25] and it might well begin at any moment.[26]

Death as discontinuity, the moment of exception – the fact that Christ's is a ritual death, marked by the sanctioned transgression and the social character of sacrifice already places it within the dynamic of taboo and violation – becomes something crucial for Christians (by which of course we mean Europeans during the greater part of two millennia), and gradually comes to be seen, as medieval deathbed imagery makes apparent, as the locus of struggle between good and evil, demons always hovering nearby in one's dying hours in the hope of capturing a weakened soul. The rituals of death, Christian and (often deeply integrated) throwback – last rites, a proper confession, talismans and distraught prayers, and centuries later, the death-bed conversion – reflect the morbid, or rather mortal, concern with the "good death," as eternal damnation or salvation was in the balance. The specific

---

25 A position that Weber would implicate in the distinctly non-Christian ethos of the post-spiritual era of Christian ethics.

26 If Socrates's was a passive, abnegatory method of approaching, of moving toward death (and the Good), a subtle transition such as Nietzsche would criticize as the sign of a suspect or misplaced optimism, Christ's was active, overtly critical as opposed to simply, however tendentiously, questioning, and the Christian afterlife is, accordingly, "salvation" rather than mere continuance, persistence, or notionally, integration, the terrible presence of God as opposed to the ghostly half-life, however enlightened. If Platonic epistemology is scopic, Christian is aural, attuned listening as opposed to passive seeing: the Word, which requires understanding as opposed to the Light, which merely enables it, and, though paradoxical-sounding, deeds as opposed to words, not sitting around chatting, but doing ("he who has faith but not works," and so on). It is to a presence, trans-human indeed, but a being rather than the abstraction of a glowing orb, to which the Christian soul is turned. The afterlife is not the seamless portal, but the eye of the needle through which one must struggle to pass, and not the realm of death at all, but of life, while there is now that other death, the death that does not die. Of course, it is always too simple to identify dichotomies. The old persists in the new, is undigested within it, the new even reverts to the old unaware of itself in so doing; we don't ever know who we are – that is our nature, necessarily so (and precisely because we die), if we follow the Heideggerian narrative.

moment of death, therefore, takes on meaning that would have been incomprehensible to Socrates or Athens, and the seed of existential despair, dread, or *Angst* comes into being right alongside the most attractive prospect ever devised by man.

With the decline of the great "humane" civilizations and the incursion of the barbarian hordes into the Roman Empire, decentralization, ruralization, feudalization, relative isolation of the populace, and, of course, the ever-waxing dominance of the new Christian world-view over the ancient conception of virtue, the European contempt for death, or rather for the fear of death, began to give way to a broad-based insecurity, which both expressed itself and was reinforced in the slowly-evolving textual bases of Christianity and in its minutely-contested if eventually systematized dogmatic structure. Although the definitive understanding and onus of guilt by which Christianity would long be burdened was virtually unknown to the early Church, already with Augustine at the dawn of the fifth century the conception of original sin (perhaps more humanly comprehensible then as *felix culpa*) would emerge and fundamentally transform a relatively sanguine, and now quite successful *community* into an amalgam of progressively more isolated, responsible individuals, a development that one readily imagines as a projection of the new precariousness of the world, which, in its obvious antipathy, might easily have been seen as a sign of God's displeasure, as in Old Testament precedent, and which would be integrated into a continuous narrative of revised covenants, new lambs, and prophetic anticipation.

This, we must always keep in mind, is a religion at whose center is a violent, unjust, and deeply symbolic death – and the overcoming of that death – which is celebrated in the holiest days of the Christian year, and in fact in every Eucharist. And, fittingly therefore, medieval life was, notoriously, suffused with death and its imagery, certainly far more so in its later centuries after the disaster of the Black Death, but from its millenarian beginnings its Christianity was always a thanato-centric creed – even its God is essentially, and not merely, as in earlier instances among more folkloric religions, accidentally or casually, the God who dies – and the organization of social life around the church (and churchyard), the enormous rate of infant and child mortality, the prevalence of war and disease, kept that fact ever in prominent focus over many centuries. Even its art thematizes death in a way that is unique in history, and kept it, and a general disdain for the flesh, before the eyes of the faithful and, more pertinently, those inclined to stray. The portrayal of the demeaned body was in fact to demean the body, to assert, and thereby reject its corruptibility, ephemeral nature, and ultimate nullity, as well as to celebrate the suffering that ransomed, and continues to ransom, the souls of the faithful. The inclusion of art in the burial regime, funeral statuary and so forth, insured the persistence of memory, and involved the living with the dead as a matter of course. The *memento mori* was a reminder of what life actually is: brief and deadly, deadly in the spiritual sense. Even the whimsical *danses macabres*, with their antic skeletal dancers and players, personifications of death, laughing in their postmortem glee, these (positive) remains of the body (of which Bataille would later speak) expressed the ecstasy of death, its transcendence, for the dead were not dead, they were in that "better place" we still sheepishly invoke, and therefore remembering them, hoping moreover, to be remembered by them in intercession with our mutual creator, insured that a "cult of death" remained vital well into modernity. And, as against the ancients, in spite of their perhaps more deeply rooted communal sensibility, every death suddenly became meaningful in a way that had been reserved only for the great and the heroic in the past, for everyone could earn salvation.[27] We were all immortals – as gods, if you will pardon the blasphemy. On the other hand, death is our shame – it was Adamic sin that somehow brought it into the world, which is another way of saying that our self-consciousness, our knowledge,[28] comes at the cost of our death, as for some later philosophers it would be death that purchases our self-awareness, and this is simultaneously our guilt (the "always-already" guilt that Heidegger would identify in the very structure of *Dasein*) and our responsibility (which both Heidegger and Levinas will make integral, in opposing ways, to their own ethics).[29]

In the same way that the exception to philosophy, to what can actually be pondered or understood, is at the heart of metaphysics from its inception, so the exception to ethics, to the paradigm of guilt and responsibility that has dominated Western thinking, namely the God who sacrifices himself for our sins, is at the heart of Christianity, which might, and not necessarily flippantly, incline us to equate Christ and death. It would, after all, be fair to say that he rules the kingdom of death and might therefore take its name – as human kings have signed themselves "France" or "Spain," he is "Death," though only in the sense that, for Christianity, while not precisely in the same way that that was true for Plato, death is true life.

Given the centrality of death in its culture, it is curious that during the long Christian interlude, including the centuries of its decay, anything interesting that might have been said about death was colored by the fact that it had been defeated (by virtue of Christ's sacrifice) and/or relegated to an invisible spiritual realm. There is little in Christian thinking about death that does not fundamentally pertain to the *summum bonum* of an afterlife to which it is hard to imagine many contemporary human beings lending serious credence, and hence it is of little current philosophical interest. If we can hardly register Augustine's glorious "Never can a man be more disastrously in death than when death itself shall be deathless," it is easy to understand why the magnificent anguish of a Kierkegaard

---

27 Baudrillard is surely not the first to observe that the doctrinal democracy of death was undermined by the actual practice of death management, the rich and powerful securing privileged access to "eternity" as to everywhere else of interest.

28 I refer, of course, to the fact that Adam ate fruit from the Tree of Knowledge (of Good and Evil). That Eve, who comes from man (i.e., nature) as opposed to directly from the hand of God, had done so first, is natural, whereas Adam's act is a choice of nature over God. It is perhaps worth noting that the very fact that they were eating might be taken to imply that death was already present among them.

29 The simple reward and punishment model of Christian ethics, or what might be seen as a laugh now pay later model, which won the loyalty of the multitudes, is veneer to the deeper problematic of faith that was most profoundly broached by Kierkegaard in *Fear and Trembling*, and which Derrida, after Potočka and Levinas, translates as the impossible, and unsatisfiable demand of responsibility.

is rendered suspect by the inevitable sense that he is thrall to a fantasy (the efforts of a Levinas or a Derrida to distill a pure philosophical position from it notwithstanding). In the wake of the afterlife, the body seemed even more abject in the eyes of the only recently Christian world, whose memory has not died graciously. The decayed faith is a spiritual ruin that still stands amidst the "modern" over-building of our thinking, just as we still see the sun rising, stars coming out, apples falling, and stand on "solid ground," as we speak of the colors and sounds of nature, of (indivisible) atoms, empty space, the flow of time, or for that matter, of "I," and even during the latter twentieth century, sophisticated philosophies found a place for the sacred, despite the ever more manifest absence of God.

In its proprietary interest in death during the more than fifteen hundred years following the demise of its founder, the Catholic Church was the first multi-national corporation, whose death-management concern monopolized all of Europe and would continue to make significant inroads in the Americas, Africa, and parts of Asia for a long time thereafter. In fact, it was during the afterlife of faith that the Church enjoyed its greatest corporate, or at least capital, success. When its trust was busted in much of Europe, the Protestant ascendency immediately abolished the relic worship (and trade) that had so effectively girded the otherwise invisible aspects of the faith, and which was such anathema to Martin Luther, as well as the sway of the image, which, after its ethics, has certainly been the most enduring cultural legacy of those many centuries, reverting to a non-iconic austerity such as would have assuaged both Muslim and Jew.

But, paradoxically, the disappearance of death imagery (as, in more modern times, the disappearance of the dead themselves) from Western culture, coincides with an increase in death anxiety, or dread, that would eventually become the crucial philosophical locus of selfhood, of self-awareness, of being itself. Evidently, when we live with death, know its powers and limitations and are comfortable with it, it is its natural, organic aspect that we see. In hiding it from view, it becomes a disconcerting mystery, possessing the power that the invisible, which thereby becomes the unknown, always exerts.[30] Of course, the Reformation was but part of an amalgam of social change that heralded the modern world, including the rise of the money economy,[31] and with it, capitalism, industrialization, division of labor, de-socialization, alienation, and so forth, and all of those developments had their effect upon newly emerging understandings of death.

With the exception of the likes of Montaigne, Thomas Browne, Pascal, and, most disconcertingly, Hobbes, death received little relevant philosophical attention in the wake of

---

30 "Indeed, the most powerful way to represent power has always been to refuse to represent it. That's why God or spirits in so many traditions cannot be shown in images; it's also why the way to show that something is truly powerful is to hide it, to render it invisible, ineffable, unknowable, utterly featureless and abstract. That which is unknown, Thomas Hobbes once remarked, is for that reason unlimited. It could be anything; therefore, you have to be prepared to assume it could *do* anything as well." (David Graeber, "Dickheads: The Paradox of the Necktie Resolved," *The Baffler*, no. 27, 2015.)

31 Another form of ghosthood, or spirit, of the dying of the thing, the work, the real.

the Reformation. A posture of meditation rather than of active thought tended to be the order of the day, and where Montaigne advocates constant attention to death, Spinoza sees no reason whatsoever to devote a moment to it when a soon to be extinguished life itself beckons us. Even the still-devout Catholic (warrior, spy, Rosicrucian, and surreptitious theorist of more-or-less-eternal life, etc.), Descartes, had little of moment to say on the matter. In fact, the recovery of philosophy from the Christian era was a long and circuitous process, and it took centuries for thinkers to cast aside the popular mythos of salvation and for death to become problematic once again, the efforts of Humes, Voltaires, and Diderots notwithstanding.

It would not be until the arrival of Hegel that philosophy would again become so self-aware as it had been with Plato, nor avail itself of such self-reflexivity to perform a sort of immanent, methodological, self-transcendence. It was with Hegel that death, too, would become not only self-aware, intimate, as it were, but would structurally serve a role analogous to that which the martyrdom of Socrates had served in Plato's thought. Here death for the first time is explicitly embraced as the guarantor of universal spiritual legitimacy, a position that even Christianity could truly imagine with regard only to its Messiah. As in Plato's dramatization, the confrontation with death reveals the higher human dimension of life that unthinking, virtually animal, existence conspires to ignore, and which calls the philosopher to turn shame upon his accusers, whose fear of death is, in principle, the humiliation that, as Kant had said (and whose dialectic of the sublime, as brilliantly elucidated by Walter A. Davis, had already contained the dynamic *in nuce*, if unbeknownst to him[32]) is the beginning of self-consciousness. In fact, for Hegel, the confrontation with death serves the dual purpose of inaugurating the recognition of self and of asserting the ascendency of the universal (and of the polity) over the individual[33] that would provoke the anti-systematic reactions of Kierkegaard and Nietzsche, as well as inspire the materialist inversion and populist fury of Karl Marx.

If we might say that Montaigne, for all that he was basically a latter-day Stoic in his exhortation to study death, enjoined us to bring death within us – for Christianity it was a foreign, repugnant, external thing, the sign of our own turpitude – it was Hegel who discovered it there already (the precursor of "our ownmost possibility"), no longer an event or a foreign realm but an abiding condition, in fact, in its universalized understanding as "negativity," a force that we are privileged to wield, but therefore from which we are no longer at liberty merely to turn away: our relationship to death becomes less and less a matter of choice in the post-Christian era. It is inherent and determining, as opposed to something we move toward or away from, and once recognized (and in the conceptual sphere of Hegel it is of course always already recognized for consciousness, i.e., "for us")

---

32 See Davis's *Deracination* (Albany: State University of New York Press, 2001), esp. pp. 46-97.

33 The individual death cannot, therefore, be valorized, as in Plato or Christianity, in fact, the individual who rejects death (the bondsman, as we shall see later), is the model for human self-realization, while the power that controls death (the lord, or in his societal incarnation, the state), remains a less than self-aware expression of the *Zeitgeist*.

the meaning of death cannot be meaningfully ignored; it is in the spiritual fiber of the race. For Hegel, death "is the very structure of what is." It defines human specificity, characterizes man's activity *vis-à-vis* the world, forms that world, and transforms the external into the internal world of thought and language, which "kills the thing" for the sake of its higher being, its truth; in yet a new understanding of the words, death remains the guarantor and the domain of truth. And it acts, functions, and operates in the world.

The "Lordship and Bondage" section of Hegel's *Phenomenology* has long been considered pivotal to his entire philosophical edifice, for it is in this scenario that consciousness (mere sentience) emerges as self-consciousness (the mode of being that is specific to humans), the rest of the *via dolorosa* of wisdom unfolding relatively methodically by comparison.[34] The struggle for recognition, which though enacted as a real-world battle of wills, presumably for the things that are actually fought over in everyday life, food, sex, goods, group dominance, etc., (though it also smacks of the sort of dramatic *Ur*-scenario that had animated the social-contract notions of the Hobbes's, Locke's, and Rousseau's), is fueled by desire (which undoubtedly introduces the profound ambiguity – my object of desire not necessarily being yours – that gradually unfolds in its dynamic right at the outset). And, as in the "natural world," so in its abstracted realm of spirit, the greater desire triumphs over the more sensitive soul. But there is a drawback to power in the philosophical domain as well: In imposing his will – gaining the "recognition" he craves – the victor is barred from attaining the self-understanding to which the timid creature now become his bondsman is opened up.[35] His victory is hollow and he will forever fall short of the triumph he had actually envisioned. He becomes, in fact, a lesser sort of being than the one he has humiliated – a slave-owner as opposed to a slave – while the latter, compelled to do the bidding of this master, develops a relationship to the world through his (initially purely compulsory) work, in which his truest human capacities are heightened and expressed.[36]

---

34 In the grim confrontation with the immediate possibility of death, I recognize that I die, that this is the fundamental and final thing about me, the kind of being I am, my essence, if you will: that it is *I* who dies. Death therefore configures or shapes the self, even if only negatively.

35 In Hegelese, the slave is the truth of the master.

36 It is worth recalling, however, difficult though that is when one is immersed in the Hegelian world, that the history that precedes such a scenario as Hegel describes is full of murder, and that the "fear" of the (eventual) slave expressed in submitting to the lesser evil in the spurious, violently imposed either/or of death or slavery, is quite reasonably predicated on the desire not to become its next victim. The victim is on the other side of death, when he dies, of course, but also when he survives, for he does not control it, does not wield it, can address it only as foreign and hostile; he succumbs to it. Death is part of his life in a way that is completely different from its role in the life of the murderer/master. He is aware that death is violence, death is terror, death is coercion, death is the theft of his humanity, and hence his view can never be "philosophical." The perspective of the murderer (whether the detached or the passionate murderer), the perspective of philosophy, generalizes death, characterizes it as and turns it into what everyone experiences, or suffers, or is subjected to, whereas the "victim" knows that it is his own death, his own unique, individual death that he is postponing or saving by sacrificing (what would and should have been) his life. The death of the philosophers ignores this singularity, fails to recognize, or rather, to acknowledge, that every death is different, unique, uniquely painful or terrified or noble or grim and small and cheated of life. The grandiose posture of "absolute knowing," in ignoring precisely what is too irrelevant to command its attention, reveals itself as an ignoble and self-serving lie, or yet worse, a lie serving the dominant interest, which is of course what Hegel's ethical and political philosophy has often been accused

Art, craft, invention, these are the province, and the gift, of the slave, while the "master" lags well behind in the realm of the spirit, a slave, if you will, to the creative work of his "inferior" subject (as he remains to his own paradoxical cowardice, since he has not actually faced death in its truth).[37] He who survives, more importantly, he who values survival (and perhaps also despises himself for it; as Nietzsche said, art is the talent for suffering), makes culture. Of course, from another perspective, we are all both master and bondsman: It is an internal struggle that most of us wage outside the mythical state of nature, and it is death or our relationship to death that is contested within it. But it is, for Hegel, the death-work of "the negative" that essentially specifies all human activity, while "real" death is merely waste perpetrated by the ignorant and unaware, redeemable only by the percipience of the philosopher; it is the motive force of both thought and work, and we might also say, of society, as the individual must "die" unto himself that it shall live.

Since death is nothing, it has always been conceived as something other by philosophy (simply in being conceived, that is), but it is in Hegel that it begins to play an explicit, or to explicitly play, a vital, role. It is no longer understood as merely "thing" or "state" or "event" or "realm" but as force and as power... and, somehow sublimely (and perhaps self-referentially), as tool. The role it plays aside, it is presumably obvious that death has now

---

of doing. Regardless of what he has managed to make out of his oppression, the slave has always lost, or rather been denied, something essential, and it is not, as Hegel implies, if against his explicit will, that it is his cowardice or inferiority that made him that way. The spiritual division into masters and slaves, a variation on which will take on such explicit force in Nietzsche, insures that neither has nor achieves the status of full human beings, though the inherent deficiency of the "master" always unfolds within the social "whole," partakes of its benefits and legitimate modes of dispute and of (illusory or even specious) reconciliation; it can be discussed and argued and refined, while the position of the "slave" is always outside and can never enter the stream of discourse as it has been established within. Its mere words burn in the ears of the slave. When the perhaps never to be integrated descendants of slaves reject, invert, and reveal the corruption of the very terms of its discourse and effectively stymie philosophy, which does not and cannot speak to them, they invoke this originary fault, suggesting a radically different possibility for an approach to death, and a different thinking altogether, the thinking of the radically other – not to say a "philosophy," which for them can never be, as loyalty to their truth, that is, to memory, must reject it in its abstraction. In the guise of a radical discourse, philosophy shows that it is actually a crypto-hegemonic tool, as Marx would soon insist, its freedom from vested interests merely the first of its lies. Its constant sense of an "us and them" (in Hegel, *we* and *it*), a better and worse, of essentially different "kinds" of people, puts it in relation to the system of inequity that it essentially accepts under the rationale that its role is to resolve, to elevate, or to "improve." There are freedom and slavery *within* the system, bound to each other inextricably, and then there is the real exception, the slave. The "traditional" mode of slave resistance in language has been literature, in opposition to philosophy, the resistance of definition, of absolute and applicable truth, of the violence of discourse, of oblivion to the unique. Art embodies the "slave value" of honest deceit, of deceit on behalf of life, over deceitful truth.
37 The one higher gift of the master to humanity might well be precisely philosophy, which from antiquity has been understood to "begin in leisure," among other things that typically at least require some leisure, such as wonder. That *Angst* plays so great a role in the history of philosophy is therefore only appropriate, regarding which, see below. We may perhaps equally well say that *Angst* begins in leisure, or that philosophy begins in *Angst*, as we might say that philosophy is the realm of justification, of excuses, excuses that are never quite good enough. In this context it might be apt to invoke Nietzsche: To those human beings who are of any concern to me I wish suffering, desolation, sickness, ill-treatment, indignities – I wish that they should not remain unfamiliar with profound self-contempt, the torture of self-mistrust, the wretchedness of the vanquished: I have no pity for them, because I wish them the only thing that can prove today whether one is worth anything or not – that one endures. (Nietzsche, *The Will to Power* (New York: Random House, 1968), p. 481)

become so figurative, so protean, that nothing, whether thing, word, concept, structure, force, or process is not fundamentally colored by its action.

For Hegel, who notoriously glorified the Prussian state in his political writing (though as always with Hegel, there is an easy, or dismissive, reading and the others), such masters, or their embodiment in the higher spiritual entity that is the polity, hold legitimate life-and-death sway over every citizen, which is demonstrated in its just (and justified) prerogative of claiming their lives, chiefly, but not exclusively, in warfare, a picture of society, not to mention of politics, that is delineated in terms of the dominance-and-submission model described above,[38] a perhaps disturbing fundamental dyad that will resurface in the thinking of Nietzsche, Freud, and Bataille.

Hegel's slave is aware that he might die, and he approaches the struggle with quite rational fear. But the dominant figure, who has set aside his fear, will nevertheless always be prey to a lurking dis-ease because he cannot, of course, trust his bondsman – after all, he "knows himself," and this means that he is therefore at odds with himself, too. In fact, the "anxiety" that will come to dominate much post-Hegelian thinking about death is the cultural contribution of the master(-race).[39] Fear of death (well, fear of harm, of predation, of becoming food) makes sense. It is completely natural and precedented among the sentient species, but anxiety, a fear with no overt object, a fear without (specifiable) cause, as it were, is where an *inchoate* version of the human cowers, and this is the legacy of the master, and of the state. It is a form of bad conscience. Which of course does not mean that it cannot and has not been experienced by just anyone at all: The master and the slave are in all of us, and all are, in principle, integrated in "absolute knowing," the presiding spirit of the work. In the "external" world, castles are the projection of *Angst*, and the rising *Angst* of the bourgeoisie, which will color the thought of the next two centuries(!) and profoundly contribute to revolution, war, and psychoanalysis, may well have been what those who held (a necessarily precarious) grip on wealth and power always felt, and which, in the waxing democratic, or let's say bourgeois, world, had now become commonplace.

In Hegel, death, or rather, actually, awareness of our death, a crucial distinction, as, for Hegel, knowing is the epitome of human activity, is for the first time seen as not only the condition necessary for human life (as opposed to for eternal life, to which it served as portal in Christianity: Christ's "you must die that you shall live" takes on a quite different cast in the context), but what *liberates* it from animal banality (which would be

---

38 The very structure of the *Phenomenology* might be said to reflect this paradigmatic moment and its social projection: "Absolute knowing," the perspective in which all of the lower, lesser, subordinate stages on the way of consciousness are integrated and from which all are judged is never in a state of equal interaction with any of them, but always stands above, has always incorporated them in its program prior to their very emergence, which is, "extra-textually," also true with respect to every reading that comes to the work. The lesser position has always been foreseen and rejected, or rather overcome. It is dominated by its totality, forestalling any possible criticism.

39 One is reluctant to go out too far on a Spenglerian limb, but a natural connection between philosophy and totalitarianism certainly seems to want to surface here.

the pre-lapsarian human state), invoking the entire breadth of the cultural adventure. And it is here that struggle as paradigm for the human experience, which would so affect the further course of nineteenth-century philosophy, in Schopenhauer, Nietzsche, and Marx, and of course Freud, would begin.

If for Plato and Jesus, the philosopher is the one who sacrifices his life that others might live, in Hegel's polity, though it is "informed by reason," the state rather sacrifices its members (and with the implicit sanction, if not the control of the philosopher). Great men make history, riding the *Zeitgeist* roughshod over peasant and philosopher alike, and they, too, will in due course submit to the "slaughtering bench of history." However, it is the philosopher (the "we" philosopher, as opposed to any particular one, though of course he is Hegel first and foremost), to whom alone, in his expansive awareness, is granted the vision in which the whole appears rational, but even in Hegel's rather simpler own time, we see him struggling to fuse elements of the grand field that are becoming intractable and which appears quite forced, if not outright ridiculous, in comfortable retrospect. It will, in part, be the patent failure to comprehend every aspect of the world in a rational scheme that invokes the division of one erstwhile system among various human and social sciences and admits the incursion of "the real world," of the genuinely heterodox, once again into the domain of philosophy, and of death.

The aftermath of the Napoleonic Wars and the spread of industrialization, with its concomitant social effects, spelled the death of the world in which such systems made sense, in which a unitary, "organic," all-embracing (or all-dominating) worldview seemed natural (though its preponderance was obviously linked to the ascent of technological control of nature), something still akin to the Platonic conception of society, in which each of the disparate social groups had its specifiable role and provided mutual support among themselves, or existed in any case for a reason beyond either the exploitation of their fellows and of nature or working themselves to near death in order to be able to wake up and do the same again the following day for the benefit of others. (Even though the state became more and more "totalized," it was only through many acts of economic and social individuation and consolidation that that was compassed: It became something like an amalgam rather than a community.) With the concentration of populations into urban centers, the personal alienation of worker from employer, abstraction of life into work, increasing economic and social disparities between classes, long working hours in de-socialized environments, insuring the expansion and isolation of the middle class, workers becoming more and more (physically) remote from their work, that is, losing manual contact with their tools and products, as well as the loss of human contact, tending of course to erode institutions predicated on community such as the Church, and the population explosion of the late eighteenth and early nineteenth centuries, a new sense of the meaning and purpose of philosophy also arose. Marx and others – utilitarians, positivists, socialists, and utopians – who had abandoned (or at least sought to abandon) philosophy proper at the outset, took a practical, materialist, approach instead of submitting to the powerful sense of despair, or disintegration that would soon color the principal trends in European philosophy, determining their language and their understanding of the world. There is no social glue any longer – the God before whom all men were brothers, and in principle equal, regardless of social position, was no longer tenable; he had, in fact, failed – and even the demeaned men for whom he had always been a comfort resented his intrusion, an ever watchful boss-figure, upon their ever more regimented and limited personal time and space.[40] The notion that God could even be dead already appears in Hegel, as it does in Kierkegaard (and Marx), before its enduring formulation in Nietzsche.[41] Even Pascal had offered a touching and elegiac foretaste of the theme two centuries earlier: "Nature is such that it signifies everywhere a lost God both within and outside of man."

If, in the perfection or perhaps the self-sufficiency of the (Hegelian) System, it offered nothing on which to build, then it could certainly be purposefully eviscerated, and its critics would take to that with gusto. So, though it produced no obvious heir for most of a century (if some might wish to designate Marx at least as a bastard), Hegel's work stimulated the most fertile reaction in the history of philosophy, his opponents carving up sacred cows right and left, and for the first time questioning even the sovereignty of reason, not only in the world at large, but even among the human faculties, and opening metaphysics to the alien ministrations of psychology, the social sciences, and even the austerer realms of science and mathematics.

It is no secret that Schopenhauer, who considered the "Hegelian aberration" to be akin to a Ptolemaic epicycle, a perverse departure from the natural course of reason, abominated Hegel and all his works. In fact, the animating assumption of the Hegelian philosophy, by and large the position of all post-Socratic philosophy, if importantly modified by Kant, namely, the notion that the world is rational (if only because it is "our" world), struck many of his most vigorous critics as simply absurd. Like a neo-pre-Socratic, Schopenhauer upended the Platonic hierarchy of the faculties (meaning also, reality), and posited Will, in which we might see echoes of Aristotelian *physis* as well as an adumbration of Freud's death drive, as the one principle of existence, otherwise hewing to the more or less Kantian epistemological position that he regarded as the true natural order of things.

It would be fair to say that Schopenhauer was the first modern Western figure outside of the Judeo-Christian tradition to explicitly consider the question of death (in its simple human, as opposed to the hyper-abstract Hegelian sense) to be central to philosophy, and he treats the matter at greater length and in more intimate detail than any predecessor of whom we are aware. Having demonstrated (to his satisfaction), prevailing upon what would seem to be an idiosyncratic understanding of Newton, that the animating principle (of human life) is immortal, and construed the particulars of its perdurance after a Brahminist/Buddhistic

---

40 Cf., Nietzsche's "Ugliest Man."

41 The projection of our mortality onto our greatest creation represents a dispiriting, or potentially energizing, watershed in human history.

model of metempsychosis, or rather palingenesis, he is at pains to resolve the tragic conse-quences of his conclusion. In a world dominated by blind will, what is to be expected by the consciousness that can experience it but cruelty, disappointment, and suffering, appar-ently, now, throughout all eternity? Although he never quite specifies just how the cycle of rebirth might function, though here again he resorts to a curious scientific mode of demonstration, nor how it might actually be broken, he posits the highest calling of reason, though it, too, be spawn of and thrall to Will, as the denial and, ideally, the termination of the abhorrent persistence of life. This is the basis of Schopenhauer's ethics, essentially, resistance to the inevitable (including of course the "typical"), which is in his view, rather refreshingly, life, rather than death.

So, death, far from cause for the terror it has sometimes inspired in human beings (who have seen only the appearance and not the truth), is the locus of hope for Schopenhauer, though a highly problematical hope, as, if it is possible at all, it must depend upon the ability of reason to penetrate appearance and then to persuade the individual will to defy the tenacious universal Will, perhaps even, eventually, to bring the wheel of rebirth itself to a halt, and with it, life. One feels here, perhaps for the first time, the frustrated *desire* for death, for death *as* death – and death has been almost everything but death in the history of philosophy – that will re-surface, if in profoundly transformed ways, in Bataille and Blanchot, and which, if also in a quite different sense, tormented Kierkegaard as well. It is what they (or "we," if you please), *mutatis mutandis*, long for, but cannot *have*, whether it be eternity or finitude that denies it.

Why all the convolution, we might well wonder? Wouldn't it be far more straightforward simply to embrace the death that is commonly believed to be final, or even to hasten it, and skip the acrobatics? Of course it would, but in that case it would be just one opinion, albeit a notionally philosophical one, amidst if against others, and it would scarcely suffice to convey the profound disdain, the abhorrence, in which Schopenhauer held life, an abhorrence that found its complex expression in a position whose "scientific" character must have gratified him. So, though he freely admits that suicide is within the rights of every being capable of it, and deeply desires the end of human suffering, he nevertheless argues that it merely supports the universal Will against which it is supposedly directed (it is even an extreme incarnation of that Will) and therefore is neither a moral nor an efficacious act. To truly embrace death, to *achieve* death, it must be a death wrested from the impossible, or at least from the vast resistance against its finality that had characterized philosophy, and all human culture, up until his day. The philosopher has his task before him, and, as so often, especially in this era of the paradoxical closing of human potential even as its technology was opening others, it is the most difficult task yet known to humanity: for Schopenhauer, the self-eradication of the race.

If death were the end plain and simple – without his notion of immortality, that is – there would be no basis for the ethics: The way of the world would be just as problematic, just as much cause for pessimism, and now irresistible, as it is in the unenlightened, unphilosophized world.[42] Pessimism itself would be futile. This is the problem that Nietzsche, too, faces and which embarks him on his own complex, "absolutely scientific" cosmo-eschatology, the "Teaching of The Eternal Return" (of the Same), though, for him, the ostensible problem was quite the opposite: how to avoid the pessimism of Schopenhauer, to reject nihilism, in fact, to embrace life with a resounding (Faustian) "Yes!" in spite of itself. For him, too, this was not merely a scientific and a "metaphysical" problem, but an ethical one. If God is dead, there is no basis for an ethical teaching (if to be a law unto oneself, assuming one is made of the right stuff, can be called a teaching)... unless, Nietzsche shrewdly discerned, we are doomed, or destined, or privileged, to repeat our every moment throughout eternity: then, it will be only those who have decisively, valiantly chosen their every act whose death will therefore also be meaningful (the death of the just? or of the philosophical? – one hears echoes of the detested Plato, in any case), a death that will be able to bear the burden, and the test, of its unending repetition.[43] Of course, here, too, the notion that within the cycle of the same there might somehow emerge that something slightly different, that recognition or that urge or that nagging *déjà vu*, that will actually fulfill the burden of ignominy for the deserving and gratify the noble, is difficult to construe, the engine, as it were, of difference within the same, just as in its negative image in Schopenhauer, for whom renunciation, à la Socrates's philosopher, was charged with the resistance against insuperable Will. But where death is the ultimate good for the latter, it is life – in spite of death, whose finitude we confront indefinitely in the cycle of eternity, almost as if to emphasize that fact with preternatural force – that Nietzsche embraces. To love life, he insists, is also to love death, the expression of a primordial unity rather than a mere fusion. Schopenhauer's might have been a passion for death, but not a true love.

Although the love of death, the ability to love one's death (and here for the first time in history, just *because* it is one's own), might not be the *differentia crucis* in Nietzsche's notorious distinction between *Untermenschen* and *Übermenschen*, it certainly offers a clue, as the ability to face death with equanimity, or sangfroid, or even indifference always has signalized the noble soul among the many, as to wherein the radical and radically dismissive, joyfully destructive, philosophy of Nietzsche joins the history it disdains, if perhaps as a *primus inter pares*: I choose death above the company of my inferiors, and not only that, but specifically as against the company of my inferiors. However, one might also note that Nietzsche's detestation of the perverse violence committed against the spirit that ignites his contempt for the so-called "slave mentality," overlooks (or ignores) the prior (biological, historical, evolutionary, what have you) fact that the imperious disdain of the master for

---

42 It would mean that, instead of a finite quotient of "souls," the potential pool was unlimited, and hence its eradication impossible.

43 Although suicide is far from *de rigueur* to the Nietzschean ideal, it is obvious that a chosen, aesthetic, meaningful death is preferable to mere accident, or incident – "Die at the right time!" as he enjoined – and Nietzsche certainly supported suicide in more than one respect. For him, the self-recusal of the weak and dispirited from life was all to the benefit of the race.

the "herd" is already a violence against "nature," in which the life-affirming value of the social is primordially inscribed.[44] Again, however, the conviction that there is more than one "nature" at play among humans re-connects Nietzsche to an abiding undercurrent in the history of philosophy, and one that, as we have seen, is the locus of aporetic disturbance in both Plato and Hegel. All the same (and apparent, or even real contradiction hardly phased Nietzsche), it is important to bear in mind that his is a *critical* moral philosophy in a way that had scarcely existed previously (though we might see Hume as something of a precursor) and that its targets did not break down strictly along class, race, religious, ideological, intelligence, or accomplishment lines. In fact, the place of death in his work represents a clear break with the principal overt tendencies of the past and an effort to bring to light their underlying motivations. And in spite of the corruption and hypocrisy he diagnosed in the history of culture in general, and of philosophy in particular, he arrived at a perspective from which to embrace the life (and death) it had been at pains to dissemble or demean, which he called the "revaluation," a possibility that we all vaguely recognize but which we generally feel incompetent to realize, that instead of the fear, distress, disgust, or despair with which we suffer rebarbative life and callous death, we can take joy in it, see it not as an insidious and deceptive spectacle engineered to manipulate or neuter us, but as a wonder of human artistry and invention, an opportunity to experience and to join in its constant re-creation out of nothingness. That it was virtually impossible to regard this as anything but a proposal to a distant future, one still far in the offing today, is all the more poignant on that account.

The two most explicit antagonists of Hegel had, naturally, begun as acolytes, and each, in going to his own root, became a revolutionary. Marx, for the realization of whose vision, death, and massive death, was a *sine qua non*, scarcely mentions it, focusing on the *work* aspect of the "lordship and bondage" relationship as opposed to its death component,[45] and beginning a long tradition among his descendants (which is not to say his disappointed descendants, such as Adorno, Benjamin, Bloch, Bataille, and Baudrillard, et al.), for whom such individual matters seem all but irrelevant to the sort of theory, or use of time, that is pertinent within the unredeemed world, (though images of violence and bloodshed certainly pervade his work).[46] And reasonably enough for a philosopher who upended

---

44 The essay "Pragmatism and Gay Science" by Barry Allen in *John Dewey and Continental Philosophy*, ed. Paul Fairfield (Carbondale: Southern Illinois University Press, 2010) offers some instructive considerations along these lines.

45 We are inclined to say that violence is *death at work*.

46 For the Marxist tradition, philosophy ignores the omnipresent and fundamental violence to which it is handmaiden and quiet support. When it speaks to its specialty, to death, it is, in the guise of a radical inquiry, of *the* radical inquiry, only asserting its essential passivity and subservience to a higher power, the power of violence, to power itself, which is the active and dominant mode of death in the world, by comparison with which the death of the philosophers is inert and powerless, and engagement with which the latter have ceded in compensation for absolute sway in their own circumscribed realm, as if to say, "Henceforth this is our department, and that is yours." To talk about death only as death is specifically to avoid talking about violence, which accordingly becomes a fact only of the world (as opposed to a fact for philosophy), something that happens rather than something we do. Not to engage death as a violent relationship to life is to do death itself violence, to twist and torture it, to ignore the terror by embracing the dread. Philosophy

metaphysics and banished the ghostly (*geistig*) shades of idealism from its halls. Action was what was needed, and the role of the thinker was merely to foment the rising up of the lethargic masses prior to standing aside and allowing them to chart their own proper destiny, or perhaps a little more than that: philosopher prime ministers or philosopher secretaries of state if not kings. Well, that was the idea. And of course, the celebration of the heroic death for the cause, of revolutionary suicide, would quite naturally become another matter, but, again, subordinated to the cause, all death for which is martyrdom and therefore an at least notionally transcendent purpose. In fact, we might well see the great swaths of revolutionary death that are implied in the very program of revolution as a sort of gift to the future, or a communal work of sacrifice on which that future will be built. But the thought of the individual death had no meaning outside of such a larger agenda. On his very deathbed, Marx dismissed the notion of the traditional summarizing apothegm, a way of saying that death was not really anything to which he gave any special consideration, a moment among those of a lifetime, and far less useful, not that his own didn't precisely serve the god of utility: "Last words are for those who never did anything."[47]

Søren Kierkegaard's work, on the other hand, is saturated with death, exemplifying his avowed philosophical mission of "thinking death into every moment." And where it is not literal death, it is death deadlier than death, whose gravitational field no thinking or writing can escape: All human space-time is warped by it. Here, explicitly, in a way that had at best been adumbrated, applied unconsciously, or theorized so abstractly that its presence remained at best ghostly, however prominent it was conceptually in earlier philosophy, there is "no sharp demarcation of life from death. It impinges on life, becoming in a way experientially present."[48] Here, death is no longer understood as mere event, nor even as opposition, force, or power, but as a, or rather *the*, way of life, a blurring of the very distinction between life and death, of experiencing death as fully integral to life, a perspective that will cast a long dark shadow into the future of philosophy.

In *Either/Or*, "A" writes,

> If I imagined two kingdoms bordering each other, one of which I knew rather well and the other not at all, and if however much I desired it I were not allowed to enter the unknown kingdom, I would still be able to form some idea of it. I would go to the border of the

---

has stood above the physical world where violence takes place, over which it rules, operating in a *meta*-physics that is therefore divorced from truth. The relatively violent milieu of Hegelian philosophy, by the standards of philosophy in general, derives specifically from the fact that the master-slave relationship is at its core: Everything in a slave-owning society is predicated on violence and the constant threat of death. And it is no coincidence that Marx's conceptual revolution is his direct response to Hegel.

47 Although I seem to have mis-recalled them, "Last words are for fools who haven't said enough" can readily be glossed as what I did recall, with the added implication that wasting words, that is, not putting them to real use, is precisely wherein philosophy has failed the world.

48 Patrick Stokes and Adam Buben, eds., *Kierkegaard and Death*, Indiana Series in the Philosophy of Religion, Kindle Edition. Paraphrased from location 397 of George Connell's essay, "Knights and Knaves of the Living Dead: Kierkegaard's Use of Living Death as a Metaphor for Despair."

kingdom known to me and follow it all the way, and in doing so I would by my movements describe the outline of that unknown land and thus have a general idea of it, although I had never set foot in it. And if this were a labor that occupied me very much, if I were unflaggingly scrupulous, it presumably would sometimes happen that as I stood with sadness at the border of my kingdom and gazed longingly into that unknown country that was so near and yet so far, I would be granted an occasional little disclosure.[49]

And such a methodology, such a *way* – in its original context pertaining to music – is applied with unrelenting vigor to the kingdom of death as well.

Death *in* life is the locus of Kierkegaard's thinking. We may not know death (*qua* death), but we can observe its effects upon and around us, we can find the kingdom of death within. In fact, for the Christian, and hardly in Kierkegaard's view alone, life consists in dying – living might indeed be more properly *called* dying – and the existential process of dying, fearing to die, longing to die, being unable to die, etc., which is after all, *ours*, enables thought to gain a purchase on the unknown realm. Whereas for Hegel, the prospect of death opens up the possibility of both self-knowledge and the annihilation of the self (in the struggle-for-recognition scenario), for Kierkegaard, the latter is impossible, which implies the even more profoundly terrifying prospect of "eternal death"; and the longing for death in its finality, the longing for the possibility of genuine suicide that despair engenders, the insuperable and almost human-life defining dread that "burns *but does not devour the soul*," only reveals the eternal life of the self. Of course, Kierkegaard "knows" what awaits the dead, which casts his thinking in a rather different light than, say, that of a Schopenhauer, for all that they both acknowledge the dreadful immortality of the soul. But at the same time, for Kierkegaard, the prospect of gazing upon the face of God is no less dreadful, and deadly, than that of eternal death: Dread is a two-edged sword.

Kierkegaard deeply felt the dread – *Angst* almost seems too quaint by comparison with what he felt – about which he wrote, the "sickness unto death" as he called it, and he had reason for profound existential insecurity, though he saw it as a necessary human condition (and not one merely his own), ascribing it even to those who seemed not to feel it at all – who even insisted they did not, a sort of "unconscious" despair, if you will, most visible precisely in their prosecuting ordinary lives as if there were nothing at all amiss! Occasionally Kierkegaard will characterize such blissfully unaware types as "too shallow to feel [the] dread" that is in them, and hence, we are compelled to conclude, as scarcely human. Indeed, in his otherwise powerfully humane thinking, one often reads of the ignorant multitudes, the distracted masses, and of the leveling tendencies of the mass culture that render us all more ordinary, stupid, and inadequate to the spiritual task to which we are called, and always in contrast to "the One," the almost impossible but longed-for spiritual companion, his true reader, himself likely to be far from having entered the sphere of the living as yet, to whom his work is dedicated.

---

49 Søren Kierkegaard, *Either/Or, Part I* (Princeton: Princeton University Press, 1987), p. 66.

Throughout the nineteenth century, we encounter the persistent theme that virtually no one is prepared to receive genuine philosophy (nor, for that matter, to encounter death, we might note), that it is, perforce, a missive to the future: For Schopenhauer there are frequently "perhaps only a few people who are prepared to understand this"; on his deathbed, Hegel is alleged to have said (apparently spuriously, but the anecdote has obvious roots in reality), "There is only one man who has understood me, and even he misunderstood me." Kierkegaard's and Nietzsche's disdain for the smugly ignorant, the masses of humanity, and particularly those who have been offered the social privileges of knowing better, is well known, though each of them, like Heidegger after them, felt a spiritual kinship with genuine simplicity (even with innocent horses). And Marx's concern that the proletariat would never sufficiently comprehend its true situation to act in its own behalf without having been led to water by the intelligentsia is outright programmatic.

We know that the individual is the fundamental "category" for Kierkegaard, that his abhorrence of the Hegelian system is based precisely on the fact that it leaves no place for the individual, the actual living and responsible person, much as the society of his Golden Age Copenhagen in its self-satisfaction cannot see the humble beggar or weary traveller who is the very embodiment of Christ, much less offer him comfort, nor, for that matter, recognize that in another sense it is their own souls who are the humble beggar. Kierkegaard often speaks of the emptiness, the virtual soullessness of his contemporaries (as of the life of the times), who are absorbed in the trivia of their daily existence and fail to see that the truly momentous (let's say their one, unique, and all-important death, for the sake of ease) is pressing upon them at every moment. In their smug congregations, for in the state Christianity of Denmark everyone took his identity in large part from his place in the church, they fail to see that "there is no common shipwreck in eternity," that belief is a matter, and a terrifying matter, between the individual and his God, and even if in the end, Kierkegaard cannot bring himself to believe that his God would actually consign even a single sinner to the depths of Hell, neither can he conscion the abdication of any sinner's supreme individual call to believe; and of course what he sees around him every day is hardly what he understands by that name. Naturally, we are tempted to view Kierkegaard's obsessive, even desperate, concern with the utterly isolated individual precisely as evidence that the era of Christianity had passed, and that therein lay the reason for his alarm. The community of Christians had been a meaningful and conditioning aspect of the early "Church," and *agape* was unquestionably the relationship to one's fellow man that defined the Christian standpoint; it was in fact Jesus's principal ethical teaching, in the context of which the panicked obsession with one's own death might appear rather paradoxical, and (at least doctrinally) misguided or self-absorbed if not outright heretical.[50] Nevertheless, Derrida

---

50 For Kierkegaard, the only true relationship to God, the absurdity of faith, *can only be* heretical, incomprehensible from the standpoint of the ethics of men, as exemplified by the actions of Abraham on Mount Moriah. The thematic that historically links the incomprehensible solitude of the vocation of the philosopher (his ethical distance in all respects from human society) to the lives and deaths of Socrates and Jesus is perhaps nowhere more pronounced than in the experience and the thinking of Kierkegaard.

sees in Kierkegaard's understanding of the "relationship" between the "singular" self and the "wholly and utterly Other" (to God) a model, in fact a homologue for the relationship between self and other in general, akin to that espoused by Levinas, a way, in effect, of exporting Kierkegaard's ethics from the realm of his ontology and of emphasizing both the unbridgeable abyss that separates individuals and the profound incumbency of the ethical burden, of the literal infinitude of responsibility. The cost, however, is an ethics that is utterly without "consequence," as Derrida will conclude, an analogue of Adorno's early criticism of Kierkegaard's conception of the radical inwardness of the subject as ultimately inert, unrelatable to anything, and hence disqualified from any ethical or for that matter epistemological standing, the most demanding and the least achieving of positions, unless of course we are to take the realm of the aesthetic a great deal more seriously (in itself) than philosophy has ever been prepared to do.[51] Even Kant's aesthetic, though the lynchpin between the pure and the practical, lived (from his perspective) only to serve them.

It was amidst a social epidemic of *Angst* (re-conceived scientifically as "neurosis," a psycho-physical as opposed to a spiritual ailment), that Freud entered the stream of intellectual history, and he long construed the occasional case of death-anxiety as rather strong reaction to less fundamental problems, or as a means of disguising what were more fundamental, if perhaps indeed utterly idiosyncratic problems, beneath a veneer of "the most important thing in the world," as if my problems are so enormous that they can only be conjured with in terms of the greatest of woes. He was, as Kierkegaard might have judged him, one of those shallow souls who never felt anything like that at all, and he was convinced that such turmoil was symptomatic of a more genuine problem harbored within the unconscious – you know, something like the fear of castration, or of abandonment. For him the sickness unto death was an actual illness.

How the death drive theory, or rather, hypothesis came to be – Freud always spoke of the death drive as hypothesis, or even as myth, and one is tempted here to invoke the lineage of the "noble lie" – in fact smacks of the repressive essence of the unconscious and hearkens back to Kierkegaard's "unconscious dread," if it rather tends to level, and of course to circumscribe, its field of action. As in any good Victorian-era bourgeois household, death was long unwelcome in psychoanalysis.

Freud came to it very slowly, even reluctantly, assuming that the symbolic law of the unconscious must be at play in death anxieties. It was by virtue of his own loss (of his daughter, Sophia), coupled with and reinforced by the overwhelming presence of death during and following the Great War, that he would begin the more serious examination of its part in our psychological economy. From the beginning, Freud's death-thoughts are intertwined with his matter-of-fact understanding of human aggression and violence – he

---

51 The genuine work of art approaches the wholly idiolectic (mystical) document as a limit, something such as we imagine the Voynich manuscript to be, for example. It demands even as it rebuffs understanding. Art is a religion whose God is inaudible, who approaches non-existence, to all but the artist.

solves the "problem of evil" without lifting a conceptual finger – and with its relationship to guilt, mourning, and the ambivalence of even the purest of human relationships, with sadism and the quandary of primary masochism, and with the repetition compulsion, and, as they evolve or mutate from half of a dualist conception of the psyche into the notion of a fundamental death drive, they become "a universal explanatory principle" (Baudrillard), subsuming the erotic drives within its encompassing sweep, which for many critics means that it says nothing at all about death, or anything else for that matter, or perhaps everything all at once, but either way more as poetry or an atavistic pre-Socratism than as science or philosophy. For them, it remains a dead-end, if a powerfully evocative, even paralyzing, dead-end that has by turns been vigorously rejected, ignored, or transformed beyond recognition by the psychoanalytic establishment.

It is as astonishing to imagine that the first "scientific" treatment of death, or let's say the first elaborate and grounded treatment of life as finitude, would take place only in the early twentieth century, as that this hypothesis by a man little inclined to see death as much of an issue in human life is also perhaps its most artful and most philosophical exposition, at once terrifying, pacifying, and measured, as if life itself were a protracted suicide in which we are complicit beyond even our ability to understand complicity. As Jonathan Lear contends, this was something new in the annals of philosophy, a "truly non-Socratic approach to human rationality. Rather than starting, as Socrates does, with an argument that mind must be rational, and then wondering how irrationality can be tacked on, [in] psychoanalysis . . . [Freud] begins with the idea that mind must be sometimes irrational,"[52] a position that philosophers were for obvious reasons loath to embrace.

Like any good scientist, Freud of course changed or revised the question, or questions, as they had previously been conceived, from "What is death?" or "What is the proper attitude toward death? or even "What does the fact of death imply for metaphysics, ethics, or politics?" to "How does death function in human life?" And the hypothesis of the death drive answers that it serves a fundamental structuring function, intrinsically operative at every moment and affecting psyche (and soma) whether or not we are at all aware of it and regardless of how we might feel about that. Death, for Freud, is neither the simple negation of life, nor the guilt-drenched (though it is in its way guilt-drenched) portal to the next life, nor, for that matter, is it surmountable [even] dialectically: it is an indestructible principle, and hence scarcely to be reckoned with at the highest peaks of the philosophical tradition. In its overtly paradoxical conjunction of death and drive, it would seem to invoke such precedents as Schopenhauer's "the aim of life is death," vitalizing death, making it a constant and ineluctable force, an intrinsic component of life, an organizing principle as opposed to an event in its putative singularity. For Freud, life is thrall to death.

The notion of the death drive, while it responds to the oppressive inevitability of death that always underlay so-called "metaphysics," and *a fortiori*, theology, to which both struggled

---

52 Jonathan Lear, *Open Minded* (Cambridge, MA: Harvard University Press, 1998), pp. 89–90.

to find a less permanent solution, if it offers no hope, like them it also, albeit oddly and in more intrinsic form, lends comfort to the dying – to us – for death, by Freud's account, *is* life. This is the horror and the solace of it. Heidegger would define death as *Dasein*'s "ownmost, non-relational, not-to-be-outstripped, certain, and indefinite possibility (of impossibility)." For Freud, even though each of us is instinct with what amounts to a very personal death, we are unable to conjure with it on its own terms: The unconscious by definition cannot accommodate the notion of the death of its subject,[53] hence death cannot be approached, or understood, except as it occurs to another, and therefore only by analogy as our own. As intimately as our death drive is *our* death drive, we cannot meaningfully imagine our death. We are not, therefore, "alone" in death, as Heidegger (as Kierkegaard before him) will insist: our relationship to death is largely configured by loss and by mourning for others (meaning as well that, though we will not be there to experience it, they will stand to us, too, in the mourning relationship). In some sense, our lives in their entirety can be understood, in Freudian terms, as a continuous process of mourning, and a continuous process of coming to terms with loss (in a variety of senses, beginning with the process of detachment from the mother), that is, via empathetic response, a fact that has inclined some commentators to elaborate a Freudian ethics of "tolerance, patience, and acceptance" on the basis of the hypothesis, which "requires us to learn the lesson of ambivalence, that life consists of fulfillment and disappointment, and that the two are inseparable."[54]

We do not experience death, we cannot *outstrip* it. It is inevitable, and we cannot get beyond it so as to comprehend it as a narratological conclusion to life, as an event in effect within life; we are essentially finite: so much is true for both Freud and Heidegger, though both of them alter the sense of death from mere event to persistent accompaniment to life and hence, its experientially uncompassable chronology aside, already insure that it "exists" for us and that it isin some sense *in* life. While it is *certain*, the fact that for Freud we are a participant of sorts in its unfolding – it is "our" individual drive toward that death that describes our very life – suggests a quasi-agency in which we are accomplices rather than mere victims, or subjects, of death. As to its *indefiniteness*, again, while we cannot specify the moment at which we will die, the fact that the death drive functions like a(n aggressively) draining hour-glass, as a theory of fate, in effect, implies that the hour is in some obscure sense appointed for it, whether specifiable or not.[55]

These ambiguities within his theory of death (as also, of course, the metaphysical aspect of an inherently un-provable hypothesis – though in what sense are so many of the philosopher's own positions "provable"?) were certainly among the reasons that inclined Heidegger to

---

53 At the same time, it is difficult not to see the unconscious as somehow the realm of death, in which the suppressed, the killed memories and desires struggle for breath again, or, as in Plato, where the truth is buried.
54 I refer primarily to Havi Carel.
55 Something along these lines is discussed by Liran Razinsky in his *Freud, Psychoanalysis, and Death* (New York: Cambridge University Press, 2013).

express surprise that such an obviously intelligent man as Freud could speak such nonsense. At the same time, both Freud and Heidegger were groping toward a position that included the alien, the un-experienceable, within the internal, the existentially intimate, as well as integrating the social within the personal; and the theoretical tensions – the tergiversation between dualist and monistic psychic structures on Freud's part and the vagaries of emphasis that unbalance Heidegger's effort to accommodate the crucial conception of being-with (*Mitsein*) into the innermost structure of *Dasein* – that that engendered would soon result in the explosion of disparate and reactionary death-thoughts by which the philosophy of the later twentieth century is signalized.

For Freud, the unhappy individual (and who among us is not from the psychoanalytic standpoint?) stood pretty much no chance of self-understanding outside the ministrations of the psychologist, almost on strict account of the structural necessity of his conception of the self in relation to the unconscious, but he did stand to recognize the existential plight of his fellow man, much as a (trained) outsider could recognize the murmurings of the analysand's unconscious. For Heidegger, on the other hand, though each individual is existentially equipped to come to self-awareness on his own, and is deflected from that course only by external forces (*das Man*/"the They"/"One"), the inertial pull, or perhaps better, the roar, of social life is such that the individuating "call of conscience" is all but inaudible to the vast majority – perhaps ironically, it is in fact "silent" within the Heideggerian auto-dynamic itself (and perhaps unaccountably spontaneous even for those who should remark it) – to the extent that only the philosopher manages to achieve a measure of "authenticity" that renders him fully individual and fully human, Heidegger's insistence that in their way all men are philosophers notwithstanding. And the great mass of men, according to Heidegger, devote their lives precisely to evading their genuine being.[56] We are pain-aversive creatures, after all, while the manifest intention of philosophy is to potentiate pain, or at a minimum to demand effort, to destabilize a "functioning" system, much as *Angst* will alert *Dasein* to the fact of its death. In a way, philosophy itself is *Angst*.

One pictures Heidegger among his beloved *Volk*, relaxing each with a pipe at the end of a long work-day, the philosopher at his desk, his comrades at their mills or forges or fields, and there is unquestionably a genuineness and a depth to his peculiar fellow-feeling, to his sense of co-immersion in the people, difficult though it might be to imagine them not laughing at him behind his back in his perhaps not yet truly folkloric Black Forest attire, even as they might be wearing it themselves. It is again the workers divorced from the land, modern workers in offices and money-men, if you will, cut off from the relationship of stuff to the human hand, who are both alienated and despised as "the They" or as "One," as they have been at least from Schopenhauer, Nietzsche, and Kierkegaard on, no doubt inspired by Hegel's supercilious ("knowing") patronization of "ordinary" consciousness and perhaps even Marx's depiction of the banality and spiritlessness of the capitalist.

---

56 As Adorno points out, "Although we have evolved beyond other species in our awareness of our deaths, we can have this experience only in a curiously abstract form, probably out of self-preservation." *Metaphysics*, p. 133.

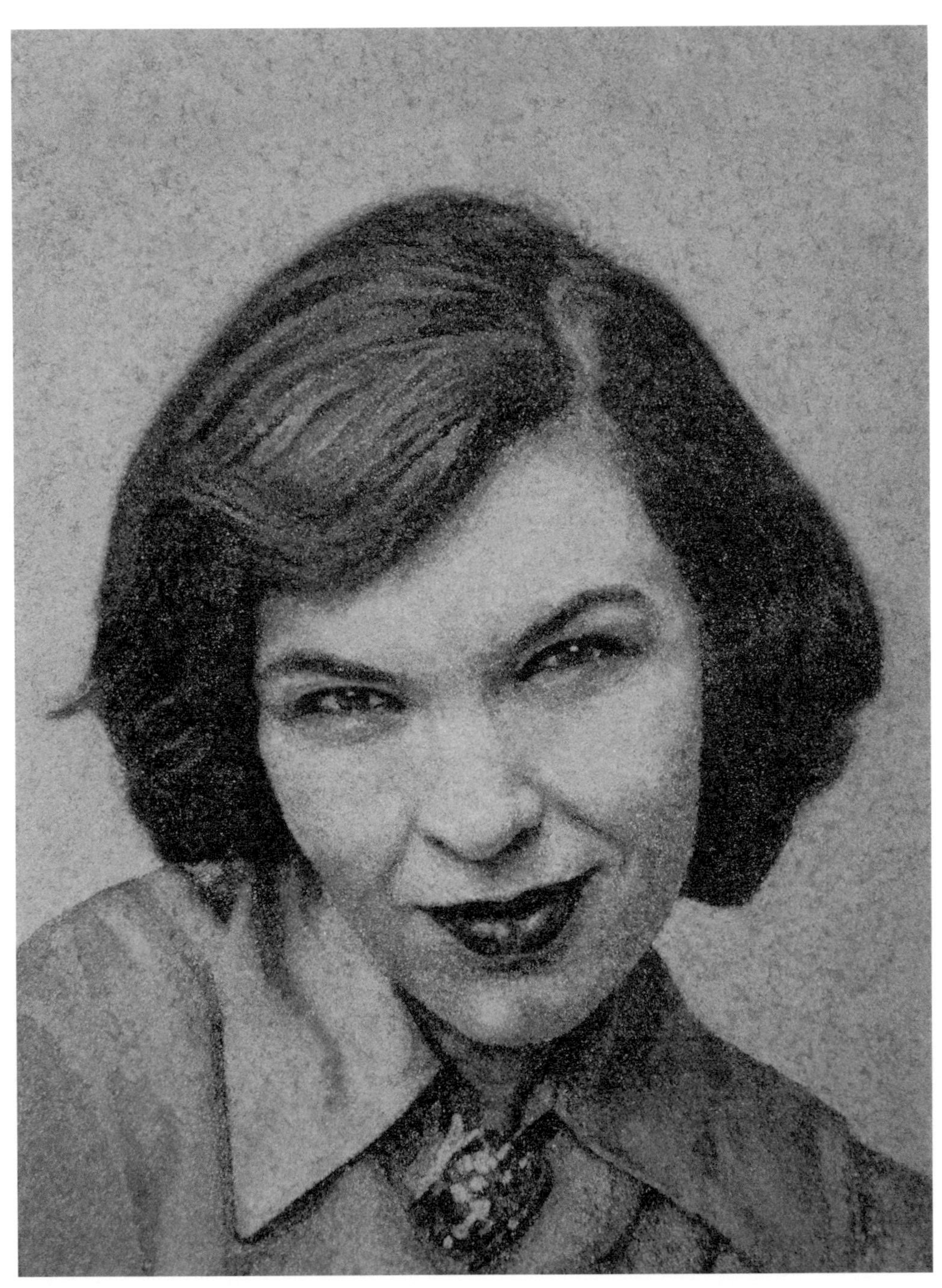

In much the same way that, for Heidegger, animals merely perish, while only humans die, it is not difficult to read the demise of the many within the Heideggerian scheme as ethically uninteresting to him, as many critics, beginning with Adorno, have, in view of the philosopher's (admittedly temporary, though bizarre and unconscionable) embrace of the Nazi program, been wont to do. As an ethicist in the Nietzschean mold, whose good ultimately derives only from the dictates of the individual's own being, unsupported or supportable by any external standard, in fact immoral or inauthentic to the extent that they are, (and of course loose or tighter connections bind *Dasein*, generally against its ownness, to the larger social amalgam), any true basis for community is at best obscure in Heidegger, while the very notion of "authenticity" is utterly contaminated by his theory of self-hood – of thrownness and *Mitsein* – and the irreducible commonality of language (the "house of *Dasein*"), that Heidegger espouses.

During and in wake of World War I, the idea that one might expect a death of one's own was deeply in question. For Freud, its shadow suggested that that we are being constantly, relentlessly, stalked by death, while for Heidegger, the ethical demand to find one's private, human, in the end, noble, or as Adorno tended to style it, "heroic," death amid the vast ignorance, oblivion, unconcern, and, as their ultimate consequence, mass slaughter, is an "ideal" that thwarts, even as it has been awakened by the terror occasioned by an omnipresent "thing" that we nevertheless collectively treat as if didn't exist and to which our individuality is almost irrelevant. It is, one is compelled to affirm, "One"/"the They" who presided over such vast swaths of impersonal death. If the ethical imperative of a personal death, then, is not exactly a call to suicide, in some respects even its opposite, an embedding in (human) "nature" perhaps, the desire for a fully embraced, consciously pursued death, of a preparing of the place for death, developed as the conclusion to a quasi-narrative that it has inspired, certainly has its assonances with it, while the Freudian death drive registers the helplessness that war visits upon the individual, even while acknowledging his complicity in it. For both Freud and Heidegger the re-imagining of the existential relationship to death can only be construed against this broader external background.

Whereas Heidegger responds to what he saw as the over-reaching, abstract, and "metaphysical," character of Hegel's conception of death as pure (unmediated) negativity – a consequence of his unique conflation, or integration of logic and experience – with a range so vast as to subsume, or at least to infiltrate everything, by preserving a core existential relationship to it in the individual experience of anxiety, which opens up his entire reconception of time as multi-vectoral – since we are always, in the nature of *Angst*, thinking ahead of or behind ourselves – and hence establishing the fundamental understanding of *Dasein* as "being-toward-death," his own best critics, who would by now have experienced the devastation, trauma, and pure depersonalized abyss of death that characterized the next World War, and would, accordingly, equally find his configuration of the *human* relationship to death abstract (or formulaic), if unlike Hegel's, spurious, pallid, insular, self-absorbed, and inadequate to the actual experience of terrified, disgusted, and dispirited living – and dying – human beings.[57] For them, the actual experience of dying had become either so intimately felt, witnessed, or imagined, or the modes of slaughter so appalling, mass-produced, and dehumanized, that to embrace Heidegger's by turns intimate and "heroic" construction of personal death seemed insulting to humanity. For them, it was the illusion of human culture itself, the illusion of philosophy, that lay in ashes. So, though much as in the wake of Hegel, little original thought built upon the Heideggerian model, as the principal locus of philosophical contention in its time, it profoundly marked the course of Western thinking (and even important strains of Eastern philosophy) ever since.

If we acknowledge the implicit Hegelian distinction between fear and anxiety, the fact that the anxiety relation to death arises from a hegemonic structure already colors Heidegger's conception of the authentic self: imperious, unconcerned about, even rather annoyed by the multitudes, by others – as Simon Critchley has characterized it, "Heidegger is one of those philosophers who has a problem with other people." Although the imperative of authenticity implies a strong, even an implacable recognition of responsibility as Heidegger's central ethical motivation, it is a responsibility only (or deeply lopsidedly) to one's self, which suggests no broader ethical mandate, or what might then seem to be no ethical mandate whatsoever. This perspective will become the locus for one of the most powerful strains of reaction against the Heideggerian philosophy, beginning with Levinas.

For all its hermetical appearance, beginning with its language – and the very notion of the occulting of Being invokes a hermetical program – Heidegger's intention was the direct approach to human experience, a project, along with the very conception of its language, that he inherited from his teacher, Edmund Husserl. For the generation that followed, this was, in some sense, the first thing to be rejected. In some sense only, because as opposed to Heidegger's occultism, for which arcane language pursues pedestrian goals (converting dross into gold and that sort of thing), theirs was often what might be viewed as a mystical approach: Though preternaturally direct, it pushes at the limits of language and hence of meaning, and at its highest pitch often achieves ecstasies which in their intensity can only dissipate before the crude light of day, in the diastole of passion. It is the thirst for the oceanic that is adumbrated in the dynamic of the sacred, which, for Georges Bataille, is all the more real for its "object" having been discovered to be of man's own creation. For the likes of Bataille and Blanchot, for all their differences, the only thing worth experiencing on the one hand, or worth writing on the other, is the impossible, the rest is just "knowledge,"[58] or words reduced to currency, imprisoned in the realm of "projects,"[59] of the ordinary, and the economy of accumulation and (false) exchange. Heidegger's "possibility of the impossible" offers only a tepid foretaste of the death that for Blanchot is brought to light as

---

57 As Adorno remarks in *Metaphysics* (p. 106), "death, in the form it has taken on, no longer accords with the life of any individual."

58 Bataille often contrasts "mere knowledge" with the genuine realm of experience, or "non-knowledge." It is self-awareness that makes human beings a "discontinuity" within nature.

59 Bataille's disdainful characterization of the practical realm of human action refers to Heidegger's terminology.

the "impossibility of the possible," and in which his understanding coincides most exactly with Bataille's: We lust for death, it is our utmost and transcendent desire, and we shall never have it. (And the melancholic sense underlying their work is that we have disqualified ourselves from having it, as if it were a tragic reversal of our banishment from the Garden of Eden.) The profound frustration of the summit of our desire is as close as we will get; in other words, the opacity of death remains perhaps not unchanged and unaffected by the millennia-long (philosophical) storming of its bastions, but maybe even rather deeper.

Bataille's orgiastic embrace of death is absurd in the face of everyday life, the principal, though certainly not the exclusive realm of Heideggerian inquiry, and hence, its (anthropologically) demonstrable universality notwithstanding, would be difficult to entertain as a (social) model. However, much as, for Freud, sadomasochism, in its eccentricity, reveals the nature of "normal" eroticism and might be explanatory even of non-sexual motivation as well, it uncovers what Bataille sees as the primary organic impulse toward re-integration in the continuity of being. The erotic, for Bataille, is thanato-tropic. And, at "bottom," absurd is definitive for human beings, infusing our "other history," and "other history of thought" that the "working" realm of life (and thought) has always been at pains to submerge for the sake of the general (broadly, economic) good. If we are inclined to see it as a version of the Apollonian/Dionysian divide, Bataille's work-taboo-transgression model of human (social) behavior versus (and inseparable from) transgression as choice, as passion, as passion unto death, must have resonated frighteningly in the post-war era (at least among the few who managed to encounter it). Bataille's death drive is more a death passion, not something to which we are merely subject but in which we lustily and against all reason, precisely against all reason, join, perhaps not exactly a choice, but not quite a fate either, a model for which Bataille must certainly have seen in the way that untold millions had so recently joined the cause of total annihilation. As a positive passion, his death urge already anticipates the thing itself in the effacement of personal identity that characterizes the sexual act – *la petite mort* – as well as all vertigoes, integrations, inexplicable ambiguities, altered states of consciousness, sacrifice, laughter, true poetry, and ecstasies, and by comparison with which the Freudian death drive appears only a tedious, if relentless, mechanism.[60]

Bataille conceives the passion for death (or sex, or sex-death, or any of the extremes of experience that foreshadow integration with the continuity of being within our discontinuous existential interlude)[61] as "sacred," though without the convenience of a sacred object,[62] whereas the actual event of death remains but the transgression of a boundary

---

60 The feeling of energy pouring wildly toward death, the exhilaration of sex, of creation, of mad disruption, is, underneath it all, for Freud, just the plodding insistence, the *basso ostinato* of the end.

61 It is difficult not to feel that Bataille's sense of oneself as a discontinuity might well reflect the alienation of the philosopher in a time of vast and incomprehensible slaughter and the urge to redeem in the flow of a harmonious nature the individual lives that can never be integrated among men.

62 Since we never "knew" that there was a sacred object, the only ostensible difference for Bataille between modern experience and that of the era of belief is in the level of self-deception involved, and the sacred "need" persists, whether out of primordial ignorance, inherent human need, inertia, habit, or an existential/structural substrate that is irreducible.

regardless of how passionately we may infuse it with the sort of Kierkegaardian longing for the unknowable that gives it (emotional) substance. Once we cross the border, our relationship to it ceases, with all the exquisite, torturous yearning that fuels the sense of enhanced reality that makes Bataille's work so compelling. But he is also about creating a model for transcendence, including especially political, and most certainly (very broadly understood) economic transcendence, the rejection of the "closed economy" of Hegelian totality, and his sense of a community, of a trans-individualist mode of being that subsists in ecstasy, in excess, in "expenditure without reserve" and the sort of fundamental mutuality that implies, demands the dissolution of interpersonal barriers and an integration of being that, again, though but an adumbration, heralds a profoundly different understanding of human existence and selfhood, one precluded to the individual, from that into which we have bumbled in the course of history.

If Bataille identified a pre-rational, pre-linguistic, if nevertheless persisting, mode of collective experience, a discovery or insight of the sort that has been crucial for the thinking of the post-Heideggerian era, presumably in reaction against Heidegger's view of language as the "house of *Dasein*," in which to locate potential hope for a social solution to the impasse of humanity, the impasse of death in its historical determination (as a consequence, that is, of its industrialization in Auschwitz, its trans-industrialization at Hiroshima), Maurice Blanchot turned its imperfectly albeit laboriously conceptualized death-work of language against the entire philosophical edifice, inverting "fundamental" ontology, even while concurring in its critique of Hegel and the Hegelian, and not only re-opening, but overturning the Platonic case against the poets and, if forbearing to put the accuser on trial, at least submitting him to a little pointed questioning.

For Blanchot, as for Levinas and Bataille, the history of metaphysics is a history of power, of domination, of violence. You might say that it reflects the rest of life that way. In absorbing all objects within the subject, the metaphysical model of thought has suppressed, in fact obliterated, all otherness, all difference, all singularity; not that it was entirely its fault, as language, from the Hegelian, some might even say the Platonic, perspective on, is the death of the thing.[63] In its vaunted "negativity," Hegelian consciousness, which lives and "sustains itself in death," conquered, or, for the squeamish, transformed, the evidently rather passive "external" world, but it lost the *world* in so doing, as well as alienating itself from (its own) authentic being, or, we might also say, its labor: it could not stand in true relation to the other because in its profligacy it had killed it (in the very broad sense in which death is operative in Hegel), nor, therefore, to itself. Blanchot locates the ultimate hubris of the (pre-apotheosized) Hegelian subject in the "impossibility" of the suicide that in its grandiosity it imagines as its fulfillment. The truth of its all-powerful negativity, its absolute freedom, is its necessary recognition that the ultimate god-like embrace of its own death as assertion of its superiority to or mastery over it, merely reveals the actual "sovereignty" of the latter.

---

63 If the house of *Dasein* is language and language is death, it might not be inapt to conclude that the house of *Dasein* is death.

In the attempt to determine my own death I am *ipso facto* "reduced" to thing-like flesh and hence never achieve *my* (unique, death-transcending) death, but only the same one that every other kind of living thing, and every other person, suffers. In the very act, my agency is rendered null. I merely die.[64] This much is already there in Hegel, the movement of the pre-self-conscious subject *toward* death that will be reversed in the all-important moment of the arrival of self-consciousness in the lordship and bondage dynamic.

Heidegger's avatar of consciousness, on the other hand, retreats from the wholesale slaughter of Hegelian negativity into what would appear to be an intimate, loving, fulfilling, and monogamous relationship with death, which rewards *Dasein* with a world of possibility, broached and textured by its considerate being-toward-death, with the one obvious (fairy-tale) stipulation, of course. But, like any relationship, it isn't all it might have seemed; things become tedious, distressing, wearying; one's bright hopes darken. Perhaps not all that we had thought was possible *is* possible; it may come to feel like living death. This perspective, representing the putative experience of Heidegger's despised and demoralized "They," is expressed in this darker side of the relationship to death, the one in which something like anxiety actually persists, weighs on one, and slowly saps the energy that the hopes and dreams of the "new" relationship (to death) might once have held out. Its once invigorating possibilities become impossible.

So much for the domestic analogy. Blanchot's critical subversion of Heidegger's tidy characterization of death as the "possible impossibility" to an "impossible possibility" (Derrida would later go so far as to say "necessary impossibility") is both the experiential recognition that we do not actually stride gloriously forth to our more-or-less-chosen deaths as (some) philosophy would have it,[65] but that we are worn down by life, by interminable dying (literally, as we of course do not "experience" death), as well as the deeper insight that the true *Being* of death, if you will, had been ignored. In its fury to overcome it, to master it, to negotiate or come to terms with it, philosophy has overlooked the actual human, the actual individual, situation in favor of a conceptual schema that makes everything, including death, the province of the subject, and an "other" as formidable as death was not likely to take that lying down. This so-called, "second death" of the subject, whose ambitious sense of possibility it had projected upon death, is in truth the impossibility of death. The philosopher, in effect, is now privileged to experience the abjection to which he (in thought at least) had consigned the multitude (of the inauthentic). The great death, the good death, and ordinary death are therefore the same. No conclusions nor ethical demands can be predicated upon what is now obvious is an illusory difference. Dying, interminable dying, becomes the human experience, and death retreats back into silence.

---

64 For the present discussion of Blanchot and Levinas, I want to acknowledge the work of Simon Critchley, particularly his provocative *Very Little… Almost Nothing: Death, Philosophy, Literature* (London: Routledge, 2004), as well as *Maurice Blanchot* by Ullrich Haase and William Large (London: Routledge, 2001).

65 Adorno had arrived at quite similar conclusions in his *Jargon of Authenticity*, and remarks in *Metaphysics*, "Death is more often perceived as something fortuitous and external, that comes upon us from outside."

In the failure of its effort to subjugate death – its refusal to accept it (as it is)[66] – which Blanchot identifies as its fundamental (and founding) project, in reducing the vast specificity of the world, and human existence to mere knowledge, of all otherness to subjectivity, philosophy's claim to pre-eminence among the human arts (and even Socrates, in the *Phaedo*, acknowledges that it is an art, if of course the highest art), comes severely into question. Philosophy henceforth is interrogated by writing. And writing concludes that philosophy, in its negativity, can express only our alienation from ourselves and from reality, never the reality or the fullness of self, and especially not the reality and fullness of the other that it had sought, curiously, just what literature will claim, or rather demonstrate, as its own "positivity": In literature (as Blanchot will reveal), there is no reality, and in writing, there is no self.

It is in literature, or "writing," which Blanchot elucidates as a different (mode of) and more essential language than the one (including, he contends, philosophy and the other "branches of arithmetic"), whose only goal is to express and convey ideas (facts, knowledge, truth, and so forth), that we encounter not merely an example of unassimilated, and finally unassimilatable "reality," an irreducible other, but a model of the infinitely "passive," responsible, attentive relationship to the other that is the only antidote to the failure of ontology. The momentarily paradoxical bouleversement of the roles of the earnest and the exulted (or "useless") modes of language follows, as his re-conceptualization of death, from the straightforward acceptance of the Hegelian metaphysical position: the word "kills" the thing in order to function, though in its place it leaves the concept. ("Where there was id, there shall be ego," we might hear echoing here.) True enough for ordinary purposes. But the very being of poetry (literature, writing, *poiesis*) precedes the "use" of language: It is the moment of address of the other itself, of the primordial creative act of naming, as Heidegger in other moments recollects, in which word and thing both exist, and neither exhausts, nor can exhaust the other.

In literature this Adamic relationship persists. Resistant, therefore, to the force of interpretation, its words remain words (as opposed to becoming ideas); the literary work remains irreducible, just as is the name (for Heidegger). And the writer, whatever his ostensible intentions, remains thrall to language, to *its* rather than to his own purposes, a fundamentally passive vehicle for its unceasing voice; he does not use language, language uses him.[67] He disappears in the work, ceases to be the "I" who creates, as the Western tradition has seen him. Writing, for Blanchot, is suicide, interminable suicide, to which the writer is driven again and again, as the work to which he is called is the impossible,

---

66 Ironically by conceiving it as a something, as specifically *my* death, as opposed to as the nothing, the pure and ineffable otherness, that in fact it is.

67 Instead of power over the "world," which would seem to be the motivating project of philosophy, literature has power over us, a motif with which one might connect the thralldom of death, the joy or ecstasy of something greater to which the Bataillean subject submits.

and of course it is therefore never truly realized in any instance.[68] To call this a mystical state would perhaps be inaccurate, though it is difficult not to see the state in which the individual disappears in the larger element of language as mystical, and Blanchot's writing itself would certainly convey that impression. There is little writing that is as impenetrable, or as resistant to interpretation, as "his."

Which makes his contention that literature essentially contributes to an ethics – and a politics – seem rather improbable (though one would typically have little hesitation in accepting the same point of view from philosophy, even though Blanchot's critique has made clear that it cannot justify its perennial claim to such a capacity, nor even to such preference.) We might well recognize, or at least be prepared to accept the notion that the person is structured like a literary work, as Jean-Luc Nancy contends in an essay to which Blanchot devoted a portion of his principal writing on the concept of community, and which seems not so far from a Lacanian perspective on the unconscious, to which in some sense the Blanchotian work of literature could be likened to as well, but exactly how, other than as analogy, that might be is initially perplexing. It is, at least *prima facie*, because it is speech, that is, language – and at this stage of his thinking, Blanchot is prepared to concede that all language can and does partake of the profound and willful impersonality of the literary – that constitutes our relationship to the other, a face-to-face, utterly vulnerable speech that is as terrifying, as insecure, and necessarily profitless as the abyssal relationship of the reader to the literary text and which demands a similar ungroundable movement of trust and an infinite depth of responsibility, (predicated precisely on "response"), a relationship that Levinas fatefully conceives as (mutual) "presence." Like literature, "ethical discourse, strictly speaking, is nonsense; but it is serious nonsense."[69]

It is one of the great curiosities of the history of philosophy that Blanchot's ethical and political thinking cannot be comprehended in isolation from that of his life-long friend, Emmanuel Levinas (whose wife and child Blanchot sheltered from the Nazis during the war while Levinas himself was held in a prisoner-of-war camp), a sort of organic, dialogic intertwining in which each thinking is implicitly modulated by, or rather responsive to the other, seems at times to *become* the other, a phenomenon that is exemplified in Blanchot's work beginning with *L'entretien infini* (*The Infinite Conversation*), in which the voice of Levinas, among numerous others, speaks and is answered, their ideas exposed, respected, and responded to, more and more without being identified "as theirs" in the later work, in what could be described as an anti-Platonic dialogue, in which thought seems never to have begun and certainly never to end, but to flow, mutate, and weave its voices indefinitely.

---

68 That it can be only hybrid, though its "purity" is the force of its critique of the philosophical, will figure in the Derridean response to Blanchot's position.
69 Simon Critchley, "Introduction," in *The Cambridge Companion to Levinas* (Cambridge: Cambridge University Press, 2002), p. 19.

Levinas's thinking, one of the crucial prongs of the anti-Heideggerian reaction, famously asserts that ethics is "first philosophy," and that it is inherently relational, irreducible to the demands of or demands upon the imperious (and imperialist) Heideggerian subject, a final derailing of the ontological prejudice, which Blanchot integrates into his larger language-based (even literature-based) depiction of human existence. It is in his notion of a community of language that literature even becomes the basis for (what under present circumstances Blanchot was compelled to consider an impossible) political community, but in which whatever such hope might remain is sustained only by the fact, and not merely the example of literature, an infinitely rich emptiness.

Where Plato/Socrates inaugurated the metaphysical tradition with literature dissembled as philosophy, or inextricably interwoven with it, prosecuting a political and social agenda on the strength of what it seems obvious t(he)y intended as noble lies portrayed as truth, Blanchot/Levinas conclude it, or at least inaugurate its long conclusion, with a philosophy so inextricably dissolved in the literary medium that while "metaphysical truth" can scarcely assert itself, actual reading, the relation to it as literature, becomes possible. Neither the one nor the other can be privileged; neither exists in the purity of its claims. Literature, the true, is impossible (becomes impure) to the same extent that it admits philosophy; it betrays itself. And the truth of philosophy is ineffable (impossible) to the extent that it admits literature. It shows where it is impossible by exactly where it admits literature. Metaphysics (as its name should always have implied) is radically heterogeneous.

Without using philosophical language in his own work, in a sort of inversion of Plato/Socrates, Blanchot/Levinas has no escape from the impasse of literature – Blanchot in some sense uses Levinas to introduce "content" that his own deeply literary inclinations would have made difficult in much the same way that Plato did with Socrates, appropriating his "story," including the putative disdain for writing, to depict a "pure" philosophy. If it is something less than literature on that account, it is also something more, something that offers an exit from the radical impenetrability of literature, and an *entrée* to discourse, which, with all its historically untoward consequences, sanctified philosophy and its relationship to society as well, at least until the latter, for good or ill, was able to slough off its shackles, while the organic relationship of literature/language to the sacred sustained an integral society which only at the end of its long, interminable, process of divorce we perceive as a purpose and a literary *history* in the profoundest sense.

Philosophy was always a mode of interpretation or inquiry and of persuasion, as opposed to one strictly of argument, and exactly because its principle subjects do not admit of truth, or rather because the truth of which they admit is not the truth of discourse; it never became more tedious than in its twentieth-century Anglo-American incarnation when it tried to sweep out the last traces of literature from its stables. Not to say wrong, exactly, or useless, but no longer even purporting to address the domain of the human unless, as is certainly not untrue, it intended to arrive there again by the (extremely) indirect route. Like tragedy, which it dispelled, it had something literary, in its powerful Blanchotian sense, namely death, at its center, something ineffable, perfect, and empty, and hence could proceed at all only by means of an amalgam of the literary and the rational or discursive, which it perforce dissembled, precisely because the literary will not submit to questioning. Perhaps it wasn't so much to refuse or to deceive death as to render it human that philosophy came into existence, and why, in spite of all elitist, hieratic, tendencies or tactics, it was intended for everyone, the impossible example, but an actual example nonetheless, whereas tragedy (also an incipiently heterogeneous mode, as Adorno insists, if perhaps for the wrong reasons) remained too enmired in the purity of literature to permit it to move, or to evolve, and only the mysteries could serve it. This self-deceit, if you will, resulted in the inherently fissured fabric of Western thought that Derrida has brought to light.

If, for Blanchot, the writer is the exemplary figure of humanity, as is the philosopher in Plato's metaphysics and all metaphysics thereafter, he is nevertheless nothing, while the philosopher is a writer who, if he has abdicated his solemn duty to language for a very deceptive mess of pottage, has remained able to speak on his own behalf, even if he is condemned to deceive. Blanchot's good life is a terrifyingly passive relationship in which the self is utterly subsumed in, or dedicated without recourse, to the other (and that must be true in the one-sided relationship with the other of death as well). There is no good death, but only death. It does not, cannot, determine the good life. The privileged status of the philosopher is abolished; he dies the way we all die. No one is any closer to truth than any other, or all are equally close to a "truth" that doesn't exist.

From the Blanchotian perspective, the relationship of philosophy and literature is the human relationship that Plato/Socrates attempted to instantiate and to teach. The good life is an ethical *and* a metaphysical question; the fusion of the "good" and "life" already silently, or perhaps too loudly, expresses that, a hybrid intention, and it cannot be approached unilaterally. Philosophy tried to "free" us from literature (indeed it is a horror and a burden), but the primordial, "true" relationship to the world that it embodies, radically poetic, is not a relationship, nor something from which we can be freed. It is us, and it is beyond us. We feel that in the Levinasian void, of which Heidegger's empty authenticity is already a premonition – as we do in Nietzsche, Kierkegaard, and Schopenhauer, the first explicitly literary philosophers after Plato – as much as in the autonomous indifference, or tortured resistance, of Blanchotian literature, which Borges and Kafka before him, as examples, had been bringing to consciousness some decades earlier, as Mallarmé and Hölderlin and Pindar before that. Where there is literature, there is truth, but ineffable truth.

So, while Blanchot didn't exactly lay death to rest, his uncovering of the other death that had for so long lain as if invisible beside the crypt of philosophy "proper" at least brought it to light in order that the work of mourning could begin, and the energies that have had a cryptic hold over thinking since Plato (or Socrates or Parmenides) could be released from their bonds of delusion. It might have seemed that death could relax a bit, but it is the "nature" of language to flow, and naturally much has been said of death in Western theory since *Writing the Disaster*, (1980). Of course, Blanchot cannot die, he was dead already, but we conclude with his contribution to the thematic, because it completes a certain trajectory (if not quite the trajectory within the trajectory from Mallarmé through Derrida and beyond) of death-thinking in that tradition, finally and definitively dislocating (if not "transcending," for that would be impossible) what Derrida would go on to call logocentrism (of which Blanchot is both the plan for escape and the profoundest embrace) and, in company with the thought of Levinas, describing the (non)basis for a (non) relationship between, or a co-existence of metaphysics and ethics, in which a sensitivity to the latter must be acknowledged as not merely equal but prior if the irreducibility of the other, of the otherness of all beings is to be honored; for we are other.

For this arc of philosophy, death is strictly speaking a literary phenomenon, a literary experience and only a literary experience. This is what has enabled it to speak about death, for outside of literature it is dead, while there it has its life. The death about which we speak exists only in texts, and there is no *hors-texte* (and no *Urtext*), which means both that death is text and that nothing is irrelevant to the understanding of it. Equally, *nothing* is relevant to the understanding of it, and its very nothingness is the capacity of language to engage it. Language thrives on nothingness, its gift is to create it, to create from and with it. The "external reality" around which these texts, this textual history, have come into existence, is as nothing. It is nothing. They exist because it does not. They are the pearl that has formed around the persistent irritation of nothingness.

In Plato/Socrates and up through the Christian era – the deaths of Socrates and Jesus are of course deaths in literature – death was a story, a connection of death to (the rest of) life itself, and from which anyone could draw conclusions and apply their examples to his own. But from the moment of its full realization, let's say in Hegel, death itself became a philosophical character, a concept, or more, the motive force of thought itself – mother of concepts – and its subsequent fortunes reflect this fact: the scope of text became unlimited, even by the ultimate limit of death (while in another sense it abides by an agenda entirely determined and delimited by death). It is indeed tempting to see the historical unfolding of the concept of death as fulfilling a Hegelian phenomenological schema at the end of which we are returned to a state of nature, as it were, but beatified by self-understanding, a state of true nature.

The wrench in the works of such satisfying resolutions is death. Real death. Because regardless of the complexity or subtlety of our strategies to encompass it, it remains resistant to (conceptual) incorporation, regardless of how much we desire that. It is forever outside, the ultimate other. In recognizing that it (or language, or writing) is not confronting the world, but that it is inherently "othered," that the *fact* of the other has resulted in the *aporias* that define it, though it does not transcend itself, thought may dislodge the inertia of its course (if only to take another). Where Blanchot's recovery of real death, of the real other of death might suggest the lineage of the Kantian *noumenon* (which Hegel contended was actually a phenomenon within thought), Derrida's recognition that they both exist (only) within thought/language/writing is akin to the true Hegelian *Aufhebung*: They continue on inseparably together, in an unequal but articulated relationship that nevertheless constantly, inertially, helplessly, moves toward (impossible) resolution or assimilation. Such "absolute knowing" as thought admits is always secretly undermined by what it refuses, ignores, or neglects, but which steadfastly remains part of it.[70] In demonstrating that the distinction between philosophy and literature is spurious, it was Blanchot's purpose to reveal that this tactic within the history of philosophy, by which its own seriousness and purity had been asserted over against a writing that is clearly and self-consciously fantastic, or purposeless, or frivolous, or useless, was quite plainly deception, and worst of all, self-deception. Once the distinction had been demolished on internal grounds, philosophy itself could be understood only as literature, which had, accordingly, never yet been fully read. So, although no ultimate resolution, no "system," could any longer be envisioned within the terms of metaphysics, it did become possible for the first time to actually *read* the history of philosophy, including the history of philosophy as the history of death (and to understand why it has necessarily been misread, or tendentiously read, or basically ignored in its actual depths heretofore: The *telos* by which it had been oriented has always been illusory).[71]

In 1994, a few years shy of Socrates's ultimate age at the time of his death, Derrida remarked in an interview, having invoked his forebear, "All of my writing is on death. If I don't reach the place where I can be reconciled with death, then I have failed.[72] If I have one goal, it is to accept death and dying." Mind-boggling though it might seem for a philosophical gentleman of a certain age, especially a philosophical gentleman of the most encyclopedic learning and most trenchant insight into even the darkest corners of his calling, not to mention the uncanny ability to locate the darkness within even its brightest rooms, to offer such a frank and frankly jaw-dropping admission (which of course must be decoded for all its disarming candor), suggests that, as Blanchot has prepared us to acknowledge, the relationship between philosophy and death is far from that of master to subject, that the philosopher would seem to stand in exactly the same relationship to his own death, as every one of us to ours, and that that relationship is infused more with fear, regret, guilt, and unfulfilled hopes, than with cool, rational, sanguine, "philosophical" acceptance, much less something more enthusiastic. In some crucial sense, Derrida would seem to be saying, philosophy does not touch the fact of death. Or we are not touched by philosophy.

---

70 In this sense, philosophy is the unconscious of culture, and precisely because it is so self-conscious that it has made its unawareness, or blindness, all but invisible.

71 We might well ask: Has its desire to dominate death, to kill death, which it knows it cannot do, and hence constantly re-invokes its own necessity, really been (only) the desire to control the discourse? Or, conversely, was it the way that the energies of the philosopher were diverted into paths well-understood by the "simpler" preponderance of humanity to be futile?

72 For Adorno, too, the notion of reconciliation (with death) seems essential. In *Metaphysics*, he suggests that only if each of us should learn to exploit his or her potential, a potential vastly beyond what we are normally willing to believe it is, would we be in a position to be "reconciled to death" (p. 133).

"All my writing is on death," he says. First, all philosophy is philosophy of death. Its subject is death, its purpose is death; as Socrates had said already, philosophy is the practice of death, which means that actual wisdom *is death*. And the Western philosophical tradition is, or was, the corpus of death. It is the place of death, where death could exist, where it could live, where we could have a relationship to it that is impossible in the other realm of life. And it is a rich and infinitely complex history which, having finally no recourse but to end itself – the dogs had been closing in on it forever[73] – persists in the afterlife of memory, of love, of the fascination we have always had with all dead things, for they have been transformed, have shown that this is not what we think it is, pointed, we still insist, toward something other. Derrida's own work is, therefore, inherently a dialogue of the dead, an investigation of death, of work that is or remains dead without the living ministration of attuned reading, as all philosophy has been, unremarked, throughout history. If not exactly an elegy (or a eulogy) for the Western philosophical project, it is, in many respects, a work of mourning,[74] a sustaining and a farewell (which sounds like a non-violent practice of the dialectic), a long farewell, honoring the traces, the scars, the imperfect if indelible memories, the defeated possibilities, in which we survive the passing of the people and things that we have loved, for the philosopher, including philosophy (which, for Adorno, "lives on only because the moment to realize it was missed").[75] And of course it is mourning for ourselves as well, for these others who have been within us, not to say "part" of us. Although we are convinced that no amount of philosophy will solve death ("real" death) – that if writing sustains a place in which something different is possible, we "know" that it is "merely" a possibility, merely writing, "hope, an infinity of hope... but not for us" – but can do nothing other than gradually come to terms with it, enable ourselves perhaps to assent to the terms of surrender that the vitality, the manifold resiliency, of mind resisted for so long, Derrida's "admission" that he has not accepted death and dying, which he reiterates in a more somber mode only weeks before his actual death, now several years older than Socrates ever became, insinuates a thought that, while errant, while vigorously denounced the moment it arises,[76] represents a fragile alternative to, or a secret trickle within the mainstream of the Western tradition (or perhaps even its Arethusa), whose obsession with death we might therefore see as not merely a matter of the slow unfolding of positions already entrenched in its inaugural performance, but a vulnerable moment indeed present

---

73 It is as absurd as the cynics think, or rather magnificently more so.

74 Etymologically, "remembering," "memory," and later anxious(!) remembering.

75 Whereas the failure of philosophy for Adorno is external, residing in its evasion of the historical world, its famous "death" is an internal, an intrinsic failure for Derrida, so the work of mourning, the work of "philosophy" in our time, is not exactly a postmortem, but rather an always-already that we had been unable to see. Though the practice of philosophy as it had been might have died, the work of (mourning) philosophy remains to be done, in the conscientious reading of its texts. To engage it, to actually listen to it for the first time, is to respect it in its mortality. As Heidegger had sought the source of Being in the hidden roots of words, Derrida finds the hidden story of death in texts that have, in their non-reading, become part of "the They," of the realm of the spoken but not heard, the mere noise of civilization, the occultation of truth.

76 Adorno likens the philosophical, and the Marxist, response to the merest hint of utopianism to the effects of throwing a rock at a police station.

in the otherwise embarrassing-seeming Socratic fable of the afterlife,[77] which might not, therefore, be merely heuristic, and deceitful, or, god forbid, literary, but the locus of the hope that, for Adorno (and more overtly, for his more sanguine counterpart, Ernst Bloch) sustains the utopian "project" (or *Ur*-human demand), the possibility of the realization of philosophy in the world, namely, the abolition of death.

Adorno's thinking constantly infiltrates and destabilizes the metaphysical stone, primarily by its insistence that the material, social, economic, historical order cannot be appropriated to thought without residue, rather that it always mediates thought, and all experience, in advance. Questioning the possibility of speaking of death at all, and certainly intending to refer to Heidegger and "existential psychology," but also perhaps to Bataille, Levinas, or the Baudrillard who would emerge only a decade later, he notes that "allegedly primal experiences are also mediated." There is no death in itself, and no personal, and especially no universal experience of death, though the typical experience under any specific historical circumstances will tend toward uniformity, and more and more so over time. Death is a historical phenomenon, and it changes with both "objective" and subjective conditions. For Adorno, the central historical event of his time, namely Auschwitz (the final dehumanization of death), implies that the wholeness of life, the culmination of a long erosion that had begun with the advent of industrialization, if not from time immemorial, no longer exists, hence the "epic," "organic" conception of death disingenuously espoused by the likes of Heidegger as the perfection of a longer philosophical arc, (or as Heidegger himself sees it, rather an arc truncated or diverted at its very inception), is mere fantasy at best, if not cynical propaganda.[78] Ironically, in "*justifying* death as the meaning of existence," Heidegger unwittingly identifies death as the *meaning* of existence, a sobering conclusion at which, as we have seen, Blanchot, too, had arrived. In his lecture series on metaphysics, Adorno writes, "The terror of death today is really the terror of seeing how much the living resemble it," and "Because the individual no longer exists, death has become something wholly incommensurable: the annihilation of a nothing." Instead of conferring meaning on life, as Heidegger had thought, modern death only, and dispiritingly, confirms its meaninglessness.

In a letter to Thomas Mann, Adorno writes, "death is a human scandal," that there is no cause to "celebrate it in the name of tragedy," and that "its abolition is morally obligatory."[79] As a (disappointed) Marxist, Adorno read the philosophical conception of death, its apotheosis as he saw it (especially in the detested Heidegger), as the veiled complicity in the degradation of life that alone makes its reflexive and vehement rejection of, its disdain for, the utopian "alternative" comprehensible. But what are we to make of this naïve, this

---

77 That "footnote" again.

78 "Heidegger's metaphysics is impotent . . . because it necessarily degenerates into a kind of propaganda for death, elevating it to something meaningful, and thus, in the end, preparing people to receive death intended for them by their societies and states as joyfully as possible." Adorno, *Metaphysics*, p. 131.

79 Quoted in Stefan Müller-Doohm, *Adorno: A Biography* (Cambridge: Polity, 2005), p. 481.

almost childish voice, this David without a rock, which insists that death simply will not do? First, perhaps, that philosophy will not give up death, *its* death, which is its power, its special relationship to the source of power, which over and over returns, against what it thinks are its deepest motivations, to the subaltern position of lickspittle to the way things are. Under the circumstances, we are more at ease with an accepted, a somehow livable disaster than with the impossible prospect of a joy whose call to conscience is nevertheless constant, an irritant in its very nature and a reminder of how we actually live, and at that, with our own passive consent. But then wasn't that true of death as well? "There is no right living when all is wrong with the world" (*Es gibt kein richtiges Leben im Falschen*), no chance of the good *life*, that is, but, exactly as art is still possible (and necessary, even after, perhaps especially after Auschwitz), a good death, a meaningful death, if improbably, still is. Which is precisely the call for its eradication. A good death is unacceptable when the good life is impossible, though "if life were lived rightly, the experience of death would also be changed radically, in its innermost composition."[80]

Utopia as resistance is a social demand. It cannot be waged in private, but the possibility of the united front, the community, that would struggle in its behalf is no greater for Adorno than for Bataille or Blanchot, and for him, too, the infinitesimal trace of that possibility also resides in the work of art, if in a form whose inevitable compromise will always eventually come to light in history.

Speaking of the recrudescence of old metaphysical notions of the good death, of a bygone, putatively integral, relationship to death (among whose perpetrators he includes Heidegger and his acolytes), Adorno remarks that "one would probably need to destroy [these old ahistorical views of death] to be free to reflect on [such] matters without ideology." Of course, Adorno knows that there is no such possibility; existing ideology can't be abolished by fiat: We can't unthink what we think so deeply that it infuses our lives, which the fact of its emergence in various quarters at this particular time confirms. But the impossible is also the spur to thought, much as death itself had set us on the course of metaphysics.

Certainly Adorno did not believe any more than Heidegger in a technological solution to a fundamental human problem; that is perhaps rather the one element of their thought in which they are in harmony. What he did believe in was sustaining the particle of hope, the germ, the gasping survivor even, or just the thought of the gasping survivor that lay beneath the mountain of mass-produced corpses, in respect to (and of) which the seed of a humanity might endure (or perhaps arise) as opposed to capitulating in death. Like Blanchot's understanding of the anonymous practice of writing as opposed to the domination of metaphysics, the force of the utopian is the force of the impossible, that is, nothing. If the long history of philosophy has been sustained by its relationship to the impossible, the nothing of death, then why not disrupt it with the equally impossible non-death?

---

80 Adorno, *Metaphysics*, p. 133.

A couple sections prior to the single passage in *Minima Moralia* in which Adorno speaks explicitly of "death," he considers the relationship of childhood to the adult world, which it understands as a vast sphere of amusement, a world-wide, never sleeping circus created for the sheer joy of it. The disillusionment of the child, and the end of (our) hope, is the moment when the deceitful practical world, the world of mechanisms, of trickery, of doing it all simply for pay – the world of death – becomes visible.[81] But the view of the child, the view we at some point believe we must shatter for her own good – "Ok, that's enough of that nonsense" – is the moment in which necessity is not (yet) necessity, in which a hope resides that perhaps we need not shatter. In what is certainly the bleakest, most unflinching, perhaps even subtlest of Western philosophy, Adorno yet abides, even insists upon, the utopian possibility, which coincides with a dour messianism, in tone if not in substance comparable with Heidegger's well-known dictum that "Only a god can save us." Both recoil at the thought of salvation by technology (as they do, in fact, at the notion that an actual god will be saving us), that it might bring something meaningful to bear on the issue of Being, or of freedom. But is it not possible, as in so many ways the questions to which philosophy had devoted itself have been adopted fruitfully by more methodical forms of inquiry and become the domain of science, that "technologies" responding to already-current thinking might radically alter our relationship to and conception of death? (Here, again, it is instructive that in the *Phaedo* Socrates embarks on a lengthy "scientific" depiction of the afterworld.) One immediately thinks of the medical conquest of aging (perhaps bionically and/or cryogenically assisted), which many quite reasonable scientists (in the lineage of Descartes) believe is inevitable, the "mind-download," cloning, or the more abstruse notion, inhabiting the realm of discovery rather than of technological enhancement, that the actual (scientific) nature of space and time is such that our notion of death is already dramatically ill-conceived, something Einstein embraced long ago[82] and which science continues to develop toward experiential means of investigating. Even the science-fiction notion of an eventual evolutionary transition to a truly social human animal, a group being, if you will, supports wildly other ways of encountering, experiencing, and understanding death, and the important strides in cognitive inter-subjectivity in recent decades already suggest a strong ontological basis for such possibilities.[83] It seems, *prima facie*, that any such developments would render a phenomenological understanding of death mere psychological history at best, whereas a thinking such as that of Adorno, which is attuned and committed to "the particular," and which is not, in any case, pledged to a metaphysical position on death, would rejoice in an achievement that, as it imagines, will further the cause of humanity. Of course, the radical differences, physical, social, and "spiritual," between the two states, including the profound effects the absence of death

---

81 In the moment of sudden change, of disillusion, *Entzauberung*, demystification, the magic is gone and we see it was a trick, but we want the illusion back. We are like animals standing over our dead in utter helpless perplexity.
82 In a letter to the family of a deceased friend, he famously wrote, "Now he has departed from this strange world a little ahead of me. That means nothing. People like us, who believe in physics, know that the distinction between past, present, and future is only a stubbornly persistent illusion."
83 Philosophy has, of course, Jules Verne-like, prefigured all of these possibilities and more.

would have on our conceptual network, make that almost as incomprehensible from our present point of view as death is already.

For Jean Baudrillard, another disillusioned, or evolved, or transcended Marxist, death as we "know" it "comes into existence" only when its understanding as a *social relation* is lost, with its separation from the life of the group, the beginnings of which are marked by the ascent of a priestly class and which becomes unquestionable with the triumph of political economy, displacing the economy of symbolic exchange (more or less as understood in the Maussian anthropological tradition), within which death and life are continuous and the dead remain vital presences within society:[84] Understood "as a universal of the human condition, death exists only when *society* discriminates against the dead."[85] "Little by little, the dead cease to exist."[86]

Although the milieu of symbolic exchange has been overwhelmed, or rather transformed by history, the fact that it is a human possibility – our behavior is entirely symbolic, in any case, only its objects and objectives have "evolved" – implies that our current conception of human possibility is no more inevitable than what preceded it, or run alongside it until it was eradicated, had been, and vestiges of such a way of life-and-death could or can still be seen in our time. In any case, it is demonstrable that a society, and a healthy, relatively untroubled and undivided society, can function under these conditions, practices, and beliefs. Our current social relationship to death and understanding thereof is neither necessary nor permanent, and a philosophical position regarding death in general is mistaken to the extent that it conceives itself as ontological. We have arrived at our death impasse historically, and it can be overcome historically.

For Baudrillard, it is precisely "in the manipulation and administration of death, in the final analysis, that all power is based."[87] We are thrall to an understanding of death that supports "real" social structures whose basis is purely imaginary, a "literally fantastic and artificial temporality" whose purpose is "repression and control," and it is in the "separation of death" from life that it has come to be. "The economic operation consists in life taking death hostage. It [i.e., death] becomes the residual life which can from now on be read in the operational terms of calculation and value . . . . Life given over to death: the very operation of the symbolic."[88] Analogous in this respect to Blanchot, for whom the literature of philosophy is used to supplant the "fantastic" (dismissible) literature of writing, modern

---

84 And they are not merely continuous, but constantly evolving companions. As Baudrillard insists, "Every moment has its death already immanent in it," meaning that there is not just one unique death, toward which we are bound in a grim existential trek, but that death changes as we change, and that, as we are not "one" once are for all, neither is it. Death has its life as well.
85 Jean Baudrillard, *Symbolic Exchange and Death* (London: Sage Publications, 1993), p. 144.
86 Ibid., p. 126.
87 Ibid., p. 129.
88 Ibid., pp. 130-131.

political economy (and the vast superstructure it supports), dismisses (as it fears) symbolic exchange, a system of social relations predicated on giving without limit and the non-rationalized, non-preferential relationship to death, as (irrational) fantasy while using its own modes of fantasy to dominate the "imaginary sphere of death" for the sake of accumulation, preference, and accountability. "The economic power of capital is based in the imaginary just as much as immortality in the church: Capital is only its fantastic secularization."[89] And modern death is merely the dissimulation of its own illusory finality within an imaginary that thereby bars access to the many. Therefore, "the revolution can consist only in the abolition of the separation of death, not in equality of survival."[90] Recognition of the indivisible unity of life and death – for Freud and Heidegger their relationship was merely a fatal conjunction – is prerequisite, for Baudrillard, to any meaningful social change.

This certainly represents a position that has roots in Marx, for whom all talk of death, which was necessarily metaphysics, was ideology; hence his own lack of interest in the subject except as a self-conscious means of achieving an end. As an aspect of superstructure, a society's conception of death does not imply or determine, and in fact hides, its infrastructure, whereas for critical theory, including Adorno, it reflects, and more pointedly, reveals the truth of its infrastructure. For Baudrillard, on the other hand, the relation specifically to death defines the infrastructure. Death is the threat on account of which a society's practices are configured: Death precedes our ways of being in society. So, while for both Baudrillard and Adorno, the social relationship to death reveals exactly wherein a society's efforts to suppress freedom reside, they construe almost diametrically opposed, and in their way, sublime, if perhaps equally improbable means of combating them.

In closing, though not as a mere enclitic: it is painfully obvious that the extensively diagnosed phallogocentrism of the Western philosophical tradition is stunningly in evidence in its historical encounter with death. Not only does something resembling a female perspective appear never to have been relevantly broached (during the long period under consideration), but the very notion that female experience might entail a divergent, and therefore utterly pertinent point of view is never even raised. That finally in the first half of the twentieth century a few women's voices are grudgingly admitted to a dialogue so compromised in advance that their voices could scarcely be called their own, instead of accentuating the loss tends rather to further obscure it.[91]

---

89 Ibid., p. 129.

90 Ibid.

91 It is previously only among the Christian mystics that something reflecting a female perspective on death can be gleaned, one in which love, passion, receptivity, openness, concern, unification, and service are prominent themes. While "their work" reveals an essential posture of self-denial, passivity, permeability, ir-responsibility, and abnegation, it may also be read in terms of deference, repudiation of (the concept of) self, of fixed identity in general, immersion in the Other, of fundamental integration, the disavowal of power or wisdom, etc., or, in general, a non-aggressive, un-self-interested, reverential, and attentive posture toward the Other, in which the final merger in death is the ultimate good. If this may be viewed as a perverse endorsement of the male ideal of the day, it also essentially undermines that

If philosophy had been a female, or a dually, , or multiply, gendered tradition, it seems quite safe to say that it would have stood in an entirely different relationship to death and would undoubtedly have proposed and developed a rather different set of concerns, and perspectives from which to elaborate them. If we look even cursorily at the foci of Edith Stein, Simone Weil, or the early Hannah Arendt, we immediately see that their work gravitates toward themes such as empathy,[92] friendship, responsibility, listening, inter-subjectivity, human transformation, and love, and imagine that, had they been able to develop their themes, they would undoubtedly have arrived at critical positions that remain ill represented in the principal trajectory of the discipline. More recently, such figures as Cixous and Kristeva embody a female perspective that is characterized by joy, laughter, creation, re-birth, and, in general, the affirmation, the embrace of life, as opposed to the grim resistance to death that has infused the work of even the most sanguine (or least sanguinary) of male philosophers. Where death is central, it is death conceived from the side of the (loving) survivor as opposed to that of the desperate self, which opens a fundamentally other *point de départ* for thought. For Cixous, death is a "gift," and in a quite different sense from that in which the tortured term is employed in Derrida's *The Gift of Death*, as the opportunity for renewal, the opportunity or the call to see beyond the given toward new ways of being. For Cixous, to write against death is to write *for* freedom, to destroy constraints and multiply possibility. It is not to death that we must be loyal, but to life. And the phallogocentric history of the concept of death merely serves to strengthen the "mind-forged manacles" by which we are bound: We need especially have no loyalty to *them*. By comparison with such perspectives, the concerns of the male philosophical mainstream seem often so small, self-righteous, or eccentric to real human concerns, so intent on the conquest of the alien, or of oneself, that we wonder that we do not always see them that way, that we so quickly enter the spirit of debate or the inertia of "the real" that just what we are debating or why becomes almost secondary: This is, if not the whole animus of philosophy, unquestionably one of its mainsprings, a dynamic upon which the Platonic dialectic, for example, constantly prevails.

In Lacan's of course intentionally provocative and far from straightforward proposition, "Woman does not exist," we have an inadvertent and disarming confession of the long-standing male view of women, especially in the intellectual vocations, whereas in truth that which is absent for psychology and for philosophy (though at least for the former its

---

ideal, and as the female mystic was among the few social roles taken seriously by the male hierarchy, it must be understood as containing a critical impetus, both inherently and often intentionally as well.

92 Regarding the notion of empathy, or the possibility of empathy, Rich Blint, invoking James Baldwin, has argued compellingly that it is an "unwitting" (or linguistically embedded) tactic, and signal, of dominance (or mastery), implying a promise that it does not actually, and cannot actually keep: It maintains distance even while making the gesture of movement toward the "other," the other for whom it cannot be mutual under the very terms of their disparity. Its function as true integration is relevant only within a securely closed system of understandings and benefits, or at least negotiated coexistence. In this light, the difference between the position of undeniably oppressed and artificially demeaned women of the dominant culture and people of the slave culture (or residual slave culture) is put into stark contrast.

absence is that to which virtually all human activity is devoted to redressing), is actually that which is always present in life, at birth and at death, and constantly in between. Her invisibility, her "lack," is merely testimony, if the history of philosophy is not evidence enough, of the philosopher's blindness or simple self-absorption, or of her everyday ubiquity. Ignore her, fail to see her, leave her out, and then tell her that she doesn't exist: philosophy as defense mechanism, as rationalization for the real abdication of responsibility by the paternal male, or as compensation for his physiological and familial near-irrelevance.

Here again, the longer arc of philosophy has been slyly anticipated by Plato, and again in subtle insinuations that we tend to read as extraneous dramatic effects or asides, or even as ironies, rather than as indications of substantive philosophical positions. We know that Socrates (or Plato on his behalf) acknowledged two masters, teachers to whom he had recourse when he sought wisdom or felt that the constant dialogue "between Me and Myself" (as Arendt described it, in reference specifically to Socrates) was inadequate to the subject at hand. These, of course, he does not mention when (inimically) surveying the landscape of wisdom in his native town, for they, perhaps uniquely, satisfied, his difficult criteria, whereas it was the loud and self-important who merely impressed the less curious with their powers that demanded to be identified and exposed. That they were both women, Diotima (of Mantinea), to whom the theory of "Platonic love" that Socrates expounds in *The Symposium* is attributed, and Aspasia (of Miletus), a *hetaera* who would become the consort of Pericles and whose home was one of the intellectual centers of Athens,[93] with whom Socrates is said to have studied rhetoric(!), suggests, on the one hand, that perhaps women were not in fact so absent from the philosophical dialogue, right here at its inception when its abiding concerns were being established, and on the other, that the value of their work, as usual (though obviously not on account of Plato/Socrates having failed to acknowledge it), has been elided in the public annals.

Not only does Socrates not disdain the wisdom of women, he would seem to value it beyond that of any of his male contemporaries. The fact that he is typically unimpressed and even ironically indulgent toward his male interlocutors, while he speaks of these female mentor-colleagues as his own teachers, not only advances the programmatic position that one would be unwise to judge too hastily of the value of another, especially on the basis of such superficial considerations as relative social standing (or of course more deeply entrenched and fundamental prejudices), but perhaps even supports the conclusion that the unreflectively disdained in society, those who are compelled therefore to observe, might well, on that very account, have an unusual relationship to wisdom, bringing them in that respect directly in correlation with the situation of Socrates himself.[94] When he

---

93 There is even a tradition that has Aspasia creating the "Socratic method," and, like Socrates, she would be subjected to public trial on charges of impiety.

94 A view that is echoed in the portrayal of the company that Jesus preferred to keep as well, and in the loyalty, kindness, solicitousness, empathy, and bravery that the women of his inmost circle displayed by comparison with most of his apostles. It is the women who keep watch over death.

proposes a radically different organization of child-rearing for the good of the new society in *The Republic*, is it not entirely possible that he intends thereby to insure that men are actually kept away from these vulnerable creatures during the crucial period of their development and instruction? That perhaps he intends even longer-term consequences and over generations, that the early exclusive company of the instinctively patient, loving, nurturing, concerned, and attentive half of the race, as opposed to the petulant, self-important, distracted, and imperious will be the true seed of the good polity? Outside, that is, of the claustral and unwholesome patriarchal dynamic of the family? It was, in any case, to women that he believed in entrusting the groundwork of the future of Athens. Of course, Athens didn't develop as Plato envisioned its future, and the course of Western history has accordingly lost the model of an alternate path along which a quite different view of life (and death) might have flowered.

Although he sent his wife, Xanthippe, home with the kids on the very day that he would die, it is certainly not because he saw the philosophical project as something for which women were unfit, or that he disdained the sorts of work that were typically considered theirs: Perhaps he regarded these last hours as merely winding up some trivial details, of setting the philosophical house in order, of hand-holding and imprinting the experience in the memory of his followers above all, while the meaningful house, always presided over by the woman, required concerted attention, in spite of, and specifically because of, his own imminent and inevitable death, and because, silently, patiently, it is she who has always undertaken the difficult work of consolation and of mourning, or explanation and reconciliation of children with the way of the world. She has been the teacher and the exegete of death through the ages, which undoubtedly has something important to do with the fact that very few of us feel much drawn to the interminable and arcane bombinating of the distracted and ever-indulged philosophers, nor believe that the lack of Heidegger might actually render our deaths less meaningful. We already have the example and the practice of women to which to refer – it is inside of us all – a legacy as ancient as death.

To my children, Sam, James, and Laura
Three distinct examples of something better.

A Conversation with Heide Hatry

Marc Pachter

MARC PACHTER: Are you bothered that people consider your work disturbing, or is that the point?

HEIDE HATRY: I have done work that people find disturbing, and I've liked it that way. I don't think I started out to achieve that effect, but I saw that it was one of the modes of an artwork's power to enter and unsettle people's relatively complacent lives. In this case, though, I certainly don't like it – if that is the outcome. In fact, it would totally disturb me, because I am trying to do exactly the opposite. My intention is to make people feel great.

PACHTER: To comfort them?

HATRY: Yes.

PACHTER: But I think with your eyes opened to this question you must suspect that in our civilization – broadly a historically Christian, European culture – dealing with the mortal remains of people in this way might be considered a form of violation. The body is seen to be a vessel and the essence is the soul. So to cling to the body rather than to return it, "dust to dust," is to do something that, it can be argued, is morbid: a challenge to the idea that we're more spirit than body.

HATRY: Although I can, of course, understand that perspective, having been a Christian myself, for me it is really disturbing that this "vessel," which was a person, becomes a mere object when the person is dead; and an object that even makes us think of it as something like a nuisance until we can get it out of sight. The person disappears and this object is left behind. However inconvenient, it nevertheless incorporates what remains of our feelings for and connection to this other, who was deeply a part of us.

PACHTER: You seem to be celebrating what is left.

HATRY: I don't know about celebrating; to me it feels more like respecting. I feel that the object is the only thing we can hold onto. We have, of course, our ideas of who the person was, our memories, our feelings, and maybe some precious artifacts. I believe, especially since I began working on this project, that *matter matters* in a weird way. I've read a lot on death and there seems to be a historically consistent connection to the thing, to the body itself, and to things that a person has touched or owned. If I can suggest a connection to my own past as a dealer in rare books: Why are we interested in having a book that is signed by the author? People don't just like signed books, they also consider them more valuable, both in price and as containing some sort of auratic quality – i.e., an aura of authenticity. If you had a copy of Kafka dedicated to Max Brod, let's say, that is so extremely interesting. But why? It is the idea that Kafka thought about it, thought about his friend, pondered their relationship for a moment, and conveyed some meaningful sense of their friendship in the book itself. That he touched it, and this copy went physically to Brod, incorporating the crucial connection between them in a gift that Brod then cherished for life.

PACHTER: Shall I give you my guess as to why? The word I would like to introduce is *witness*. We understand that these people and their objects actually existed in such and such a time and place. But there is emotionally something in us that requires verification. This is a core reason why we hold on to and exhibit them in museums and in our own family holdings. These objects are witnesses to that existence.

HATRY: That's a concept that I find elegant, and respectful – very much as I see these portraits. A witness is a quiet observer who nevertheless offers eloquent, or fundamental, testimony to truth. So what about seeing my pictures as witness to this person? Something like that captures what makes them so important to me. And from my point of view, I can't imagine anything worse than throwing the ashes away; getting rid of this precious residue of what the person was, but which is also the truth that this person actually existed. The DNA is there, to put it in more contemporary but still primal terms. I have this urn of DNA; I have the REAL thing, the thing you rightly call the reason we collect our most meaningful heritage in museums or, on a more intimate register, the reason people place urns on their fireplace mantles.

PACHTER: Does it bother you that you yourself, as portraitist, are not usually a witness? Certainly with your father and with your friend you were witness to their lives. But when someone comes to you and gives you the ashes of a life you never knew *in* life – that, in fact, you can only come to know through a photo – doesn't that challenge your claim?

HATRY: Absolutely not, because I am not making it for me. I'm making it for that person. The artist, in general, still has something of the social function of the shaman, standing in for the deep spiritual needs of others and mediating between them and the future, or the past – which are both the same in their essential non-existence. For the images of my father, of my friend Stefan, and for James Purdy, the making process was important. I needed to transform my own feelings of loss into something that was saved and stayed with me. At the beginning I found this comforting and consoling. I thought those feelings came from the necessarily rather contemplative process of making, but I realized later that this wasn't true.

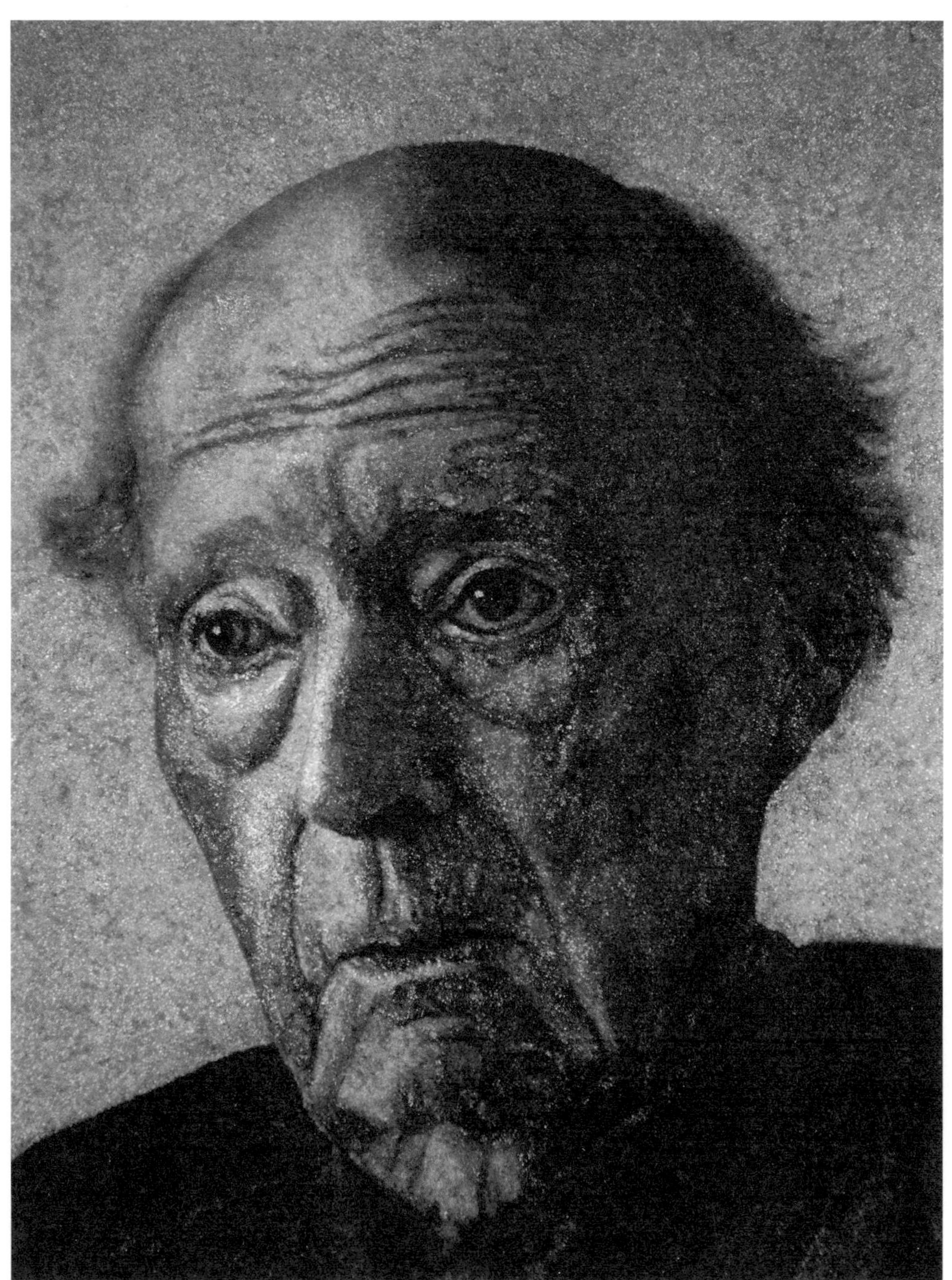

I found the thing itself consoling: that the ashes are consoling, that to have the ashes *look* at you is consoling. That to speak to the ashes, or to listen to them, is consoling.

PACHTER: That's an important statement: the ashes *look* at you. Cremation is known in many cultures. We realize we can look at those ashes in an urn. But now you are saying that in a sense it is important for the ashes to look back. It's an interesting idea. Everything you say about the *witnessing* of the ashes I can understand. But why is it so necessary for the face to be replicated? Why be so literal?

HATRY: It's absolutely necessary; and it's necessary that the portrait is as realistic as possible because even though, as I said, the portrait of my father is not technically made from his ashes, I imagined having his ashes, and that's what that portrait means to me. I imagine that he's looking at me, or a bit off into the distance, as if we can't quite connect immediately any longer given our divergent existential states. I feel his presence is intensified through seeing his face. The face is where we understand communication is happening. Even when we see other aspects of the body as eloquent, the face is template for interpersonal communication, for capturing all the subtleties that make us human. The very idea of a face-to-face confrontation thus takes on an ethical function. Other ways of reading a person are incidental or filtered through this. If you say, show me a picture of somebody, I won't normally show you a picture of his hands or feet. I'll usually show you a picture of his face.

PACHTER: But in portraiture, more and more artists are beginning to understand that personality can be in every element of the body.

HATRY: Yes, a perfect example that springs to mind are the "portraits" by John Coplans.

PACHTER: Yes, they are brilliant! But it is interesting that you mention his work, because although it's his body, literally, that is photographed, he reduces its individuality. I would argue that he makes himself an abstraction, and so does not actually produce a self-portrait. But one can think of so many people whose most personally expressive feature to be portrayed might be, for example, an arm rather than the face.

HATRY: Have you seen the new photo book about Louise Bourgeois by Alex van Gelder? He photographed mostly her face, but also quite often her hands, and you can recognize her in those with equal force – which I suppose makes perfect sense for an artist, especially of her type. They're beautiful!

PACHTER: We can agree that if the goal, as I think of your project, is keeping someone permanently in our company, the face is the most natural way to do this. But I have another question about portraiture to pose for your project. It is a fixed way of looking at a person. The reality of being with somebody and knowing them is that they are not fixed; they float into many manifestations, both physical and in expressions of personality. Is that a problem for you, given your goals?

HATRY: I have thought a lot about how to make portraits, and, of course, these in particular. But with this project I'm concerned about their essence, and what it means to portray in general. In the beginning I was interested in making them as realistic as possible; that seemed, even if it is somehow secretly determined by a photographic aesthetic or ideal, to capture what I was driving at. And then some people asked: Why don't you make more conceptual or analogical portraits, for example of a pond or a tree, a garden or a landscape that s/he liked? Well, I don't find that interesting, and I think for exactly the reason that I don't like the idea of scattering ashes in a place someone happened to like. The place where the dead still live is in our memories, or more generally, in some amalgam of our sensorium and our memories, and to disperse their ashes just seems to me to deny them access to us. The conceptual aspect of scattering can be poignant, of course, but it also insures that one potentially powerful access to memory is abandoned.

As to the notion that the portrait in general misrepresents because it offers a fixed image of a dynamic being, I think that's a bit of a linguistic problem rather than a phenomenological one. The whole point of art is to capture what is vital in a static medium, and we have evolved lots of strategies to address that: symbolism, quasi-abstraction, ambiguity, and various means of insinuating emotion, all of which potentially contribute to more living representation. But to return to the photographic aesthetic that I think dominates our notion of portraiture nowadays even when it is not actually employed, life stops at some point. Possibility is arrested, or the multiple has narrowed down to the singular. It has been observed that the photograph is essentially preterite, a *memento mori*, and I think that in embracing this tendency in portraiture in general I am more or less subconsciously insinuating the notion of death. I think when you see these pictures you know that the subject is dead; but they also exude a calm and reassurance that comes from their very specificity in a past, or singular time. Or, perhaps it suggests the necessary affectlessness of the dead, which can also be one of the preternatural aspects of the photographic portrait. For death, one moment is as good as another, time has ceased to flow, and with it the vicissitudes of personality: our tendency to narrow our view of the dead, especially in seeing the good in them, might be another example of the psychological truth that the "static" portrait contains. This was me; that it wasn't all of me is irrelevant because I am showing you what we all have in common, even while I remain specific.

I told you that I had expanded this project at one point and memorialized things as well as people. For example, I bought this huge wooden dollhouse, burned it, and then made a painting of the house out of its ashes. A connection like that makes sense to me, but to make a house out of the ashes of a person doesn't, or at least not in my conception of this particular project.

PACHTER: I, of course, agree.

HATRY: I did think about making portraits that are not so fixed – and making them blurry, like the Gerhard Richter paintings of members of the Baader-Meinhof Group from the 1970s. It seemed like a perfect solution to this problem, because that way the person seems gone, far away, not possible to grasp, eluding us as s/he recedes into memory, and with an unclear quality that exemplifies our relationship to the most enigmatic thing in life: we just can't grasp what is going on, or what it means, or how we should deal with it; and those Richter images are haunting for these sorts of reasons – I even find them highly reminiscent of the "spirit photographs" of the late nineteenth century. In fact, they touch on the fleetingness of experience and of memory in general especially poignantly because they come from newspapers, which had documented the most powerful or horrifying things of that moment and are now almost as illegible as that horror or power in their distance from us, in our ignorance of them.

I showed people for whom I was preparing to make portraits of their beloved, examples of Richter's blurry pictures – which I think are philosophically and emotionally truer, because they make it much clearer that the depicted person is gone and that, while the idea of them is still there, it is becoming blurry in our minds pretty quickly.

But almost everybody disliked that idea. They explained to me that they want to remember that person, want the art to be more solid than memory can be (even if that means a distortion). That the whole point is to look the deceased again in the eyes and talk to him or her, and therefore she or he has to look as realistic as possible. They were afraid that the blurring is happening anyway in their minds and that they will forget too soon how she or he looked… Maybe they are right, but I did blurry faces as well. And I like them both.

PACHTER: Yours is a project that might breed comfort for some and stir accusations from others. Let's deal with some of those possible accusations. At least one of the theories of grieving is that you go through stages and eventually come to terms with death. This takes a while; the process should not be rushed. It might be suggested that you stick people permanently in one of those stages of grieving. That certainly can provide comfort at the time. But they don't move on.

HATRY: When we live with an artwork, much as with an actual personal relationship, we grow into it, our relationship changes, things mute or expand in a natural, unprescribed way, and one day we discover that the relationship as it had existed is just different; or we don't even discover it, it just is different. I think that these works tend to become part of our lives in that way, not desperately clinging to something that can no longer be, but a natural extension into the future of an important past, the specific quality of which can't be predicted. The change happens in us, not in the thing, but we see it differently as we change.

Let me start by telling you about my own experience. I was stuck in the grieving over my father's death for 15 years. When my friend Stefan committed suicide eight years ago,

I was so afraid that this would happen again – he meant so much to me, and at the beginning it was even worse. But after I had made the portraits of my father and of Stefan, I found that I could cope with both deaths after a relatively short period of time. First I was in terrible pain, but then I talked to the portraits, told them why I was so angry, disappointed, and devastated… And then I started to calm down and started to understand and accept and was consoled by their "presence."

I should say now that I equated their deaths not just because of the degree of my pain and the loss of both, but also because I believed at the time that my father's death was also the result of suicide. I only recently learned that this might not be the case.

A friend of mine who is a psychologist said that this is a wrong approach, that I have to let go and I shouldn't try to keep the person, because if you can't let go you will never get over it. But I experienced something completely different, and I think she was wrong. I know, for example, that James Purdy is dead because I have his ashes; this is evidence that he is dead! And I feel that he is here because his ashes are with me and I can see his face and he smiles at me and I smile back. This was probably one thing that was so difficult for me about my father; that I couldn't understand that he was dead, maybe because I didn't have the possibility to see him in death, which is supposed to help a lot to understand that a person is actually gone.

PACHTER: Well, this is the famous question of the open casket. Some abhor it, but others say unless I witness the dead body I don't emotionally believe.

HATRY: And, therefore, I believe that my solution is so perfect; in the open casket you don't necessarily even recognize your beloved one.

My friend, the poet Franz Wright, died last year. (Do you know him? He was a brilliant poet and the son of a brilliant poet as well, James Wright. Both of them won a Pulitzer Prize. We collaborated several times.) He had lung cancer and was supposed to die a few months after he was diagnosed. But he somehow lived and was extremely productive for four years, writing some of his best work.

When he died, his wife Beth kept him at home; he was never taken to a funeral home. He stayed in his bed and was lying on special ice and you could go visit him where he had lived. The room was cool and dark and filled with nice spices and smells. In the last two days they covered the body with linen; you could still touch him and it was consoling, and everybody who wanted to see him could say good-bye. It's not legally necessary to embalm a body, and I was really impressed by how beautiful it was to do it this way.

PACHTER: But of course what you're doing is not saying good-bye.

HATRY: It is. I think these portraits can help you to understand, ultimately, the bare fact of death.

PACHTER: I think, perhaps, there are also underlying cultural assumptions. You are a European who lives in the U.S.; so you are a participant in both worlds. I'm interested in some of the assumptions going into your work when we think of European and American cultures. They are the same, as Western, but also not the same. It is often commented on that Europeans are more comfortable with death, in the sense that it is integrated into the idea of life. America, it is said, mostly denies, emotionally, the inevitability of death.

HATRY: I think everybody denies death, which I don't necessarily see as a bad thing. It has a lot to do with how we can proceed with our lives, unhobbled by despair, or at least anxiety.

PACHTER: But it still seems to me that, as a European, you are willing to contemplate death and how we deal with it more than most American artists. At least those I know of. But to be honest, I am trying to decide whether your approach reconciles us to the inevitability of death or is another form of denying it. Perhaps that is what concerned your psychiatrist friend. Do you think denial is at the core of your project?

HATRY: Although I can't control how others might see it, and the interpretive spectrum of such a large subject is also going to be vast, for me, in my relationship to the work, absolutely not.

PACHTER: Then might we call this an embrace?

HATRY: Embrace is too strong. I think it's coming to terms with it – a way of getting it, and moving on. And this isn't just skipping denial; it's really dealing with it. I dealt with my father's and friend's deaths in a way I've never dealt with anyone else's death. I was thinking about them. I was talking to them.

Having the portrait is almost like having a psychologist. I don't have a shrink, probably because we Europeans still don't believe so much in psychologists, we might still tend to think of that as something of an anomaly of our bourgeois past. But having the portrait was like someone (and not just someone, but specifically the person in question) was listening and making me think about our relationship and about their life. It was a healing process to interact with them. And now they are here and I smile at them when I walk by or see them.

PACHTER: That's the core of what you're trying to do.

HATRY: [Pointing at an installation on the wall.] Yes, I know this looks like it is still a big part of my life. But it's not, at least in that way.

PACHTER: It does look like an altar.

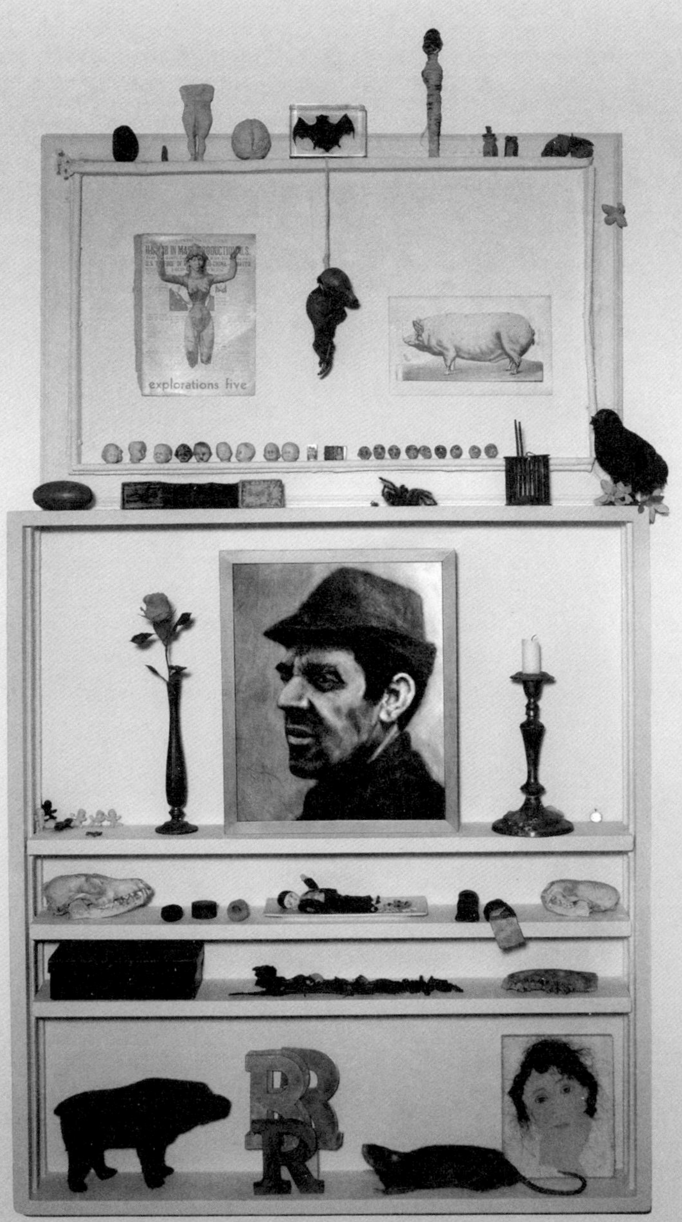
explorations five

HATRY: Yes, it is an altar, and I like it; but it's really not there to console me, because I don't need consolation anymore. It's more like a touchstone and an often surprising reminder. It gives me a reason to have a brief thought about my father, and it's sweet. More often than not, though, I encounter it as an artwork, and it makes me now think of Josephine Meckseper – you know her, she is the one who displaces artifacts of daily life (like newly bought stockings, or panties, or jewelry on a mannequin), advertisements, and other shiny things, and elegantly arranges them in vitrines. I never got what she was driving at, as it always seemed rather random to me: which might be what she intended, to give an insight into the fundamental particularity of the person, even in a world full of manufactured needs and circumscribed desires but what I do understand is the idea to arrange artifacts, which reminds me of something like the impulse behind Joseph Cornell's work, which is certainly memorial in its essence, memorial of the world's forgotten course.

PACHTER: So, let's talk about the altar part of this. Do you expect that the people for whom you are doing this will create an altar?

HATRY: They might, but how they interact with the work is for them to decide. I had originally planned to offer options like that; for example, a hanging box with shutters that they could use as an altar in which they could put things that are precious to their memory of the person. Or a mausoleum of sorts, in which things connected to the dead person could be displayed. But I decided against that part of the project because it seemed to be exerting too much control and diffusing the focus of the work itself; which might actually hinder the process of letting go. And in New York City it wouldn't have been so easy anyway since most people have rather small apartments and certainly not space for an additional room within them.

PACHTER: But it's not just that. Perhaps also it is a way for an individual to personally participate in the memorializing, even if they have not done the portrait.

HATRY: That would be an argument *for* the mausoleum. And people can of course build their own mausoleum, they can also do what they want with the picture.

PACHTER: One comment and then a question. The comment is that of course in the case of people having taken their own lives, the anger is so natural. It would enrage anyone left behind. But I would argue that the impulse of anger is a lot more common even when suicide is not the cause of death because people feel abandoned even when it was not the intention of the person to die.

HATRY: That anger can extend to someone else, too; for example, in an accident. And of course what we are really dealing with in grief is the rending of ties within ourselves.

Something is being torn out of us against our will, and so we react with confusion as our whole being responds to this violence.

PACHTER: But even if they just die, in the fullness of life, in their 80s, for example, a grown child often feels abandoned by his or her parents.

HATRY: But is that really anger?

PACHTER: That's a fair question. I think anger goes into grief because it's irrational. Anger is not just felt because you are wondering whether or not the deceased is responsible for their death. Anger is something you feel when you are alone and you need that person to be there.

On the question of how we memorialize: as you know, I spend a lot of time in Asia and now think of two Asian traditions; one Chinese, and one Thai. The Chinese have a great tradition of after-death portraiture. There's much less a tradition of life portraiture. After someone dies, usually the distinguished father or mother of a household, portraits of them are painted.

HATRY: Really? And how did they do it, before the person died? Or on the death bed?

PACHTER: I don't know. Certainly this tradition predates photography.

HATRY: I don't think you have to go to Asia to find a tradition of post-death portraiture. In Egypt they painted portraits on the sarcophagus.

PACHTER: And of course there is the tradition of icons in ancient tradition and even now of portraits after death based on photography.

The other Asian tradition I want to mention comes of recent experience with friends in Thailand. There cremation is universally done among the Buddhist majority. It's worth noting how they deal with the ashes, at least in the ceremony I know of. They assemble a small representation of the human body in the form of a stick figure, made out of the ashes of the just cremated body, and is then presented in a bowl. This is the closest to what you are seeking to do. But it is temporary. In the end the ashes will be placed in an urn. I thought you would find this interesting.

HATRY: May I ask is this ritual taking place while you meet with all the friends and family? Who makes the figure? How long does it take?

PACHTER: The presiding monk, I think, does it. And presents it to the mourners. There are also assembled photos of the deceased. It's all quite elaborate. Funerals are very important.

To turn to another matter, perhaps one of the most difficult challenges to your project. There are those who may find it particularly unnerving to hear of a German working with human ashes. How do you deal with this possible cultural challenge to your work?

HATRY: That is a serious problem for me. As I told you before, I have used my alter ego, Betty Hirst, as the ostensible creator of my art when I didn't want to reveal that I am German. I so often had this feeling that I don't want to be German, and that I don't want to have this history and this guilt, and that I don't want to not be able to do what I want, what I am passionately inspired to do, simply because I am German. But I am, and I guess I am responsible for what I am doing being German. And that's a huge part of my thinking, and dealing with, and feeling about so many things.

PACHTER: But that hasn't stopped you.

HATRY: No, for example with the book *Skin*. That was my first project and the first time I made something out of pigskin, and I was criticized for doing the same things that Nazis did when they made things, like lamp shades, out of human skin. There I saw no correlation between the practices, except the – as I thought – obviously negative one. Some critics (and I don't necessarily mean professional ones) latched onto the superficial resemblance and, therefore, failed to enter into the real space of the work. Nazis used human skin to degrade human beings, to show how worthless and at best merely instrumental these people were in the Nazi mind.

PACHTER: It was the final process of dehumanization.

HATRY: Yes, and what I did with the pigskin was the opposite: I was trying to redeem despised "cultural" materials precisely to remind the viewer, or, I hoped, the experiencer, that these had been living beings and that we are complicit, our whole civilization is complicit, in their unnecessary and un-thought-about mass destruction; to make people aware of how we treat other sentient beings. And the assonances that might connect that with Nazi practices were meant to reflect back upon ourselves, to make us think about our own actions in a rather brutal and unflinching way and not simply accept the flow of history as it leads to, or even is rooted in, brutality. Naturally, it tended to have the opposite effect, as we always try to protect ourselves from really seeing the horrors we've neutralized in order to live.

PACHTER: So, if we look at what the Nazis did to human beings, they eviscerated their humanity and individuality.

HATRY: That definitely was in my mind soon after I conceived this project; and it is precisely for that reason the most difficult one I have ever worked on. I am working with human ashes. People entrust me with the final remains of people they loved, and at the same time it is inevitable that the work will be, especially in view of the fact that I am German, connected with Nazi mass destruction of human beings, burning millions of bodies and dispersing their ashes: covering Europe with the all but invisible evidence of their unspeakable inhumanity.

I have been working on this project for eight years, and at one point, I think it was about two years into it, I had given up because of this problem. I couldn't see a way around it. When I researched what the Nazis did with the ashes of their victims, however, I learned that they tossed them into rivers and ponds and that they used Jewish labor to crush the bones as finely as possible so that no traces would remain; as if their victims had never existed and as if their slaves were mere instruments.

It was actually my friend, the wonderful novelist, Luisa Valenzuela, who got me back to work and encouraged me to continue because she is convinced that it is such a powerful and humane project. She even wants me to make a portrait of her ashes one day.

My relationship to the dead people I portray is the complete opposite of the barbaric Nazi intention. My effort is entirely to preserve the sense of a person, of her or his individuality; to lovingly preserve that quality even in death, in memory, and with it the integrity of the human lineage through generations. But I must admit I still have trouble coming to terms with the reflexive connection to Nazi atrocity.

PACHTER: The Nazi process aimed not just to dehumanize but to negate the particularity of a life. They began with the abstraction of race and subsumed all that was individual in millions of human beings into that category. And, having eliminated individuality, they did what they could to destroy the category itself. It is significant that you are reaching for the particularity of a life, even when it may be said that cremation initially eliminates it, reducing the body to indistinguishable ashes.

HATRY: Exactly what I have in mind: returning indistinguishable ashes to the particular. In some ways a lot of my work is about re-literalizing, trying to return to the traumas, or the site of the traumas, that have been subsumed in culture. It seems to me to be a way of keeping alive what is always in danger of being lost or forgotten, or – more pertinently – ignored.

PACHTER: We don't trust memory. It fades, literally as we grow older, but also culturally. Probably when we suffer loss, our greatest fear is not of losing this person: we have lost them, they are dead. The greatest fear is losing them in our memory. You offer one solution.

HATRY: What about the fear of your own death?

PACHTER: An important question, of course, but something in me says that we basically don't think that we will die. Even at my late age, some two or three decades ahead of you, I don't emotionally believe it. I think the greater fear is the loss of others. Something I need has disappeared. My own death is unthinkable.

HATRY: It's funny. Why is it unthinkable for us? I just started realizing it now, that I too will die – and it startles me.

PACHTER: It goes back to our reality. Everything that is the world we distill through our senses. That's the only reason we believe that there is a world. And so if our senses go, then the world must go. So how can we die? We are the agent of the world's existence. I remember having a conversation with my daughter about the service after my death. At a certain age you're supposed to have that conversation. She stopped me. Not because it was too terrible to discuss. She's very unsentimental, in a very good way. She said, "It has nothing to do with you." It was the perfect answer, because it doesn't. That is the unimaginable world after me. I won't exist. It will be up to my children to do what they need to do. I think that you are precisely dealing not with the needs of the deceased but the needs of the living.

HATRY: That's a very good argument in response to a critic who said that it is very disturbing that I have done these pictures without the consent of the people who died. I don't think I need their consent. But I always tend to take seriously whatever sensitivity seems to be affronted by this particular body of work, since that is the opposite of what I am trying to achieve.

PACHTER: You may not need their consent, but it is interesting to think about the assumption that is built into their position. It is the assumption that we possess the memory of ourselves. So, often people want to construct their own memory.

HATRY: Absolutely, we do this all the time; when we're alive it's about our reputation.

PACHTER: Much of art and history is not allowing people to control the interpretation of their lives. We despise the powerful person who tries to control everything. So, many important people who know they will be written about often burn their letters, or now, perhaps, delete their e-mails and messages. It is a human enough impulse. I don't think we own our own narrative exclusively. Certainly not after we go.

HATRY: I find it a very difficult notion that we don't own ourselves, even though I completely accept the fact that everything we do, at least as artists, comes into its real being only when it interacts with others. The reason why people make art is at least in part to build this immortal *whatever*, that encapsulates their ideas, themselves, as perfectly and finally and immutably as they can. Or at least satisfies their needs for accurate portrayal of them as they understand it.

PACHTER: But if it is art it will have a life of its own and it will read differently. The motivations that went into the artist's work will be the lesser part of its final value. The better the art, the less important the original intent. Of course we do things out of ego, and we yearn for a kind of immortality, but that doesn't convey ultimate value. If it is only you then it is not very good. It has to touch things that even you do not know you are touching in the process of creating it.

HATRY: I think the secret domain of art that is revealed only as it enters into the experience of others, is analogous to the way that the death of those about whom we care reveals the complexity of their effect on our souls. I think that mourning makes it clear that death is inherently a social phenomenon for people, and only through mourning is the actual meaning of death made real. If we can say that the work becomes a work of art only when it is engaged by its viewer or reader, we can equally say that without mourning death is the pure unknowable emptiness or cipher that the core Western philosophical tradition considers it. That is summed up in Wittgenstein's proposition that we do not experience our own death.

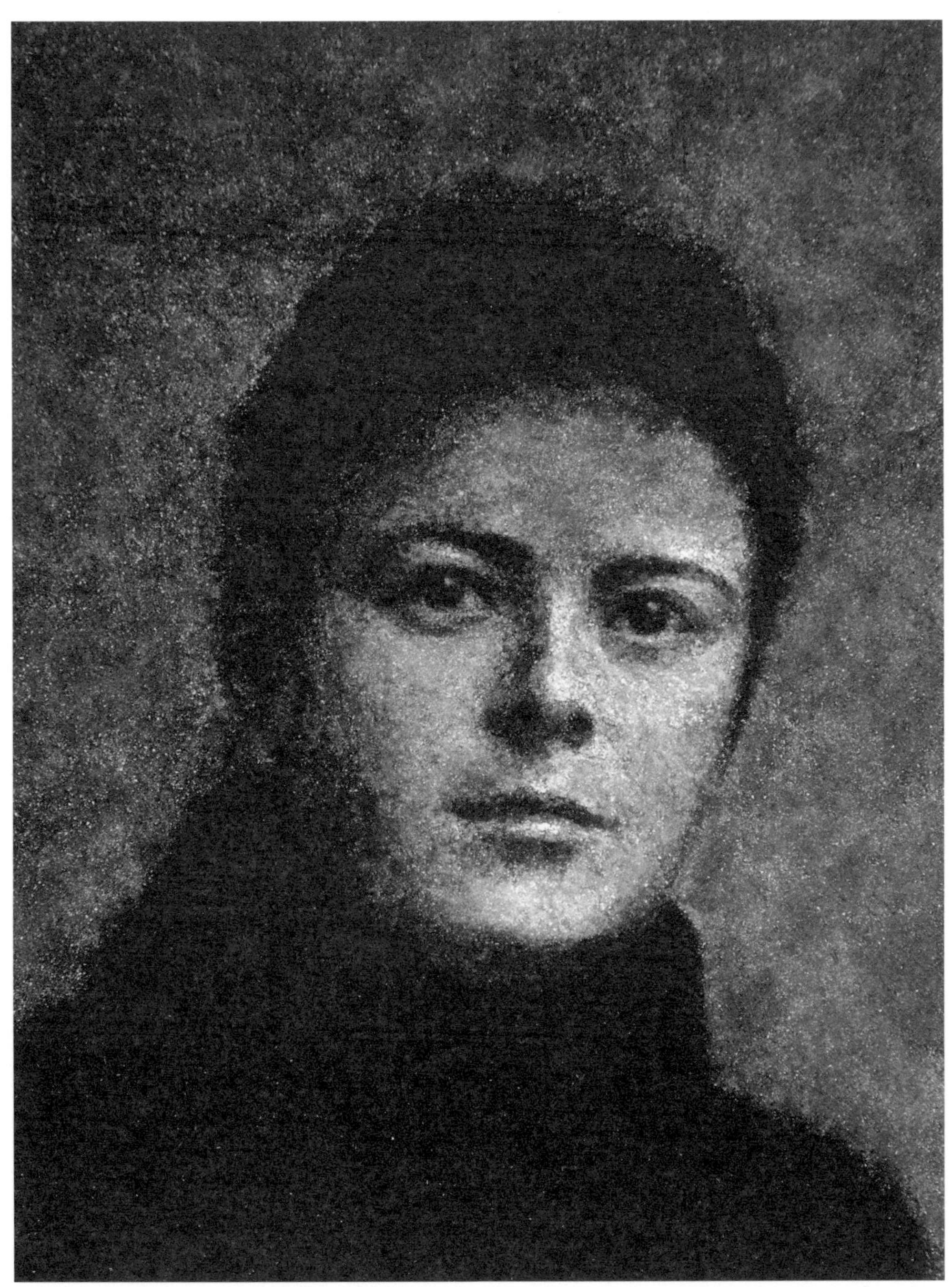

Image and Death: Embodiment in Early Cultures
Hans Belting

To speak of the image and death is to evoke two themes that are today surrounded by uncertainty.[1] The old, symbolic power of images seems to have faded, and death has become so abstract that the question of its meaning scarcely arises. We no longer have images of death that compel our questions – and, more than that, we are even getting used to the death of images, the field in which we once exercised our fascination with the symbolic. In the process, the analogy between image and death, which seems as old as image-making itself, is falling into oblivion. If, however, we follow images far back into their history, they will themselves lead us to the great absence that is death. We are still aware today of the way in which the image conveys a contradiction between presence and absence, and that contradiction has its roots in the human experience of death.

The embodiment of the dead who have lost their body raises the question of what role exactly it is that death has played in the decision to erect images of man's own invention. Today this appears a very remote question, for images nowadays are more likely to invite the living to an escape from the body than to attempt to represent the body of the dead. We are today more concerned with the images' loss of meaning than with the role that death has played in their invention.[2] And yet we cannot understand the one without the other. The anthropology of the image must, therefore, probe the origins of the image and of its connection to death in order to advance our understanding of the ways in which we interact symbolically with the image. But whenever a philosophy of the image has been advanced, the origins of the image have been quickly passed over. When Plato questioned the meaning of images, for example, he was thinking of the advanced art of illusion of his day, which aimed at a mimesis that he thought deceptive and therefore abhorred.

The Greeks of Plato's day hardly remembered that images had once served as vessels of embodiment, replacing the lost bodies of the dead. The notion would have been quite

---

1 This is a revised and expanded version of Hans Belting, "Aus dem Schatten des Todes: Bild und Körper in den Anfängen," in Constantin von Barloewen, ed., *Der Tod in den Weltkulturen und Weltreligionen* (Munich: Diederichs, 1996).
2 On this see Barloewen, ed., *Der Tod in den Weltkulturen und Weltreligionen*; Thomas Macho, *Todesmetaphern: Zur Logik der Grenzerfahrung* (Frankfurt am Main: Suhrkamp, 1987), "Vom Skandal der Abwesenheit," in Dietmar Kamper and Christoph Wulf, eds., *Anthropologie nach dem Tode des Menschen* (Frankfurt am Main: Suhrkamp, 1994), p. 417ff.; Karl S. Guthke, *Ist der Tod eine Frau? Geschlecht und Tod in Kunst und Literatur* (Munich: Beck, 1997); and especially John Taylor, *Body Horror: Photojournalism, Catastrophe and War* (New York: New York University Press, 1998), on the contemporary media image of death.

foreign to him that an image might be called to life through an act of animation, that it need not remain always a lifeless artifact. We too are apt to disparage animation as the relic of a "primitive" worldview that saw a magical identity connecting the image and what it depicted, an identity that obscured any genuine understanding of the image as such. Moreover, historical movements that were dedicated to enlightenment in general and to the enlightened use of images in particular, often took exception to images in a cult of the dead, seeing them as incompatible with a rationalistic conception of the world. Physical pictures of the dead were rejected in favor of mental images of them, on grounds that only the latter could be *living* images.[3]

Maurice Blanchot once posed the metaphysical question, what is it that we learn about death when we look at it.[4] Paradoxically, we come to see something that is not there at all. Similarly, an image finds its true meaning in the fact that what it represents is absent and therefore can be present only as image. It manifests something that is not *in* the image but can only *appear* in the image. An image of the departed was therefore not an eccentricity, but rather an early and rather literal statement of what an image essentially is. The dead have always been absent in person, and their unbearable absence – that is, their death – was made good by the presence of images. It is for this reason that we fix the dead in a chosen location (the grave) and give them an *immortal body* in the image; that is, a *symbolic body* in which they are re-socialized while their *mortal body* dissolves into nothing. The image that represents the dead thus acquires a counter-meaning to that other image, the corpse.[5]

At the moment of death, the corpse indeed becomes an image, a rigid image that merely resembles the living body. That is why Blanchot can say that, being no longer a body, "the corpse is its own image." No body can resemble himself. Only in the image or as a corpse is this possible. The living, those who are the observers, reacted to this perplexing discovery time and again with the supposition that along with life, the soul, too, left the body. But is a body from which life has departed still a body? Answering in the affirmative would mean reducing the body to dead matter, the opposite of life. The body belongs to life, just as the image that takes its place belongs to death, regardless of whether that image anticipates the inevitable death or merely represents it after the fact.[6]

---

3 This antithesis was first articulated by Plato. See also Iris Därmann, *Tod und Bild: Phänomenologische Untersuchungen* (Munich: Fink, 1995), passim.

4 Maurice Blanchot, *L'espace littéraire* (Paris: Gallimard, 1955), "Les deux versions de l'imaginaire" (1951).

5 Philippe Ariès, *Bilder zur Geschichte des Todes* (Munich: Hanser, 1984); Paul Binski, *Medieval Death: Ritual and Representation* (Ithaca, NY: Cornell University Press, 1996); Claudia Schmölders, "Das Gesicht der Toten," in Christoph Ransmayr, ed., *Kursbuch 114: Todesbilder* (Berlin: Rowohlt, 1993), p. 19ff.; Nigel Llewellyn, *The Art of Death: Visual Culture in the English Death Ritual c.1500 - c.1800* (London: Victoria and Albert Museum/Reaktion, 1997), p. 53, on the corpse and effigies. The corpse as an image of the body is not the same theme as a picture of the corpse.

6 On this see Roland Barthes, *La chambre claire: Note sur la photographie* (Paris: Gallimard, 1980). On the corpse and the anatomical gaze see Robert D. Romanyshyn, *Technology as Symptom and Dream* (London: Routledge, 1989), p. 114ff.; for a different perspective Jean Baudrillard, *L'échange symbolique et la mort* (Paris: Gallimard, 1976).

What is alarming about death is the fact that a speaking, breathing body is transformed into a mute image before our eyes, in an instant. And it is a fleeting image at that, for in no time at all it begins to disintegrate. There was nothing people could do but stand helpless before the realization that life, when it dies, is transformed into its own image. They had lost the deceased, who had been part of the community, to a mere image. And so quite sensibly they made an effort to defend themselves against their loss. They created a different image, one that enabled them to make death, the incomprehensible, into something that they could understand on their terms. This new image would be an image of their own creation that they themselves would marshal against the image of death, the corpse. Through this act of making an image, they would cease to be passive before the experience of death. The enigma that already surrounded the corpse would be shared now by the image: the paradoxical *absence* that speaks so loudly in the *presence* of the corpse would be heard now also in the *presence* of the image. It is with this paradox that the mystery of Being vs. Appearing begins, a mystery that has never ceased to exercise the mind of man.[7]

A fascination with this paradox may have begun as soon as man realized that by creating a man-made image in response to the mystery of death, he was in fact creating a new mystery. The making of the image was an active response to a disturbance in the community, more important in fact than the actual possession of the image, for this act of making reestablished the natural order: the dead were given back a status that they needed in order to maintain their presence in the social group. On the other hand, when the body became an image, it underwent what Louis Marin has called an "ontological transfer."[8] The image was given power to act in the name and place of the body. This is just the kind of transfer of power that normally takes place between bodies, and it effectively endowed the image with a new kind of authority. The image was no longer merely compensation for a loss but had, in the very act of representing a body, acquired "Being" in the name of that body. Its presence, precisely because it was delegated to the image, surpassed that of an ordinary body – quite apart from the fact this new image-body, as part of a cult of the dead, had now acquired a sacred character. Through images and their use, the social realm was now expanded to include the realm of the dead. And as the social realm acquired this new dimension, the realm of the living became less precarious.

We possess few images older than the skulls from Jericho. Though actual skulls, they are images to the extent that they were covered with a layer of plaster and painted. But images of what? A skull is an *image of death* by its very nature. And even if it is painted, that does not make it an *image of life*. A more accurate way of posing the question therefore would be: an image *for* what? The answer arises from the demand made by the cult of the dead;

---

7 Usually, the question of Being vs. Appearance is treated outside of the theme of death and therefore truncated. On the hierarchy of Being and Appearance, see the illuminating juxtaposition in Hannah Arendt, *The Life of the Mind, Volume 1* (New York: Harcourt Brace Jovanovich, 1971), p. 23ff.

8 Louis Marin, *Des pouvoirs de l'image* (Paris: Éditions du Seuil, 1993), p. 9ff.

namely, the demand for a medium to reestablish the presence of the dead. A new face possesses the social signs of a living body, yet it belongs to a stranger, because it attests to the incomprehensible transformation that is death. Through the transformation of the skull into a specific person, however, the deceased returns to a community that is able to interact with him in a "symbolic exchange" of signs.[9] In Polynesia, too, there was an ancestor cult that involved the veneration of statues surmounted by real skulls: the places in society that the dead had left empty were repopulated in the course of cult rituals celebrated in the midst of a living community. In so-called "primitive" cultures death is not the fate of an individual but of the community, which must protect itself from dissolution.[10] In the Neolithic "skull cult," the living secured a means of interacting with their ancestors, of preserving their presence. The transformation of the corpse into an *effigies*, as the Romans later called the double or likeness,[11] was still in that context a measure taken in the interests of preservation, as was the mummy.

The image has a variety of roots, including depictions of animals on the walls of Stone Age caves and female fertility idols, but what concerns us here is not its overall genealogy, but only the emergence of the image as a reflection on the experience of death.[12] Humans responded to death by erecting stones and memorials devoid of image. These were generally followed – although we cannot trace a neat evolutionary path – by funerary images. Just as there is a nearly inexhaustible richness of ideas about the nature of death, so too is the variety of images of death virtually infinite: mummies, stelae, and anthropomorphic funerary urns; one thinks also of the dolls that were used in death rituals when a community wished to rid itself of the contagion of contact with its dead. Both the presence and absence of the dead, howsoever close or contradictory the relationship between the two might be, were symbolized by images that were intended either for collective memory or for the brief ritual of exorcism. Used in this sense images are carriers or vessels, even if what they convey is merely a conception of the dead, a conception that they render visible in a representation.

IMAGE BODIES AND IMAGE MAGIC IN THE CULT OF THE DEAD

We enter now on an area in which the anthropological material immediately presents us with uncertainties as to what, if any, general concepts can be appropriately applied to its interpretation. In fact the material itself is contradictory and obscure, the more so the

---

9 Baudrillard, *L'échange symbolique et la mort*.

10 The ethological literature on this subject is extensive. On the cult of the ancestors in Rome, see note 11.

11 Attested especially in Cicero. On effigies in the modern period, see Horst Bredekamp, *Thomas Hobbes visuelle Strategien: Der Leviathan, Urbild des modernen Staates: Werkillustrationen und Portraits* (Berlin: Akademie, 1999), p. 97ff. On effigies in the Middle Ages, see Kurt Bauch, *Das mittelalterliche Grabbild: Figürliche Grabmaler des 11. bis 15. Jahrhunderts in Europa* (Berlin: Walter de Gruyter, 1976), p. 249ff., and Wolfgang Brückner, *Bildnis und Brauch: Studien zur Bildfunktion der Effigies* (Berlin: E. Schmidt, 1996).

12 A comprehensive account of this discussion is in Margaret Wright Conkey et al., eds., *Beyond Art: Pleistocene Image and Symbol* (San Francisco: California Academy of Sciences, 1997).

further back we trace it. It is dangerous to look for archetypes, even though we know that images of death are foundational for most cultures; for when we attempt to search for a unified meaning, we only find *local truths* of the sort that already drew a smile from Herodotus. (He tells an anecdote about the Persian king Darius, who could no more persuade the Greeks to eat their ancestors, which is what a tribe of Indians did, than he could persuade the latter to burn them, as was the Greek custom.)[13] Moreover, when we encounter images in the cult of the dead in one culture, they often defy comparison with those of any other culture. And yet, they raise the common questions: why do they exist in the first place; and what function is it that they were created to fulfill?

In the 1920s, the topic of the image and death possessed an importance, among artists and ethnologists, that it has subsequently lost. Carl Einstein, a champion of the Paris avant-garde, presented his "methodical aphorisms" in the series *Documents*, edited by Georges Bataille. "The image," he tells us, "is a consolidation and a defense against death. Our existence is unalterably an experience of space. It is in this sense that art serves the dead: by restoring a space for their representation." If their images were seen as living, it was because of the "fear of death" and out of a wish to secure the "continuation of the family," which would include always a place for the "spirits of the dead." The images of the ancestors, "a kind of petrified memory," deprived death of its power to destroy duration. "In this sense one can speak of a religious naturalism," in which the dead "prove superior to the living."[14]

In the cult of the dead, images were at first accessories to performances – masks, makeup, costumes, and disguises. Only later did they separate from the body and replicate the latter as a doll or a fetish. In the first instance they were borne directly on the body of the person; in the second, they received an independent existence so as to invoke a *body comparison* and to assume the place of the body. The goal of the substitution was either to transform a body into an image or to duplicate a body. The *image body* did not need to demonstrate its fundamental resemblance to a body because it was created solely for the sake of this analogy and thus could not resemble anything other than a body – not a particular body, but *the body* as such.

And yet the analogy was fatally flawed, for the image remained mute. The silence of the image – a shortcoming that we today overcome through the use of moving images and sound – did not disturb the onlooker, however, until the image lost its connection to the death cult.[15] So long as it remained a part of ritual practice, it was animated by performers who gave it voice. It might even be said that through this animation the ultimate purpose

---

13 Herodotus, *The Histories*, 3.38.
14 Carl Einstein, "Aphorismes méthodique," *Documents* 1 (April 1929). See Carl Einstein, *Werke, Volume 3, 1929-1940*, ed. Marion Schmid and Liliane Meffre (Berlin: Medusa, 1985). On Einstein, see Hans Joachim Dethlefs, *Carl Einstein: Konstruktion und Zerschlagung einer ästhetischen Theorie* (Frankfurt/Main: Edition Qumran im Campus, 1985).
15 On this see Hans Belting, "Die Ausstellung von Kulturen," in Wolf Lepenies, ed., *Jahrbuch des Wissenschaftskollegs, 1994-95* (Berlin: Nicolai, 1996), a discussion with Diawara.

of the image was achieved, namely the embodiment of life. Take away the cult, the magic if you will, and the image is reduced to a medium of remembrance. But even remembrance, when it takes place in a living body, is a kind of embodiment. The image now transfers its embodiment, via representation, to the beholder's imagination. Personal remembrance replaces the collective imagery of the cult. When this point is reached, the embodiment of a person in an artifact becomes suspect. It is viewed as "image magic," as an atavistic misuse of images. In modern times, "image magic" has been relegated to the dark realm of demonology, to such practices as abusing a double (a doll or the like) in order to inflict harm on a living person. Tales of corpses raised from the dead to a hideous, uncontrollable shadow existence belong in the same category. Once disconnected from the cult of the dead and its ritual control, the image moved into a murky realm in which it contaminated life with its touch of death. Today, when we have nothing remotely like a cult of the dead, we are apt to mistake the meaning of the human production of images. For example, Ernst Kris and Otto Kurz, in their book *Die Legende vom Künstler*, traced the "likeness as magic" back to a "confusion" for which they held the "primitive races (*Naturvölker*)" responsible.[16] As they saw it, the confusion was created when humans asserted the magical "identity of the image and the depicted" without according the image a status of its own.

The notion of a "magical worldview" is, however, a modern one, and it does not take account of the power of symbolization of the ritual act.[17] The medium symbolically closes what Kris and Kurz term the "gap" between image and person. The existence of this gap was the motivation for the making of physical images invested with an old tradition of symbolization. Kris and Kurz introduced the concept of "image magic" with the intent of situating the artist within a genealogy that traced his descent from the magician.[18] When image magic dropped away, they maintained, the role of the artist could begin in earnest. In the likeness he created a new bond between image and person. Likeness, so the argument went, was required of art once images were no longer animated by magic. What Kris and Kurz have described as the emergence of the concept of art could also be understood, however, as a structural change that began when the image was detached from the cult of the dead. In cult usage "likeness" meant ontological identity, a meaning that went missing when what was once a cult object became an object to be admired for the skill with which it was made, in other words as a work of art.

16 Ernst Kris and Otto Kurz, *Die Legende vom Künstler: Ein geschichtlicher Versuch* (Frankfurt am Main: Suhrkamp, 1980).

17 Even psychoanalysis was unable to eliminate this schema, from which the discourse of the image legitimated itself by differentiating itself from animism.

18 Conversely, Jean-Hubert Martin, in his Paris exhibit in 1989 entitled "Magiciens de la terre," used the term in a general sense for a global community of artists.

The Ones Who are Left Behind:
A Short History of Lamentation in Western Art

Michaël Amy

I. Preliminary Thoughts

The cities, towns, villages, and suburbs we inhabit are the outcome of decisions and interventions that were made by people who are now long dead. The dead have also left their footprint upon our natural environment.

The house I live in was designed, constructed, and enjoyed by people, most of whom are dead. While much of the music I listen to was composed and performed by musicians who are no longer with us, their work comes to life every time I slip a compact disk into the CD player – and thus, these artists rise, briefly, from among the dead. The dead remain within arm's reach.

The same is true when I look at a work of art or architecture, watch a movie, look at photographs, or read a book. I remember marveling years ago when reading Plato, at the freshness and directness of the Greek philosopher's language and at the fact that I could so clearly hear a voice that reached across a span of almost 2,500 years.

I am similarly struck when reading authors who are chronologically much closer to me, such as Madame de Lafayette, Madame de Sévigné, Voltaire, Diderot, and Rousseau, who speak to me in my mother tongue. Now, when I pick up a book, I am filled with wonder when I am directly engaged by a person who is, in fact, dead. I am roused by these writers in ways so many among the living seem incapable of stimulating me.

Additionally, the actors in the book, painted on canvas, projected on screen, or seized in the photograph come alive when I engage with them; and when viewing photographs or movies of a certain age, I cannot help but think that those people who seem so alive to me are, in fact, dead.

The list goes on, of course. I continuously handle objects that were invented, designed, made, or cherished by people who are now dead – such as the chair I sit on, the table I work at, the cup I pour my coffee into, and the spoon I use to stir a little sugar with; chairs, tables, cups, spoons, coffee, and sugar being inventions of considerable antiquity. But we do not think in these terms, or at least not much – perhaps not enough?

The moral codes that inspired the laws that steer our lives down mostly predictable channels, were established by people who are all long dead. My genetic code is determined both by the dead and by the living (namely my parents), and my identity is as well – to a large extent – by the dead, and the dying. The dead rule us in more ways than we care to acknowledge.

As we come last, we are the ones who are left behind – to look back and ponder.

What I am stating here is so terribly obvious that it seems almost redundant to commit it to print. I am saying in so many words that the world we inhabit is the product of millennia worth of man-made interventions. The wine I drink at the end of a long day was invented over 8,000 years ago, at the beginning of civilization – though our modern wines are, happily, thinner and smoother.

The dead are part of the fabric of our lives. We would, quite literally, be nowhere without them. To playfully paraphrase George Kubler, they have *shaped our time* – much more so than do most of the living. Leopold II, Stalin, Mussolini, Franco, Hitler, Mao, Pol Pot – to name only a few among the more infamous mass-murderers of the blood-soaked twentieth century – and their somewhat less noxious ilk, constituted exceptions to this rule, when they were alive and kicking, but they, happily, constitute a minority.

Major figures from the fields of politics, the social sciences, science, technology, and culture, to limit myself to these areas, may mark our societies during their very lifetimes – think of how Bill Gates and Steve Jobs (deceased in 2011) have changed our world, and not only for the better – but I would argue that their impact is less than that made by the now dead, viewed collectively. The issue is one of magnitude and scale.

The dead I have alluded to so far are not part of our entourage – regardless of how much they may appeal to us, intrigue us, or repel us, as we contemplate them from a distance. Our immediate circle matters in a different way, though not necessarily to a greater degree, when it comes to issues of life and death. When death strikes at the workplace, or among one's friends, or within one's family, it touches one in ways that the death of someone we admire or disdain from a distance does not.

I am not saying that the former instance of demise is necessarily more intense, as it may not be; for the passing of a favorite writer may affect us more deeply than that of a family member one has little in common with. But unless one suffers from delusion, one recognizes that one has some shared history with the family member, which one does not have with the writer – regardless of the extent to which the latter may speak to one.

With the passing of the writer, a point of view or mode of expression one cares for has suddenly lost one of its more compelling spokespersons. An entire world of accrued knowledge and feelings is instantly wiped out, and all potential future contributions are nipped in the bud. With the death of the family member, shared private experience withers away. That affects us in a different way. The circle tightens.

Not all deaths bring us sorrow, or even something close to indifference. Some deaths bring relief or pleasure. My wife walked down to the dining room where I write during much of the year, leaned forward and whispered into my ear that the Associated Press had announced that Supreme Court Justice Antonin Scalia had been found dead at some rich man's ranch in Texas – *en flagrant délit*, I might add.

This news was met, as Milina expected, with joy on both sides, a joy commensurate with the ardor Scalia applied in gutting the rights of all but the wealthiest and most powerful people in the United States. The deaths of Ronald Reagan and his partner in crime Margaret Thatcher was met with similar satisfaction on my side, one which will pale, I assume, in comparison to what I will feel when Henry Kissinger finally bites the dust – from old age, and in the lap of luxury, I fear, and not in the prison cell in which he should be rotting away.

The reactions to death announcements listed in the two preceding paragraphs are, I suspect, unbecoming, but like the ones that are listed earlier, they strike me as being perfectly human. If one does not have this full gamut of reactions, it seems to me that one isn't quite alive.

Above, we have underscored the continued relevance, or should we say *omnipresence*, of the dead. I should now like to look at some responses to the dead, as relayed to us by select works drawn from the history of Western art.[1]

II. The First Death

> After the first death, there is no other…[2] – Dylan Thomas

We come to works of art with bodies of personal experience – or, we should strive to do so, by opening ourselves up, and being prepared to receive and interpret. By the time we have

---

1 The subject of mourning in Western art is vast. Most of my examples will be drawn from the fields of painting and sculpture, and the scales will be heavily tipped toward Christian art of the Renaissance and Baroque periods. The theme of lamentation is, obviously, not exclusive to Western art. Additionally, the subject of lamentation in Western culture, beyond the history of art, is a vast and rewarding subject, as mourning is explored in, among other areas, poetry, plays, fiction writing, essays, instrumental music, song, opera, and film. I imagine this essay as constituting a handful of tesserae within that much larger and richer mosaic, which should also include the arts that lie outside the confines of the Western world. The works that are listed in this essay can be found through Google Images and/or Wikimedia Commons. Alternatively, I invite the reader to visit the websites of the museums where these works of art are preserved, or, even better, visit these museums.

2 James Ellroy, "James Ellroy on The Black Dahlia," *The Guardian* (October 29, 2014) http://www.theguardian.com/books/2014/oct/29/james-ellroy-the-black-dahlia-book-club. The verse cited by Ellroy is the last verse of Dylan Thomas' poem: "A Refusal to Mourn the Death, by Fire, of a Child in London," published in the collection of poems titled *Deaths and Entrances* (1946).

reached adulthood, almost all of us have experienced a death that touches us first hand, and most among us have found ways of processing it. Thus, we are differently equipped to interpret the subject of mourning in, for example, painting than we were before our personal confrontation with death.

The first death that brought me to tears was that of my kitten Sheba, when I was about seven years old. On the evening in question, I performed as the lead male singer in a school production I had trained for over several weeks at the Abraham Lincoln School in Kampala – as I had a better than average voice. As my classmates and I crossed an avenue in the Ugandan capital on our way to the performance venue, a car moved toward us without stopping, and my friends and I pulled apart just in time to allow it to pass between us without hitting us.

Later that night, as my father steered our car down the driveway leading toward our house in Katalemwa, he spotted my cat's corpse lying in the grass, where Patrick, our gardener, had laid it after finding Sheba by the side of the road. I have always imagined that the vehicle that had almost hit me some hours earlier miles away from where we lived, had run over my kitten just outside of our garden. I imagined that if that car had hit one of us as we were crossing the boulevard, it may have been delayed in Kampala, and thus may not have run over my kitten. I remember looking out of my bedroom window, as I watched my father dig a grave, in the dark, at the back of our garden.

I was heartbroken – but young hearts mend more quickly in such situations than do, I suspect, aging ones, besieged as their owners are by the deaths of members of their circle, and concerned as seniors are about their own continuing decline. Sheba's death girded me for future confrontations with death, though I remember my distress years later, both when I lost a small plant I cherished to lice I was unable to fend off (as I only visited my mother's apartment on weekends) and when my brother's wonderful Flemish rabbit died in our garden in Antwerp.

The death of people from my own circle affected me differently, though not in all cases less. One person I was close to and lost years ago appeared in my dreams for weeks on end, and then far more sporadically, though to this very day. When I wander through a flea market, he is often right there with me in my thoughts, and then once more gone – as looking for hidden treasures was an activity we indulged in together in the late morning on Sundays in Antwerp.

The shelves packed with books at home remind me both of him, my mother's erstwhile boyfriend (a producer for the Belgian radio, and an art and literary critic), and my paternal grandfather (a lung specialist with expertise in tuberculosis). The latter, who engaged daily with outstanding works of literature, took me at a tender age to the Corman bookshop in the heart of Brussels to ply me with Voltaire and Dickens. He carried a paperback copy of

Jacques le Fataliste in his inner coat pocket, and announced at a gathering he had planned for weeks with distant cousins of his, that he had recently had his eighteenth-century, leather-bound collection of works by Voltaire restored just for me. That night, as he turned off the lights in his bedroom, he said to my grandmother: "Et les vins étaient délicieux." These were my grandfather's last words.

When my mother's former boyfriend died in Antwerp after a two-week long hospitalization, I proceeded to visit an art collection in Washington, DC, as planned, as I was by then well aware of the soothing effect art had upon me, and the next day I immersed myself in the lovely exhibition of ancient Mayan art at the National Gallery of Art. A few days later, I flew back to Belgium to be with my mother, attend Freddy's funeral at the Schoonselhof Park, read his eulogy at Galerie de Zwarte Panter, in Antwerp, and empty his apartment.

When I work in my garden, I think back to my paternal grandmother, who so loved gardening – and thus that activity brings us together again. The dead are close by – or, as John Berger has stated, "The dead do not stay where they are buried."[3]

These last observations bring me to my next point. Byron, Shelley, and Keats live on, but millions upon millions of later people are forever lost, as all trace of their existence and all living memory of them has vanished. My father's mother is slowly disappearing, as the people who knew her die off, the letters she wrote are discarded, and the photographs of her get thrown away. This is our lot. We commoners die twice.

Perhaps this is best.

The theme of the lamentation in Western art takes us back to Greek antiquity. On the *Dipylon Krater* (attributed to the Hirschfeld Workshop, terracotta, Metropolitan Museum of Art, New York), a grave marker of circa 740 BCE from the Dipylon Cemetery in Athens, we see women – in the second register from the top – mourning a deceased general with their arms raised in such a way that their hands must be tearing away at their hair. I can hear these women wail, as I heard comparable cries when approaching the Greek island of Naxos by boat in the late 1970s, and saw a funeral procession ashore.

In this masterwork of the painter's art, seven women, presumably all relatives of the deceased, stand one beside the other, spread across the available space in such a way that their bodies do not overlap – to avoid all visual confusion, and establish a rhythmic pattern – at either end of the bier. This is a public ceremony; such events are more closely proscribed than are semi-private or completely private ones. Beneath the register where the man's body is laid out (the *prothesis*), there is the procession (the *ekphora*) of his soldiers, on foot and in horse-drawn chariots.[4]

---

3 John Berger, *Here Is Where We Meet* (New York: Pantheon, 2005).
4 John Roberts, ed., *The Oxford Dictionary of the Classical World* (Oxford: Oxford University Press, 2005), p. 203.

As I look at this rigorous arrangement of extraordinarily stylized human and animal forms surrounded above and below by abstract geometric patterns, my thoughts take me to a much later frieze-like arrangement of standing figures, likewise in painting, though in this case produced with oil applied to a wide expanse of flat canvas, namely Gustave Courbet's *Un enterrement à Ornans* (*Burial at Ornans*, oil on canvas, 1849, Musée d'Orsay, Paris).

From where we stand, we see three rows of overlapping figures in the French artist's painting, the thick mass of which is echoed on a smaller scale by the cliffs in the distance. The latter optically press down upon the actors in the foreground and near middle-ground – mostly in the right half of the picture – thereby accentuating their far more restrained public display of grief than is found on the Greek krater. Only the diminutive figure of Christ, the Savior, raised at the end of the tall cross held by one of the clergymen, breaks through the dipping horizon line. Jesus is profiled against a bank of clouds. His redeeming death opens a pathway to Heaven.

There is – unsurprisingly – far greater differentiation of type, pose, gesture, expression, and dress in the figures painted by the leader of the Realist school in French painting, than there is in the highly stylized repetitive figures on the grave marker from Athens. In fact, the men and women on the krater are all naked – perhaps to underscore the arrangement of different genders within the two registers containing figuration, as funeral ceremonies were not conducted in the nude during the Geometric period, in Attica.

When looking at Courbet's canvas, it is worth remembering that one behaves differently when dressed for formal occasions, as one is sensitive both to the kind of ritualized theater such instances call for, and to the extra effort one has made to look just right, as one hopes to garner more than the usually allotted amount of attention, or, instead, blend into the conforming crowd. Witness the way people strut around at weddings, or deport themselves during baptisms, which events, in their adherence to an unusually high degree of decorum, are reminiscent of funerals: people are more conscious of their gestures and utterances, speak and laugh more loudly, or more quietly, depending upon the moment, and throw their heads somewhat further back.

While clergy members partake in the funeral in the nineteenth-century picture – and, in fact, play a lead role during this type of ceremony – priests are absent from the scene depicted on the krater; for in ancient Greece, priests did not participate in funerals, for fear of incurring pollution.[5] In the mural-sized oil painting, the men and women are solemn, many with eyes downcast. One of the more gripping figures presses a handkerchief with her black-gloved hand against her mouth.

We do not see the body of the deceased in the painting by Courbet – in fact, we do not even see the coffin the corpse is laid in. The latter lies at the bottom of the shaft that is truncated

---

5 Ibid., pp. 203; 591-592.

by the picture's lower margin, so that the deceased, whose identity is unknown to us, is transferred to our realm. We live among the dead. A priest stands close to the hole in the ground, reading from his missal.

III. "Speak, Memory…"

The men and women dressed in black in Courbet's picture take me back – as art will do – to the first funeral I attended, around the age of ten, in my native Antwerp, after my maternal grandfather suddenly died of his second infarct within a span of about twelve hours. Having been raised an atheist, I was struck by the gleaming black hearse covered with wreaths, the painfully long ceremony, and the expertly drawn out expressions of those who were paid to join us in mourning, and remember standing in line to shake hands with the many men and women I had never seen before and would never see again, to receive their commiserations, and thank them for attending my grandfather's funeral. My younger brother and I were then dispatched to my great aunt's house, on my father's side, built by a great grandfather I never knew, to be spared the actual entombment and what my father had referred to as the *koffie klatch* – i.e., reminiscing over coffee and pastries.

I remember my father calling his father from his bedroom in Deinze, to ask if he should take his two young sons to their maternal grandfather's funeral. My paternal grandfather – who I would eventually grow very close to, and whose corpse both I and his eldest and only surviving daughter would wash in his bedroom following his own demise – thought that would be fine.

About a year earlier, my mother – who was fixing up the house we had recently moved to, following our return from Africa – loaded a large brush with blue paint and wrote *J'en ai marre* on the white wall of my parent's bedroom – a little in the style of Motherwell's *Je t'aime*, but stating the opposite. Shortly afterward, she walked out on my father. As I stood there in the bedroom as my father called his father, I could clearly read my mother's words of discontent through the overlapping coats of white paint.

My maternal grandmother dressed in black, from head to toe, for exactly one year, almost from the very instant my grandfather passed away, and then, suddenly, no more. The period of obligatory mourning had passed. We are ruled by tradition – though some among us are so far more than others – and thus, we are governed by the codes of conduct set down by people who are long dead. I found such unquestioning ritualized behavior troubling, even at my tender age.

IV. Jackie Kennedy and the Holy Virgin Mary

Another scene of public mourning I should like to turn to was the outcome of the violent demise of United States president John F. Kennedy on November 22, 1963. Caught live on film (excerpts of which were soon published as photographic stills), this very public assassination – unsurprisingly – deeply shocked the American public, which proceeded to watch the ensuing developments on television. There was no more *public* a funeral prior to Kennedy's. The ceremony was watched, heard, and/or read about worldwide.

The American artist Andy Warhol closed in on the widow of the deceased statesman in both paintings and prints, as he sought to encapsulate the grief of a nation. He had developed this compositional strategy in his earlier photography-based portraits of beautiful, glamorous, tragic women, which was inspired by the promotional shots of film actresses and starlets he collected since his youth.

> WARHOL: When President Kennedy was shot that fall, I heard the news over the radio while I was alone painting in my studio. I don't think I missed a stroke. I wanted to know what was going on out there, but that was the extent of my reaction . . . . Henry Geldzahler . . . wanted to know why I wasn't more upset, so I told him about the time I was walking in India and saw a bunch of people in a clearing having a ball because somebody they really liked had just died and how I realized then that everything was just how you decided to think about it. I'd been thrilled having Kennedy as president; he was handsome, young, smart – but it didn't bother me that much that he was dead. What bothered me was the way the television and radio were programming everybody to feel so sad. It seemed like no matter how hard you tried, you couldn't get away from the thing. I rounded up a bunch of people and got them to come over and we all went out to one of the Berlin bars on 86th Street for dinner. But it didn't work, everyone was acting too depressed. David Bourdon was . . . moaning over and over, "But Jackie was the most glamorous First Lady we'll ever get."[6]

In the *Sixteen Jackies* polyptych (1964) at the Walker Art Center in Minneapolis, the First Lady of the United States is shown beaming on the morning of Kennedy's assassination – dressed in what we know from color photographs and journalistic accounts, to be the pink ensemble she wore in Dallas on the day of the shooting – in the four panels in both the top and bottom registers of the painting. The sense of delight radiating from these small canvases will accentuate by contrast the grief displayed by the widow in the two middle rows of this composition.

In the second register from the top, Jacqueline Kennedy is shown in close-up, almost in pure profile toward the left, only hours following President Kennedy's assassination, and still wearing her blood-stained pink ensemble. On the verge of flying off to Washington, DC, with the coffin holding her husband, Jacqueline Kennedy was unexpectedly asked by Vice President Lyndon B. Johnson to stand by his side on Air Force One in order to witness his swearing in as the next President of the United States.[7] This moment was captured by photographer Cecil Stoughton, and the most well-known image that was shot

---

6 Andy Warhol and Pat Hackett, *POPism: The Warhol '60s* (New York: Harper & Row Publishers, 1980), p. 60.

7 See Robert A. Caro, "The Transition: Lyndon Johnson and the Events in Dallas," *The New Yorker* (April 2, 2012), http://www.newyorker.com/magazine/2012/04/02/the-transition.

was dramatically cropped by Warhol – to such an extent that Jackie's face and hair fill almost the entire available space of each panel located in the second row of the painting, counting from the top.

The mourner is numb with grief, and in a seemingly catatonic state. A quick check of the visual materials that are available on the Internet confirms Jacqueline Kennedy's state of utter despair – as her expression and stance have not changed one bit in two other photographs shot around the same moment, while Johnson turns away from her in one of these photographs and, compassionately, toward her in the other. Jackie's body is frozen. Her mind is clearly tied up elsewhere.

In the register beneath this one, we see Jackie three days later, at her most statuesque, at her husband's funeral – dressed all in black, with a soldier standing somewhat deeper in space, on the right. The repetition of this and the three other images, four times each, echoes the seemingly endless repetition of the news cycle – as others have noted. Interestingly, we find both repetitive patterns and the use of registers to organize different types of information, on the body of the *Dipylon Krater* – and later, in the layout of newspapers and magazines, which constituted such important sources of imagery and compositional strategies for Warhol.

Warhol understood how reiteration blunted meaning. He underscored loss by closing in on the state of one survivor just prior to and following a sudden death – and then perversely rips the rug from under our feet by echoing the mind-numbing strategies of the mass media, thereby also subverting the meaning of painting. For all we know, the general represented on the *Dipylon Krater* may likewise have succumbed to a violent death, and like John F. Kennedy, Commander in Chief of the U.S. military, he too was a leader of men. Warhol and the anonymous Greek master underscore the suffering of one woman and many women respectively, to stand in for the mourning of far larger numbers of individuals, both male and female.

Closing in on the heart of the matter is not new in the history of art. Witness the following image-type – which constitutes an apt transition from the work of an artist of Polish Catholic descent, who dealt with mourning in such a highly idiosyncratic way. I am referring to the image of the Virgin Mary cradling the corpse of her full-grown son Jesus, an anonymous, German-Gothic invention known as a *Pietà* – a theme without parallel in pre-existing Christian accounts.

In the painted Gothic wooden statuette from the Rheinisches Landesmuseum in Bonn, the smaller seated figure of Christ is seen with his body in profile, placed at a right angle to the body of Mary, who is seated in frontal view. Mary holds her Son's back upright with her right hand, and holds His thighs in place on top of her own with her left. Christ's head falls back as far as it will go, with the face turned toward us so that we may contemplate the closed and swollen eyes and the mouth that is agape. Mary tilts her head toward the left as she contemplates her Son from the corner of her eyes, with her mouth twisted in agony. This category of *Andachtsbild* (the German term for a *devotional image*, serving as an aid for prayer) became especially popular in Germany and France.

The *Pietà*-group was distilled from the biblical scene of the *Lamentation of Christ*, which became popular in Western art during the Romanesque and Gothic periods. In *Lamentation* scenes, Jesus is mourned by his mother Mary, John the Evangelist, frequently Mary Magdalen, and – in many instances – three additional women named Mary, plus Joseph of Arimathea, and Nicodemus, following Christ's deposition from the cross upon which He was crucified and upon which He died. However, more mourners may be included, as in the *Lamentation* (also known as the *Pietà di San Remigio*, tempera on panel, circa 1360, Galleria degli Uffizi, Florence), by Giottino (Giotto di Maestro Stefano), which includes two female donors (rendered on a smaller scale) who are presented by their two male patron saints (one a monk, the other a bishop), or Giotto's *Lamentation* fresco in the Scrovegni Chapel in Padua, of 1305, where a crowd of mourners is cropped by the left border of the painting, and wailing angels dot the sky.

Among the great inventions in the latter painting one must count the two women seated in the foreground with their backs toward us, so that their faces cannot be seen. Only their postures and one exposed hand express their suffering, thereby compelling us to use our imagination to fill in the blanks.

The many mourners in Giotto's mural take me back to Cimabue's altarpiece of the Crucifixion of circa 1280, painted on the wall in the left transept arm of the Upper Church of San Francesco at Assisi, in which Jesus' agitated followers are all situated on His proper right (thus to our left) and His attackers, equally numerous in number, are placed on His left – symbolizing the more sinister side. Cimabue packed a considerable amount of drama in a field three-and-a-half-meters tall by almost seven meters wide. Pietro Lorenzetti – who saw Cimabue's mural in the Upper Church, having worked in the Lower Church several decades later – produced a deeply moving scene of the Crucifixion on an intimate scale intended for private devotion, showing the Virgin Mary who has passed out from agony (Pietro Lorenzetti, *The Crucifixion*, tempera and gold leaf on wood, 1340s, Metropolitan Museum of Art, New York).

In less crowded Crucifixion scenes, the persecutors of Jesus are not present – we conclude that they walked away, following the death of their victim – and only the Virgin Mary and John the Evangelist may appear respectively on Christ's right and left side, as in Rogier van der Weyden's painting at the Escorial (*Christ on the Cross with Mary and St. John*, oil on panel, circa 1457-64, Real Monasterio de San Lorenzo de El Escorial), or ter Brugghen's picture in New York (Hendrick ter Brugghen, *Crucifixion*, oil on canvas, circa 1624-25, Metropolitan Museum of Art, New York). Mary Magdalen may eventually be added to this group, weeping at the foot of the cross, as in Allegretto Nuzi's *Crucifixion with the Virgin Mary, St. John the Evangelist, and St. Mary Magdalen* (tempera on panel, circa 1365, Birmingham Museum of Art), in which she occupies a position akin to that of St. Francis in Cimabue's large mural in Assisi.

This excursus reminds us that mourning the Christ precedes the Lamentation – witness, for example, the gripping depictions of the Deposition by Rubens in Antwerp (Pieter Paul Rubens, *The Descent from the Cross*, central panel of a triptych, oil on panel, 1612-14, Onze-Lieve-Vrouwe Kathedraal, Antwerp) and Rembrandt in Munich (Rembrandt van Rijn, *The Deposition*, oil on panel, 1633, Alte Pinakothek, Munich).

Mourning the inevitable is actually accelerated from the onset of Christ's Passion. Not surprisingly, it continues beyond the Lamentation – i.e., until the Resurrected Christ is recognized by his followers. As far as the former point is concerned, witness Caravaggio's *Entombment* (Michelangelo Merisi da Caravaggio, oil on canvas, 1603-04, Pinacoteca Vaticana, Rome) for an altar in Santa Maria in Vallicella, the *Chiesa Nuova* of the Oratorian Fathers in Rome.[8] Carlo Crivelli places the mourning Virgin Mary, John the Evangelist, and Mary Magdalen in the sarcophagus together with the Christ, who is held upright, in a seated stance, as if He were alive, thereby intimating at His Resurrection (Carlo Crivelli, *Pietà*, tempera on wood, gold ground, 1476, Metropolitan Museum of Art, New York).

V. In Search of a Theology of Mourning

Upon re-reading this essay, I notice that almost every death I list is that of a male protagonist. I should like to correct this state of affairs, however slightly, and wonder whether a female author would have easily achieved greater gender balance when covering the subject of mourning in Western art. The Apostles' response to the death of the Virgin Mary – to whom devotion in the West increased dramatically during the Gothic period (beginning in 1140, in the Île-de-France) – is rendered with arresting intensity by Hugo van der Goes (*The Death of the Virgin*, oil on panel, circa 1480, Groeningemuseum, Bruges) and Caravaggio (*The Death of the Virgin*, oil on canvas, 1605-06, Musée du Louvre, Paris) – the latter adds a female, most likely the Magdalen, bent over in sorrow, in the foreground of his picture.

In the context of a faith in which death plays such a prominent role, mourning the deceased who perished for their convictions is key. The Christian martyrs, the saints, and God

---

8 In light of that altar's dedication to the *Pietà*, it is worth noting that the Christ in Caravaggio's picture is informed by the one carved by his namesake Michelangelo for his marble *Pietà* in Rome (1498-1500, New St. Peter's, Rome). Howard Hibbard, *Caravaggio* (Boulder, CO: Westview Press, 1985), pp. 171-179; 312-315.

Himself, die for the cause, and Christians gather in churches and chapels to commemorate these heroes, in a celebration tinged with grieving. Martyria, chapels and churches, which are all associated with tombs – for consecrated altars are also tombs, as they contain relics – are places where Christians go to mourn. There is plenty of lamentation in Christian art, and in Christian life.

Let us return to the theme of the *Pietà*.

When one's child dies, whatever the circumstances, all else is obliterated, for there can be no greater loss. It is the elimination of all of the rest to focus on the last communion between the parent and the dead child that results in the *Pietà*, in which the grieving parent happens to be the Mother of God (*Theotokos*) – whose status as such was confirmed at the Third Ecumenical Council held at Ephesus in 431,[9] long before the Gothic period – and the child happens to be the second person of the Trinity, the Son, Christ, who took on the flesh in the womb of a young virgin in order to be sacrificed upon the cross for the redemption of humankind.

The image of the Virgin holding the Christ Child was codified during the Early Byzantine period.[10] I now wonder to what extent that model inspired the inventor of the *Pietà* to imagine that same mother holding her child one last time, thirty-three years later – witness those *Pietàs* showing the Virgin holding a much smaller dead Christ upon her lap, somewhat reminiscent in scale of the Christ Child. In Byzantine as well as later images of the Virgin and Child, Mary may be shown filled with sorrow as she holds or contemplates her Infant, for she has foreknowledge of the divine plan (Giovanni Bellini, *Madonna Adoring the Sleeping Child*, tempera on panel, early 1460s, Metropolitan Museum of Art, New York).[11] Thus, a *lamentation* of sorts actually begins decades prior to the Crucifixion. Witness Mary's apprehension in more than a few scenes of the Annunciation – Simone Martini's wary Virgin in his *Annunciation* in Florence (Simone Martini and Lippo Memmi, *The Annunciation and Two Saints*, tempera and gold leaf on wood, 1333, Galleria degli Uffizi, Florence), and the *sinopia* (underdrawing) for the fresco of the *Annunciation* by Ambrogio Lorenzetti for San Galgano in Montesiepi, come to mind. Every birth brings a new death into this world.

Placing a full-grown dead man on top of the lap of a middle-aged woman and creating a compelling composition was no easy feat, as an overview of *Pietàs* produced both during

---

9 Hans Belting, *Likeness and Presence: A History of the Image before the Era of Art*, trans. Edmund Jephcott (Chicago: University of Chicago Press, 1994), pp. 32; 558.
10 Ibid.
11 Even in those works of art in which Mary doesn't appear filled with sorrow when in the presence of the Christ Child, she does seem apprehensive, as in the *Schöne Madonna* from Krużlowa (circa 1400-10, National Museum, Kraków), the terracotta statuette of *The Virgin with the Laughing Child* attributed to Antonio Rossellino (circa 1465, Victoria and Albert Museum, London), and Leonardo's *Benois Madonna* (1478, State Hermitage Museum, St. Petersburg).

the Gothic age and after teaches us. A further reductive process eventually ensued, and the mourning figure of Mary could be examined in complete isolation, as in Adriaen Isenbrandt's *Our Lady of the Seven Sorrows* (oil on panel, 1521, Onze Lieve Vrouwekerk, Bruges), which constitutes the right wing of a disassembled diptych.[12] In other depictions of this subject, either one or seven swords pierce Mary's chest, to highlight her suffering.

This development came about once Mary's role as co-redemptress was firmly established, a role that was underscored in Rogier van der Weyden's extraordinarily gripping *Deposition* (oil on panel, circa 1439, Museo del Prado, Madrid), in which the arrangement of Christ's corpse is echoed by the pose of his Mother, who has passed out from grief.[13] In this early Netherlandish painting, the suffering of the mourners is highlighted by excising both the figures and the cross from their landscape surroundings and placing these upon a shallow stage – inspired by the carved wooden altarpieces then popular in Germany and the Netherlands – and in front of a gold ground.

Leonardo noted how difficult it was to render the movements of the soul:

> The good painter has to paint two principal things, that is to say, man and the intention of his mind. The first is easy and the second difficult, because the latter has to be represented through gestures and movements of the limbs . . . . That figure is most praiseworthy which best expresses through its actions the passion of its mind. The movement which is depicted must be appropriate to the mental state of the figure. It must be made with great immediacy, exhibiting in the figure great emotion and fervor, otherwise this figure will be deemed twice dead, inasmuch as it is dead because it is a depiction, and dead yet again in not exhibiting motion either of the mind or of the body. The motions and postures of figures should display the true mental state of the originator of these motions, in such a way that they could not signify anything else.[14]

Images flow through my mind as I read these lines, and Niccolò dell'Arca's fiery life-sized terracotta *Lamentation* group lingers on (circa 1462-63 or 1485-90, Pinacoteca Nazionale, Bologna).[15] That *tableau vivant*, produced for a church founded by the Congregation of Battuti (also known as the Flagellati, or flagellants), has the *energia* of Cimabue's great Crucifixion scene in Assisi.

---

12 The large family of donors is represented on the left wing, in the company of the husband's and wife's patron saints. See Maximiliaan P.J. Martens, ed., *Bruges et la Renaissance: De Memling à Pourbus* (Paris: Ludion-Flammarion; Bruges: Stichting Kunstboek, 1998), pp. 128-129, fig. 40.

13 Otto G. von Simson, "*Compassio* and *Co-Redemptio* in Roger van der Weyden's *Descent from the Cross*," *Art Bulletin*, XXXV, no. 1 (March 1953): pp. 9-16. The subject of Mary fainting from grief is frequently depicted, including by the likes of the Magdalen Master, the Master of the Fogg Pietà, Petrus Christus, Sandro Botticelli, Raphael, Antonio Begarelli, Correggio, Federico Barocchi, Ludovico Carracci, and Annibale Carracci.

14 Martin Kemp, ed., *Leonardo on Painting: An Anthology of Writings by Leonardo da Vinci with a Selection of Documents Relating to his Career as an Artist* (New Haven, CT: Yale University Press, 1989), pp. 144-146.

15 Joachim Poeschke, *Donatello and His World: Sculpture of the Italian Renaissance*, trans. Russel Stockman (New York: Harry N. Abrams, 1993), p. 453.

VI. The Classical Heritage

Losing one child is awful, losing one's only child may be worse, and losing all of one's children amounts to death by one thousand cuts. The latter tragedy is the subject both of the *Niobe* group of over life-sized marble statues at the Galleria degli Uffizi (Roman copies of figures in a Hellenistic group of either circa 300 BCE or, more likely, the first century BCE), and the red-figure calyx krater by the Niobid Painter (circa 450 BCE) at the Louvre in Paris. Homer tells us in the *Iliad* that Niobe, daughter of Tantalus, had six sons and six daughters, and that she mocked the Titan Leto (the Roman goddess Latona) for having no more than two children, namely the twin deities Apollo and Artemis (the Roman goddess Diana). Apollo exacted revenge by killing all of Niobe's sons with his arrows, and Artemis did the same to all of Niobe's daughters.[16]

The sculpture group shows the moment of climax when the children are struck, and when the once proud mother realizes what has befallen her. One kneeling daughter – with bottom bared – is pressed by Niobe against her abdomen in an effort to shield her, as if to return her to the womb, as the mother looks up with pleading glance, though all in vain.

The agony of Niobe, surrounded by the many dead and dying children is echoed, in a sense, in the Christian subject of the *Massacre of the Innocents* (Matthew 2:16-18), so strikingly rendered by the likes of Giovanni Pisano, Giotto, Duccio, Matteo di Giovanni, Lucas Cranach the Elder, Marcantonio Raimondi (after Raphael), Daniele da Volterra, Pieter Brueghel the Elder, Tintoretto, and Rubens. I say "in a sense," as here too the many victims are children, though they belong to different mothers.

The result of the wrath of another goddess, Athena, is captured in the Hellenistic *Laocoön* group (Athanadoros, Hagesandros, and Polydoros of Rhodes, *Laocoön and His Sons*, marble, copy of the early first century CE probably after a Hellenistic original of circa 200 BCE, Musei Vaticani, Rome). As recounted by Virgil in book two of the *Aeneid*, the goddess sent two sea serpents ashore to strangle the Trojan priest *Laocoön* and his sons, after the former revealed the ploy of the Trojan Horse to his fellow Trojans. I join Winckelmann in interpreting the agonizing expression of the father as a response to the impending death of his two sons.[17] Here as elsewhere, mourning begins before the actual passing.

VII. A Deadly Virus

One of the most gripping images of mourning I know is the one shot in 1990 by journalism student Therese Frare of the dying AIDS patient David Kirby, with a care giver (reduced

---

16 Homer, *The Iliad*, trans. Richmond Lattimore (Chicago: University of Chicago Press, 1951), p. 491; XXIV: 602-17. See also Ovid, *The Metamorphoses*, trans. Horace Gregory (New York: New American Library, 1960), VI; pp. 167-172.
17 Francis Haskell, Nicholas Penny, *Taste and the Antique: The Lure of Classical Sculpture, 1500-1900* (New Haven, CT: Yale University Press, 1982), p. 244. I was not able to consult the original source.

to an outstretched arm) on the left and the man's father, mother, and sister on the opposite side of the bed. What makes this picture so unforgettable is the father's boundless sorrow, as well as the contrast between his heft and the skeletal shell of his son. The father gives his child a last embrace, resting his face – with his wailing mouth open, and his weeping eyes closed – against his child's forehead, as he ever so gently cradles the wobbly head with his right hand, while holding his offspring's boney elbow with his other hand. I imagine that at this moment, he remembers holding that vulnerable child for the very first time, in his arms, as a newborn. This is the end. Alpha meets Omega.

Frare's photograph makes the accuracy in the rendering of loss and lament in, for example, the *Laocoön*, Giotto's *Lamentation*, and Rubens' *Massacre of the Innocents* all the more mesmerizing. In Pietro Lorenzetti's *Deposition of Christ from the Cross* (fresco, 1320s?, Lower Church of San Francesco, Assisi), the Virgin presses her face against the forehead of her Son, which is upside down in relation to his Mother's, in such a way that their eyes align. For me, this counts as one of the great inventions in the history of Western art – one that may have inspired Picasso's entangled faces.

In the photograph shot by Frare, the overweight mother leans in a direction opposite to that of her husband in order to embrace her young daughter as she looks at her son, who, with tilted head, mouth partly open, and blank eyes, seems no longer capable of registering the world around him.

VIII. The Classical Heritage, Continued

Mourning prior to the actual passing is rendered in a classicizing vein in Jacques-Louis David's picture of *The Death of Socrates* (oil on canvas, 1787, Metropolitan Museum of Art, New York) – a popular subject in late eighteenth-century painting. The women, the last of whom are seen in the distant middle ground, are sent away, as Plato reported, and the responses of the mostly young men range from peaceful to agitated despair. Socrates, the most lively figure in the composition – with his limbs flung wide apart, though admirably calm – is tendered the cup of hemlock by a follower who turns away and covers his eyes. The figures in the foreground are arranged in a relief-like fashion, characteristic of neoclassical painting and reminiscent of sarcophagi fronts – an appropriate source, considering the subject of impending death.

Lamentation scenes occur, as one would expect, on classical sarcophagi, such as in the carved relief at the Louvre showing the *Death of Meleager* (marble, Roman sarcophagus front, circa 180 CE, Musée du Louvre, Paris). The grieving woman left of center (with both arms flung back far enough to make the shoulders pop out of their sockets) – or a woman just like this one (as such scenes were repeated on other sarcophagi fronts) – inspired the St. John (who constitutes a mirror image of the woman) in Giotto's *Lamentation*.

Scenes of mourning also appear on other types of funerary monuments, such as the late-classical *Athenian Grave Stele of Thrasynos* (circa 375 BCE, The J. Paul Getty Museum, Los Angeles), showing the deceased young man standing as he shakes the hand of his seated mother – a gesture signifying the ongoing link between the living and the dead. In the *Cenotaph of Maria Christina of Austria* – a monument singularly devoid of Christian imagery – grieving children, women, and an elderly man walk toward the door at the center of the large pyramid (Antonio Canova, *Cenotaph of Maria Christina of Austria*, marble, 1798-1805, Augustinerkirche, Vienna).

Unsurprisingly, the subject of one-on-one mourning in Western art precedes the appearance of the medieval *Pietà*. The much-restored *Pasquino* (marble, Roman copy of the Flavian era after a Hellenistic original of the third century BCE, with modern restorations, Loggia dei Lanzi, Florence) was recognized in the late eighteenth century as showing Menelaos carrying the body of Patroclus after he was fatally wounded by Hector (*Iliad*, books XVI and XVII).[18]

The *Pasquino* is tied to war, which occasion brings its fair share of death and mourning. The classical sculpture-group shows the closeness of brothers in arms, which brings up the subject of the loss of a friend; in other words, of someone who is more or less an equal. This is a subject we have barely touched upon thus far, with our focus upon the relations between mothers or fathers and their offspring, and between revolutionary thinkers (Socrates, Christ) and their followers. Montaigne's essay *On Friendship* merits pondering at this point.

IX. Love and Loss

Let us now turn to yet another subject involving mourning, namely the death of the person one is in love with. Nicolas Poussin interpreted the story of *Venus Weeping for Adonis* (oil on canvas, 1626, Musée des Beaux-Arts, Caen), tenderly, in his warm and early manner so profoundly marked by Titian. Venus kneels to pour nectar onto her lover, who lies on top of drapery laid on the ground, as if he were merely resting, though Adonis' body is ashen.[19]

In Poussin's ravishing picture of *Echo and Narcissus* (oil on canvas, 1628-30, Musée du Louvre, Paris), Narcissus lies in the foreground with his body turned toward us, as Echo in her grief over his death leans against a rock in the middle ground, and withers away. Narcissus' body has not yet turned into the flower named after him, and Echo has not yet been reduced to only her voice, which echoes ours. This picture constitutes a glorious ode to unrequited love, and to the effects of intense, ongoing grief upon body and soul.[20]

18 Ibid., pp. 291-296, no. 72.
19 Ovid, *The Metamorphoses*, X: pp. 295-296.
20 Ibid., III: pp. 95-100.

I conclude this brief consideration of grief over the loss of the one we love intensely, and in a different way than the friend or the family member, with Giovanni Battista Tiepolo's *The Death of Hyacinth* (oil on canvas, circa 1752, Thyssen-Bornemisza Museum, Madrid). Here, as in the story of Adonis, we have the love of a god for a mere mortal. The body of Hyacinth is displayed in frontal view, with the head thrown back in profile, with feminine languor. Tiepolo shows us the lover Apollo who has rushed forward and raises his clenched right hand to his brow as he throws back his other hand in horror, when seeing the youth whose color has turned a waxy beige. From the boy's spilled blood, Apollo made the flower named after the youth, in memory of him.[21]

> ARISTOTLE: A lover enjoys talking or writing about his loved one, or doing any little thing connected with him; all these things recall him to memory and make him as it were present to the eye of imagination. Indeed, it is always the first sign of love, that besides enjoying someone's presence, we remember him when he is gone; and we love when we actually feel pain because he is there no longer. Similarly there is an element of pleasure even in mourning and lamentation. There is grief, indeed, at his loss, but pleasure in remembering him and as it were seeing him before us in his deeds and in his life. We can well believe the poet when he says: "He spake, and in each man's heart he awakened the love of lament."[22]

In the many works mentioned above, we join one or more persons in mourning the deceased, or the dying. The image of the *Pietà* was tailored to induce empathy – as medieval prayer manuals make clear. After the Virgin bid her Son farewell, His body was laid in the tomb, all by itself.

X. THE LONELY DEAD

Hans Holbein the Younger illustrates this apparent "end" in *The Body of the Dead Christ in the Tomb* (oil on panel, 1521, Kunstmuseum, Basel). The right side of Jesus' body is shown to us in profile, in full length, as if we had sunk underground and one wall of the tomb had been lifted. Thus, we become the privileged mourners who can see the dead Christ. We are left to our own devices, as no one is there to show us how to grieve this God who has taken on the flesh in order to die upon the cross for the salvation of humankind.

The same is true of many Crucifixes, either painted, carved or cast, in which the body of the Redeemer is presented in singular isolation – I am thinking of those by Brunelleschi, Donatello, Verrocchio, Botticelli, Michelangelo, Cellini, Giambologna, Rubens, van Dijck, Duquesnoy, Bernini, Zurbarán, Velázquez, and Dalí.

---

21 Ibid., X: pp. 278-280.
22 Aristotle, *Rhetoric*, Book I, Chapter 11, in *The Complete Works of Aristotle: The Revised Oxford Translation*, ed. Jonathan Barnes, trans. W.D. Ross et al., 2 vols. (Princeton, NJ: Princeton University Press, 1984), II, p. 2182. The verse cited in this passage is drawn from Homer, *The Iliad*, XXIII: 108, p. 453; and Homer, *The Odyssey*, trans. Richmond Lattimore (New York: Harper & Row, 1975), IV: 183; p. 70.

The Christ in Michelangelo's Roman *Pietà* (St. Peter's) informed the pose of the French revolutionary leader in Jacques-Louis David's *Death of Marat* (oil on canvas, 1793, Royal Museums of Fine Arts of Belgium, Brussels). Killed – as was Jesus – Marat is presented to us as a martyr for the new, post-revolutionary age. Lying in the tub in which he was assassinated, he is presented to us in singular isolation, his quill in hand, signifying his ideas that will live on.

We who look at this painting are placed in the position of mourners, as we are also when looking at Stefano Maderno's statue of *Santa Cecilia* (marble, 1600, Santa Cecilia in Trastevere, Rome), Jacques-Louis David's unfinished painting of *The Death of Bara* (oil on canvas, 1794, Musée Calvet, Avignon), Picasso's close-up of the head of his friend, a suicide, in *The Death of Casagemas* (1901, Musée National Picasso, Paris), Ferdinand Hodler's drawings and paintings of his dying and – eventually – dead lover Valentine Godé-Darel (1915, Kunstmuseum, Basel; 1915, Kunstmuseum, Solothurn), or Man Ray's photograph of *Marcel Proust on his Deathbed* (November 20, 1922, J. Paul Getty Museum, Los Angeles).[23]

XI. THE LONELY MOURNERS

As alternative to the isolated corpses I have just listed, we have the lonely mourners, such as Picasso's *Weeping Woman* (oil on canvas, 1937, Tate Modern, London), or his *Weeping Woman* (oil on canvas, 1937, National Gallery of Victoria, Melbourne), which paintings have their source in the lamenting female holding the dead child on the left in *Guernica* (1937, Reina Sofía National Museum and Art Center, Madrid), Picasso's pictorial "howl," in black, white and gray, against the bombing of the eponymous Basque town. However, when they are presented in this way, all alone, in close-up and bust-length, Picasso's weeping women become ambiguous, as the reason for their sorrow is unknown.

Picasso's pictures of an isolated grieving woman have an antecedent of sorts in Titian's *The Virgin Dolorosa with Her Hands Joined* (oil on panel, 1554, Prado, Madrid) and Titian's *Mater Dolorosa with Open Hands* (oil on marble, 1555, Prado, Madrid). I say "of sorts," as Titian's pictures were designed to be paired with an image of Christ placed to the proper right of the Virgin (our left), and because Titian's tearful mother – inspired by northern European models – is a private, Christian, devotional image, in which Mary should also be seen as interceding with God on behalf of the viewer, in this case Titian's patron, the Holy Roman Emperor Charles V.[24]

Mourning is an act of remembrance. Through the workings of memory, the dead stay with us a little longer. Works of art and literature are among the tools we have at our disposal to keep memories of past events, things, and people alive.

---

23 Picasso's and Man Ray's images inscribe themselves within a pre-existing and ongoing tradition of postmortem painting and photography.
24 https://www.museodelprado.es/en/the-collection/art-work/the-virgin-dolorosa-with-her-hands-joined/6caedf60-c6 5c-4fe1-b821-9de7b2e0b0a9.

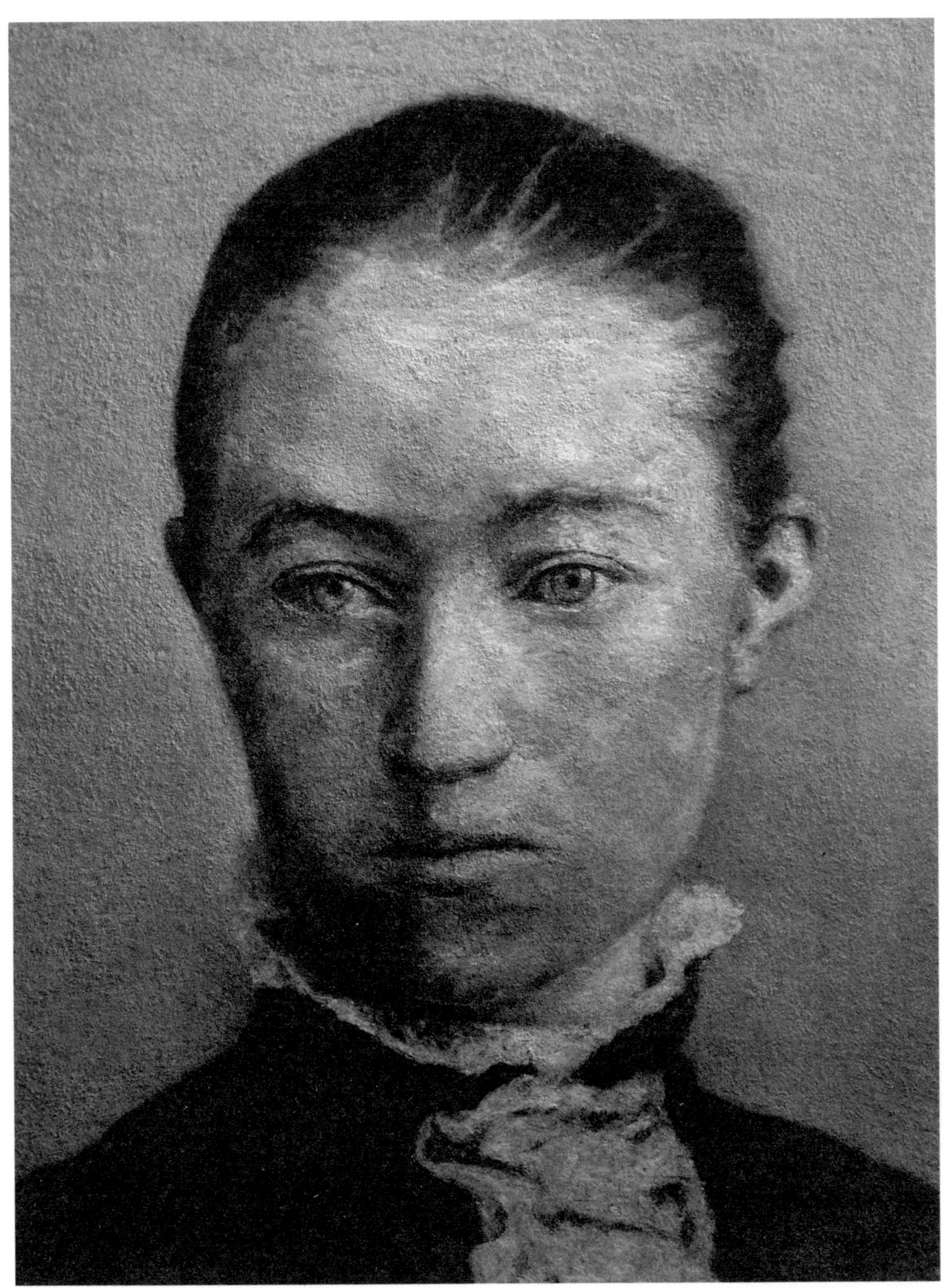

Corruptible Bodies: Catholic Morbidity

Eleanor Heartney

> Death is the mother of beauty; hence from her,
> Alone, shall come fulfillment to our dreams.
> And our desires.
> – Wallace Stevens, "Sunday Morning"

Wallace Steven's great poem "Sunday Morning" is essentially a conversation about the meaning of death and the nature of Paradise. Couched as a dialogue between two voices, it lays out a pair of arguments, which take us to the heart of our modern ambivalence about mortality.

The poem sets the stage with a description of a dreamy Sunday morning, as the unnamed female interlocutor drifts from the comforts of her immediate surrounds to a meditation on the religious meanings of the day. Rebelling against the Christian preoccupation with death, she offers a counterproposition. Invoking the beauties of nature she declares, "Divinity must live within herself." Not one of the religion's trappings of shroud and spirit "has endured/ As April's green endures; or will endure/ like her remembrance of awakened birds, Or her desire for June and evening…" Thinking further, however, she notes that this proposition is not wholly satisfying ("But in contentment I still feel the need of some imperishable bliss").

Her conundrum is addressed by an omniscient voice which makes the case for the inseparability of death and life. Declaring "Death is the mother of beauty," this voice invokes the pathos of a paradise without death – where ripe fruit never falls and perfection abolishes all change. Instead, the voice suggests, what makes life precious is the presence of death in our midst. Casting back to the theological speculations which open the poem, the female interlocutor finally understands the Christian fixation on mortality:

> She hears, upon that water without sound,
> A voice that cries, "The Tomb in Palestine
> Is not the porch of spirits lingering.
> It is the grave of Jesus, where he lay."

"Sunday Morning" beautifully captures the tension in Western culture between our fear and our fascination with death, and links this dilemma to the legacy of Christianity. Among the

Christian rites were the preservation of relics, the accumulation and display of corpses in charnel houses, and the creation of graphic and even grisly images of martyred saints and the dead Christ. In more recent times, American Christianity (this includes both Protestant sects and even post-Vatican II Catholicism) have downplayed what Stevens refers to as "the domain of blood and sepulchre" in favor of an emphasis on spiritual rebirth.

In his monumental study, *The Hour of Our Death*, Philippe Ariès takes on Western culture's changing attitudes toward death.[1] He describes a medieval world in which death is an incident in a larger vision of life, which begins with birth and ends with the reunion of body and soul at the end of time. He notes the shift from a pre-Christian and Jewish tendency to view the dead as unclean and to keep them at a distance from the living to the view that the presence of the dead sacralizes the spaces of life. In keeping with this new sensibility, in the early Christian era, burials moved into the city and then into the churches, and graveyards became centers of social life.

Later, around the fourteenth century, beliefs about the nature of death changed again. No longer a sleep shared by all until the Last Judgment at the end of time, death, defined as the moment the soul leaves the body, became a moment of truth in which one's salvation or damnation was determined. This lead to a new anxiety about death which manifested itself in a covering of the corpse and a remarkable flowering of artistic representations of the macabre.

Medieval art from the fourteenth to the sixteenth century reflects a consciousness of death as the fearsome moment when one's eternal fate is decided. The tradition of the *vanitas* or *memento mori* incorporated symbols of death and decay into representations of earthly abundance. Transi sculptures lovingly reproduced the half-decomposed corpse in all its gruesome detail. Prayer books were full of *tableaux* in which God and Satan vie for the soul of a dying person. Also popular were images of the *Danse Macabre* in which the dead and living dance together as rotting mummies taking the hands of robust men and women. Similar representations live on today in Mexican celebrations of the Day of the Dead.

The new reform movements that followed the Reformation tended to view the pre-Reformation focus on dead bodies as morbid and unhealthy. Ariès quotes New England Puritan leader Increase Mather: "When the soule departs this life, it carries nothing away with it but grace, God's favour, and good conscience."[2] The body, once viewed as an indivisible feature of human identity, becomes for Mather simply a useless shell to be disposed of without ceremony once it has served its earthly function. He notes:

> The body, when the soule is gone, will be a horrour to all that behold it, a most loothsome and abhorred spectacle. Those that loved it most cannot now finde in their hearts to look

1 Philippe Ariès, *The Hour of Our Death* (New York: Alfred A. Knopf, 1981).
2 Ibid., p. 342.

on it, by reason of the griefly deformedness which death will put upon it. Down it must into a pit of carions and confusion; covered with wormes, not able to wag so much as a little finger, to remove the vermine that feed and gnaw upon its flesch.[3]

Ariès charts a general post-Reformation trend away from a preoccupation with physical death. Images like those above were seen as gruesome and distracting, "vain fantasies" in the words of John Calvin.[4] The Catholic sacrament of Extreme Unction, or Last Rites, in which a sinner could be absolved of all sin on his deathbed was anathema to Luther. So was the Catholic concept of Purgatory, that intermediate state between heaven and hell from which souls of sinners can be released to heaven through the prayers of the living. Instead of worrying about death, and the long process of negotiating one's fate after death, the faithful were enjoined to focus on life.

The dethroning of death accelerated in the twentieth century when death left the home and became ensconced in the sterile impersonality of the hospital. As a result, death largely disappeared from sight. Survivors were counseled to "move on" and avoid morbid attachments to the dead. But, as Ariès notes, the attempt to "modernize" attitudes toward death by banishing fear, superstition, and fatalism simply made it unmentionable. By 1969, in her groundbreaking book *On Death and Dying*, Elisabeth Kübler-Ross could write that death is a "dreaded and unspeakable issue to be avoided by every means possible in modern society."[5]

Despite a Protestant tendency to associate the cult of death with Catholicism and to see morbidity as a residue of Papism, Ariès notes that these attitude changes engulfed Catholics and Protestants alike. However, he concedes that residues of medieval beliefs about death retain a powerful hold on the modern psyche. And, indeed, many of the practices decried by Protestants and downplayed by the Catholic Church were very much a part of my pre-Vatican II Catholic childhood. I remember wearing scapulars, cloth badges which were said to insure the wearer against unexpected death. I recall reciting prayers and novenas which, my prayer book promised me, would relieve a designated number of years in Purgatory. Like a bank account, these could be redeemed for oneself or transferred to a soul currently languishing in Purgatory. The assumption was that this grateful soul would later intercede for its deliverer at the time of one's death. These practices disappeared with the modernization of the Catholic Church in the 1960s. However, in Latin cultures and in parts of the United States with large Latin populations, the cult of death survives in such rituals as the celebration of the Day of the Dead and the rite of the Sacred Heart.

But the contemporary aversion to death is countered by an equally powerful pop culture fascination with morbid and gruesome images of death. The loving recreation of flying

---

3 Ibid.

4 Ibid., p. 300.

5 Elisabeth Kübler-Ross, *On Death and Dying* (New York: Macmillan, 1970), p. 14.

body parts and blood-drenched corpses in films by such popular directors as Quentin Tarantino and Wes Craven reveal a willingness to embrace the spectacle of death as mass entertainment. Another case in point is the success of the HBO series *Six Feet Under*, which takes place in a funeral home in which dead bodies laid out on gurneys serve as a backdrop for the unraveling of convoluted personal dramas. Further evidence of the seductions of the morbid can be found in the enormous crowds (forty million) who flocked to *Body Worlds*, anatomical exhibitions which appeared in more than ninety cities featuring dozens of plastinated, real flayed bodies stiffened with silicone and arranged in lifelike poses.

Located at a nominally safe psychological distance, death makes for pleasant diversion. But when it comes closer to home, it has clearly not lost its sting. Following the collapse of the World Trade Center towers in 2001, photographs of people jumping to their deaths from the burning Twin Towers were quickly removed from print and broadcast view. In the subsequent wars in Afghanistan and Iraq, American photographers found themselves following an unspoken code which forbade the depiction of actual bodies or body parts. In a war diary report aired on National Public Radio on April 15, 2003, photographer David Leeson explained the dilemma. "Photographing the dead is very difficult," he reported.

> Today, when I approached this man in his vehicle with the intention to photograph a civilian casualty, [I] couldn't quite do it . . . This man had been shot behind the wheel of his car and when I got to the car he had no face. So, it was entirely too sad and too gruesome at the same time. It just didn't seem fitting for human life to be photographed in that state. So, I just didn't do it. I walked away from it and went and found something else to photograph.

Thus while graphic images of military and civilian deaths were released by news outlets in Europe and the Middle East, American audiences rarely saw them. One cannot help wondering about the extent to which this unspoken interdiction against explicit representations of war's carnage helped keep American support high during the conflict.

Such contradictory attitudes toward death formed the subtext of a court case in 2002 which sent a young Cincinnati artist named Thomas Condon to prison for five months. During the course of his trial and imprisonment, Condon became known as the "morgue artist" for a series of photographs he had taken of cadavers at the city morgue. Believing he had secured permission to pursue this private art project in the course of negotiations with the coroner's office about making a training film for employees, Condon photographed corpses juxtaposed with various objects meant to signify the cycle of life and death, among them shells, toy ladders, and sheet music. He planned to crop the photographs to hide the identity of his subjects.

However, when he sent several sets of negatives to be developed commercially, the developer, alarmed at the content of the pictures, passed the negatives to the police. They promptly arrested Condon and seized his photographic equipment. The negatives then were mysteriously leaked to the press, where they were printed in local tabloids and reproduced on local television news stations. Although Condon had intended to crop the photographs to obscure the identity of the bodies, these leaked images contained clearly identifiable features, stirring understandable outrage among the relatives of the deceased.

The result was a predictable media circus in which local pundits denounced Condon's project as "sick" and "repulsive," and demanded his incarceration. After considering various charges, among them breaking and entering and pandering obscenity, the prosecutors eventually indicted Condon for corpse abuse, a charge which carried a salacious odor of necrophilia and body snatching. After a brief trial overshadowed by a heavy media focus on the anguish of the families of the deceased, Condon was convicted and imprisoned in the spring and summer of 2002, shortly after which he was released pending appeal.

The legal issues were complicated, involving issues of permission, ethics, and the definition of "corpse abuse." The situation was further complicated by the general atmosphere of Cincinnati, a city with a long and litigious relationship to avant-garde art. It was in Cincinnati that the Mapplethorpe controversy came to a head, when local prosecutors tried Dennis Barrie, then the director of the Contemporary Arts Center, on obscenity charges for presenting the artist's retrospective. Five years later, the city prosecuted the Pink Pyramid bookshop for renting out a video of Pasolini's *Salò, or 120 Days of Sodom*. The Condon case was also aggravated by a simmering feud between the coroner's office and the county prosecutor which involved several cases in which bodies had been mixed up and improperly disposed of.

But one thing that emerged clearly from the murk was the ease with which the public's discomfort with death could be manipulated by a unscrupulous media. After all, Condon is hardly the first artist to use photographic images of dead bodies in his work. His direct inspiration was Andres Serrano's 1992 *The Morgue* series. He also was following in the wake of artists like Jeffrey Silverthorne, who created a series of photographs, which overlaid images of the living and the dead to suggest the continuity of life and death. (Silverthorne wisely secured permission for his project from the Attorney General of Rhode Island, where the morgue in question was located, and he made sure that his images were not exhibited locally.) Going farther back in time, one could cite the mangled bodies in the appropriated disaster photographs of Andy Warhol, as well as the now classic images by the photojournalist Weegee of the gory aftermath of gangland shootouts and grisly murders.

Such precedents carried no weight in Condon's trial. Underlying the official outrage was the assumption that the depiction of dead bodies in and of itself is somehow obscene and that people need to be protected from a direct visual contact with death. Condon's photographic project ran counter to the unspoken cultural taboo against the unvarnished depiction of dead bodies. As Cincinnati Coroner Carl Parrott told the *Cincinnati Enquirer*, "Not only is it probably illegal, it's immoral."[6]

Raised Catholic, Condon evidences a more accepting attitude toward representations of our mortal remains. Noting that, "In these photographs, people have just come from death," he explains, "I wanted to show the split second fragility of life." He adds, "I wanted to help people come to an acceptance that this is what the body is. The body represents a life lived. It's a road map to the person's life. When the body is opened up and exposed this way, it's a very beautiful thing."[7]

In this statement Condon echoes the sentiments of Andres Serrano, an artist whose work was an important influence on him. Serrano is best known to the public for *Piss Christ*, the photograph immortalized in the mass media as "the crucifix dipped in urine."[8] The brouhaha, which ensued when this work was included in a traveling exhibition partly paid for by the NEA in 1989 obscured the fact that *Piss Christ* is part of Serrano's ongoing exploration of the spiritual dimensions of base matter. Over the years he has explored this theme through a succession of photographic series, which led him to frame overtly allegorical works using animal parts and costumed models with a set of more abstract "immersion" works of which *Piss Christ* is one. In these works, symbolic objects have been photographed through various body fluids. The fluid photographs were followed in 1990 by portraits of such diverse groups as New York homeless people, Ku Klux Klansmen, and members of the Catholic clergy.

Serrano's morgue series consisted of photographs taken in an undisclosed morgue of bodies awaiting autopsies or removal to funeral homes. Many had come to the morgue as a result of violent and unexpected deaths, and Serrano noted this in titles like: *The Morgue (Rat Poison Suicide)*, *The Morgue (Knifed to Death)*, and *The Morgue (Death by Drowning)*. These wrenching titles provided a disturbing counterpart to the ravishing beauty of the images themselves. Using dramatic lighting, zeroing in on telling details and carefully cropping out identifying characteristics, he maintained the corpses' anonymity. Losing their specificity, they were transformed into studies reminiscent of Renaissance religious themes like the Nativity or the Deposition of Christ. *The Morgue (Fatal Meningitis II)* presents the head of a child whose lower features are covered with a white cloth, bringing to mind traditional depictions of the swaddled Christ Child. *The Morgue (Knifed to Death I and II)* is a diptych of a pair of hands, fingers blackened with ink for fingerprinting and wrists punctured with the coroner's scalpel. Serrano presents the outstretched hands so that they face each other, echoing the touch of God and man in the Creation panel of Michelangelo's Sistine Chapel.

---

6 Dan Horn, "While County Considers Charges, Others Defend Artistic Motivation," *Cincinnati Enquirer* (February 4, 2001), p. 1.
7 Eleanor Heartney, "Is the Body More Beautiful When It's Dead?" *The New York Times* (June 1, 2003), p. 37.
8 Passim.

Another work, *The Morgue (Rat Poison Suicide)*, focuses on the stiffened arms of a woman who died of ingesting rat poison. Her arms are raised in a defensive gesture as if, in the artist's words, "she is fighting off demons."[9]

Thus, despite the often grisly circumstances of death, Serrano invests these images with a luminous beauty, which reminds us that in the Christian tradition death is simply a threshold between two states of being. Like Condon, he presents them redeemed by beauty. Serrano has said of this series, "I never saw the bodies as cadavers or corpses. I called them my models, my subjects. I was interested in the way they still had a human presence, that something of their soul was intact."[10]

The morgue series is an extension of Serrano's preoccupation with beauty as a manifestation of the divine on Earth. As he once noted, "You can't have the sacred without the profane . . . . What is wrong is to make something that isn't beautiful."[11] What makes his work both provocative and profound is the way he creates this beauty from raw materials that are conventionally considered disgusting or sordid. Dead bodies certainly fall under that rubric. So do body fluids like blood, milk, semen, and urine, which form the basis of the *Immersion* series to which the much maligned *Piss Christ* belongs.

Serrano's focus on degradation echoes that of Joel Peter Witkin, another artist with a conflicted personal history. However, while Serrano deals with "subjects that border on the unacceptable," he exalts and beautifies them. Witkin also traffics in the images of the dead and the dispossessed, but his approach is quite different. In Witkin's photographs, dead bodies are clearly, often gruesomely dead, their exposed entrails visible, their limbs bloated or stiffened in *rigor mortis*, their skulls cracked and limbs severed. In one image, a cadaver sits on a chair with its head cut off. In another a decaying head of an old man has been sliced and rearranged so that his profiles fuse and join lips in a gesture that recalls Brancusi's *Kiss*. In yet a third, a massive masked nude woman lies in a pose reminiscent of Caravaggio's *Bacchus* but grasping three preserved fetuses.

While Witkin's most notorious photographs use dead bodies or body parts, he does not limit himself to that subject. An ad placed at the end of one of his books contains a plea for models which solicits, among others:

> pinheads, dwarfs, giants, hunchbacks, pre-op transsexuals, bearded women . . . twins joined at the foreheads, anyone with a parasitic twin, . . . people with tails, horns, wings, fins, claws, reversed feet or hands, elephantine limbs . . . . Anyone born without arms, legs, eyes, breasts, genitals, ears, nose, lips. All people with unusually large genitals . . . . Hermaphrodites and

---

9 Robert Hobbs, "Andres Serrano: The Body Politic," in Patrick T. Murphy, *Andres Serrano: Works 1983-1993* (Philadelphia: Institute of Contemporary Art/University of Pennsylvania, 1994), p. 42.
10 Eleanor Heartney, "Postmodern Heretics," *Art in America* (February 1997), p. 32.
11 Celia McGee, "A Personal Vision of the Sacred and Profane," *The New York Times* (January 22, 1995), p. 35.

teratoids (alive and dead). A young blonde girl with two faces. Any living myth. Anyone bearing the wounds of Christ."[12]

These models become elements in carefully constructed photographic *tableaux* which inhabit a bizarre territory which is part Bosch, part Coney Island. They include traditional still-life aspects, mingling organic produce and body parts, "freak show" imagery, and demented restaging of famous paintings. In Witkin's works hermaphrodites pose as classical gods and goddesses, people with deformed limbs are outfitted with wings to play the role of angels, and severed heads are served up on platters à la John the Baptist.

Curiously, given the potentially inflammatory nature of his photographs, Witkin has never been the subject of a full-fledged controversy – this despite having received NEA grants and major museum exhibitions. The closest he has come to Serrano or Mapplethorpe type dustup came in 1993 when NEA foes featured his print of a testicle stretching figure in some anti-NEA literature. It is possible that his work has evaded right wing scrutiny because his photographic technique makes it difficult to discern how much is real and how much the result of post-production manipulation. Witkin always photographs in black and white, and often scratches his negatives and then prints them through tissue paper to slightly blur details. He completes them by mounting them on aluminum, applying pigments and covering the whole with polished beeswax. The photographs that result have a faded daguerreotype quality whose illusion of temporal distance helps aestheticize their admittedly shocking subject matter.

Though he has been denounced by evangelist Pat Robertson as a Satanist, Witkin himself declares that he is a practicing Catholic. At a conference I attended in Arizona, he noted that he sees his work as a sacred act and that he prays over his subjects, dead and alive, before he photographs them.[13] Some commentators have seen this confession of faith as a cynical effort to cultivate a perverse public persona, but his history suggests a genuine spiritual search.

If one can get beyond the grisly details, his photographs are marked by an absurdist sensibility that comes close to a quality described by literary critic Mikhail Bakhtin as the "carnivalesque." Taking his cue from the folk culture of the medieval carnival, Bakhtin posited the notion of a subversive humor in which all hierarchies and official orders are temporarily suspended. In their place, he maintained, was a liberating chaos in which different spheres were fused, normally hidden sexual and scatological body functions like farting, defecation, and copulation were put on public display and death became a joke instead of a threat. This, he declared, was "carnivalesque."[14]

---

12 Richard Woodward, "Joel Peter Witkin: An Eye for the Forbidden," *Vanity Fair* (April 1993), p. 192.

13 "Ethics and the Arts Conference," Lincoln Center for Applied Ethics, Arizona State University, Tempe, Arizona, October 28, 2001.

14 Mikhail Bakhtin, *Rabelais and His World*, trans. Hélène Iswolsky (Bloomington: Indiana University Press, 1984).

Critic Wayne Booth summarizes Bakhtin's influential idea thus:

> Carnival laughter, the intrusion of everything forbidden or slanderous or joyfully blasphemous into the purified domains of officialdom, expressed a complex sense that the material body was not unequivocally base: every death contains within it the meaning of rebirth, every birth comes from the same region of the body as does the excremental. And the excremental is itself a source of regeneration – it manures life . . . References to the lower body were . . . used to produce a regenerative, an affirmative, a healing – finally a politically progressive laughter.[15]

In Bakhtin's view, this emancipating frivolity has largely disappeared from an overly atomized and individualistic society. He remarks, "It must be recalled that the image of death in medieval and Renaissance grotesque (and in painting, also in Holbein's or Dürer's "dance of death") is a more or less funny monstrosity. In the ages that followed, especially in the nineteenth century, the public at large almost completely forgot the principle of laughter presented in macabre images."[16]

From this perspective, Witkin can be seen as a purveyor of a kind of transformative laughter that subverts boundaries in order to bring us back to our essential humanness. This playful attitude toward death remains visible today in the Mexican celebration of the Day of the Dead and in the idea of Halloween, its Anglo counterpart. While Halloween has largely become a means of acting out fantasies, the Day of the Dead remains tied to the idea of the dead among us. It is an occasion for festive interaction between the living and dead, marked by the preparation of meals for the dead, the exchange of special foods like sugar skulls, chocolate skeletons, and special Bread of the Dead which is ornamented with bone motifs, and in some locations processions in which townspeople dress up as ghouls and carry an open coffin with a smiling "corpse" within.

The raucous embrace of death represented by the Day of the Dead points to an important aspect of contemporary Catholic flirtations with the macabre. This fixation tends to persist most powerfully in Latin versions of Catholicism, which were shaped by the meeting of the medieval Catholic morbidity of the Spanish conquerors with the death cults of the Aztecs and other indigenous American peoples. In some cases, the fusion of the two consciousnesses was quite deliberate, as when Spanish priests moved the Aztec celebration of Miccailhuitontli, dedicated to the goddess Mictecacihuatl ("Lady of the Dead"), to the first two days of November so that it coincided with the Catholic observance of the All Saints and All Souls Day. (These latter were the days the faithful honored the saints who had been accepted into heaven and prayed for the souls of those still waiting release from Purgatory.)

---

15 Wayne Booth, "Freedom of Interpretation," in Mikhail Bakhtin, *Bakhtin: Essays and Dialogue on His Work,* ed. Gary Saul Morson (Chicago: University of Chicago Press, 1986), pp. 161-162.
16 Bakhtin, *Rabelais and His World,* p. 50.

Such religious fusions reinforced tendencies toward the embrace of death that, as Ariès points out, were beginning to wane even among Roman Catholics in post-Reformation Europe. The blending of pre- and post-colonial religion remains powerful in the culture of Mexico and Latin America to this day, finding manifestation in the merging of Aztec goddess Tonantzintla with the Virgin Mary in the figure of the Virgin of Guadalupe and the incorporation of undercurrents of the Aztec ritual of human sacrifice with the sacrificial death of Christ on the Cross. From this perspective, as Shifra Goldman points out, the playful skeletons of the Day of the Dead have antecedents in the pre-Columbian belief in the duality of life and death.[17]

Thus, it should come as no surprise to realize that many of the contemporary artists most deeply involved in the imagery of death have Latin roots or connections. Serrano comes from a mixed Afro-Cuban and Honduran background. He is somewhat ambivalent about his Hispanic identity, happy to embrace it, but unwilling to be pigeonholed as a Hispanic artist. He describes his obsession with religious imagery thus: "It's a Latino thing, but it's also a European thing."[18]

Witkin is not ethnically Latin. However, his natural penchant for the morbid has clearly been reinforced by his long residence in New Mexico, where the Hispanic influence is particularly acute. Some of his works make explicit reference to this influence.

Witkin's embrace of the more macabre aspects of Hispanic culture takes place in the context of his private search for God. Michael Tracy, another Anglo who has immersed himself in the Latin cult of the dead, does so, at least in part, in the service of a political agenda.

Tracy has employed performance, installation, and sculpture. These works mingle materials that signify the excess of Baroque religious art – gold leaf, bronze and wood, with organic matter – flowers and hair, and body fluids like blood, semen, and urine. He creates paintings encrusted with gold leaf and dried blood and constructs crosses and icons pierced with bronze spikes, knives, bones, and shards of glass. At times his works evoke holy relics, their bits of human matter bearing witness to the never-ending saga of human suffering.

Over the years he has orchestrated several elaborate quasi-religious ceremonies one of which culminated in the ritual murder of one of his most important paintings by stabbing and immolation.

---

17 Shifra Goldman, "The Heart of Mexican Art: Image, Myth and Ideology," *New Art Examiner* (December 1993), p. 14.
18 Lucy Lippard, "Andres Serrano: The Spirit and the Letter," *Art in America* (April 1990), p. 241.

In a sculptural triptych entitled *Tríptico Para Los Desaparecidos* (*Triptych for the Disappeared Ones*) from 1982-83, he pays homage to the thousands of victims of El Salvador's death squads. Here the three panels are riddled with knives, swords and a machete, as well as surrogate torture devices like knitting needles and shards of broken glass.

At Artspace in San Francisco he created *Santuarios* (1989), re-making the gallery into a chapel dedicated to both the recent war dead of Nicaragua and El Salvador and the continuing plight of Mexican "mojados" or wetbacks who die in their efforts to cross the border into the United States. In this work, a selection of ritual objects – cruciform assemblages, blood-encrusted shrines and paintings were set off against gridded wooden chairs and partitions meant to evoke the confessional. During the run of the exhibition, Mass was held twice in this space, once for the local community and once to pray for the victims of AIDS.

But perhaps Tracy's most spectacular sacrificial ritual took place on the Rio Grande river outside San Ygnacio on Good Friday, 1990. This is the day that the town's populace traditionally restages the Stations of the Cross, the path taken by the bloodied Jesus Christ on his way to his Crucifixion. Tracy's *The River Pierce: Sacrifice II, 13.4.90* also took the form of a Stations of the Cross procession, but the object to be sacrificed was one of his largest sculptural crosses, a ten-foot-high accretion of horns, milagros, crosses, mud, and flowers. Carried on a horse-drawn cart and accompanied by a train of invited clergy, artists, and select townspeople, it was carried to the edge of the river, set afire and pushed by the wind to the Mexican side of the river.

Tracy dedicated this ritual to the Rio Grande itself, which he sees as a victim of the environmental indifference of the Mexican and American governments. The work also celebrates the river as the lifeline that connects two countries across a difficult and contested border. The "sacrifice" of the cross, like the sacrifice of Christ, was offered up for the redemption of an entity that seemed otherwise condemned to death.

Over the years, Tracy's works have often taken on the qualities of shrines and memorials. Their explicit references to blood, broken bones, and instruments of torture evoke traditional rituals for the veneration of Christ and the martyrs who died for the faith. But they also turn our attention to the continuing horrors of social injustice. Thus the Catholic language of death becomes a means to espouse a politics of life.

Catholic morbidity takes on a female coloration in the work of Ana Mendieta. In what became a cause célèbre, dividing the art world into hostile camps, Mendieta died at age thirty-six when she plunged from a window in her SoHo loft after an altercation with her husband, the well-known minimalist sculptor Carl Andre. At issue was whether she was pushed or fell, a controversy that did not die down even after Andre was acquitted of her murder after a highly publicized trial.

Many saw an irony in Mendieta's early death. A Cuban-American, her work involved symbolic burials and blood-based rituals, which she herself maintained were at least partially inspired by the Afro-Cuban religion of Santeria. Santeria fuses the African religions of the slaves imported to the Americas with elements of Catholicism (some of them adopted as a kind of camouflage behind which adherents could continue to practice forbidden rituals). It is an animistic religion, based on a principle of universal energy. Adherents follow such traditional practices as sacred drumming and dance, trance possession as a means to communicate with the ancestors and deities, and animal sacrifice. Today Santeria claims many adherents of Hispanic and Caribbean descent who also count themselves as Catholics.

Mendieta was exposed to Santeria during her childhood in Cuba. (Her sister recalls that, while her parents looked down on Santeria as superstition, the two girls learned about it from the family's servants.) However, it did not become important to Mendieta until much later, when, as an adult, she began to confront the enormous chasm which divided her childhood in Cuba from her later adulthood. The chasm opened up when, at age thirteen, Mendieta and her sister Raquelin were sent to Iowa without their parents as part of the Pedro Pan Operation. This program, initiated by the Cuban Catholic Church, was designed to preserve the Catholicism of young Cubans in the wake of the Communist revolution there. Mendieta was not to return to Cuba for twenty years, by which time she had become an established artist.

Her early performances have elements that echo the experimental body art being practiced by many artists of the day. She transferred mustache hair from a male friend to her face, distorted her features by smashing her face into a nylon stocking, and pressed her naked body against a pane of glass.

Such works made it clear that Mendieta was interested in gender issues at this early stage. But she also began to employ more shocking elements of blood and bone, which pointed back to her ethnic and religious roots. In a performance entitled *Sweating Blood*, she was filmed with her eyes closed as blood trickled down her face. In *Blood Writing* she pushed herself against a wall and slowly sank down, leaving a blood trail as her hands dragged against the surface. In an untitled performance from 1972, a naked Mendieta embraced a skeleton, breathing life into its mouth and covering it with her body in a movement that was at once sexual and protective. In *Death of a Chicken* (1972), she made explicit reference to Santeria, as she stood naked holding a beheaded chicken as its blood spurted over her body.

Such works suggest that Mendieta was seeking a way to reconnect with a heritage from which she had been forcibly separated. Looking back on her student days, she later told Judith Wilson, "I started thinking I would have to act it out and work from my own experiences, my own sources – I started immediately using blood – I guess because I think it's a very powerful, magical thing. I don't see it as a negative source."[19]

In a posthumously published interview, she told Linda Montano, "I don't think you can separate death and life. All my work is about these two things, about Eros and Life/Death."[20]

Mendieta is best known for a series of works entitled *Siluetas* (Spanish for silhouette). In these works, which exist today only as photographs or films, she pressed her body onto the landscape and marked the shape with a variety of symbolic and evocative materials.

The first work in this series was executed in a Zapotec tomb in Oaxaca (Zapotecs were a Mesoamerican people who resisted the Aztecs). For this work she climbed naked into the shallow rock cavity and covered her body with long stems and white flowers. The photograph which records this work is hauntingly beautiful. Her body seems literally in the process of disintegrating into a cloud of white and green foliage.

The presence of a physical body is unusual in this series. More commonly, the *Siluetas* present the female form as a void, cut into earth or sand and filled with moss, water, flowers, blood or mounds of rocks. One, entitled *Anima* (and recorded in a short film), consists of a female outline formed of lit fireworks, which gradually burn out, leaving nothing but ashes.

The *Siluetas* are canny celebrations of death and rebirth. The figural cavity is at once a womb and a grave, and the elements that fill it become surrogate souls whose natural processes point to the cycle of decay and rebirth.

Mendieta followed the *Siluetas* with a related series, *Fetishes*. These consisted of bodies molded from earth and penetrated in various more or less violent ways. The fetishes were marked with blood, branded with an iron, or pierced with sticks. Thus, their implied anger at female victimization suggests a more overt feminism than is found in the *Siluetas*.

Art historian Miwon Kwon has pointed out that Mendieta's use of her body almost always involved some form of erasure or negation.[21] Though her body was the initial reference, it constantly disappeared, to be replaced by a surrogate of earth, fire, rock or flora. Thus, in marked contrast to the death-related work of Serrano, Witkin, and Tracy, her works are imbued with a sense that rebirth is inseparable from death. She was fond of a quote by

---

19 Judith Wilson, "Ana Mendieta Plants Her Garden," *Village Voice* (August 13, 1980).
20 Linda Montano, "An Interview with Ana Mendieta," *Sulfur* 8, no. 1 (Spring 1988), p. 66.
21 Miwon Kwon, "Bloody Valentines: Afterimages by Ana Mendieta," in *Inside the Visible*, ed. M. Catherine de Zegher (Cambridge, MA: MIT Press, 1996), pp. 167-168.

Octavio Paz which appears in one of her artist statements. It says, "Our cult of death is also a cult of life in the same way that love is a hunger for life and a longing for death. Our fondness for self-destruction derives not from our masochistic tendencies but also from a certain variety of religious emotion."[22]

Unlike Serrano, Witkin, or Tracy, Mendieta internalized death, using her own body to evoke its constant presence in our lives. In the process, she gives the idea of death and resurrection a decidedly female spin. Mother Earth is both our origin and our destination. The blood of birth and the blood of death commingle, placing us in a never-ending cycle of dissolution and regeneration. In the process death loses its horror and menace, and becomes, instead, as Stevens suggests, the lair "in whose burning bosom we devise/ our earthly mothers waiting, sleeplessly."[23]

This text is a slightly amended version of a chapter from Postmodern Heretics: The Catholic Imagination in Contemporary Art, *published by Midmarch Arts Press, 2004.*

22 Unpublished artist statement, with reference to Paz, *The Labyrinth of Solitude* (New York: Grove, 1961), p. 23.
23 Wallace Stevens, *Harmonium* (New York: Knopf, 1923).

Melancholic Relics
Adele Tutter

So quotidian, so inevitable, death, when it greets us, is nevertheless inconceivable. Comprehensible in theory, we face it uncomprehendingly. "How can they be dead?" one asks. It is not a rhetorical question. "It makes no sense to me... it *cannot* be. How could they be here, and then not? How is it possible? How *can* it be possible?"

I am often asked these questions, questions that have no answer. What we think is the gradual "acceptance" of the reality of a death is, for a long time, merely the gradual inability to forget it, such that it becomes a familiar fact, a numb ache. Until that happens, we forget, and then we remember, and we are shattered, dumbstruck, over and over again. Wakening is excruciating.

The notion of actual absence – the void left in place of the other – is so unsettling as to be unthinkable. It sets into motion an endless search. After a death, many wish it for themselves, sometimes to literally rejoin the dead. A psychoanalytical view implicates in this impulse identification with the dead, a melancholic being-with-them. But to die is also to repudiate having been left behind.

For the ancient Greeks, the simulation of reality so keen as to achieve verisimilitude was something close to magic; the artist was a magician, sorcerer, conjurer. In the Renaissance, the likeness of a lost loved one was cherished for the comfort it brought the bereaved. Today, bombarded and barraged by images and videos (indeed by "virtual reality"), the humble portrait, and much more often the photograph of the deceased may stir memories, but these images carry little of the magic they did in times past. Sometimes, it seems, they serve less as a reminder of the deceased, and more as a reminder of the brevity of life.

In *Camera Lucida*, Roland Barthes details his struggle to locate the essence of his beloved late mother in stray photographs of her; in contrast, images of her material *things* would do, albeit for a short moment.

> In order to "find" my mother, fugitively alas, and without ever being able to hold on to this resurrection for long, I must, much later, discover in several photographs the objects she kept on her dressing table, an ivory powder box (I loved the sound of its lid), a cut-crystal flagon, or else a low chair, which is now near my own bed.[1]

1 Roland Barthes, *Camera Lucida*, trans. Richard Howard (New York: Farrar, Strauss & Giroux, 1981), p. 64.

It is this materiality, this physicality that we seek – the substantive evidence, the corporeal trace that we crave. It drives the survivors of catastrophe to grasp for the smallest scrap of flesh or shard of bone of the disappeared; to not find that iota of being, to bring it back into communion with us, is its own trauma. When there are no material remains, when there is no sense of the secure presence of the dead, one exists in a vacuum. Even a gravestone, marking the ashes or corpse buried below, is grounding.

The words "relic" (and the related "reliquary") stem from the Latin *reliquiae*, or "remains" (plural of *reliquus*, "remaining" or "residue," which in turn derives from *linquere*, "to leave"). "Relinquish" (from *relinquere*, "to leave behind") also shares this root. A relic does not deny death; indeed, it is at least in our times a sad reminder of it, less an animistic fetish than some have claimed. But at the same time the material relic defies the total relinquishment of our hold on the other that death would otherwise impose, long after the dead have relinquished their hold on life. We still have a part of the departed, who are still a part of us.

When a home is destroyed, the vestiges of its structure – a window, a doorknob – become precious, physical traces of life, of time and place. For my parents, we designed a tombstone in the shape of the provincial Baroque façades of the Czech Republic, my father's relinquished country. We made for them a reliquary, a little house for the dead. Years later, I saw a sarcophagus in Naples in the shape of a house, its stone doors permanently closed. A Holocaust survivor whose entire family was murdered told me that to have no graves, no place to commune with the mourned, is to be without a home. Left behind, you are lost, adrift, atomized.

Heide Hatry's constructions of image from ash are not literal reconstitutions of presence, of course; nor are they purely symbolic. They are metonymic in their imagery – every portrait is of this order – but they also incorporate and re-organize the material trace: what remains when we are left behind. They are both likeness and facsimile; both reliquary and melancholic relic.

A year or two after his death, I saw my father in a dream. He was looking down at me mournfully through a second-story window of a house somewhere in Nová Cerekev, the village of his birth. He held the lace curtains aside, the glass window the only thing between us: a transparent boundary, but as absolute as the stone doors in Naples. This dream image, a purely mental reconstruction, was (and still is) as (or more) vivid as my "actual" recollection of the living man, and consoling in a manner, although his mournful face speaks to the sad fact that we can be reunited only fractionally, only in the dream world. Less evanescent are the traces he left behind – the things he touched, the things he made, things that bear his impression. Melancholic relics, they too are parts of him, restoring my memory of his presence, and his presence in my memory.

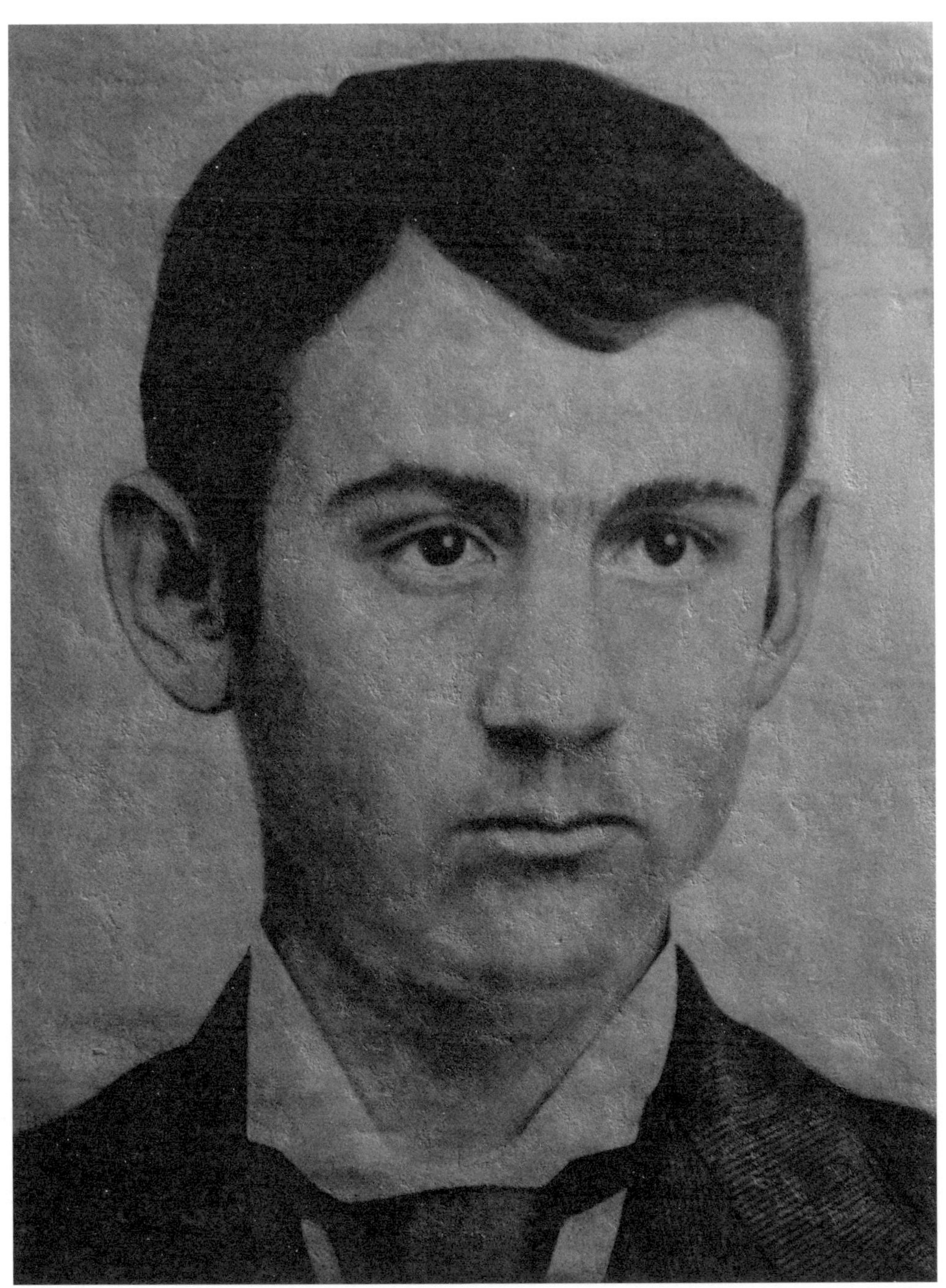

Postmortem Photography in Europe and America
Stanley B. Burns and Elizabeth A. Burns

Postmortem photographs are special mementos with deep meaning for mourners. Photography offers the opportunity to visually "embalm" the dead. These keepsakes become special icons that help survivors move through the bereavement process. The human bond, our connection with others, is a strong guiding emotion and thus influences our fears and actions. These images represent confrontation with our loved ones' mortality, as well as our own. Healthy grieving ultimately distances us from the dead. Today, when loved ones die, their images remain behind in depictions of celebrations and other important events. Just as such photographs bring back memories of loved ones at particular moments in their lives, postmortem photographs concentrate our thoughts and feelings on the entire life of the deceased. These photographic links to lost loved ones help give vitality to our memories.

In photography's earliest years, death was a natural part of everyday life. People took photographs of their cherished departed with a reverence little understood today. These photographs were a normal part of the culture, and are testament to a time when the magic of photography offered the hope of extending relationships. At the moment people were most vulnerable, photography provided a memento that seemed real – a tangible visual object that allowed continued closeness to the deceased.

The differences in the cultural applications and practices of American and European postmortem photographs are significant. Postmortem photography in America has historically been used for private expressions of personal loss. Europeans often made and publicly displayed postmortem photographs of royalty, nobility, the wealthy, and other notables. In America, postmortem photographs of public personalities and political leaders were not taken. These traditions mirror differences in the overall practice of photography on the two continents. In Europe, early photography was an elitist pursuit taken up by artists as a profession and by the well-to-do as a hobby. In the United States, it was a common person's trade and could be practiced by anyone, anywhere.

The historian's task is not simply to cover eras and events, but to uncover significant patterns of human life and elements of the human condition. Both in Europe and in America, postmortem photographs were used as part of the bereavement and memorial process. However, their place in the culture was lost over time due to changing perceptions and beliefs. The social structure of European countries, many of them monarchies, dictated that their deceased leaders be photographed and presented to the populace. This practice was perhaps the manifestation of a paternalistic outlook: as the "father" of the nation passed, its citizens, his "family," would mourn him.

Postmortem daguerreotypes and ambrotypes from the Continent, like other early European photographs, were presented in wall frames. In contrast, American postmortem images were cased and, for the most part, private. To display American images, the cases were opened and placed on mantles and tables. American expatriate practitioners influenced English daguerreian portraiture to the extent that postmortem photographs in England are found in either style, framed or cased, although most were cased. In Europe, the practice of openly displaying photographs of the dead was simply the extension of a longstanding artistic tradition. Mortuary paintings or portraits of the dead were artworks of sufficient quality to be shown to the public. European daguerreotypes and ambrotypes were prepared in glass *passe-partout* mounts sized for standard frames. If a frame was not affordable, a clasp for hanging the mount was attached and the photograph hung. By the 1860s, American and European postmortem photographs followed similar presentation patterns with the establishment of photographic paper prints as the predominant format worldwide. By the 1880s, the standard in both Europe and the United States was to frame and display paper prints larger than four by six inches.

In the early years of photography, images of entire families posing with the dead were much more common in America than in Europe. Photographs of parents with their deceased children, however, were made in both places. In the United States, postmortem photography for the middle and working classes ended by the 1930s. However, immigrants who followed the traditions of their countries of origin, as well as populations in some areas of rural America, continued to have professional postmortem photographs taken. In addition, the development of Polaroid instant photography and easy-to-use amateur cameras allowed people to take postmortem photographs surreptitiously throughout the century.

Most American memorial images are unattributed. Content, rather than authorship, predominates in these remarkable images. These anonymous photographers, in the presence of death and the sanctity of deep loss, were able to produce captivating images. In many cases, it is quite likely that the families dictated the composition of these scenarios. Though some parents wanted to hold their dead child, others did not – or could not. Art photographers brought their own styles and presentations to memorial images. As most photographers in Europe came from an artistic tradition, European postmortem photographs followed the styles of deathbed and mortuary paintings. While both European and American families used photography in the mourning process, the traditions of each society dictated the presentation and usage.

One of the styles of nineteenth-century postmortem representation was the posthumous mourning portrait. There are critical differences between "posthumous mourning" and "mortuary" photographic portraiture. The typical mortuary presentation was deathbed depiction, alone or with family. The posthumous mourning portrait images portrayed the dead as if still alive, not simply by having the deceased's eyes open, but sometimes creating a *tableau*. These two distinct postmortem photographic endeavors followed painterly traditions. In general, curators and collectors have recognized the artistry and poignancy of posthumous mourning photographs, but have not recognized they are a separate category of postmortem photography. In photography's earliest era (1839-60), European posthumous mourning photographs are rare.

During the latter half of the twentieth century, most American postmortem photographs were taken privately and kept private. In the past decade, however, public display of these photographs has increased. Openly photographing our dead and dying loved ones has become acceptable. Noted photographers and documentary filmmakers have focused on the subject of dying parents and loved ones. Photographing stillbirths and neonatal deaths has also become more common. Some hospitals are giving one-time-use cameras to parents whose infants have died and others have professional photographers on staff. Bereavement centers are advising mourners to use such images to aid themselves in the grieving process.

We can feel the power of these photographs generations after the images were made. We relate to these pictures of strangers because they speak a universal language of emotions – tenderness, affection, need, hope, loss, and despair – uniting the human family in common experience.

For more information about postmortem photographs and to view those pertinent to this article (listed below) please visit the *Icons in Ash* section on www.burnsarchive.com.

Little Drummer Girl: A Posthumous Mourning Portrait. Sarah A. Lawrence of 119 Hudson Avenue Green Island, Albany County, New York. Daguerreotype 1/6 plate, Tinted, circa 1847. Posed as if she is still alive, this spectacularly tinted daguerreotype must have been the only photograph ever taken of this young girl. Certain conventions, such as flowers in one hand or a recumbent pose, are typical of early postmortem portraiture, and were not generally used in portraits of the living. The cloth behind this girl is another fairly good sign of a postmortem photograph; the wrinkles in it show she was lying down or propped up against it. Images of adults and children can often be identified as postmortems by the blanket, sheet, or other cloth placed beneath the body so as to absorb any secretions. Despite the efforts on the part of Sarah Lawrence's parents and her photographer, they could not hide the telltale signs of her death. Sarah is presented in one of the most beautiful and vibrant daguerreotypes ever taken. It has kept her alive for her family and for us. The photograph transcends time to become an important example not only of postmortem photography, but also of all daguerreian art.

Mother and Daughter. A.D. Hopper, New York City. Daguerreotype 1/6 plate, circa 1854. For postmortem daguerreotypes, older children were usually laid out on a couch, chair or bed. Yet, this mother chose to hold on to her daughter, presenting her as if she were still living. Her unwillingness to release her child is seen in the firm grip of her arm, as well as her glazed look. Parents frequently posed with their children in order to document family bonds and to keep the child in the family for as long as possible. The ending of family touch and presence is an admittance of loss and final separation. Recently, many hospitals have returned to taking postmortem memorial photographs of deceased new born and neonatal children with their parents. Although abandoned for a long time, this practice has been determined to be a psychological aid in the bereavement process.

Bald Man in Bed. A Daguerre, Grand Gallery, Passage Jouffrey, #44, Paris, Gesso Frame 10 1/2 by 12 1/4 inches. Daguerreotype 3/4 plate (5 1/2 by 7 1/4 inches), circa 1850. This daguerreotype was taken in the style of the centuries-old European tradition of the deathbed portrait painting. Most of these artworks concentrated on the deceased's head lying on a pillow. These images were made to accurately document people's features in their "last sleep." They were the photographic equivalent of death masks, which had been done of the rich and famous for centuries, but fell out of favor as photography produced an acceptable alternative. As with all French portrait daguerreotypes, this image was framed for hanging. Only the inner part of the frame is shown here.

Religious Family with Daughter in a Red Dress. Daguerreotype 1/4 plate, Tinted, circa 1848. This father solemnly holds a Bible, documenting the family's strong religious beliefs. The Bible was a frequent prop in family loss images. In the daguerreian era, crying, smiling, and other expressions of emotion were not part of the photographic tradition. Rigid facial expressions were most likely the result of having to hold steady for the long exposures dictated by primitive photographic chemistry. Thus, the apparent lack of grief in these images may be an artifact of the technology. In the 1880s, photos of people crying and displaying grief became popular. This image is an example of the tradition of pink/red clothing in postmortem daguerreotypes.

Scottish Parents with Their Child. Great Britain, Gesso Frame 7 by 8 inches. Ambrotype 1/6 plate, Tinted, circa 1858. Made in Paisley, Scotland, the shawl is not the only identifying mark of this British Isles image. The clothes, as well as the quality and nature of the painting, positively identify its origin. The early daguerreotypists in London introduced detailed coloring, setting the trend. Thus, most painted British postmortem daguerreotypes and ambrotypes were often done with extreme detail. Continental postmortems with such fine detail coloring are rarely found. American colored images are more subtle and painterly, with little or no pointillist detail. Owing to the influence of expatriate American photographers, British daguerreotype or ambrotype images are found either cased or framed. This ambrotype is housed in a gesso over wood frame typical of the era.

"Mad" King Ludwig of Bavaria, The Drowned Swan King. von Frz. Werner, Munich, Cabinet Card, 1886. King Ludwig II of Bavaria (1845-86) was noted for his bizarre behavior, attributed perhaps, to syphilis. He drowned under mysterious circumstances in Lake Starnberg, three days after being declared legally insane. Ludwig Friedrich Wilhelm's extravagances ranged from his obsession with swans to the building of fairy-tale style castles to his patronage of composer Richard Wagner. His excessive behavior kept him in the public eye. It earned him many nicknames, including "Mad Ludwig," "The Swan King," as well as "The Dream King." His unusually designed anachronistic castles, such as Neuschwanstein, are now important Bavarian tourist attractions. The castles were inspired by Wagner's operas. Most postmortem photographs of European leaders and nobility are simple dignified compositions. However, this postmortem image of King Ludwig II, with his casket surrounded by candles, was perhaps inspired by his love of Wagnerian opera. He is depicted as a quintessential Wagnerian hero returning as a warrior to his maker.

Relics of Death

Deborah Lutz

> Every spirit passing through the world fingers the tangible
> and mars the mutable, and finally has come to look and not
> to buy. As shoes are worn and hassocks are sat upon . . . finally
> everything is left where it was and the spirit passes on . . .
> – Marilynne Robinson, *Housekeeping*

Death brings the tragedy of transforming people into objects. But might it also lend inanimate matter a new life? The prophet Elisha's bones, in a tale in the Bible, transfer animation when touched – starting a dead man back to life. In 1549, St. Patricia's shriveled corpse bled, according to the faithful, when an ailing Roman knight drew one of her teeth from its socket. All of his bodily ills then disappeared. Believers in saints' relics – the Virgin Mary's breast milk, St. Edmund's nail parings, St. Petri's ligament, the finger of St. Stephen – felt that earthbound matter could be miraculously infused with the spiritual, thus maintaining a numinous vitality. For medieval Catholics, physical objects were fertile, "maternal, labile, percolating, forever tossing up grass, wood, horses, bees, sand, or metal."[1] The relic, "linked by a bond to the whole stretch of eternity," according to Victricious, the fourth-century Bishop of Rouen, skips over the full stop of death, of temporal finality.[2] While relics were suffused with limitless time, they were also deeply localizing, requiring closeness to specific material objects. In order to harness their technology, pilgrims had to travel to be in their presence or even to touch them. Inscriptions on ancient tombs certify this: *Hic locus est* (Here is the place).

Yet for secularists, beloved bodies can hold some of the sublime, fetishistic magic of holy relics. According to folk customs, a corpse transfers meaning to mourners through touch – pressing or kissing the brow or cheek – or even just presence. The deceased's strength or good luck might be passed on, for example, instead of being taken to the grave.[3] Funeral feasts grew, in part, out of the belief that the food consumed stood in for the body. Mourners "eat" parts of the corpse, thus incorporating the materials of death into the motions of still-vigorous bodies. Positive attributes could be "consumed"

---

1 Caroline Walker Bynum, *Christian Materiality: An Essay on Religion in Late Medieval Europe* (New York: Zone Books, 2011), p. 233.
2 Peter Brown, *The Cult of Saints* (Chicago: University of Chicago Press, 1981), p. 78.
3 See Ruth Richardson, *Death, Dissection, and the Destitute* (Chicago: University of Chicago Press, 2000); and Bertram Puckle, *Funeral Customs: Their Origin and Development* (London: T. Werner Laurie, 1926).

from the moribund, or the living could take on the "sins" of those about to be judged. A marginalized or destitute individual was sometimes hired, becoming a "sin eater."[4] In a different register, John Donne celebrated the bracelet made of the woven hair of a lover in two poems. In both, the corpse speaks out, worried that someone will disturb the "bracelet of bright hair about the bone," which testifies to a love now secret and unknowable. Through sympathetic magic, the bracelet represents the body of the missing lover, so that it provides a way "To make their souls, at the last busy day,/ Meet at this grave, and make a little stay."[5] A lock of hair once belonging to the dead is emblematic of the body in its most mysterious state – still or motionless. With its frozen movement, hair divorced from a breathing, growing body calls to mind the moment in time: how it disappears forever after its brief existence. It makes apparent the dreadful poignancy of the body's change into mere matter, re-enacting that hour – the sadness of its singularity – again and again. The meaning of bodily relics is always in their referent. To gaze on them is to fall into the reverie of memory, to bring to mind the absent being. The matter disappears, becoming pure symbol and pointing only outside of itself. Yet its texture, its substance as an object in the world, as an actual fragment of a person, can bring one back from reverie to realize its obstinate "thingness," its blunt reference to nothing but its presence. Heide Hatry's pictures carry within them these complexities: they are the "thing itself" (the body), the representation of the thing, and also a call to remembrance. "The body is a thing among things" and also a sort of container for things.[6]

In pondering a picture of his dead mother, Roland Barthes decides that the photograph is also a relic, since light has emanated from a body in order to create its shadow on the sensitive apparatus. Both the photograph and the relic provide a kind of proof that the absent beloved really did exist, that she "has been absolutely, irrefutably present."[7] This "that-has-been" quality can bring on deep longing, can bring home the fact that a unique being has been lost, a whole that can never be replaced or even encompassed. Relics especially substantiate this utter singularity of the person, or of the material sample of a body, that can never be duplicated or given to grow again. Barthes finds that the photograph can make him feel, all at once, a wholesale loss, causing him to fully understand that when his mother died he lost a living, changing entity, the "grace" of "an individual soul." Emblematic of the "radiant, irreducible core," relics speak the truth of the beloved body, a particularity unable to be universalized, just as the lock of hair or collection of cremation ash can never be reproduced or copied.[8]

---

4 See Puckle and Richardson for more about funeral feasts and the practice of "sin eating."

5 John Donne, "The Relic." In "The Funeral," the bracelet is referred to as "That subtle wreath of hair which crowns my arm" (line 3). Donne based his idea for "The Relic" on a Latin poem by the Augustan Propertius, showing his awareness of a much longer history of secular hair jewelry.

6 Bill Brown, *A Sense of Things: The Object Matter of American Literature* (Chicago: University of Chicago Press, 2003), p. 4. See also Susan Stewart, *On Longing: Narratives of the Miniature, the Gigantic, the Souvenir, the Collection* (Durham, NC: Duke University Press, 1993).

7 Roland Barthes, *Camera Lucida* (New York: Hill and Wang, 1981), p. 77.

8 Ibid., p. 75.

One doesn't need an actual part of the body to feel reverence for materiality. In the cult of saints, a second-class relic is defined as an object that touched the body of a saint (first-class is a body or body part). A strip of green ribbon with buttons shaped like olives is believed to have been the Virgin Mary's belt. Pilgrims travel for the rosary, white cape, shoes, traveling bag, purse, and umbrella of St. Bernadette Soubirous as they once did for St. Thomas Becket's boots and penknife; the coals that burned St. Laurence; and the comb of Mary Magdalen. St. Bernard's staff, resembling a shepherd's crook, has been encased in gold and silver. In ancient folk beliefs, death had a strange influence on the lives of possessions. Clocks sometimes stopped when their owners died, many believed, "as if the machine was somehow identified with the allotted span of a particular human life."[9] Covering mirrors when a family member passed away was a holdover, in some cases, of fears of omens or haunting, with evil spirits able to reside in reflected images.[10] Leaving open doors and windows let the soul easily drift out, and, conversely, dark clothing and hangings could protect from malignant forces hovering around death.[11] The personal possessions of a beloved or admired individual can also work as witnesses. Musing on the jacket of a dead friend, Peter Stallybrass realizes that "he was there in the wrinkles of the elbows, wrinkles which in the technical jargon of sewing are called 'memory.'"[12] Books are a special sort of second-class relic. Carrying traces of their pasts, in certain cases even residue of bodies that have handled them – sweat, saliva, blood – books are contact relics, like clothing. They can also hold matter: a fern or flower to be pressed, a letter or a clipped article. Books, like relics, can call on all the senses. Their smell, their texture, and their wear tell the reader something about their biography or the biography of their owners. Or they might be like reliquaries, when the things stuck in them matter more than pages with their words.

A nineteenth-century book-receptacle at the British Library illustrates the way flesh, paper, and text can meld more thoroughly than through ordinary reading (hands turn pages, press open boards).[13] Created by Thomas Wise, a scholar and bibliophile, the large tome, bound in red levant morocco, is entitled *Percy Bysshe Shelley: His Last Days Told by His Wife, With Locks of Hair and Some of the Poet's Ashes*. A kind of album of death, the keepsake encases letters and official documents that describe Shelley's demise and the afterlife of his remains. Set inside the front cover are two glass cavities, one containing a lock of Shelley's hair and the other a curl from the head of Mary Shelley, his widow. In an urn-shaped chamber in the back cover is a pinch of Shelley's ashes and fragments

---

9 Richardson, *Death, Dissection, and the Destitute*, p. 27.

10 In Jewish tradition, however, covering mirrors and not bathing during a wake is a means to honor the dead by putting aside all considerations of personal appearance.

11 Richardson, *Death, Dissection, and the Destitute*, p. 27.

12 Peter Stallybrass, "Worn Worlds: Clothes, Mourning, and the Life of Things," in Dan Ben-Amos, Liliane Weissberg, eds., *Cultural Memory and the Construction of Identity* (Detroit, MI: Wayne State University Press, 1999), p. 39.

13 The book (Ashley MSS 5022) is dated 1822, as are most of the documents in it. But Wise probably bound the volume much later, possibly as late as the 1890s or the 1910s.

of his skull.[14] There is something emphatic about this artifact, something excessive in its reiteration of meaning on different levels of representation: through language, inscription, hair, charred corpse, bone. Written proof is somehow not sufficient to attest to this life and its end; parts of the thing itself (the body) must be included as well.

While Shelley's death was in many ways exceptional, his wandering corpse parts and their framing and binding were less so. He was neither a saint (whose relics might work miracles) nor exactly an ordinary individual; but the treatment of his corpse tells of a different approach to the dead, one rarer today. Shelley was just short of thirty years old when the schooner he was manning went down in a storm in the Gulf of Spezia. The shock of his sudden loss was compounded by the difficulty in locating and identifying his body – ten days passed before the badly decomposed corpse washed up on the shore along with those of his two companions. Shelley had to be identified by his clothing and by a volume of Keats's poems, tucked into his jacket pocket and pressed open as if he had been reading as the storm hit. Worse was the decision by the Italian quarantine authorities that the corpse must be immediately buried on the coast where it was found. Cremation, rare for the time, was the only means to move his body. Six months after the initial burial, his friends Edward Trelawny, Lord Byron, and Leigh Hunt arranged for the Italian health officials to incinerate him in a furnace on the beach at Viareggio. Trelawny, the only one of the three who had the stomach to watch the burning, claimed that Shelley's heart "remained entire," and he was able to snatch it from the flames.[15] While most of Shelley's ashes were buried in Rome's Protestant cemetery, where Keats was interred, Mary took the heart (or a small pile of ashes, according to some sources) back to England. She stored it in a large-format, paper-bound copy of Shelley's *Adonais*, now at the Bodleian, in a page torn off and folded in four (or wrapped in silk, some accounts report). While the heart was eventually buried with his son, many Shelley relics can still be found in museums and archives, including parts of his skull at the Pforzheimer Collection at the New York Public Library and fragments of his jaw, at the Keats-Shelley Memorial House in Rome. The tragic, sensationalistic nature of Shelley's early death and the relative disembodiment of this demise might go some way to explain the need, with the British Library volume, to curate a little museum or archive of mourning. Wise remarked that the "tiny heap of Shelley's ashes" let into the rear doublure "is an object of deep and pathetic attraction."[16]

Yet many Romantic-era celebrities, especially poets, were memorialized by the treasuring of their physical remnants. Snippets of Keats's hair are shelved in at least six libraries or

---

14 Wise included authentication letters in the volume, tracing the provenance of the hair and ash. Despite this evidence, the "relics" are probably not from Shelley's body, as they passed through the hands of well-known fabulists, such as Trelawny and Wise himself, who was an occasional forger. Nevertheless, both Trelawny and Wise were Shelley lovers of the highest order and strong believers in the powers of relics. Wise also compiled an edition of Elizabeth Barrett Browning's *Sonnets from the Portuguese*, which included in the binding locks of her hair and Robert Browning's.

15 Edward Trelawny, *Records of Shelley, Byron, and the Author*, 1878 (New York: New York Review of Books, 2000), p. 145.

16 Thomas Wise, *A Shelley Library* (London: Printed for Private Circulation, 1924), p. 11.

museums. When Robert Burns's wife died in 1834 and his tomb was opened to include her, his skull was removed for a casting and a few curls were collected. A long scrap of flesh claimed to be Napoleon's penis, reputedly severed by the abbé who administered last rites, went on display in England.[17] These are just a few famous examples of a commonplace Romantic-era mourning ritual, which continued into the Victorian era and was practiced by individuals of all classes. The cherishing of secular relics that reached its height of popularity from the late eighteenth to the early twentieth centuries emerged in part from a Romantic belief in the centrality of the individual. Mid eighteenth-century Enlightenment thought that continued in various forms into the nineteenth century shifted allegiance from religious figures to national and personal ones. The resulting cult of personality fed into the Romantic fashion for the sentimental, for a sophisticated cultivation of ardent emotion expressed by an intimacy with one's immediate environment and the bodies and personalities of others. This current of desire and longing lent objects – including corpses – a rich texture, a new ability to be the source of meaning and narrative. A gothic sensibility added a dark tinge to this sentimentalism, imbuing cemeteries, ruins, decay, and the mortal body with a melancholy, erotic attraction. The beautiful death, a subject many eighteenth- and nineteenth-century writers and artists took up, gave the perished body a certain radiance.

Death, thus aestheticized, had the fecund quality of narrative. Corporeal fragments became the starting point for stories or vital lyricism, rather than their end. Yet, by the beginning of the twentieth century, the remains of the dead were less likely to be treasured, and it became much rarer for a lock of hair to be kept and worn as jewelry. Dwelling on the deathbed scene, lingering upon the lips of the dying to mark last words, and recording the minutiae of final hours in diaries, letters, and memorials were no longer common practice. Rooms of houses became less likely to hold remains, and nobody had died in the beds where the living slept. Walter Benjamin lamented this turning away from death and felt that it led to the disappearance of the art of storytelling.[18] He found his early twentieth-century contemporaries "dry dwellers of eternity" because "today people live in rooms that have never been touched by death."[19] By avoiding the sight of death and dying, these "dry dwellers" failed to experience the instant when life becomes narrative, when the meaning of being is illuminated in its ending.[20] Benjamin celebrated the shared moment of death, when many would gather around the dying to listen for final words of wisdom, to find out perhaps, in the end, the whole story.

---

17 For more on Napoleon's wandering penis, see Judith Pascoe, *The Hummingbird Cabinet: A Rare and Curious History of Romantic Collectors* (Ithaca, NY: Cornell University Press, 2006), pp. 100-101.

18 Benjamin also discusses the "aura" as a type of authenticity that was lost in the nineteenth century with mechanical reproduction. See his essays "The Work of Art in the Age of Mechanical Reproduction" and "Little History of Photography."

19 Walter Benjamin, *Illuminations*, ed. Hannah Arendt (New York: Schocken, 1968), p. 94.

20 For more on the late nineteenth- and early twentieth-century denial of death, see Philippe Ariès, *The Hour of Our Death* (New York: Knopf, 1981); and Patricia Jalland, *Death in the Victorian Family* (New York: Oxford University Press, 1996).

A relic, such as Shelley's tress, was a text of experience; it could be "read" for its past. Binding human remains in a book literalized the belief that death's materials made a life legible. Keeping books tethered to bodies could bring consolation that both would remain animated. The Shelley book at the British Library was created for all these reasons, but its expense made it a rare example of this connection between book and embodiment. Simpler, cheaper means were more common, such as inscription. Handwriting on a page provided evidence that fingers brushed the paper, that a particular person had handled a volume at a specific place and time. A unique identity, impressed onto the book, marked it out from all other copies. When the inscriber died, the book became, in some cases, a relic for those who loved or revered her.

The association of the physical self with paper was one that would have already lingered in the minds of Shelley and Wise's contemporaries. Before the rise of wood pulp paper in the late nineteenth century, most reading material was made from old rags. Through a long chain of recycling, clothes that had kept limbs covered became reading matter. Printed paper was then re-used in turn as food wrappers and toilet paper. Ingestion and defecation were stages of the biography of most books, linking them closely to parts of the body other than eyes (to read) and hands (to open and hold the book). In fact, skin could do more than merely touch a book. Using human skin to bind books – called anthropodermic bibliopegy – went through a sort of fashion in the first half of the nineteenth century.[21] Books covered in tanned human skin can be beautiful (if poignant) objects, the "leather" generally soft and buttery to the touch, with the follicles visible. Rumors spread about the Hungarian master binder Joseph Zaehnsdorf, who established his business in London in 1842, taking orders from doctors, lawyers, and other well-off patrons to sheath volumes in the integument of unclaimed corpses.[22] While this was mostly gossip, he did finish a handful of books with skin, such as a copy of Holbein's *Dance of Death*.[23] Anatomy and medical books bound in skin were popular, their material reflecting their contents, like with the Holbein.[24] Dr. Stockton Hough, a bibliophile and amateur bookbinder, tanned flesh from the back of a man who died in his care in the 1880s. He incorporated it into the binding of his French medical encyclopedia.[25]

---

21 Patricia Fumerton, in *Cultural Aesthetics: Renaissance Literature and the Practice of Social Ornament* (Chicago: University of Chicago Press, 1991), relates an earlier example of using the body to bind books. When Charles I was executed, a poem "upon the King's Book (the Icon Basilike) bound up in a cover," was "coloured with his blood," p. 9.

22 See "Books Bound in Human Skins," *The New York Times* (January 25, 1886). This rumor obviously contained a political agenda, and a *Blackwoods* lampoon of 1838 that recommended the use of pauper's skin for leather also referenced class injustice, similar to Swift's "A Modest Proposal."

23 This edition, dating from 1816, was rebound by Zaehnsdorf in 1893 and is now at the John Hay Library, Brown University.

24 A copy of Vesalius's anatomy book, *De Humanis Corporis Fabrica*, bound anthropodermically in the nineteenth century can be found at the John Hay Library. A particularly strange example of binding mirroring content is a copy of Thomas à Kempis's *Imitation of Christ* bound in human skin, which the late-Victorian pornographer Leonard Smithers claimed to own.

25 Folio 610B P215, 1857-89, University of Pennsylvania Special Collections.

He used the skin of a young woman named Mary L., who died of consumption, to bind three other books.[26] In some cases, anthropodermic bibliopegy was a form of recycling the corpse. The historian Ruth Richardson tells the story of a radical who wrote a text in 1829 criticizing burial as a "romanticization of human remains." He argued that everyone should follow him in creating wills that direct executors to not only dissect their bodies, but also tan their skin for re-use, such as to upholster chairs. His bones he wanted to go to a turner to create "knife-handles, pin-cases, small boxes, buttons, etc."[27]

Akin to the Shelley tome at the British Library, volumes about executed criminals were sometimes bound in their skin. At the Bristol Royal Infirmary is an account covered in "the true skin of John Horwood" of his murder of a girl, his trial, death, and dissection in 1821.[28] A number of relics from the famous "Murder in the Red Barn" of Maria Martin in 1827 by William Corder can be found at the Moyse's Hall Museum, in Bury St. Edmunds, Suffolk, including details of his trial bound in his skin.[29] In some cases individuals requested that their flesh be integrated into a book about themselves. At the Boston Athenaeum are two volumes of the autobiography of the American George Walton (also called James Allen), a professional thief, who wanted them to be bound with his own skin, after his execution in 1837.[30] With this auto-icon, his "corpus" (and this word takes on all its meanings here) might live on as the warm hands of readers resurrect the dead words and enliven the book-crypt. His skin sheaths his narrative, much like the skin holds together the self (or soul). Skin shows its kinship with paper; the body can be engraved, be read. To think of this another way: if the body is the binding, then it is the interiority that is the "writing." Such a book is difficult to read when the individual still lives. Yet, in death that skin might give up its secrets and the body might become narrative.

---

26 These volumes reside in the College of Physicians, Philadelphia. See "Dr. John Stockton Hough: Medical Bibliophile and Bibliographer," *Transactions – Studies of the College of Physicians of Philadelphia* (1989), pp. 355-361. See also Laura Ann Guelle, "Anthropodermic Book-Bindings," *Transactions – Studies of the College of Physicians of Philadelphia* (2002), pp. 85-89.

27 Quoted in Richardson, *Death, Dissection, and the Destitute*, pp. 168-169. Teeth found on the battlefields of Waterloo and the American Civil War were used to make dentures. See John Woodforde, *The Strange Story of False Teeth* (New York: Routledge, 1983).

28 "Human Skin as Binding," *Bookworm: An Illustrated Treasury of Old-Time Literature* (January 1, 1891), p. 148.

29 The account of Corder's trial is written by the journalist James Curtis, and the surgeon who dissected him, George Creed, tanned the skin. The *Bookworm* reported in 1893 that the library of the Prince of Wales at Marlborough House contained two volumes made from the skin of Mary Patman (sometimes called Bateman), a Yorkshire "witch" hanged for murder in the early nineteenth century. "Human Skin as a Binding," *Bookworm: An Illustrated Treasury of Old-Time Literature* (January 1, 1893), p. 103. Other examples include: a book bound with the skin of George Cudmore, who poisoned his wife and was executed for it in 1830; an edition of Samuel Johnson's dictionary bound in the skin of James Johnson (relation unknown), hanged in Norwich in 1818; and a pocket-book made from the skin of the notorious "body snatcher" William Burke, after he was hanged in 1829 for murder (now at the Museum of the Royal College of Surgeons, Edinburgh).

30 The full title of the two-volume collection is: *Narrative of the Life of James Allen: Alias George Walton, Alias Jonas Pierce, Alias James H. York, Alias Burley Grove, the Highwayman: Being His Death-bed Confession, to the Warden of the Massachusetts State Prison.* See Oliver Robinson, "Bound for Glory: The Macabre Practice of Book Bindings Made of Human Skin," *Rare Book Review* 33 (2006), pp. 29-31.

Books worked as traces of bodies, as things that bodies left behind. Yet new technologies came along that slowly loosened this braiding of text and flesh. Photography, invented in the late 1830s, became a popular means to commemorate the dead by the 1850s. The easy availability of the *carte-de-visite* photograph in the late 1850s started a fashion for photo albums, which began to largely replace earlier albums that were collections of objects (such as valentines, labeled specimens of flowers, leaves and seaweed, or curls of hairs and even fingernail parings). Photographs, tipped into books, were, despite Barthes's theories, disembodied memory devices, with no need to have touched the body they memorialized. Reproducing without taking a sample of the real, the photograph lost the embodied intimacy of the snippet of hair, the heap of ash. Texts drifted further away from skin when handwritten manuscripts began to be replaced by typewritten ones by the end of the nineteenth century. Other technologies increased the gap. The telegraph, telephone, film: all record or transmit the person, but in such a way that needn't include the nearness or touch of the body remembered. E-mail has no interior; a lock of hair cannot be included as an attachment. Nothing can be tipped into an electronic book. Might the de-materialization of the book, of texts, have some relationship to the disappearance of the widespread treasuring of the dead body? Relic culture and its intermingling with book culture shows a willingness to linger over objects replete with mortality, to see death's materiality as woven into the texture of living.

I thank Cabinet Magazine *for permission to reprint here a revised and expanded version of "Skin Book," which originally appeared in issue 49 (2013), pp. 92-95.*

Anthony Haden-Guest

It's unsurprising that most of us should find that artists, writers, and performers are at least as reliable tipsters on life as preachers, pundits or philosophers. But do they help us deal with death? That, of course, depends on what help you are hoping for. Certainly some artists pick up on the significance of death – which almost all of us successfully manage to deny almost all of the time – pretty early.

"As a child what I most wanted to do was illustrate stories," Alberto Giacometti wrote. "The first drawing I remember was an illustration to a fairy tale. Snow White in a tiny coffin and the dwarfs." And an artist can find breathtaking symmetries in the most horrid and unappealing facts. As with Artemisia Gentileschi's painting of *Judith Slaying Holofernes*. Or Goya's *Disasters of War* and the fields of crashed airplanes Paul Nash painted during the First World War.

Francis Bacon hugely admired *The End of the Game*, Peter Beard's book of photographs of the massive die-off of elephants in Kenya's Tsavo National Park in the early 1960s. Bacon wrote to Beard: "For me the most poignant are the ones of decomposing elephants where, over time, as they disintegrate, the bones form magnificent sculptures which are not just abstract forms, but have all the memory traces of life's futility and despair."[1] Franz Kafka, more tersely bleak, wrote: "The meaning of life is that it stops." Voltaire contrived to stave off the preachers until the literal end, his deathbed. "Now now, my good man," he reproved a priest who was urging him to renounce Satan. "This is no time to be making enemies."

Death is traditionally the occasion for grief, of course even if the shows of grief are sometimes purely ritualistic and sometimes not quite even that. "Well, the cunt died today," said the movie star, Bette Davis, a woman who took no prisoners in her conversation, when she heard that her rival, Joan Crawford, was no more. "You should never say bad things about the dead, only good. Joan Crawford is dead. Good!" The American writer, Ambrose Bierce, faced death with admirable sangfroid. "If you hear of my being stood up against a Mexican stone wall and shot to rags, please know that I think this is a pretty good way to depart this life," Bierce wrote in a letter from that country in December 1913. It was his last letter. He disappeared. Another mysterious disappearance in Mexico a couple of years later was that of Arthur Cravan, the writer nephew of Oscar Wilde, who had been the light

---

1 Personal conversation with Peter Beard in 2015.

heavyweight boxing champion of France, and was in Marcel Duchamp's circle in New York. There were supposed sightings of Cravan for many, many years, as there had been supposed sightings of Arthur Rimbaud.

Artists and writers can occasionally have deaths almost as cultish as those of some preachers. And sometimes the two can morph, as with Philip K. Dick, perhaps the greatest of science-fiction writers, who believed he had been pierced with a mystically illuminating beam of pink light when the sun struck a fish pendant worn by a young woman who was delivering the pain reliever, Darvon, began to experience hallucinations and came to believe he had also been a Christian persecuted by the Romans. He died in 1982 and it's curious that he has not generated a religion, the way L. Ron Hubbard did. Well, not as of yet, anyway.

Can the arts help deal with death? A reasonable question. The narrative and/or symbolic content of much of the art in all cultures before modern times was religious, so death was very much part of the story. And there is actual evidence. Some months before he died, the English poet John Donne (1572-1631) commissioned a portrait that would show him rising from his grave at the Apocalypse. Donne's biographer, Izaak Walton, better known for *The Compleat Angler*, a celebration of fishing, described the poet's sitting for the artist:

> Several charcoal fires being first made in his large study, he brought with him into that place his winding-sheet in his hand, and having put off all his clothes, had this sheet put on him, and so tied the knots at his head and feet, and his hands so placed as dead bodies are usually fitted, to be shrouded and put into their coffin, or grave.

Donne hung this image on his wall and an accomplished portraitist Nicholas Stone turned it into a sculpture, which was installed in Old St. Paul's Cathedral, when Donne was buried there. In 1666 the cathedral was gutted by the Great Fire of London, but the sculpture survived, and can be seen in the rebuilt St Paul's. It's startling. Tomb sculptures in all cultures almost always show their subjects reclining at their ease, but the poet Donne is standing on an urn, eerily wrapped, chrysalis-like, in his winding sheet, on the alert for what is to come.

It's a luminous tale: Death/Art/Faith. Grünewald comes readily to mind as an artist well acquainted with mortality and I have read speculation that he became a convert to that fierce anti-art cult, the Iconoclasts. Hence his stoppage of production. But faith seldom seems part of the package with artists in our Po-Mo times, of whom Damien Hirst may well be the most gleefully morbid. As a grinning seventeen-year-old art student, he had himself photographed next to a severed head in a morgue in Leeds. This entered Hirst's oeuvre as *With Dead Head* after he kick-started his career with *The Physical Impossibility of Death in the Mind of Someone Living*. He cemented it with the tremendous *A Thousand Years* and sent it into the peculiar space it occupies today with his diamanté skull: *For The Love of God.* Deliciously gothic work all, but I think we can ignore the title of the last. This is not a Death/Art/Faith oeuvre. "I've got an obsession with death," he has said. "But I think it's like a celebration of life rather than something morbid."

Or there is the Mexican artist, Teresa Margolles, well, the arts and popular arts of Mexico have always been full of virile morbidity and Margolles, who also works in a Mexico City morgue and has studied forensic medicine, does not disappoint. *What Else Could We Talk About?,* her show in the Mexican Pavilion at the 2009 Venice Biennale dealt with the 5,000 plus murders in Sinaloa the previous year. Hanging outside was a banner dyed with blood collected where the murders had taken place. But her work is about outrage, not faith. It is perhaps a prayer for the living.

Which brings me, inevitably, to Heide Hatry. I first came across Hatry's work in a Chelsea gallery a few years back, namely some portraits fabricated from… well, hide sounds nicer, but let's call it what it was, skin. Powerful, unsettling stuff. We duly met. I learned that she had grown up in Baden-Württemberg, in southwest Germany, not far from Stuttgart.

"I grew up on a factory-farming pig farm," she told me. "I had to cut them up into pieces, so that I could put them in bags and label them. I was fascinated. I knew all the organs that were in pigs and how they were connected. My father wanted me to be a butcher."

So Hatry's pictorial vocabulary began to be formed. She gave a talk about her work in the Goethe Institute.

"I was wearing a pigskin dress," she says. "The pigskin was straight from the slaughterhouse." And she wore a brooch made from fresh tongues. "It was duck tongues. A *lot* of duck tongues connected."

Did people notice?

"Oh, yes, everybody was saying something. But they were more shocked about the dress than about the brooch."

Yes, shock. It is shocking. But, God, have we ever needed to be shocked more? Most of us have always denied death but now we have an ever-growing list of undeniable things to deny. Heide Hatry's art requires us to live with death. Knowingly.

Her most recent show was made up of disturbingly convincing flowers assembled from body parts. In-your-face shock was again a weapon she deployed. You could say that Hatry's work moves through phases of grief and that the body parts works are a phase of acceptance. So what of this new body of work?

I began by observing that our species is conditioned to deny death. Nothing wrong with this. Our survival mechanisms depend on that conditioning. But when the cold everyday realities of death strike really close to home, becoming impossible to wipe from the mindscreen, what is the artist to do? Cartoony skulls, zombie movies and Hallowe'en fright wigs won't work their cutesy magic here. What Heide Hatry does is use the ashes of the dead to paint their portraits. Here I am. Look at me. In Death, in Art, in Life. This phase of grieving might be called Consolation.

It takes, it should be said, a certain fortitude for an artist to take this road in our irony-saturated postmodernist era. From Classical times through to the nineteenth century past artists have dealt with emotion more directly than we are generally inclined to do. But these works were commissions, they have a job to do. And many individuals who have commissioned Heide Hatry's ash portraits have told her that, yes, they do feel consoled. It's art that works.

When death comes unexpectedly last lines can be surreal. Lucio Fontana said to his brother "Go and buy me *Playboy*." Lee Krasner had walked out on Jackson Pollock and gone to Paris. Pollock was drunk, enraged and in a blue Oldsmobile with his girlfriend Ruth Kligman and her friend, Edith Metzger who were insisting that he take them to a party. "You want to go to this party?" he barked, gunning the motor and losing control. He hit a pole, which killed Metzger instantly, and the car somersaulted, flinging him fifty feet into a birch tree where he also died.

Where death is foreseen, though, for artists, writers, performers, the prospect of death can be liberating. "I want to go to sleep now," said Byron. He was thirty-seven. It was 1824. "Death will be a great relief. No more interviews," rejoiced Katherine Hepburn. "It's my party. And I'll die if I want to," said the hugely missed ornament of the Warhol Factory, Taylor Mead. "I am dying. I haven't drunk champagne for a long time," observed Anton Chekhov. The final entry in the appointments diary of the photographer, Diane Arbus, in 1972, the day she took her own life with a blade and barbiturates read: LAST SUPPER. Anna Pavlova's haunting last words were "Get my Swan costume ready." I'll come up with something as good as that if it's the last thing I do.

The source of most of the quotes appearing in this essay are from the personal notebooks of the author.

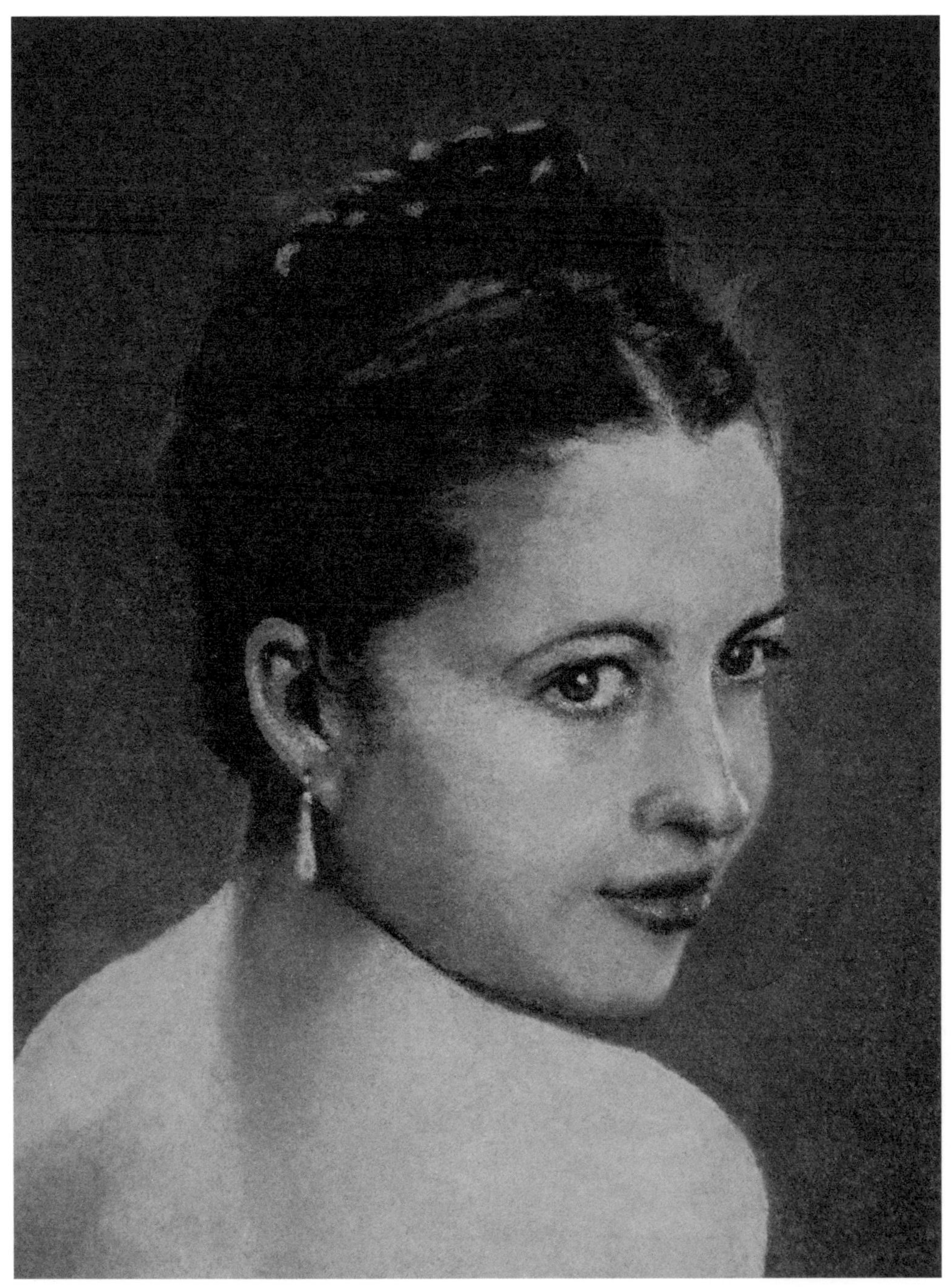

Art and the Many Ways the "Disenchanted Body is Enchanted Again and Again"
Thyrza Nichols Goodeve

Dedicated to the memory of Michelle Cliff

One nineteenth-century artist was so upset to learn that his paint was mixed from real human bodies that he took all his tubes of this pigment into his garden "and gave them a decent burial."[1]

I. Matter, My Mother

We knew the ashes were hers because of the titanium screws.

I can still taste the particles – gritty, like soft stone. They decidedly did not feel like those grinding unwelcome traces of years of broken down matter – sand – mixed by the ocean wind into my mother's homemade egg salad sandwiches I ate as a child at the beach in Martha's Vineyard. No, these particles were less sharp, more like chalky dust; matter,

my mother.

We were throwing her ashes into a river by a theater in Vermont, housed in a beautiful old church set on the riverbank of the West River in Weston. Here she and my late father spent some forty years attending theatrical productions. That day in 2009, the river's cool wind swept the cloud of ash up away from its banks, back at us, dusting my brother's hair as I opened my mouth to take a breath. And so, I swallowed my mother. In a millisecond, that once-living, bloodstream of muscles, mucous, breath, and biology, who I began inside of as an egg + sperm

– this essence of my existence –
slid down my throat
cold flesh and bone to ash
to
parted lips

---

1 Victoria Finley, *Color: A Natural History of the Palette* (New York: Random House, 2002), p. 106.

tongue
digestive system
genetic material
accretion into bloodstream
to become *enchanted*
my skin and bone and self
until I too
die
becoming a body stripped bare.

II. How the Beloved Could Turn into Earth

> It begins to devour itself within minutes, as the enzymes that had once turned food into nutriments start dissembling the body that no longer needs them in their old job.[2]

In Thomas Laqueur's formidable 711-page study, *The Work of the Dead: A Cultural History of Mortal Remains*, the Cynic Diogenes serves as the ultimate arbiter of what Laqueur calls the ultimate "disenchantment" of the dead body. In other words, death stripped bare of meaning; the body as pure meat. For this man, known as the dog philosopher, death contains no moral, no story, not even the hint of signification. Death is just a moment of transition without enchantment, when our bodies become pure physiological referent. It is neither sign, nor spirit, just brute refuse set to decompose. And yet, "I was trying to figure out what it was all about, what happens after death. She was so there and so not there,"[3] says artist Sally Mann as she stares at the frozen carcass of her favorite greyhound, Eva, who died suddenly in 1999.[4] After Eva's burial, Mann exhumed and photographed the canine's bones and skeleton because "I just wanted to see how something that beloved could turn into the earth. It was a way to come to grips with the finality of death."[5] Mann was not after transcendence. This modern day Diogenes, a dog philosopher in her own right, grasped after death by photographing the stages of physical deterioration of a canine body that meant more than the sum of its skin and bones to her.

And then in 2003, Mann produced nothing less than a Diogenesian masterpiece called *Body Farm*. She spent several months photographing the various stages of the human body's decomposition at the Forensic Anthropology Center or, Body Farm, at the University of Tennessee. One of six such farms in the United States, the Tennessee facility is the oldest, founded in 1981 by anthropologist William Bass for forensic anthropologists and law

---

2 Thomas W. Laqueur, *The Work of the Dead: A Cultural History of Mortal Remains* (Princeton, NJ: Princeton University Press, 2015), p. 2.

3 Malcolm Jones, "Love, Death, and Light," *Newsweek* (September 9, 2003), http://www.newsweek.com/love-death-light-136365.

4 Ibid.

5 Ibid.

enforcement to study the precise permutations of decay that the dead body undergoes – step by step, stage by stage.[6]

> The bodies are exposed in a number of ways in order to provide insights into decomposition under varying conditions. Observations and records of the decomposition process are kept, including the sequence and speed of decomposition and the effects of insect activity. The human decomposition stages that are studied begin with the fresh stage, then the bloat stage, then decay, and finally the dry stage.[7]

One of the most extraordinary images in Mann's project features a biomorphic ready-made, in other words, a found-object, no longer human, skin slab of elemental abstraction. The form has been captured at the point of ooze. Its shape has the feel of a deviant Barbara Hepworth or Henry Moore maquette. Because the head is obscured, and the form is caught in the bloat stage (more like the melt stage), only a curved arm with decomposing hand signifies the once living human this forensic grotesque once was.

Among the effects of abstraction is Mann's choice of black-and-white photography. And yet, she exclaims to an interlocutor, "You should see the colors – they're really beautiful."[8]

III. Color – The Astonishing Discovery

> In 1691 William Salmon, a "Professor of Physick" working out of High Holborn, gave a recipe for artificial mummy as follows, "Take the carcass of a young man (some say red haired) not dying of a Disease but killed; let it lie 24 hours in clear water in the Air: cut the flesh in pieces, to which add Powder of Myrrh and a little Aloes, imbibe it 24 hours in the Spirit of Wine and Turpentine…" It was a particularly good remedy for dissolving congealed blood and expelling wind "out of both Bowels and Veins," he said.[9]

It was a particularly good remedy.

In Victoria Finley's *Color: A Natural History of the Palette,* we learn of "the astonishing discovery that English artists once smeared dead humans onto their canvases."[10] In other words, Diogenes' abject body, stripped bare of metaphor and meaning, is set to an alchemical

---

6 According to Wikipedia: "Over 100 bodies are donated to the facility every year. Some individuals pre-register before their death, and others are donated by their families or by a medical examiner. 60% of donations are made by family members of individuals who were not pre-registered with the facility. Over 1300 people have chosen to pre-register themselves. Perhaps the most famous person to donate his body for study was the anthropologist Grover Krantz, as described by his colleague David Hunt at the Smithsonian." The University of Tennessee Body Farm is also used in the training of law enforcement officers in scene-of-crime skills and techniques. https://en.wikipedia.org/wiki/Body_farm.
7 Ibid.
8 Blake Morrison, "Sally Mann: The Naked and the Dead," *The Guardian* (May 29, 2010), https://www.theguardian.com/artanddesign/2010/may/29/sally-mann-naked-dead.
9 Finley, *Color: A Natural History of the Palette*, pp. 104; 106.
10 Ibid., p. 2.

process that leads to re-enchantment. According to Finley, "the two most controversial browns in European art history are asphaltum and mommia ("mummy"). While mommia is made of dead Ancient Egyptians,"[11] asphaltum does not use dead bodies, yet it too traffics in death. Made from oily bitumen taken from the Dead Sea, it is a material that disintegrates over time. For this reason, the use of asphaltum was an unwitting death sentence to every painting in which it was used, as in the case of the work of Joshua Reynolds who never found out, "alas, that many of his pictures are now in ruins."[12] The paint decays, the color fades, like a certain carmine pigment used by Frederick Turner "that day in 1835" when he made *Waves Breaking Against the Wind*, where "he chose his brightest red even though he knew it would not last."[13] In fact, "Mind your own business" was his response when Winsor (of Winsor and Newton) cautioned him not to use it.[14] Only the present tense of color interested Turner. If a hue lost its vibrancy – died over time – so be it.

But in some instances, the color red, like the brown mommia, or bone black, said to be made from human corpses,[15] is literally death put to work by a body of a different kind. Before the invention of artificial dyes, carmine was made from the blood of crushed pregnant female insects known as the cochineal. And until Change.org blasted Starbucks with petitions, the company used the cochineal to color its specialty drinks.[16]

So, while Simon Schama amends the notion that bone black is made from human remains by stating unequivocally that it "is uncontroversial powdered and burned scraps from the slaughterhouse's remainder pit,"[17] today, lipstick, carmine, crimson, and food coloring additive E120, is made from the crushed carcasses of female cochineal bugs – pregnant, simultaneously to the introduction of a new trend in art, "Dead animal art is back in fashion."[18]

– roadkill
– taxidermy

---

11 Ibid., p. 104.

12 "Asphaltum is an oily bitumen from the Dead Sea and was first used in the sixteenth century as a lustrous brown. But as the artist Holman Hunt told the Royal Society of Arts in his impassioned speech of 1880 about how painters could no longer remember how to use paint, by the time Joshua Reynolds decided to use asphaltum in the 1780s he 'had not had experiments of generations to show him the course of safety… and it is owing to this, alas, that many of his pictures are now in ruins.'" Ibid., p. 104.

13 Ibid., p. 134.

14 Ibid., pp. 134-135.

15 Simon Schama, *Rembrandt's Eyes* (New York: Penguin Books, 1990), p. 216.

16 James Johnson, "Starbucks No Longer Using Dead Insects to Color Specialty Drinks," *Inquisitor* (April 20, 2012), http://www.inquisitr.com/222782/starbucks-no-longer-using-dead-insects-to-color-specialty-drinks/#Oseosw2yr Dkf0HkJ.99. The use of the cochineal bug, additive E120, is common in food coloring. See http://www.laleva.cc/food/enumbers/E120-E130.html.

17 Finley, *Color: A Natural History of the Palette*, p. 103.

18 Martin Chilton, "Dead Animal Art Is Back In Fashion," *The Telegraph* (February 25, 2015), http://www.telegraph.co.uk/culture/art/art-news/11433699/Dead-animal-art-is-back-in-fashion.html.

Art and the dead bodies of the non-human animal in the twenty-first century is the new material grotesque brought forth from technologies of death such as factory farming, the automobile, the fur and leather industries, and our maniacal enchantment with munitions.

Take Yang Maoyuan's inflated taxidermy.[19] An unnaturally bright yellow horse hide, with head and hooves still attached, is inflated into a perfect bloated balloon-body, producing a ghoulish, cartoony comic-horror of a sculpture, which, like the bone black limbs of lambs, bears witness to the work of the dead.

Or Jennifer Angus' *In the Midnight Garden*:[20] A pinkish floor-to-ceiling wash – a dye extract that comes from the cochineal, a scale insect – gives the whole scene a Day of the Dead feel. *In the Midnight Garden* was produced from an archive of 30,000 insect specimens. The artist uses them to create a room of "orderly parts – neatly arranged patterns of concentric circles, squares and other shapes."[21] The variety of insects used includes:

thorny sticks (*Heteropteryx dilatata*),
moving leafs (*Phyllium giganteum*),
white-winged cicadas (*Ayuthia spectabilis),*
clear-wing cicadas (*Pompoina imperatorial*),
blue-winged cicadas (*Tosena splendida*),
brown-winged cicadas (*Angamiana floridula*),
katydids (*Sanaa intermedia*),
green stag beetles (*Phymateus saxosus*)
and several varieties of grasshoppers.[22]

Like Heide Hatry's *Not a Rose*,[23] a book and exhibition of images of exotic flowers of astonishing aesthetic allure (but beautiful as a biomorphic corpse), such works partly or wholly conceal the secret of their origins. Hatry's flowers were constructed from flesh and biological material: the detritus discarded from the slaughterhouse that cannot be recycled into the consumer market; bits of non-human animals such as vaginas, claws, eyeballs, tongues, and penises. These monstrous creations were then photographed in color to resemble an otherwise innocuous coffee-table book on flowers (a florilegium).

Meanwhile Fabian Peña uses cockroach wings and crushed flies to draw a picture of a boy aiming a rifle,[24] while Jordan Eagles uses animal blood "to create vibrant, abstract panels

19 See https://cakeheadlovesevil.wordpress.com/2010/01/11/yang-maoyuan-inflated-taxidermy/.
20 Alicia Ault, "How Thousands of Dead Bugs Become a Mesmerizing Work of Extraordinary Beauty," *Smithsonian Magazine* (November 6, 2015), http://www.smithsonianmag.com/smithsonian-institution/assemblage-dead-bugs-becomes-mesmerizing-work-extraordinary-beauty-180957050.
21 Ibid.
22 Ibid.
23 Heide Hatry, *Not a Rose* (Milan: Charta Books, 2012).
24 "Fabian Peña," David Castillo Gallery, http://davidcastillogallery.com/artist/fabian-pena/#22.

that appear to glow from within" to which writer (Robin Wilkey) adds: "(Fret not, PETA: all blood used in his art is procured from a slaughterhouse.)"[25]

Pigment out of waste and putrescence,
the bodies of animals
– crushed
– slaughtered
– discarded.

The function of art here is the repurposing of mortal remains
– human (*mommia,* brown)
– insect (carmine, red)
– animal (bone black).

Or, the artist Jill Magid using the ashes of the architect Luis Barragán, to make them into a diamond?[26]

IV. The Paint That Kills

> Gentlemen, I send you by this same post a little French box of – so-called – "safe" colours. We have various scares here about scarlet-pink – giroflée – and carnation-darnation fevers; and I've just given this dozen of mortal sins to a young convalescent of six. Will you kindly analyse the temptations and see if they're – not worse than apples and currents – if only mildly licked? And if really right – will you please make me another box, like this exactly, for ten pence.[27]

And then, of course, there is the paint that kills – *and see if they're not worse than apples and currents – if only mildly licked?* One has only to think of Laird's "Bloom of Youth Foundation," produced in the 1870s, the white paint of death; a female cosmetic. White – what it takes for the European woman to pass as feminine at the very same time that such nations as France, Belgium, and England are colonizing the black, nutmeg, and brown of the West Indies, India, the Congo, North Africa, South Africa, and in the case of the United States of America, initiating genocide against the "red man."

Juxtaposition of skin tones (racial configurations)
– white death
– putrid brown

---

25 Robin Wilkey, "Jordan Eagles 'Haemoscuro': New Exhibit Makes Art of Animal Blood," *The Huffington Post* (April 17, 2012), http://www.huffingtonpost.com/2012/04/17/jordan-eagles-haemoscuro_n_1432259.html.

26 Antonio Pacheco, "Shine Bright Like a Diamond: Jill Magid Transforms Luis Barragán's Ashes into a Two-carat Diamond," *Architect's Newspaper* (July 27, 2016), http://archpaper.com/2016/07/luis-barragan-ashes-diamond/.

27 Letter from John Ruskin to Messrs, Winsor & Newton, August 9, 1889. Finley, *Color: A Natural History of the Palette*, p. 134.

– *mommia*
– the color line.

Imagine the bodies of slaves
Free Enterprise[28]
as pigment

in Turner's *Slavers Throwing Overboard the Dead and Dying*, one of the great paintings of
the mercantile ferocity of the Middle Passage where in a few smudges of brown: "My eyes
were locked on the foreground of the painting, where a few brown arms, some lengths
of chain, and one brown leg glanced through the waves, alongside magnificently colored
fish."[29]

Colors,
you should have seen them (Mann)
the bodies of
white women
dying to be white, as "lead white was made by the poor and it poisoned the poor"[30]
or
brown bodies
used
as chattel
material
the astonishing discovery
dead Egyptians
– unspeakable
Ruskin: *I've just given this dozen of mortal sins to a young convalescent of six*
pigment as death
the color line
where, in the Anglo world, the mixing of colors is an abomination.[31]

V. YOU

> I am writing my story as if I were a statue... I wish they had carved me from the onyx of
> Elizabeth Catlett. Or molded me from the dark clay of Augusta Savage. Or cut me from
> mahogany or cast me in bronze. I wish I were dark plaster like Meta Warrick Fuller's *Talking
> Skull*. But I appear more as Edmonia Lewis's *Hagar* – her striations caught within.[32]

---

28 *Free Enterprise* is the name of the experimental montage novel by Michelle Cliff.
29 Michelle Cliff, *Free Enterprise* (New York: Dutton Books, 1993), p. 73.
30 Finley, *Color: A Natural History of the Palette*, p. 123.
31 See Michelle Cliff, "The Laughing Mulatto (Formerly a Statue) Speaks," in Michelle Cliff, *The Land of Look Behind:
Prose and Poetry* (Ithaca, NY: Firebrand Editions, 1985).
32 Cliff, *Free Enterprise*, p. 85.

I wish you could regenerate like the "many animals that can regenerate complex body parts with full function and form after amputation or injury."[33] You who I am told as I write about the work of mortal remains "died last Sunday under medical care" – decades too soon, making these words of ashes, of carcasses, killed, incinerated, and crushed bodies – "the human decomposition stages that are studied that begin with the fresh stage, then the bloat stage, then decay, and finally the dry stage"[34] – now shudder with your remains.

This very instant the person I knew is a corpse, incinerated and dumb. This matter without consciousness that wrote about color – onyx, black, bronze, red, nutmeg, and brown bodies – twisted by white death, as in *Free Enterprise* where Mary Ellen Pleasant (an actual nineteenth-century, African-American abolitionist and entrepreneur) writes to Annie Christmas (a fictional, mixed-race Jamaican) about a dinner party she was invited to by Miss Alice Hooper (fiction) celebrating the unveiling of a painting by the Englishman Turner. The painting is *Slavers Throwing Overboard the Dead and Dying, Typhoon Coming On* (1840). MEP is asked by the hostess to explain what incident Turner depicts but "I wasn't at all sure. Which of the hundreds that came to light?" An answer that disappoints Miss Alice until a lecturer from Harvard, Mr. Bodley, explains to the dinner guests; "Turner based the painting on a ship named Zong, an infamous case in which the traders threw slaves, living and dead, overboard, to collect the insurance money and not lose the investment." For MEP this brings up the question, who insured the investment, the loss of property, the "few brown arms, some lengths of chain, and one brown leg glanced through the waves, alongside magnificently colored fish." She is grateful "that the artist portrayed it thus, indicating the horror of the thing aslant, by these few members, and a reminder of their confinement, the irons which would take them down."

It got to Mary Ellen Pleasant. It got to you. It gets to me all these associations between your writing, the color of a smudge of paint, the dead bodies, brown, which Turner portrays, you, now a body, "a disenchanted body, a disenchanted corpse, a 'corpse without consciousness': bereft, vulnerable, abject."[35]

Diogenes helps here to let go of this matter; the you who lived in prose so poetic you could not go on. Secrets soaked in anguish. We are left wondering – Did you, did you really, light your entire life on fire at the end; paper, letters, body into ash?

"Mr. Bodley was about to turn the question of where to hang the painting into a parlor game, with each trying to be cleverer than the next." You see, the painting was so painful for Ruskin, "eventually he had to conceal it." A dinner guest speaks up, offering her own way of dealing with, really concealing, the pain: "The thing is behind us; surely we can enjoy the art it engendered. The man had a brilliance with form, color."

---

33 See http://www.eurostemcell.org/factsheet/regeneration-what-does-it-mean-and-how-does-it-work.
34 Ibid.
35 Laqueur, *The Work of the Dead*, p. 1.

As did you.

I think of you and your ink, "dark liquor of cuttlefish when they are afraid,"[36] a lifetime of books written in a hand so fine, never ash. If only we could make you into pigment using your prehistoric defense, like octopus ink, but you prefer to be left in shades of color that disintegrate – *asphaltum* or the no-color of ash. "Ashes and decomposition was how I described the non-colors dismissively to a conservator friend, before my research had really started."[37]

As Victoria Finley learned, there is no such thing as *no-color* when it comes to the incinerated or decomposed body (Mann again: *You should see the colors!*). Ash, after all, has a color even before it is mixed with a medium or glass in the case of cremation art.[38] Cremation art memorializes the incinerated matter of the beloved. It fixes what otherwise is ritually thrown to the wind near a river, spread over soil, into a garden bed, atop a mountain, across the New York Harbor, and even in one case I know, sprinkled covertly into a pair of shoes at Barney's. Or the woman "who told me the tattoos on her knuckles were made from ink that had been formulated with her grandmother's ashes"[39] or how a woman and her mother "had taken the ashes of her father, a professional photographer, and put them in 35mm film canisters that they would be leaving in the venues around the world where he had taken pictures."[40]

Luis Barragán – the no-color of a diamond.

To turn dead matter into an object is a ritual of enchantment and yet it is the inverse of sand painting, which celebrates life's impermanence. In Tibet a *chak-pur* sieve is used to make Buddhist mandalas which are destroyed the minute they are complete. Like 30,000 years of Aboriginal art, the painting made of colored sand is not made to last because a kind of death is integral to the process, as in the dry paintings that flow through Navajo hands producing images that are not to be seen because, "To create an authentic sand painting solely for viewing would be a profane act."[41]

The color line again: red skins "refers to skin color or the use of pigments by certain tribes"[42] and how *they* (white people) "gave a name to the mutilated and bloody corpses they left in the wake of scalp hunts: redskins."[43]

---

36 Finley, *Color: A Natural History of the Palette*, p. 103.

37 Ibid., p. 70.

38 See: http://www.cremationsolutions.com/other-cremation-options/cremation-portraits.

39 Laqueur, *The Work of the Dead*, p. 550.

40 Ibid.

41 See: https://en.wikipedia.org/wiki/Sandpainting.

42 See: https://en.wikipedia.org/wiki/Redskin_(slang).

43 Ibid.

Here we enter the realm of atrocity, where, *the dead do not matter,* in ways horrific and obscene: lampshades made from the skins of Jews, homosexuals, Roma, or footballs made of pigskin, a bear rug on the floor, or the human animal who attends auction night at Christie's draped in a silver fox stole.

I once wrote an essay on an exhibition featuring art made only of meat, which a celebrated animal advocate and feminist condemned. As if I had no clue or commitment to the ethics of slaughter. How she misunderstood what it took to write about art made from the remains of torture and death.

Raw flesh is not aesthetic; it is not pigment.

And so are the ways we re-enchant dead matter in manners both heartless and cruel. Or in the case of artists Xu Bing, Ed Ruscha,[44] and Cai Guo-Qiang, use the materials that kill to make art. Or Xu Bing's tiger rug made out of 500,000 cigarettes, works that signify the aestheticization of our will to kill. In fact, to the Chinese artist Cai Guo-Qiang, his paintings made out of gunpowder are indeed *think pieces.*[45]

In the end, we are bought back to paint, to pigments made from ash, and crushed and decomposed animals and insects, to photographs of mortal remains. Indeed, to agree with Diogenes, "there is nothing behind the veil of the corpse"[46] except what we bring to dead dumb matter. T.S. Eliot is right when he tells us in *The Four Quartets*

> human kind
> Cannot bear very much reality[47]

And so, the astonishing discovery is how often and with what care – and yes, at times, with what heartless disregard – *the disenchanted body, the disenchanted corpse, without consciousness… is nonetheless enchanted again and again.*[48]

---

44 See "Ruscha Gunpowder Ribbon Drawings," Craig F. Starr Gallery, http://www.starr-art.com/exhibits/Ruscha_Ribbon_Drawings.

45 Quoted in *Wu Hung on Contemporary Chinese Artists*. Cited in footnote 29 of *Ink Art: Past as Present in Contemporary China,* ed. Maxwell K. Hearn (New York: Metropolitan Museum of Art, 2013), p. 191.

46 Laqueur, *The Work of the Dead,* p. 35.

47 T.S. Eliot, *The Four Quartets,* http://www.coldbacon.com/poems/fq.html.

48 Laqueur, *The Work of the Dead,* p. 550. This essay could not have been written without the scholarship and research of Laqueur's book, particularly the formulation of the enchanted versus the disenchanted body.

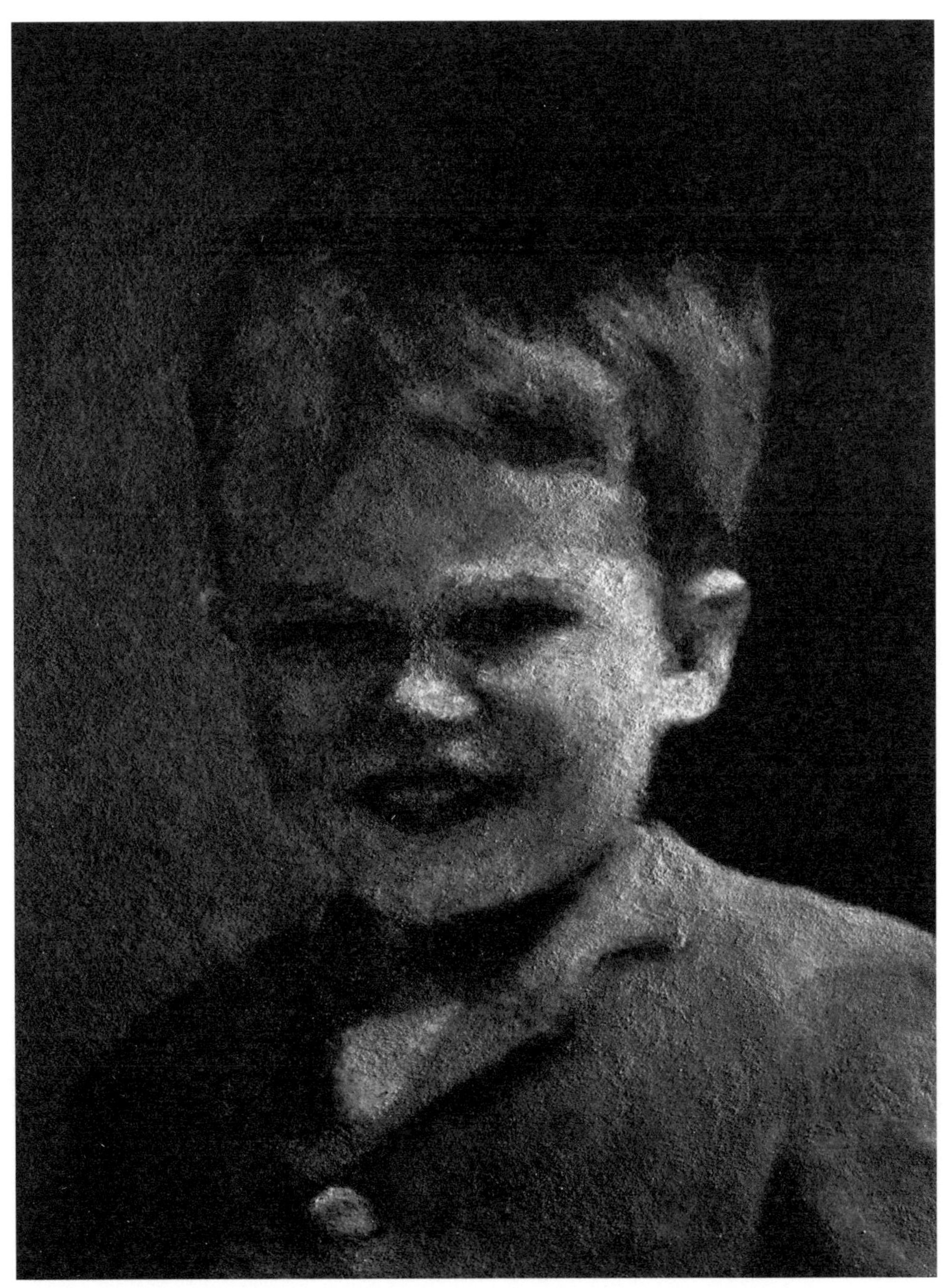

The Matter of Ashes
Thomas W. Laqueur

The ashes of the dead have always borne the most attenuated relationship to the flesh and blood of the human beings from which they come. Moist, warm, subtly colored and clearly ordered – head, torso, arms, legs, fingers, toes – while alive the dead body remains for some time not unlike the living one. In the ground or fed to the birds, it takes some time to become truly something else. But within the span of a day, fire renders it into dry, brittle, chalky white – or darkened by smoke – fragmented, disorderly remains. In the old days there was still something human about the dead body, even after cremation. A corpse would be placed in full view on a great pile of wood; more fuel might be added over the day and part of the night it would take to finish the process. Even the most thorough old-school funeral pyre would leave some semblance of a body behind: the more or less intact large bones of the leg and upper arm; recognizable bits of skull and rib. This is how we recognize cremation in archaeological sites.

But all this changed in the late nineteenth century, when the reverberatory furnace was adapted from the production of steel to the burning of the dead. Fuel and the material being processed – i.e., bodies – were now kept scrupulously apart, hidden from view, in an enclosed chamber where hot gases were allowed to circulate. This constituted a break in the history of human ashes. The brilliant Austrian jurist Daniel Paul Schreber, whose paranoid schizophrenia had so engaged Sigmund Freud, got this right: "In special crematoria, by means of excessive heat, cutting off atmospheric aid, etc., total destruction is methodologically aimed at and probably achieved." "Nothing," he writes, "remains of the human being after death but a small heap of ashes."[1] This was to him unprecedented.

All of the physical properties of bodies – their many variations of color, size, shape, hardness and softness – are gone, leaving only tiny cinders: more or less coarse; somewhere in color between light and dark gray. Most of the body – 95-98%, all the moisture of the flesh and blood – has escaped into the air; the rest, the basic elements – nitrogen, potassium, calcium, phosphorus, chlorine, with traces of others – fit into a box the size of a fat novel. A cremated dog or sheep would yield less, a cow or a horse more; the exact percentage of various elements might vary slightly in their remains. They may be a little brown. The fuel

---

1 Daniel Paul Schreber, *Memoirs of My Nervous Illness*, trans. Ida Macalpine, Richard A. Hunter (New York: New York Review of Books, 2000), p. 297.

used makes some difference. But basically all ashes are the same. And this is why it is so remarkable that we can make so much of them; so much from so little. We can conjure the dead from the merest matter whose relationship to the living body – to any living body – is vouchsafed, at best, by its provenance. Nothing inherent in the ash identifies it as belonging to a human, but less to the remains of a specific human being. We are here at the limit of representation.

And yet, in various arenas intimate and public, we make a great deal of these infinitely inconsequential ashes. As I was writing my book *The Work of the Dead*, I heard many stories.[2] One woman told me that she had divorced her former husband in large part because he was more interested in sex with himself than with her. Many years later, she was with him when he died; she recovered his ashes and has put the urn next to a jar of Vaseline in her bathroom. Another told me that her grandmother's ashes colored the ink with which she was tattooed. The family of a professional photographer put his ashes into 35mm film cartridges and buried these in the various places all over the world where he had worked.

I can contribute also a brief, anthropological account of what happened to the remains of an old man, a hunting buddy of one of my childhood friends in rural Appalachia and a lifelong Christian. He died at the age of eighty and had a traditional open-casket funeral at the Jordan Methodist Church in Pulaski, Virginia. His body was there for all to see. Then he was cremated, and his ashes were dispersed among friends and relatives. Some went to his fellow deer hunters, one of whom is my friend. They took their share and headed for the cabin Ed had owned along Little Walker Creek and apportioned it as follows: some was loaded into cartridges and shot into the air using the musket loaders that Ed had made; some was scattered on the deer lick to be ingested by the game which in future seasons they would kill and eat; and some was scattered around the rock where it had been their custom to pee together. These rituals – leaving out what his wife and sons did with their shares – takes syncretism to new levels and makes one despair of a coherent hermeneutics of practice.

Ashes are recuperative in public spaces: "Here, in an urn, bits of earth mixed with ashes brought back from Auschwitz perpetuate the memory of martyrs," reads the epitaph on a memorial at Père-Lachaise Cemetery in Paris, near the Mur des Fédérés, which commemorates the dead of the 1870-71 Commune. "Under this stone [is] a bit of ash [from the] seven thousand French martyrs murdered by the Nazis at [the] Neuengamme [Concentration] Camp – they died for us to live free – their families and comrades," says another monument built by survivors in 1949. Ashes retrieved from Poland and Germany to France bring back the dead. So does the work of Heide Hatry who incorporates the ashes of individuals in postmortem portraiture: auto icons both painfully immediate and hopelessly distant from a living human being. In this tension is their poignancy.

---

2 Thomas W. Laqueur, *The Work of the Dead: A Cultural History of Mortal Remains* (Princeton, NJ: Princeton University Press, 2015).

How is all this conjuring with ashes possible? In some way this question represents only a special case of an equally mysterious, more general version: why do we – we humans – give the inert material remains of the dead so much attention? Why does this matter so much? These remains are perhaps a few steps closer to individual lives than grains of common elements that high temperatures have fused together, but they are still on one side of an uncrossable chasm that separates them from warm flesh and blood. I have no real answer to either the specific or the more general question but will retell a story that I tell in my book and that represents the best answer I can offer.

More than a decade after we mixed my father's ashes – he was the first of my lineage to be cremated – with the clay soil of Virginia, I was invited to lecture in Germany. My wife suggested that I take some of his ashes with me and mix them with the soil on the grave of his father, my grandfather, in Hamburg's spectacular Ohlsdorf Cemetery. He had died in 1927, a decorated veteran of the Great War and a passionate, deeply conservative German patriot despite his pained awareness of the rise of anti-Semitism in the last years of his life. I had never been to his grave, but knew what it looked like because my grandmother who had barely managed to escape Hitler – she left in December 1939 – had a picture of it on her desk all through my childhood.

I replied to my wife's suggestion that, as she well knew, I had no ashes; they were by now leached away by the snows of winter and rains of summer; there were not a lot of them to begin with – less than the contents of a five pound fertilizer bag – and these had been spread more than a decade earlier over a sizable flower bed. Nothing of him could possibly be left. After some discussion, I finally decided to take a small bag of dirt in which there might have been a homeopathically small number of inorganic molecules that had once been in my father and to mix these with the soil of his father's grave. This gesture of repatriation would have been regarded by my father as an act of rank superstition.

And so, I suppose, it was. If there were any molecules that had been part of my father's body in the bag of dirt, they were indistinguishable from the soil amendments I had added to the garden: mostly calcium, sodium and potassium salts – sulfates and phosphates and carbonates, plus some trace elements of this and that. But it did seem right that some of him – however attenuated and basely material – should be back where he had once felt both comfortable and troubled; and it did make me understand that he was dead. And it united him with the father he had lost when he was seventeen years old, with whom he had been exceptionally close. It seemed a gesture that mirrored my insistence on giving lectures in German in Germany, even to an audience like that at the Kennedy Institute for North American Studies in Berlin, where everyone's academic English is better than my academic German. Like the return of dirt pretending to be ashes pretending to be a body pretending to bear some relationship to a person I had loved, there is little that reason has to say about all this. Such is the work of culture.

I number myself among the unenchanted; I take the work of the dead – in this case the work of ashes – to be perhaps the greatest and most mysterious triumph of culture. There is, I am sure, nothing "real" behind it. It has always taken a leap to make something, but not too much, of corpses. (The past must not bury the future.) I believe that the power of the dead has always worked and still does by sleight of hand, but of a profound sort. Magic.

If the things magicians did were in fact "real," they would lose much interest to us moderns. If we watched their shows always thinking of the tricks that were being played on us, they would become empty and cold. Unmasking may have its place, but this is not my purpose. Instead, as the art critic Dave Hickey writes of a show in Las Vegas, we watch elephants disappear without inquiring how this is done, and we listen to a chorus asking that they be made to reappear in the same spirit. We understand that

> the whole tradition of disappearing things and restoring them is located where it should be: in rituals of death and resurrection. [We] simply take pleasure in seeing the impossible appear possible and the invisible made visible. Because if these illusions were not just illusions, we should not be what we are: mortal creatures who miss our dead friends, and thus can appreciate levitating tigers and portraits by Raphael for what they are – songs of mortality sung by the prisoners of time.[3]

---

3 Dave Hickey, *Air Guitar: Essays on Art and Democracy* (Los Angeles: Art Issues Press, 1997), pp. 189-190.

Death Strategies:
Coping with Loss through Ritual and Art
Phoebe Hoban

One might consider that the birth of religion – of all faiths – is humanity's way of dealing with its own mortality, its consciousness of death. (Our knowledge of death gave birth to the concept of an afterlife: perhaps the most famous of all death images is that of Christ on the cross.) While animals are known to mourn their dead, we have no way of knowing if they understand, as we do, from early on, that the days of the living are numbered. The human species alone is cursed or blessed with this special, as it were fatal, information. And an argument could well be made that most – if not all art – is, at its core, an instinctive effort to defy death by creating something immortal that endures beyond the life of its maker.

The impulse to express something of oneself that remains after death is an innate impulse of the living; perhaps the most positive aspect of the complex human conundrum of dealing daily with mortality. Quite literally, the most primal form of creation – procreation itself – in addition to its evolutionary necessity of propagating the species, is emotionally and psychologically spurred by the desire to leave a legacy. Just as fundamental as such life-affirming responses to death are the flip side, the grieving and mourning that form an inextricable part of life's cycle. Thus, the living have devised intricate strategies to cope not only with the knowledge of their own inevitable demise but with the loss of those they love.

From the earliest days of recorded time, humans have memorialized their dead. Through elaborate funeral rites that celebrate the life of the departed or vanquish evil spirits, or through symbolic relics, like locks of hair or funerary urns, people have invented unique ways to deal with death's profound enigma. These range from the bizarre to the beautiful, from quickly disposing of the corpse to posthumously wining and dining it, and many of them are still in practice.

In Tibet, for instance, the rocky terrain itself has made burial difficult if not impossible, giving rise to the tradition of "sky burials." These burials involve cutting up the corpse (or sometimes leaving it intact) so animals and birds of prey can devour the remains. Some cultures have gone much further, eating their own corpses, a practice known as endocannibalism; or, like the Yanomami tribes of South America (in Venezuela and Brazil), ingesting their ashes and ground bones, sometimes mixed into plantain soup.

Anthropologists puzzled by the fossilized human remains found in feces in the ancient Anasazi ruins in New Mexico attributed it to enemy factions eating each other's dead. But it is just as possible that the Anasazi, whose culture had complex religious rituals, might well have been eating their own dead, like the Fore people in Papua, New Guinea. In some cultures, this was thought to be a way of ingesting the wisdom, bravery, or other good attributes of the deceased.

The incomprehensible pain of death engenders many strange rites. The Dani tribe, in Papua, New Guinea, for years practiced a well-documented custom of amputating their own fingers, a metaphor for the injury of losing a relative to death, thus combining physical pain with emotional pain. The amputated fingers themselves became part of the ritual; they were burned or stored in a sacred place.

There is a similar practice among the Mafulu Mountain People of British New Guinea and the natives of the Fiji Islands. "When the little finger is cut off, the fourth finger is said to cry itself hoarse in vain for its absent mate," writes Effie Bendann in her classic 1930s book, *Death Customs: An Analytical Study of Burial Rites.*[1]

She goes on to recount that when a King of Tonga died, it was customary to amputate one hundred fingers. Meanwhile in Australia, she reports, laceration of all types is a widespread custom. In Victoria, Australia, a widow burns her breasts, arms, legs and thighs until exhaustion, takes the ashes of her husband and rubs them into her wounds, and scratches her own face until she draws blood. The Kurnai of South East Victoria cut themselves with stones and tomahawks, in view of the deceased one's relatives. The women of the Alatunja of the Alice Springs Group use sharp yam skins to cut themselves during the death ritual, while the men use stone knives.

While so-called civilized communities don't engage in self-mutilation, the well-known Jewish tradition of Kriah, which calls for rending one's clothes upon learning of a death, may fulfill a similar function, by enabling the survivor to physically express great anguish or rage. It has been hypothesized that Kriah originally evolved from the pagan custom of tearing one's own flesh or hair. It fulfills the survivors' need to express deep grief, sometimes in a violent manner. "Although our culture gives no symbolic expression to anger, a considerable number of others have done so," writes Geoffrey Gorer in *Death, Grief and Mourning In Contemporary Britain.*[2]

Sex and death (Eros and Thanatos) have always been entwined (consider the French term for orgasm: *le petite mort*) and have been psychoanalytically linked by Sigmund Freud as

---

1 Effie Bendann, *Death Customs: An Analytical Study of Burial Rites* (New York: Kessinger, 2003), pp. 95-96.
2 Rabbi Maurice Lamm, quoting Geoffrey Gorer, "Keriah: the Rending of Garments," http://www.chabad.org/library/article_cdo/aid/281558/jewish/Keriah-The-Rending-of-Garments.htm. Keriah is also called Kriah. See: Geoffrey Gorer, *Death, Grief and Mourning in Contemporary Britain* (New York: Anchor Books, Doubleday, 1967).

opposing drives. Viking burials apparently enacted this somewhat literally, with forced sex followed by human sacrifice. According to some accounts, when a Viking chieftain died, he was buried for ten days while new clothes were tailored for him. Meanwhile, one of his slave girls was chosen to join him in the afterlife. After being forced-fed alcohol to the point of anesthesia, she was required to have sex with the village men, culminating in the act with another chosen six before she was ritually strangled, then stabbed by the village matriarch. In order to continue to serve her master in the afterlife, her body was put alongside that of the chieftain's on a wooden platform, or in some cases a wooden ship.

After cremation, Vikings commonly buried their deceased in the ground, under a mound called a tumuli, evidence of which can be seen in Scandinavian countries from Norway to Sweden and Denmark, including the extraordinary Borre mound cemetery in Norway, which contains seven large mounds beneath which are graves, some of them fashioned like ships, equipped for the afterlife with weapons, goods and crafts, and many containing the remnants of animals – and in some cases human sacrificial remains. So-called "stone ships" (stones arranged in the form of a boat) were often used to mark the graves, as they are at Jelling, in Denmark.

On the Eros side of Thanatos, are the funeral-strippers, brought in to vanquish wandering spirits and to give the dead a proper send-off, but also, in modern-day Taiwan and China, to help draw a crowd to the funeral service, a mark of social status. Their use has become so common (and so publicized on social media and YouTube) that the Chinese government has recently cracked down on it.

Funerary pole-dancing might seem extreme, but perhaps not as extreme as dancing with the corpse itself. There are several cultures – like the Malagasy of Madagascar – where it is common to ceremonially exhume the corpse every few years, and dance with it, or include it in family gatherings. In Tana Toraja, Eastern Indonesia, the burial ceremony includes music, dance and a feast, and water buffalo are slaughtered to carry away the soul of the deceased. But the body of the deceased may be kept in the survivors' home for years, treated like a convalescent, and even fed. Paul Koudounaris, author of the book *Memento Mori*, was told by a Torajan guide that as a child he and his brothers slept next to their grandfather's mummy, which every morning would be taken out of bed and dressed before being put back to bed at night, "because they loved him." In Bolivia *ñatitas*, (or "little pug-nosed ones") are kept in shrines in the home, and honored as family members.[3]

Bodily material, such as hair or bones, whether that of the deceased or the survivors, has always played a part in death rituals. Some ceremonies require widows and children to shave their heads. From early on, saving a lock of the deceased's hair was a way of preserving their memory. Widows in the Kaitish tribe in Central Australia believe that unless they

---

3 Paul Koudounaris, *Memento Mori: The Dead Among Us* (New York: Thames & Hudson, Inc., 2015), pp. 18-19.

cover themselves with campfire ashes during the entire funeral ceremony, the spirit of their husband will tear the flesh from their bones, while the women of Koombokkaburra cover their heads with clay and ashes and the men blacken their bodies with burnt bark and grasses. Averting their gaze from the deceased's face, the Reindeer Koryak wipe it with wet moss.

Interestingly, some rituals require distancing oneself from the corpse – and even its kin – due to the contagion of death, while others require intimate acts. In Mumbai, India, the Zoroastrians bathe the corpse in bull's urine, lay it out in linen, bring in a dog to cast away evil spirits, and then place it in a "Tower of Silence" where it is eaten by vultures. But some cultures insist on close communion with the dead. In South Australia's Encounter Bay, for instance, one of the nearest relatives must sleep on the head of the corpse.

The use of bones to commemorate death reached an apotheosis among the early Christians, who built charnel houses and catacombs to store skeletal remains, such as the famous catacombs in Paris, Rome, Palermo, and Venice. Sometimes the skulls or skeletons were used as architectural elements in chapels and churches. One such ornate "ossuary" is located in Sedlec, Czech Republic. First contained in a small chapel, it was renovated in the 1860 by Rint, who was hired by the nobleman Karl Joseph Adolph von Schwarzenberg. Skulls and bones were used to festoon the space, arranged, say, in the shape of garlands. Churchware, such as chalices, were also fashioned from bones; and, most conspicuously, an elaborate ossified chandelier, plus a bony replica of the Schwarzenberg coat of arms. The San Bernardino Alle Ossa cathedral in Milan, Italy, built in the sixteenth century, and reconstructed in the 1750s, contains thousands of skulls used as large parts of interior arches and vaults, vying for attention with the painted mural in the church ceiling.

Sometimes the entire skeleton became part of the structure, as in Campo Maior, Portugal, which has three skeletons of victims of a fire built into its walls. A less decorative use of bones are the hundreds of martyrs' skulls lining the wall of the ancient cathedral in Otranto, Italy, remains of a long-ago Turkish invasion and a *memento mori* within the Cathedral, which is used to this day for weddings.

Skulls could also serve as talismans. In a bone room in Oppenheim, Germany, it is the custom for visitors to rub their foreheads against that of a skull. This practice has taken its toll; many of the skulls bear a worn patch in the center of their foreheads.

The Torajan culture, based on the Indonesian island of Sulawesi, in addition to keeping mummies at home, is also known for its burial caves, where bones that remain when the wooden coffin has decayed are arranged as a public display within the burial cave, which is also adorned with carved wooden dolls or effigies known as "tau tau." In the Philippines, in addition to "hanging coffins," which were placed high up in the cliffs, there are also burial caves, including the enormous collection of skulls in the Opdas Cave, which contains hundreds of skulls methodically arranged on stone ledges.

In some locations, mummies, rather than bones, were put on display in churches and catacombs, as in the church in Rome known as Santa Maria della Concezione. In Palermo, the Capuchin monks originally interred their mummies in crypts beneath the church, displaying them in niches, a practice that became popular among secular people and a good source of income for the monks, who even built galleries to exhibit the mummies. The Palermo Catacombs contain 3,000 mummies. The practice became common throughout Sicily.

Even more extreme is the living mummification once practiced in Asia. There, monks practiced a ritual called Sokushinbutsu, which involved fasting over a period of one thousand days, drinking a poisonous tea potion for another thousand and then spending one thousand days in a locked tomb. The ultimately mummified monk was considered sacred, and some were even coated in gold, and served as holy statuary – a sort of whole-body death mask. Eventually this ancient practice was banned. (A modern-day venerated mummified monk is Luang Pho Daeng, who sports a pair of glitzy sunglasses. Prior to his death in 1973, he requested that his mummy be displayed, and it has become a popular tourist attraction at the Khunaram temple on Thailand's Koh Samui island.)

The Bolivian culture regularly – and joyfully – consorts with the dead through their ongoing relationship with *ñatitas*. It is quite common to keep a *ñatita* in the home, where, as Paul Koudounaris writes in *Memento Mori*, it serves as a guardian, spiritual guide, shaman and good-luck talisman. According to Koudounaris, the Bolivians perceive death as just another stage of life, and therefore continue to view the deceased as a valued family member.

The *ñatitas* might have individual specialties that attract visitors – such as expertise in medicine. Indeed, one home boasts not the typical single *ñatita*, but fifty-four of the little pug-nosed ones. And a police precinct in El Alto, Bolivia, the FELCC (special anti-crime force), has a famous pair of *ñatitas* ensconced in its homicide division: Juanito and Juanita, garbed in caps and sunglasses. These skulls are given questions on slips of paper, rewarded with offerings like candy and cigarettes, and credited with serving as psychic mediums who have successfully solved numerous cases.

Ñatitas even have their own day of celebration, November 8, the Fiesta de Las Ñatitas, when they are taken en masse to local cemeteries. They are dressed up for the occasion in hats or flowers, wearing sunglasses, or even given a cigarette, the ashes of which are used to predict the future. Cotton balls are often placed in their eyes, and their mouths might be re-shaped with wax or foil. After being brought into the chapel to hear a mass, the *ñatitas* are placed on temporary outdoor altars, where they are given offerings of thanks for their faithful vigilance over the living. This festival is not designed to mark death; rather it celebrates the unique and lasting bond between the living and the dead.

A less anthropomorphized use of skulls as commemorative objects are the decorated skulls in Austria and Switzerland. These are individually painted, often with the name of the deceased labeled on the forehead. In Asia, skulls are turned into sacred objects by coating them with gold leaf, and even studding them with rare jewels. In Tibet, skulls called *kapala* are heavily ornamented with gems. With their hinged, silver-lined crania, they are used as ritual vessels to drink wine or store cakes that are used to transfer the attributes of the deceased to the living.

For sheer magnificence, the gem-covered skeletons of early sixteenth- to eighteenth-century Christian martyrs of the Roman catacombs are non-pareil. They were painstakingly created by skilled nuns, and often shipped to Germany, Austria and Switzerland. Clothed in jewel-encrusted armor, with eyes made up, say, of pearls and sapphires, their elaborately jeweled garments and headgear rival those of royalty.

*

The leap from gilded mummies and jeweled skeletons to sacred skulls and death masks is not a great stretch, really more a matter of degree (and, of course, culture). Death masks date back at least to ancient Rome, where a wax mask, made from the deceased's face was ritually worn by someone in the funeral procession. They were especially popular in the nineteenth century, for everyone from noblemen to bandits. Jesse James and Billy the Kid's faces were immortalized in plaster, but then so was the visage of Emperor Napoleon Bonaparte, made shortly after his death on St. Helena in 1821, and auctioned for about $350,000 in 2013. In fact, there were several versions of Napoleon's death mask: one in bronze; and one on painted plaster. One even resides at Boston University's Mugar Memorial Library. One purpose of the death mask was to preserve the faces of the royal or venerated dead when they lay in state, to enable long-distance travelers to view them. Without the mask, the real face, even embalmed, could not be viewed because of decomposition.

Death masks were not only for the rich or famous; the masks were a common method of preserving the faces of unidentified corpses, perhaps destined for Potter's Field. Indeed, photographs of the gently smiling death mask of the anonymous *Unknown Woman of the Seine*, made around 1900 in Paris, are frequently reproduced; and her face has inspired several artists, including Man Ray.

One of the best-known experts in the creation of death masks was Madame Tussaud, who started her career making masks of victims of the French Revolution. In fact, she was called upon to make a plaster cast of both Marat, murdered in 1793, and of Robespierre, executed in 1794. (She is supposed to have stationed herself next to the guillotine to make a cast of his decapitated head.)

A sampling of famous death masks includes, in no particular order: Mary Queen of Scots; John Keats; William Blake; Ludwig van Beethoven; Benjamin Franklin; John Dillinger;

Oliver Cromwell; Vladimir Lenin; Robert E. Lee; Ulysses S. Grant; James Dean; Isaac Newton; Frederick the Great; and Theodore Roosevelt. In 2002, the Musée d'Orsay, in Paris, exhibited a show called "The Last Portrait," which ranged from death masks (including some of the above) to paintings by such famous artists as Tintoretto, Monet, Ensor, Munch and Hodler, to photographs, including one of Marcel Proust on his deathbed, taken by Man Ray, plus deathbed photographs of songstress Edith Piaf and the recently sainted Mother Theresa.

Preserving the face of the dead is a venerable and ancient art. Fayum mummy portraits date back to ancient Egypt, from the Roman period, starting after Cleopatra's death in 30 BCE and peaking in the period of 138-192 CE. These beautiful, flat, but realistic images, painted in tempera or encaustic on thin wooden panels, were placed on the linen death shrouds, with the portrait covering the mummy's face. Many such portraits were found in a region called the Fayum Oasis, about sixty-five miles from Cairo. Designed to accompany the dead into the afterlife, they are considered among the world's oldest portraits. Yet they remain somehow eternally fresh. As John Berger wrote in an essay in his book, *Portraits*, which has a mummy portrait on its cover, "The Fayum portraits touch us, as if they had been painted last month."[4] Sigmund Freud found them especially compelling: excellent examples could be found in his Vienna study among his famous collection of ancient artifacts.

One could almost think of them as Egyptian instagrams destined for eternity. It is hypothesized that the portraits were either done from life – or shortly before or after death – and often used after the subject's death to identify remains after burial. Indeed, Holland Cotter, reviewing a show of Fayum mummy portraits, "Ancient Faces," at the Metropolitan Museum of Art in February, 2000, wrote, "The faces certainly seem familiar. The prettiest girl from high school is here and that smug 10-to-6-er she married . . . . Didn't you see that elderly gent in the subway and brush past that unisex youth in the street?"[5]

As the Metropolitan's exhibition notes observe, "In their artistic style and technique, the portraits on wood panels followed the Greek painting tradition of depicting the subject in three-quarter view, with a single light source casting realistic shadows and highlights on the face."[6] The portraits, especially those painted with encaustic allowed for a certain degree of brush strokes and impasto. They might also incorporate thin gold-leaf for the background, or to depict ornamentation. Some mummy portraits were three dimensional – with slightly molded faces made of clay or plaster. And, in other instances, the linen shrouds that wrapped the mummy were painted with a full-length portrait.

---

4 John Berger, "The Fayum Painters," *Portraits: John Berger on Artists* (New York: Verso, 2015), p. 7.

5 Holland Cotter, "Expressions So Ancient, Yet Familiar," *The New York Times* (February 18, 2000), http://www.nytimes.com/2000/02/18/arts/art-review-expressions-so-ancient-yet-familiar.html.

6 "Ancient Faces: Mummy Portraits from Roman Egypt," The Metropolitan Museum of Art (February 8, 2000), http://www.metmuseum.org/press/exhibitions/2000/ancient-faces-mummy-portraits-from-roman-egypt.

The mummy portraits were created in keeping with ancient Egyptian beliefs about the afterlife. But throughout time, artists (even those totally devoid of a religious context) have been moved to paint the beloved dead. During the seventeenth century in the Netherlands, the deathbed portrait was popular among the bourgeoisie, who could afford this last souvenir of the dearly departed.

Then there were those artists who felt compelled to capture the final repose of their beloved. Take Claude Monet's famous portrait of his dead young wife, Camille (*Camille on Her Deathbed*, 1879, also known as *Madame Monet on Her Deathbed*), portrayed Ophelia-like in a wedding veil, with a garland of flowers. The artist wrote in his journal that as she lay dying he couldn't stop painting her face. Tintoretto similarly painted his dead young daughter. And Ferdinand Hodler chronicled the terminal illness of his partner, Valentine Godé-Darel, culminating in a haunting deathbed painting.

With the invention of photography in 1827, the death portrait took on a stunning new dimension, which reached its apogee during the Victorian age, where postmortem photographs were both hugely popular and a conventional part of a family's grieving process. These weren't simply small images worn in lockets (although those were also common). These were group portraits of the living family with their dead loved one, posed as if still alive. To this day it is possible to peruse thousands of sepia images of dead babies sleeping in their mother's arms, dead wives stiffly propped on settees, whole families arranged around a dead father in his favorite armchair with his dogs. Often this last photograph, not an inexpensive prospect, was the first the family had ever commissioned, a testament to its importance in their efforts to deal with their loss.

The photographers found various means of propping up the corpses, sometimes using another family member, as in the case of three brothers, the two living brothers propping their dead sibling between them on a sofa, or surrounding a young girl with her dolls, or even using a stick to support the back of a man's standing corpse. To today's sensibility, these images might appear somewhat morbid; but at the time they were taken, they were a source of comfort and pride to the surviving family members.

*

The popular tradition of honoring the dead by saving ashes in funerary urns is as old as recorded time. And the ritual sprinkling of the ashes, often at sea or at a favorite haunt of the deceased, is also a common – and timeless – funerary rite. In the past few years, a small cottage industry has also arisen around incorporating the ashes into objects – either the funerary urn itself, or other items, such as a picture frame, or even a knife blade. Theodore Nazz, a New York based bladesmith, blended the ashes of his childhood friend into Damascus steel, to create rings for his friend's mother and father. He also carburized three kitchen knives with his grandparents' ashes and gave them to his aunt, uncle and mother. They are now in daily use. "My aunt proudly told me, 'I regularly cook with my father,'" he remarked.[7] (When he went online to post his intention to mix his friend's ashes with Damascus steel, he was instantly answered by "Steve," who recounted that when his father died, he was offered a silver picture frame made from his ashes, but had allowed this memorial artifact to pass on to his mother and sister.)

Maria Munroe, a Los Angeles based artist, has been using ashes to create crematory sculptures and urns for decades. She uses a variety of materials, including silver, lead crystal and ceramic, to produce vessels – so-called "Eturns" – that contain the cremains, and ashes may also be mixed directly into the material. One example is a star-shaped silver sculpture that holds the ashes of Jeffrey Blumberg, in the silver trade, who died in 1996. She also incorporates ashes into crystal orbs and meditation beads. And in Korea, there is a current-day rage for condensing cremation ashes into beads, often turquoise, which are worn by the survivors. Indeed, the one percent have taken it a step further, encapsulating ashes into diamonds and other rare stones.

There is an ever-increasing myriad of choices for commemorating cremains. Since 1997, a company called Celestis, based in Houston, Texas, has offered a service which launches cremains into space – either into Earth's orbit, on the lunar surface or into deep space. Their first such launch sprinkled counter-culture pioneer Timothy Leary's ashes into the cosmos. They run about two private space launches a year.

For those who prefer water to air as a burial site, Eternal Reefs in Sarasota, Florida, creates "green burials" using a combination of a funerary urn, the loved one's ashes and sustainable artificial reefs in the form of igloo-like concrete structures (or "Reef Balls") that serve as marine-life habitats. Or, as the company puts it, "living environmental memorials." Using cremated ashes as fertilizer for plants or a garden is an organic way to deposit the ashes and simultaneously contribute to the growth of a tree, flower, or entire garden. But caution must be taken; unadulterated cremains have a high pH and sodium level that can actually harm plant life, so the ashes must be mixed with either a specialized product, or good-quality potting soil before use.

Perhaps the most intimate commemorative act using ashes is to have them mixed into tattoo ink and imprinted on your skin. While the jury is still out on medical concerns that have been raised regarding this process, it has nonetheless become a popular trend in the tattoo industry – whether it is tattooing a name, a meaningful quote, or even the deceased's image.

Heide Hatry's art marks an inventive step in the millennia-long evolution of death rituals and portraiture, and eloquently merges both the ritual aspect, the preserving of ashes, with the artistically commemorative convention – memorializing the deceased with a death

---

7 Phone interview with Theodore Nazz, September 20, 2016.

mask or portrait. Originally created out of her own anguish at the early death of her father and the suicide of a friend, she realized that creating images of them out of their own ashes not only honored their memory but also provided her with a deep sense of personal consolation and closure.

The process of creating the portrait itself is quite subtle. Hatry, who has formerly worked with animal organs to create gorgeous flora out of offal, takes loose ash and embeds it into warm beeswax. The ash is not wholly absorbed by the wax, but remains granular. She then uses a custom-made mechanism to delicately place a mosaic-like image onto the warm layer of wax. This results in a kind of alchemy: Not only does she produce a recognizable likeness of the dead; it is, as it were, not flesh of their own flesh, but ashes of their own ashes. As Lucian Freud once remarked, "I want paint to work as flesh… I would wish my portraits to be *of* the people, not like them. Not having a look of the sitter, *being* them."[8] Hatry has made ashes, not paint, work as flesh. After all, ashes – or dust – is what all flesh eventually becomes.

In her creative leap, which originated in a spontaneous impulse to comfort herself and cope with her grief, Hatry has made a significant contribution to the way in which we, the living, honor our dead. As my father, the late writer Russell Hoban, once wrote,

> Reality is ungraspable. For convenience we use a limited-reality consensus in which work can be done, transport arranged, and essential services provided. The *real* reality is something else – only the strangeness of it can be taken in and that's what interests me: the strangeness of human consciousness; the strangeness of life and death; the strangeness of what the living and the dead are to one another.[9]

People die, but our relationships to them live on. Hatry has found a unique way for the living to commune with the dead; and in so doing has affirmed a fundamental aspect of humanity.

---

8 Phoebe Hoban, *Lucian Freud: Eyes Wide Open*, Icons Series (New York; Boston: New Harvest; Houghton Mifflin Harcourt, 2014), p. 38. Freud made this remark to Lawrence Gowing who wrote the first monograph on him; Lawrence Gowing, *Lucian Freud* (London: Thames & Hudson, Inc., 1982).
9 Russell Hoban, "Foreword," *The Moment Under the Moment* (London: Jonathan Cape, 1992).

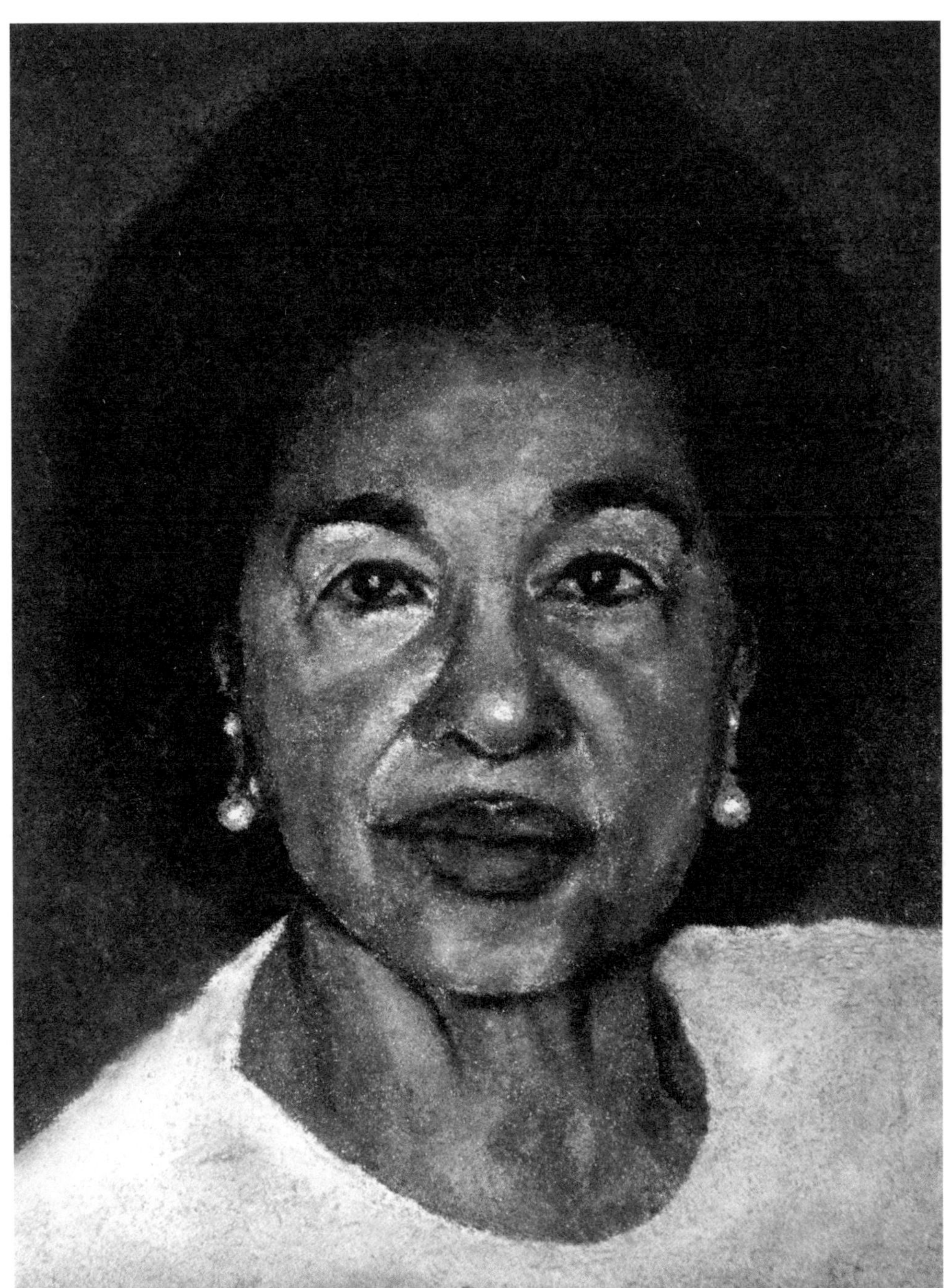

Mind and Body, Form and Essence, the Unbearable and the Inconceivable

Steven Pinker

The death of a loved one is not just a tragedy but also a mystery. When we interact with people, we don't treat them as what science tells us they really are, namely as stupendously complex networks of neurons firing in patterns. We treat them as *minds,* as loci of beliefs and desires – colorless, odorless, immaterial, silent abstractions. Cognitive scientists call this feature of our psychology "mentalizing," "mind-reading," and "theory of mind" (the intuitive theory of the beholder, not the formal theory of the psychologist). We are all intuitive dualists. Not even the most reductionist, materialist biologist can avoid thinking of another person as a spirit or soul rather than as an incarnated neural network.

Together with the invisibility of patterns of neural firing, people have always had plenty of evidence that souls can part company with the body. During a dream, a delirium, or a trance, it appears that some part of us has slipped the surly bonds of the body, which remains anchored to the bed while we walk or hover over the Earth. A reflection in a mirror or still water, or a shadow that follows us, preserves the form and motion of the body while being made of nothing. And in death, the body seems to have been stripped of some force or power that animated it moments before.

No wonder that a belief in the soul or spirit – a ghost in the machine – is ubiquitous across religions and cultures, or that it emerges, untaught, in young children. Indeed, until modern science explained shadows and reflections and dreams, the soul hypothesis was a perfectly reasonable theory. Brilliant nineteenth-century scientists such as Alfred Russel Wallace, the co-discoverer with Charles Darwin of the theory of natural selection, and my hero William James, the founder of cognitive and evolutionary psychology, were confirmed spiritualists.

Of all the data that support the soul theory, death is surely the most compelling. Notwithstanding the carnival tricks of séance charlatans, we know that death is final: Aunt Mabel's spirit does not go to some other place where she can tell us the floorboard under which she hid her jewels. Yet even the hardest headed scientists, knowing full well that a brain has surrendered to entropy and ceased its patterned firing, cannot truly wrap their minds around the fact that a person or a mind has ceased to exist. How is this possible, we ask ourselves? Machines break, cars rust, wood rots, bodies decompose. Yet how could an ethereal web of thoughts and feelings suffer this ignominious fate? How can the entire world that is a person somehow just no longer be? It's a small step from a belief in an immaterial soul to a belief in an immortal soul – and that's even if you put aside the socially convenient corollary that people might be liable to reward and punishment in an afterlife for the sins and good deeds that escaped notice or were excused when they were alive.

How do we deal with the thought – not just unbearable but inconceivable – that someone we love no longer exists? We can no longer have all of them, body and soul, but we struggle to keep some part of them in perpetuity. In some cultures they pickle or mummify the corpse, like Lenin or King Tut, or an organ or two displayed as a relic, like the heart of Brother André, which greets the visitors to St. Joseph's Oratory not far from where I grew up in Montreal. Yet for most of us, preserving the cadaver of a loved one crosses a line into the macabre, to non-sexual necrophilia. And a body, no matter how ingeniously embalmed, inevitably falls into the uncanny valley between the living person we knew and an unrecognizable corpse.

More commonly we are guided by the primitive intuitions that underlie sympathetic magic or voodoo. We are formalists, and believe that the soul may be captured in a likeness or effigy that preserves its form despite being made of a different material. At the same time we are essentialists, and believe that the soul may be captured in a portion of the stuff of the body, in some invisible ingredient that preserves its essence after the form has been disaggregated, disabled, dismantled – for example, a lock of hair, or perhaps a razor or hairbrush or sweater with specks of the person still affixed. Often we succumb to the intuition of transmission by contact, and preserve an article of clothing, or a pair of eyeglasses, or a favorite object.

In Heide Hatry's *Icons in Ash*, ineluctably, these paradoxes come together in a new artistic medium, filled with fascination and pathos. Each work is a likeness of a person made from a part of them, a union that conserves both their form and essence. It reaches to the deepest and most superficial, the most primitive and most sophisticated, ways in which we relate to that ultimate mystery – another person.

An Artist's Reply to Evolution's Impersonal Cynicism
Wolf Singer

It is commonly held that the mechanisms governing biological evolution, the generation of diversity and the selection of the fittest, led to the emergence of species that are well adapted to the biotope in which they evolved. The fitness criterion is reproductive fitness. The organisms need to survive until they have produced offspring carrying their genes. In order to assure this transmission of genes – the only immortal component of multi-cellular organisms – a number of requirements need to be fulfilled. Above all, organisms have to be able to survive in an uncertain and dangerous environment, they have to feed and respond adequately to challenges in order to maintain their structural and functional integrity. In case of sexual reproduction, they need, in addition, to identify possible mating partners, select the fittest, engage in mating, and, depending on the species, invest some time in the nurturing of the offspring. These are the functions that have been optimized by biological evolution. Longevity beyond the end of the reproductive period has not been a prime target for selection. On the contrary, organisms no longer contributing to reproduction become competitors for common resources and hence a burden. It is only in species endowed with the cognitive ability to learn from others that the cumulative experience of the old, of the silver backs, can be exploited to increase the fitness of the group. Yet, this "cultural" fitness criterion holds only for species with highly evolved cognitive functions living in cooperative groups and obviously has not outweighed the advantages of limiting life span to the reproductive period. As a consequence, genetic programs are installed that terminate the continuous repair processes required for the maintenance of life and finally cause the "suicide" of the organism.

So far so good. One cannot but be humbled by and admire the efficiency of this evolutionary process that has brought forth a mind-boggling diversity of species employing admirably sophisticated strategies for survival and reproduction, most of which are in addition aesthetically appealing to us.

However, there is one issue where evolution has dramatically failed. Because evolutionary mechanisms evaluate only outcomes – that is, cannot anticipate consequences and correct errors only with great delays, in extremis with extinction – mishaps are unavoidable. Unless one adheres to scientifically untenable positions of creationism or creation myth, there is no intentional agent to be blamed. If there were, s/he would have to be accused of cruel cynicism that exceeds what Greek drama writers were able to imagine when interpreting fatal constellations as consequences of fate or intentional acts of rivalling gods.

Here are the ingredients of the fatal plot. To increase the chances for survival, to find the appropriate mating partners and to assure the necessary care for the offspring, certain cognitive functions are advantageous. Coping with the environmental challenges that menace the integrity of organisms requires knowledge about the world. The more an organism knows about the conditions of the embedding environment in which it evolves, and the more it understands the rules that govern processes in this world, the easier it is to generate well-adapted responses to challenges. In order to generate such an internal model of the world relevant signals from the environment have to be captured by specialized sense organs and be subject to cognitive operations that permit recognition of relevant constellations, learning from experience and the formulation of predictions. It is obvious that organisms that excel in these cognitive functions have a competitive advantage, in particular as improving cognitive abilities is fraught with only few if any adverse side effects. Investing in running, climbing, swimming and flying skills, body size, armoured skins, craws, and teeth also enhances fitness, but it comes with the prize of specialization. If conditions change, what has been advantageous may become a problem and evolution is rich with examples where specialization led to extinction. Investing in cognitive abilities circumvents this danger because it increases the ability to adapt to changing conditions. Most likely this is the reason why evolution has brought forth nervous systems of ever increasing complexity and sophistication, a trend that has so far reached its culmination point with homo sapiens. And again, even though we are still far from understanding the precise neuronal mechanisms that are at the root of our cognitive functions, we can only humbly admire the unimaginable complexity of the human brain, the organ that is ultimately responsible for the transition from biological to cultural evolution. This transition has led to the emergence of social realities, a novel class of phenomena that differ ontologically from those characterizing the pre-cultural reality: that is, it has slowly produced our belief systems, moral attributions, artistic activities, metaphysical extrapolations – in brief, phenomena that constitute our mental or spiritual dimension.

The evolutionary optimization of cognitive abilities has apparently led to the emergence of skills that go well beyond the purely utilitarian functions required for reproductive fitness – a luxury that we enjoy when engaging in artistic exploration and diving into the realm of novel realities created by artists. In addition to optimizing cognitive skills, evolution has also selected for internal drives that support survival and successful sexual reproduction. Virtually all organisms are endowed with mechanisms that allow them to distinguish between dangerous and beneficial conditions, and in cognitively evolved organisms these mechanisms generate emotions and drives. Internal evaluation systems attribute emotional connotations to perceived conditions and classify them as aversive, in which case one experiences fear or disgust, or as desirable, in which case there is wanting and satisfaction.

Given the selective pressure for survival and reproduction it is only natural that one, if not the strongest drive is to stay alive, to cling to one's existence, to protect oneself, and to be maximally afraid of life-threatening events. Equally natural, and sometimes as strong, is the drive to reproduce and, in certain species, the desire to bond with the mating partner and the offspring to assure nurturing in a safe environment. This drive for bonding is particularly pronounced in primates, humans included, as the development of babies toward sexual and cognitive maturity is very prolonged in this species, providing unique opportunities for adaptation by learning. Again, one might say that evolution has endowed us with wonderful abilities that are at the root of great joy: *la joie de vivre*, love, sexual ecstasy, bonding, and confidence.

Nonetheless, here comes the tragedy put on stage by the blind mechanisms of evolution, a tragedy that an empathic designer would have avoided by all means. The investment in cognitive functions, the fitness factor devoid of the disadvantages of specialization, led to brains increasingly capable of generating realistic models of the world, to become conscious of their own abilities and to extrapolate from observations on future developments. Great achievements indeed! However, with the appearance of modern men, evolution went one step too far. We seem to be the only organisms capable of developing not only a model of the world but also a self model that allows us to predict our own future and to realize that we are finite, that we have a limited life span, that we are bound to die. And if this were not enough of a burden, we are in addition endowed with the ability to kill ourselves, to commit suicide, which tremendously augments our autonomy but also our fragility. What else than cynicism would one attribute to a designer who endowed creatures with mighty emotions and drives that make them cling to life and attach to the beloved, experience horror of death and deep sorrow about the loss of the dear – and to allow the same creature to realize that death and loss are unavoidable.

As soon as men became aware of their tragic condition they sought for remedies, this conflict between Eros and Thanatos probably being the major drive for creativity, even more so than curiosity and sensation seeking. Accepting death as the endpoint of one's life, of one's unique existence, as the moment of the irreversible farewell to all beloved is definitively the most difficult cognitive exercise. Believing in resurrection, rebirth, or continuation of an immortal soul is certainly the best remedy and the consolation most frequently opted for culturally and personally. Some relief can also be derived from the confidence that those remaining will engage in rituals of mourning and conserve memories, thereby delaying complete extinction. Yet others opt for leaving lasting traces by inscribing their name in halls of fame or by associating their names with "immortal" creative acts. Needless to say, the motivation behind most of what constitutes our culture, the masterpieces of art as well as the realm of ideas and discoveries, is ultimately the hope to leave behind something that is intimately associated with our existence and outlasts our life. This effort to leave traces also contributes to mitigate the moaning of those left behind. It helps to overcome the loss, known to be definitive, if memories are kept alive. Objects dear to the disappeared and above all concrete representations of the defunct get integrated in the daily lives of the survivors: for centuries, paintings, sculptures, and death masks served as permanent reminders. The attempt to preserve the presence of the defunct in the world of the living found its most natural solution in mummification, the most extreme variant being the perfectly conserved, preciously dressed mummies in the Catacombe dei Cappuccini in Palermo. Then photography took over and permitted everyone to generate without great effort quite detailed and realistic pictorial representations. Since then pictures of those who passed away populate countless photo albums, embedded in the accidental context of their daily lives. And more recently, with the advent of movie cameras, movements and voices of the defunct can be archived equally effortlessly and replayed in home cinemas and on smart phones *ad libitum*. And one might argue that this is so far the best way to keep the memory of the dead alive in our memories.

Or is there something missing? Are we satisfied with the seamless embedding of the defunct in a context that is no longer theirs? Are we blurring and playing down the categorical transition from life to death? Are we trying to overcome our fear of death by simply ignoring our finiteness, by avoiding the confrontation with death, by eliminating the experience with death from everyday experience? It does not take much to interpret characteristic features of Western lifestyle in the context of repression: the denial of aging; unbounded consumption; the hiding of death behind the walls of hospitals and retirement homes; and, finally, the abandonment of death cult and moaning rituals.

The very first artistic creations of men were the polished hand axes that were not designed to be functional but to satisfy aesthetic criteria. They served as funerary objects to dignify the defunct. It is in this tradition that I see the ash paintings of Heide Hatry. In establishing new relations between the formerly unrelated – the essence of creation – Hatry found a contemporary formulation of the *memento mori* that has pervaded art since the very beginning of culture. The combination of ash, the ancient symbol of impermanence and mortality, with photography, the most recent technique for the generation of permanent representations, creates a metaphor for the in-between; for the ephemeral presence of the dead in our lives. Creating these ash paintings has the connotation of rituals, like the fabrication of Tibetan sand paintings. It requires meticulous mastering of the material, patience and mindfulness. It renders dignity to those who made the step into the forever unknown. An artist's response to the most difficult challenge imposed on us by evolution.

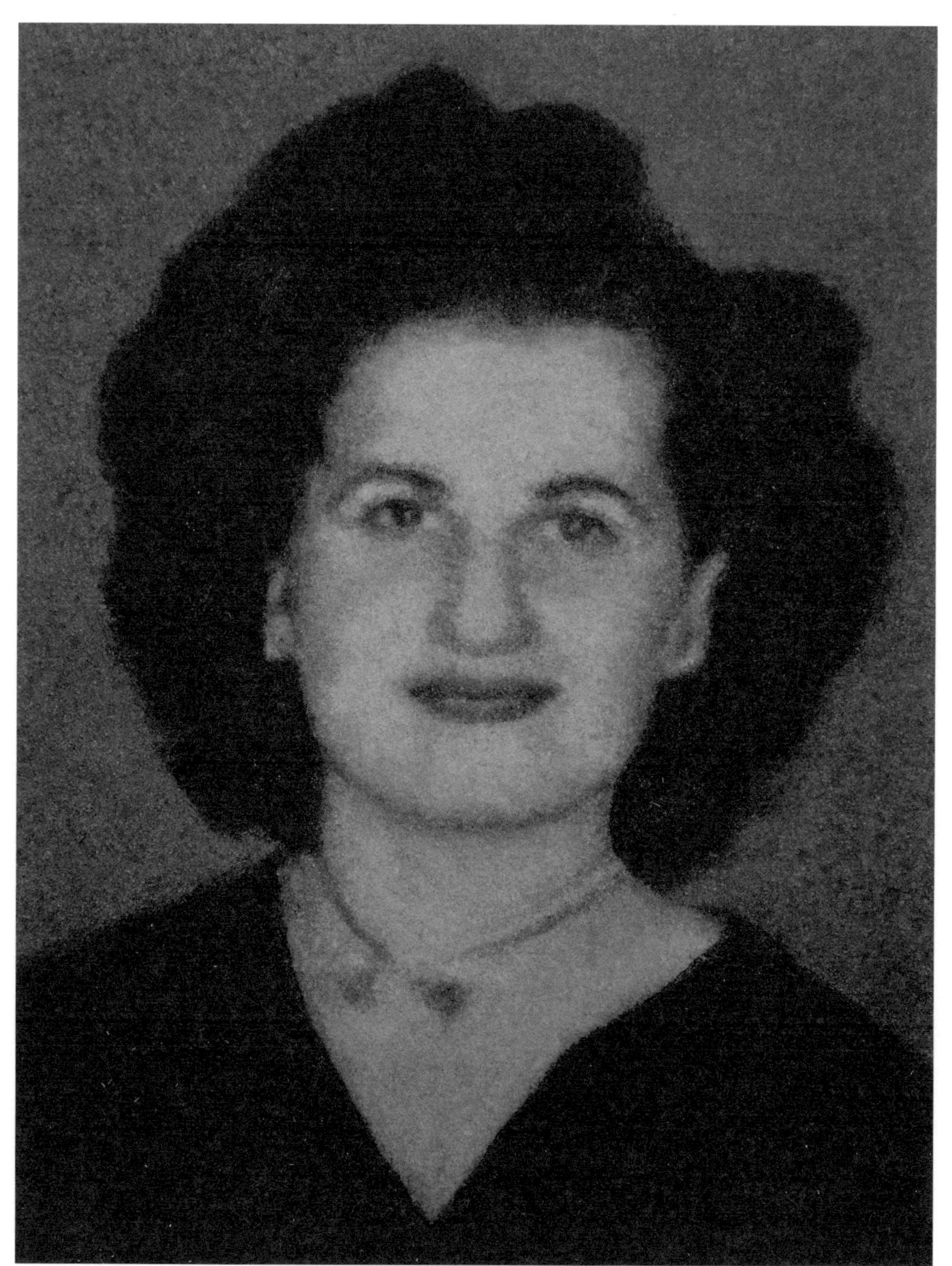

Death and Life

Peter Weibel

> If on opportunist grounds Man now fixes
> the term of his life at three score and ten years,
> he can equally fix it at three hundred, or three thousand…
> – George Bernard Shaw, *Back to Methuselah*, 1920

The greatest puzzle of life is, paradoxically, death – the fact that the improbable gift of life is taken from us again in a monstrous manner. So far there have only been two rational answers to the questions raised by the existence of death, the existence of an end to existence. One of these answers is provided by the theory of evolution, and the other by psychoanalysis.

Freud and the Death Drive

In his 1920 essay *Beyond the Pleasure Principle*, which followed the discovery of the unconscious in 1912, Freud published another core element of his theory: the discovery of the death drive. Prior to this, he had made the dualistic assumption that mental activity is governed by two principles, namely the pleasure principle and the reality principle. But in *Beyond the Pleasure Principle*, he replaced these with a still more fundamental psychological opposition, between the life drives, encompassing sexual and self-preservation drives, and the death drive. While treating neuroses, Freud had noticed the phenomenon of "repetition compulsion," an urge that means we bring back even those past experiences that contain no potential for pleasure. This compulsion forces someone to repeat an experience that brings *unpleasure*. It arises from something repressed in the unconscious, and obviously puts an end to the dominance of the pleasure principle. The repetition compulsion, which recreates unpleasure, overrides the pleasure principle in every way. So, there was something deeper and more powerful than the pleasure principle. Freud began to wonder what that might be and how the drives (sex drives, ego drives, self-preservation drives) were connected with the repetition compulsion. His first answer was that we should see the drives not only as the force urging us toward change and development, but also as its opposite, an expression of the conservative nature of living things. Drives, then, are "an urge inherent in all organic life to restore an earlier state of things" (Freud, *Beyond the Pleasure Principle*). The ultimate aim of all organic life is therefore not an unprecedented state, but an old one, a starting point. Thus Freud reaches the paradoxical-sounding conclusion: "The goal of all life is death" and "the whole life of instincts serves the one end of bringing about death."[1] In this view, life is merely a complicated detour en route to death, an extension of the path toward death. The sex drives, which lead germ cells to meet each other and thus reproduce life, are also conservative, in that they bring back earlier states of the living substance, but this makes them the true life drives. Sex drives represent the efforts of the living substance to restore a state of life.

Once his thoughts on the repetition compulsion had led him to discover the conservative character of libidinal life, Freud was forced to differentiate between two types of drive. Both are conservative, since their goal is the restoration of a state impaired by the development of life, but the ways in which they go about this restoration are different, meaning that their results also differ. Freud's second response to the repetition compulsion was therefore to differentiate between the life drive and the death drive, which replaced the dualism of the pleasure principle and the reality principle. Based on the repetition compulsion, the conservative character of libidinal life, speculations about the beginning of life and biological parallels, Freud concluded that "besides the instinct to preserve living substance and to join it into ever larger units, there must exist another, contrary instinct seeking to dissolve those units and to bring them back to their primaeval, inorganic state. That is to say, as well as Eros there was an instinct of death. The phenomena of life could be explained from the concurrent or mutually opposing action of these two instincts."[2] Life is a compromise between the drives of Eros and Thanatos.

Freud's theory of a death drive, which he developed further in *The Ego and the Id* (1923) and *Civilisation and Its Discontents* (1930), still meets with fierce resistance today. The work of the death drive can be proven by phenomena such as masochism and sadism, but its existence destroys many illusions about human nature. It is easy to recognize sadism and masochism as a mixing and unmixing of libidinous and destructive energies. The work of the death drive can turn against the outside world and other living things, and manifest as aggression and an urge to destroy. "In this way the instinct itself could be pressed into the service of Eros, in that the organism was destroying some other thing, whether animate or inanimate, instead of destroying its own self."[3] Masochism, Freud says, is a primary destruction, not displaced onto an object, but directed against one's own self.

Of course, accepting that a death drive exists in humans has wide-reaching, uncomfortable implications. Freud's reasoning at first seems to go against all experience, because it forces us to give up many positive assumptions about human nature. Freud himself writes: "Many of us will also find it hard to abandon our belief that in man himself there dwells an impulse toward perfection, ... But I do not believe in the existence of such an inner impulse, and

<hr>

1 Sigmund Freud, *Beyond the Pleasure Principle* (London: The International Psycho-Analytical Press, 1922), pp. 30-31.
2 Sigmund Freud, *Civilisation and Its Discontents* (New York: Norton & Company, 1961), pp. 65-66.
3 Ibid., p. 66.

I see no way of preserving this pleasing illusion."[4] There is an obvious case for identifying the destructive drive with the principle of evil. Since Freud, then, it has become impossible to deny the existence of evil, or of the aggressive tendency of an original, independent instinct in human beings. In sadism, a partly sexual drive, we see the desire for love alloyed with the destructive drive; in masochism, an inwardly directed destruction linked to sexuality. The pleasure principle seems almost to be in the service of the death drive. The obstacle that can disrupt the death drive is culture. Human culture is thus built on sublimation and the suppression of drives. Culture is the struggle between Eros and death, the life drive and the destructive drive.

According to Freud, the life drive and the death drive are subject to the same principle, which he called the Nirvana principle after Barbara Low: the mind's efforts to restore an earlier state, and therefore to reduce, to keep constant or remove internal tensions. In his theory, then, death is a part of life; life and death are causally coupled, they have the same source: "The emergence of life would thus be the cause of the continuance of life and also at the same time of the striving towards death," is how it is stated in a cryptic passage from *The Ego and the Id* (1923).[5]

In developing his theory of the death drive, Freud was not immune to the influence of the evolutionary theory of his time, and he quoted some of its authors in *Beyond the Pleasure Principle*, in particular the neo-Darwinian A. Weismann.[6] From Weismann's work comes the idea of dividing the living substance of metazoans, multi-cellular organisms, into mortal and immortal halves. Only the soma, the body in the stricter sense, is subject to natural death. The germplasm, by contrast, is potentially immortal, insofar as it is capable of surrounding itself with a new soma. And just as Weismann distinguishes between two forms of living matter – the soma, which is enslaved to death, and the germplasm, which serves reproduction – so Freud distinguishes between two forces or drives active within living matter: one which propels life toward death, and another which constantly seeks and achieves the renewal of life. There is admittedly an important difference here. Weismann does not see death as an original characteristic of the living substance, as an absolute necessity founded in the essence of life. For him, death is a late acquisition for the multi-cellular organism. But death does serve an evolutionary purpose: following the subdivision of the body's cells into soma and germplasm, the unlimited lifespan of an individual has become an inexpedient luxury. The individual can pass away, because the germplasm ensures the continuation of life.

Freud does not agree with this differentiation. His theory is served only if death drives are not an invention of higher organisms, but stem from the beginning of life on Earth.

---

4 Freud, *Beyond the Pleasure Principle*, p. 33.
5 Sigmund Freud, *The Ego and the Id* (London: The Hogarth Press, 1949), p. 38.
6 *Über die Dauer des Lebens (On the Duration of Life)*, 1882; *Über Leben und Tod (On Life and Death)*, 1884; and *Das Keimplasma (Germplasm)*, 1892.

For him, death drives are an original characteristic of living matter, just like reproduction. Weismann only considers reproduction to be an original characteristic of living matter, like growth, from which reproduction proceeds. Freud believes that the forces that propel life toward death are active from the start, just as the life drives are. The ego-drives, which serve the self-preservation of the individual, are therefore most threatened by the id, which itself is subject to the silent death drives. And that makes death an accomplice to life.

The Theory of Evolution and Death

The second answer to the problem of death, which evolutionary theory attempts to provide, also theoretically couples death to the conditions of life. "An Infidel Half Century," George Bernard Shaw's one-hundred-page preface to his five-part drama with the distinctive title *Back to Methuselah* (1920), and the drama itself, which represents the second of his legends of creative evolution after the dramatic parable *Man and Superman* (1901), approach these questions of death and eternal life from an evolutionary perspective. Shaw was an adherent of the idea of "creative evolution" (Bergson), which holds that the impetus for evolution is creative. In his "Metabiological Pentateuch," as he calls his play, Shaw refers to Empedocles, Button, Wallace, Darwin, Lamarck, and Butler. He turns against neo-Darwinists, arguing that natural selection alone is not enough to drive the engine of transformation that sees organisms become ever more complex, because it merely replaces one meaningless coincidence (or existence) with another. Shaw follows Lamarck, whose basic tenet is that living organisms change because they want to change. The great factor in evolution, he says, is the use or non-use of organs. Shaw illustrates this process with the example of automatic, unconscious habits like riding a bike or breathing. According to Lamarckian principles, "circumstantial selection" does not even need to operate in the process of perfection (the process Freud disputes). We live and want to live more intensively and for longer. We have a desire to expand our consciousness, our abilities, and our lives. Our efforts are directed toward acquiring the new organs and new ways of using them needed for this expansion. This principle also comes into play with purposeful, directed selection – breeding – says Shaw, because careful selection follows an aim, the purposeful passing on of desired characteristics and habits. Who forbids us to think that alongside blind, circumstantial selection, nature does not also implement a guided, desired selection, a steering mechanism to optimize the achievements of living things?

Darwin famously avoided speaking of will, purpose, and intent in his explanation of evolution, putting circumstance or coincidence in their place. Because some leaf-eating animals happen to have longer than average necks, they happen to survive better when the trees have been stripped of their leaves up to the average height, and these animals then find taller mates and thus, coincidentally, breed long-necked giraffes. Circumstance therefore brings about what looks like purposeful selection, breeding. But the coincidence of natural selection can't be entirely blind, because there is at least one drive – hunger – which needs to be satisfied, and which provides a direction, a directedness; the satisfaction of drives is an engine of evolution, which is to say that Eros, the drive to preserve life, even in long-necked animals, can be interpreted as directedness. Whether we call it modification, transformation, functional adaptation or evolution, the aim is always survival. The classical theory of evolution only gives one criterion, one mechanism for survival: those who survive are those who have adapted best to the changed conditions of their environment. This adaptation occurs through circumstantial selection. Or, that is Darwin's brief.

The theory of evolution implicitly assumes a life drive to which it does not give further methodical consideration. The crucial point here is that for the Darwinists, evolution effectively means the same as selection. But this selection obviously has death at its core. Even if it is coincidence that decides over death and life, extinction or survival, death remains the crucial engine of change. Selection rests on the principle of death, on the Thanatos principle. Without death there is no selection, without selection no change, without change no evolution. Evolution requires death.

There is no way for the theory of evolution to explain the transformation and development of species without selection, and therefore without death, which weeds out living things that are unfit. The theory of evolution sees life as a struggle between these two tendencies, making the situation as paradoxical as it is for Freud, who sees life as a compromise between life drive and death drive. The origin and the end of species through natural selection is thus ultimately founded in death, origin (or adaptation) and end converging in, on the one hand, the emergence of new species, and, on the other, the extinction of species that have proved unable to adapt. The development of species therefore rests on the same principle as the extinction of species, "Destruction as the Cause of Coming into Being," as Sabine Spielrein called a 1912 article, which anticipated Freud's theory of the death drive. If the evolutionist says that to prevent selection is to prevent evolution, then he is also saying that to prevent death prevents evolution, because selection relies on aging and mortality.

In the theory of evolution, then, death is inseparable from life; it is fettered to the preservation of life (in species) and the development of diversity. Within the theoretical framework of evolutionary theory, it is unthinkable that the dinosaurs could go on living alongside other old and new lifeforms; they provide the perfect illustration of how evolution develops through selection, through the survival of a species that happens to adapt, and the extinction of another species that happens not to. Put simply, the argument is that death ensures the constant renewal of life without overpopulating the planet. Death ensures the development and growth of variety among species.

This is the fatalistic element in the dismal death theory of psychoanalysis and Darwinism: the fact that death is interpreted as a condition of life, as inseparable from life; and that death is claimed to be the *conditio sine qua non* of the human condition. This also mirrors the anti-life element in Christian doctrine, whether the same or not, with its triumphal declaration that the human condition is suffering and death (albeit, the suffering and death of Jesus). Only through death do we gain eternal life, the Church tells us; this is the absolute mastery of death over life. Christianity is not a philosophy fed by love and Eros, but by the death drive. The fatal thing about the classical theories of death is their fatalism, their affirmative attitude toward death, the fact that they submit to and justify death with their theories, instead of combating the injustice of death with every means at their disposal. Shaw, on the other hand, coolly declares that circumstantial selection does not provide an explanation for natural death. "Nobody can explain why a parrot should live ten times as long as a dog, and a turtle be almost immortal," he says in the preface "An Infidel Half Century."[7] Shaw claims: "Among other matters apparently changeable at will is the duration of individual life."[8] To make this fantastical thought more entertaining, Shaw writes that he has written *Back to Methuselah* as his contribution to the modern Bible. Of course the Bible speaks of a man named Methuselah, who lived an unusually long time: 969 years.[9]

Shaw thus terminates the contract drawn up by the neo-Darwinists between evolution and death. He uncouples the death question from the question of the origin of species through circumstantial selection. Shaw peels back the natural justification from the death problem. Death as an absolute law of nature is no longer a universal, eternal law. (Thus the epigraph, as above, and its extravagant claims: "If on opportunist grounds Man now fixes the term of his life at three score and ten years, he can equally fix it at three hundred, or three thousand…") Death, which all sides situate and underpin theoretically as an absolute boundary, as the most iron of laws, as an insurmountable wall, as the end of all striving, as inevitable, as the universal condition of life, now holds an additional terror, because science also fails in the face of this greatest of problems, accepting and legitimating death in natural and human philosophy. The biological wall of death is joined by another, theoretical wall. When Shaw uncouples death and evolution, lifespan and life, as he demonstrates with the Methuselah myth of near-immortality, he is taking a stand against the absolutization of death.

This text was translated from the German by Ruth Martin.

---

7 George Bernard Shaw, *Back to Methuselah* (New York: Brentano's, 1921), p. xviii.
8 Ibid., p. xviii.
9 Genesis 5.21.

Dead Talk

George Quasha

> The dead taking refuge in art seek language
> from a perspective scarcely known to us,
> and art that hears their call speaks their unknown.
> − Ontononymous the Particular

Inter-incursive Art

Art seems to make every effort it can to get beyond death. Yet it can rarely leave death alone for long. Obviously there's a strong mix, a witch's brew, which gets our attention whenever the dark story slips back into view. The occasion here is a unique one: speaking to an artist's lifelike portrait crafted with the ashes of the dead.[1] This is not a matter that falls easily within my comfort zone, and that helped convince me to accept its interesting challenge. My intention accordingly is to lay the matter bare in writing, as far as I can, and in a way that brings alive the bite of the issue − the dead who are by art so risen.

To put it more simply, this is an experiment, by way of grasping the real matter, so difficult to name, to see if I can perform in language, not an equivalent of what the artist is doing in the particular art act of portraiture, but a *telling simulacrum*. I would characterize this "real matter" as *inter-incursion with the dead*. Some part of such an act does not properly belong to the apparent maker. The artist is the apparent maker of the portrait series in question, just as I am the apparent maker of this text. If you look at any of the artist's portraits you might focus on the lifelike photographically precise face of the person deceased. A living observer naturally sees a living image whenever possible. The fact that it is, so to speak, a vision from beyond the tomb is not a visual fact as such, but it is a conceptual one, perhaps also an experiential one. At some point you become aware that you are looking at a rather vibrant dead person, and, further, that what you are seeing is constituted by the actual ashes of the deceased person in the portrait. That fact changes everything in your mind. Nevertheless your eyes have a life of their own, just as the image has a life of its own: Eyes gaze upon a person's portrait and convey that person's life.

---

1 The work in question is Heide Hatry's portraits of the deceased, but I will primarily refer to her as *artist* in that the present text is not intended as "art criticism" but an exploration in art/language transformative function.

I'm speaking to you in writing that I do not regard as particularly *mine*, but, impersonal as it is, there's no denying that in some sense I'm doing the speaking here. Nevertheless, I'm somewhat ambivalent on this point. It's in "my" English, a language we are sharing here, whatever else may be true of us, and it comprises the interface between us that holds us to this momentary communication – or perhaps *communion* may turn out to be a better notion, since what can be said must remain, although shared, quite inconclusive. A question persists: What is the force of language here? The unexampled ambiguity of the life/death interface of the portraiture destabilizes any discourse addressing it.

Language by its nature is a site of mutual exchange, and it forms a porous membrane between us. Pursuing our metaphor, likening the text – site of an actual language interchange – to the artist's portrait of a deceased person, perhaps the ink constituting the physical words on the page might serve as stand-in for ashes; however, since the words, not the ink, are coming from "me," as the ashes used to "ink" the portrait come from the cremated body of the deceased, we could designate the *inked words*, the real "substance," as embodying the body-in-place – the presumptive physical other to which – to whom? – one is connecting. (If we view it as remains of a corpse, it's "to which"; if to a being, then "to whom.")

Obviously there's something intangible as well that stands in here, an incursion into the physical drawing and lingual analog, something inspiriting, a breath-like living current that keeps this process going – something non-physical. It *goes on*: You continue gazing at the portrait, just as you are still reading the text. Such writing as this implies that someone is speaking to you; likewise a portrait looks you in the eyes – but is anyone at home? You can experience the text as something *like* a voice coming from my vocal cords and striking your ear drums, yet it is actually entering through your eyes (reaching through to your optical nerve and generating a neurological event); reading as a textual process relates, albeit obliquely, to what a portrait does. So, a question is: Where you might think to be hearing "my" voice, what is it you imagine receiving from the deceased person? A ghostly presence? A soul life? Spirit? Imaginality?

Coming into question here is the status of the event of transfer between the work and the observer, who in this case would be you. Imagine a living link between "you" and "me" peculiar to the present experiment and right now in the process of being realized. For all you know I'm dead too, since you're reading this at some point after the time of writing, just as for that matter the artist may also not be living in *your* now, even as the person portrayed was not alive in the artist's initial portraiture in ash. So, for all you know everyone's dead but you, at least potentially. Oddly that doesn't much alter our relationship. Of course that's a commonplace of life itself, which can be gone in a flicker – and yet "it" goes on. You're talking on the phone, there's a long pause, the other person could suddenly be dead, but the phone call is still happening; no one hung up and you're still hanging on. This is an art moment, living time experienced amidst unlimited death; after all, in the

Metropolitan Museum of Art, with its vast and overwhelming art charge, the putative sources, the makers, are for the most part long departed. Not only are certain intensities enhanced by death (an obvious one being art's market value), but experience of the art communication, where the life status is fundamentally ambiguous, challenges the status as well of the primary opposition: life versus death. At any given moment we stand at the threshold – the limen of life and death, and where this liminality becomes conscious there is a charge that partakes of both; and not one without the other. The charge is between.

The portrait is a bounded space, the site of a certain charge, a stored intensity.[2] There's a charge of course in any portrait, even without the factor of an unprecedented and unrepeatable composition, here the ashes of the person portrayed. Yet that factor seems to add an alternate dimension, somewhat as a note written in one's blood has unexampled force for almost anyone. What kind of force is this?

To press this question further: Consider that, as a conceptual performance piece – call it mortal self-portraiture – I decide to write my autobiography in my own blood and continue until I've used it up, which also uses me up, depending on how fast I write and my sustained energy level: I'm thereby offering myself and my story in the same finite performative gesture. Inevitably I find myself in an energetic life-death struggle at the edge. (I note that even suggesting such an action raises the ante in our discourse here; as I wrote the above idea something stirred in the gut, a not particularly pleasant excitement.) If a person, by binding agreement, chooses to have her portrait made by the artist, to be executed postmortem with her own ashes, she performs a somewhat related conceptual performance gesture, indeed, a *performative* act in that the agreement seals the deal: instantly the life-death bond is fully in place. (Did she feel any special excitement upon signing up, a brush with darker energy?) Its further execution is projected into future time, yet once the word is recorded it's a done deal. And when the portrait is finally completed the person will have fulfilled her end of the bargain by dying and handing herself – her last remains – over to the artist's "ink" supply, rather than to the more common choice, the earth.

Now, by writing her story, spelling all this out, and even in a sense embodying her action in discourse, do I become part of the bargain? What's my relationship to it when I put this question in your mind, meanwhile invoking the energetic charge of its life and death art matter? Let's say I'm the one offering my ashes and I'm reporting it to you now, promising to die into a future portrait: does that change the status of these words, do they have more blood in them? Do they have *duende*?

---

2 Joseph Beuys seems to have considered an art work to be like a battery, which carries a charge whether or not one appreciates the work or perhaps even notices it – art as stored energy. A literal example was his piled sheets of felt between two copper plates.

TALKING *DUENDE*

To ground whatever *frisson* might be mounting here, I turn to the great and influential 1933 essay by Federico García Lorca, "Play and Theory of the *Duende*,"[3] which has lastingly focused the key term as it speaks to art, including music, dance, and poetry:

> "All that has black sounds has *duende*." . . . Those black sounds are the mystery, the roots that cling in the mire that we all know, all ignore, the fecund silt from which comes the very substance of art. "Black sounds" said the man of the Spanish people, agreeing with Goethe, who speaking of Paganini landed a definition of the *duende*: "A mysterious power that everyone feels and no philosopher has explained."

> So, the *duende* is a power, not a labour; a struggle, not a thought. I heard an old *maestro* of the guitar say: "The *duende* is not in the throat: the *duende* surges up inside you, from the soles of the feet." Meaning this: it's not a question of skill, but of true living style; it's in the veins; it's of the most ancient culture of immediate creation . . . in sum, the spirit of the earth . . . .[4]

In the culture of southern Spain that Lorca embraces, the *duende* is a close encounter with the other side. The master torero sustains a heightened state of near-death energy (often said to be a necessity for the presence of the *duende*), and, indeed, many of the major heroes, famous for the level of intentional risk and repeated brushes with the surging horn, die thereby – the deadly *cornada*. It's a state of art in which life and death are equally present, a dynamic of interlacing realities, and one that includes, at least in the case of the bullfight, an almost intimate bond between man and bull and between performer and observer. Many thousands (48,000 in the world's largest bullring in Mexico) have been felt to virtually suspend breathing simultaneously at the most charged passes of the cape (*muleta*) and final thrust of the sword (*estocada*). It's as though their life hangs on the matador's action; if he triumphs, they triumph, life triumphs over death; if he cheats death cheaply he may fear for his life – from the people! If he escapes shamed, he may insist on returning for another fight to seek redemption, only possible in the arena before common eyes. Lorca refines our perception:

> The bull has its own orbit, the torero his, and between orbit and orbit lies the point of danger, the vertex of terrible play.

> You can own the muse with the *muleta* and the angel with the *banderillas* and pass for a good bullfighter, but in the cape work, while the bull is still free of wounds, and at the moment of the kill, you need the *duende* to drive in the nail of artistic truth.

---

3 See also Christopher Maurer's translation in *In Search of Duende* (New York: New Directions, 1998). Freely downloadable at http://www.poetryintranslation.com/PITBR/Spanish/LorcaDuende.htm, trans. A.S. Kline. The essay was a lecture Lorca gave in Buenos Aires in 1933.
4 All citations of Lorca's essay are in my translation from the online original, "Teoría y juego del duende," at http:// usuaris.tinet.cat/picl/libros/glorca/gl001202.htm, with reference to the above noted translations by Maurer and Kline.

> The bullfighter who terrifies the public with his bravado is not bullfighting, but lowering himself to a ridiculous level, doing what anyone can do, playing with his life. But the torero who is bitten by *duende* gives a lesson in Pythagorean music and makes us forget that he is always throwing his heart over the horns.

Duende is notoriously difficult to define or translate, and there's no satisfactory word in English covering the range of meanings suggested by Lorca.[5] He does not define it much beyond words like "power," "force," and "struggle," but talks at length about the rarefied conditions of its appearance, the extraordinary acts or moments. (He spoke of calling it up before his own public readings of poetry.) Yet its commonality in southern Spain, especially Granada or Seville, comes with the notion that a certain singer or dancer *has duende*; but it's only for the moment, the action in which the *duende* shows up. No one has it all the time. It can't be owned.

In Lorca's famous description of the celebrated Gypsy singer Pastora Pavón, known as *La Niña de Los Peines*, following a performance before an audience of aficionados in Cádiz which had elicited an insult:

> [She] leapt up like a madwoman, trembling like a medieval mourner, and downed a huge glass of fiery spirits, and began to sing with a scorched throat: without voice, without breath or colour, but… with *duende*. She managed to tear down the scaffolding of the song but left the way open to a furious, burning *duende*, friend to sandstorm winds that make listeners tear at their clothes with rhythm like the rites of the Blacks of the Antilles, huddled before the statue of Santa Bárbara.
>
> *La Niña de Los Peines* had to tear apart her voice because she knew experts were listening, who demanded not form but the marrow of form, pure music with a body lean enough to float on air. She had to rob herself of skill and security, banish her muse and become helpless, so her *duende* might come and deign to struggle with her up close. And how she sang! Her voice no longer at play, her voice a jet of blood worthy of her pain and her sincerity, it opened like a ten-fingered hand around the nailed stormy feet of a Christ by Juan de Juni.
>
> The arrival of the *duende* always means radical change in forms, brings unknown and fresh sensations to old ways, with the quality of a newly created rose, miraculous, generating an almost religious enthusiasm.

It lives in flamenco music and dance, especially the *cante jondo* (deep song), in particular *siguiriyas*, linked by Lorca to an ancient art (something like an *Ur*-flamenco) evolved in Andalusia independently of flamenco tradition, with Arabic influence and elements transmitted to southern Spain by Roma, who migrated centuries before from northern

---

5 A common etymology is *dueño* or *duen de casa*, "master of the house," meaning a sometimes troublesome household spirit, a meaning more common in the north of Spain and referring to a fairy- or goblin-like creature, a sprite or elf. Lorca distances his usage from this mythology.

India. Did the *duende* come with them? Lorca sees it as an *earth spirit* phenomenon with international play in a range of artists, who are not particularly ethnically identified (e.g., Goya); yet the *duende* is evident on the surface of traditionary Spanish culture of the South, especially the Romani current, and popularly revered there.

Lorca famously distinguishes *duende* from angel and muse:

> Angel and muse come from outside us: the angel brings light, the muse form (Hesiod learned from her). Loaf of gold or fold of tunic, it is her form the poet receives in his laurel grove. The *duende* must be awakened in the furthest habitations of the blood.

It's an energy too fierce to endure outside the work, and so it requires a medium — an art powerfully evolved enough to contain it, yet forged in an art matrix beyond the illusion of formal or stylistic protection as such:

> There are neither maps nor disciplines to help us seek the *duende*. We only know it burns the blood like powdered glass, that it exhausts, that it rejects all the sweet geometry we have learned, that it shatters styles, that it makes Goya, master of the greys, silvers and pinks of the finest English art, paint with his knees and fists in horrible bitumen blacks . . . or it clothes Rimbaud's delicate body in a saltimbanque's costume, or puts the eyes of a dead fish on the Comte de Lautréamont at dawn on the boulevard.
>
> The great artists of Southern Spain, Gypsy or flamenco, whether singers, dancers, or musicians, know that no emotion is possible without the arrival of the *duende*.

It also requires an art of retention, one capable of continuing in the most intense and relentless state of inner focus; one that knows a power beyond pleasure and personal satisfaction; one with a singular temporality that is perhaps really a timelessness:

> Neither in Spanish dance nor in the bullfight does anyone enjoy himself. The *duende* charges itself with making us suffer by means of a drama of living forms, and clears the way for a move outside the reality that surrounds us.
>
> The *duende* works on the dancer's body like wind on sand. It changes a girl by magic power into a lunar paralytic, or brings an adolescent blush to the cheeks of a broken old man begging in the wine shops, or gives a woman's hair the odour of a midnight seaport, and at every instant works the arms with gestures that give birth to the dances of all the ages.
>
> But it's impossible for it ever to repeat itself, and it's important to stress this point. The *duende* never repeats itself, any more than do the waves of the sea in a squall.

Atemporal Autonomous Zones

This idea plays against a major contribution to ontological-anarchist non-hierarchical social theory by writer and poet Peter Lamborn Wilson, writing as Hakim Bey in *T.A.Z.:*

The Temporary Autonomous Zone, Ontological Anarchy, Poetic Terrorism (1991).[6] Focusing on ways of creating temporary social zones free of control structures, he discusses historical examples of TAZ, such as "pirate utopias," and explores the principle of releasing the mind from inherited mechanisms of control – what William Blake called "mind-forged manacles." No doubt the history of the nomadic Roma was for centuries a continuous search for autonomous zones that, in their long oppressive history, gave over to many degrees of assimilation in cultures besides southern Spain. On another plane, Wilson has also written extensively on entheogens, including speculations on the substance behind the Vedic Soma (notably in relation to Ireland[7]), which in certain cultures may well be the site of *duende* experience; indeed, psychotropics could be considered a contemporary individual path to an "autonomous zone" that revives ancient shamanic practices.[8]

Blake says, in essence, the reason revolutions fail and autonomous zones are so unstable (the temporary ones tend to be very short-lived, according to Wilson) has to do with the level of conception, the mind-set, the state of consciousness that produces and attempts to sustain them. This is a big subject, yet without wishing to oversimplify, I want to recall that all levels of the question of reality status, including order (social, political, personal) and individual awareness, are intertwined. Blake recognized that no revolution could succeed (not turn into tyranny) until human consciousness evolves or awakens to a certain point of openness to unexampled human/planetary possibility. Speaking here about Lorca and Roma we must never forget the tragic social and political context in which they lived (and many Roma continue to live); and yet I'm invoking them now for the power of their engagement with the most profoundly challenging level of life-death experience, particularly as registered in art. Thinking in a way that allows levels of reality to interlace actively in the present moment, we may open, as Blake said, "the doors of perception" somewhat further – and if we do it radically enough we may discover "the infinite which was hid."[9]

The question of *duende* is of this nature. We don't know whether to say "the *duende*," as if an entity of some kind, or just "*duende*," as if a state of mindbody, and it's probably unwise to pretend to know the answer. Pastora Pavón *had duende* when she was able or so focused, and yet it was like an ally that came into her service at the most intense moment. If one

---

6 The full text of the Autonomedia book is freely downloadable at http://hermetic.com/bey/taz_cont.html.

7 Peter Lamborn Wilson, *Ploughing the Clouds: The Search for Irish Soma* (San Francisco: City Lights, 1999). The view of Soma as a mushroom, in particular the *Amanita muscaria*, was first proposed by R. Gordon Wasson, founder of the field of ethnomycology, in *Soma: Divine Mushroom of Immortality* (New York: Harcourt Brace Jovanovich, 1968).

8 Entheogens in general are associated with ecstatic experience, but the tryptamine family (including psilocybe mushrooms and ayahuasca) comprises the probable sites of *duende*-like experience. See, for instance, Terrance McKenna's *Food of the Gods: The Search for the Original Tree of Knowledge* (New York: Bantam, 1992).

9 William Blake, *The Marriage of Heaven and Hell*, "A Memorable Fancy": "If the doors of perception were cleansed every thing would appear to man as it is, Infinite." See William Blake, *The Complete Poetry & Prose of William Blake*, ed. David V. Erdman (New York: Anchor Books, 1988); also the online Blake Archive for this and other Blake texts in the Illuminated editions: http://www.blakearchive.org.

witnesses comparable contemporary *cante jondo/siguiriya* performance, especially by certain Roma and Spanish from Granada or Seville, one can experience and study the complexity of the embodiment issue, and indeed see why Lorca can say something like *duende* "changes a girl by magic power into a lunar paralytic." The faces of Roma singers instantly contort and the eyes look beyond the ordinary as if entering the nearly unbearable condition of ecstatic song.[10] The great flamenco dancers move with almost violent suddenness, twists, and percussive striking of heel to ground, and eyes seeing into what no one sees, lips moving in conversation with… what? It's not a stretch to feel the presence of *duende* at those moments, to register it in one's own body. You can feel that the transmission of the state of *duende* is like a transfusion of an alternate substance, quite like blood, crossing the membrane of physical and non-physical.[11]

Duende only shows up as embodiment within a medium – the body, the eyes, the voice, the guitar, the poem… And yet it doesn't quite stay *in the thing*. Something nevertheless remains in the recordings and films, for instance, of the great moments of *cante jondo*. It seems to happen again in our registration now – provided that we have attained a comparable focus and know how to refocus – or as John Cage said, *unfocus* – to allow the event to take place inside us. It means leaving behind what we already know. It's like a sudden identity that happens in a state of between, a conscious liminality, a being at the edge of what is and is not oneself or one's known reality. The art that embodies this possibility creates an alternative possibility of *viewing, listening, reading*. I italicize the words to invite a little shimmer in the thinking, because at the level of concept we're nowhere near *duende*. It's the present act of connection that matters. You don't witness *duende* art so much as undergo it. It shakes any confidence in knowing what art is before it happens. You are the site of its happening, so you are in question. There's a disturbance of boundary, an inter-incursion – at once in performer, observer, the outside.

What then would comprise an atemporal autonomous zone? An artist's motivation for working at the margin of life would seem to aspire to what is not limited by temporality. *Duende* thrives at the threshold of time and timelessness. It rises from the ground and

---

10 For instance, Dolores Agujeta (born 1960), viewable on YouTube, is a master Roma singer who carries an Andalusian lineage of *duende*-embodying singers from Jerez (Cádiz), following the tradition of Manuel Torre.

11 Fortunately there are very many videos of true flamenco on YouTube: search "*cante jondo gitano*," "*siguiriya*," and by name the powerful flamenco performers: from the highly accomplished and widely known dancers (the great Romani, Carmen Amaya, and our contemporaries like Eva La Yerbabuena, Beatriz Martín, Mercedes Ruiz, Patricia Guerrero, Gema Moneo, Karime Amaya, and many others – all in a sense descendants of Carmen Amaya as powerful women innovators who also sustain the great tradition) to the passionate local scenes in Granada, Seville, Barcelona, et al. The cabaret scenes there (the famous *peña flamenca* and *tablao* or *café cantante*) represent the raw local traditions Lorca was indicating. And, of course, the many great singers (starting with the greatest of all, the Romani, Pastora Pavón and Camerón de la Isla, and today's masters of *cante jondo* like Estrella Morente or Dolores Agujeta) and guitarists (beginning with the transformative Ramón Montoya and the greatest of our time, the late Paco de Lucía). Many non-traditional performing artists may be seen as manifesting *duende*, such as Diamanda Galás's "vocal terror," Janis Joplin, John Coltrane, Cecil Taylor, Marilyn Crispell, Rashaan Roland Kirk, the blues…

through the feet to play through the body. Death passes in the charging bull, enfolded in the cape as the flamenca lifts the gown with the lightest grip. In the time-suspended free zone the dead speak under cover of art. And we can choose to meet there, either speaking *of* ashes or *in* ashes.

The work as (a)temporal free zone is a place of connection, a crossroads of self-(re)patterning, where we learn to live multiple lives in our one. A work of the order of Blake's "Illuminated prophecy," *Jerusalem: The Emanation of the Giant Albion* (1804-20), offers itself as a gate to another dimension of reality, the poem an immense and intricate structure within the visionary theater of which total transformation is possible: and one enters by the Door of Death. Blake said that the poem was dictated to him from elsewhere – an *incursion* of text. The promise it offers is not a pre-constructed paradise supported by belief or dogma, but a state of imaginal engagement which Blake called speaking in Visionary Forms Dramatic. He writes:

> I give you the end of a golden string;
> Only wind it into a ball,
> It will lead you in at Heaven's gate,
> Built in Jerusalem's wall.[12]

Jerusalem is a two-way bridge traveled both ways at once, a state of feedback with continuous oscillation between earth and not-earth, self and not-self, work and not-work. Staying closely conscious of and within what leads us, definitive step by definitive step, following the language as it arises, takes us further into the core action of the work, the event. It's a performative reception retaining the matrix of its own possibility. *Duende* incurs as if the living dead speaking with performative force, what can only happen now, as never before, non-relative and atemporal, absolute only within its singularity. It leaves us rising up as never who we were, barely what we are.

---

12 From *Jerusalem*, plate 77: Blake, *The Complete Poetry & Prose of William Blake*, p. 231.

Dead Religion
Mark Dery

I. *Imagoes*

"An image of the parent buried in the unconscious from infancy and bound with infantile affect" was Dr. Hannibal Lecter's admirably pithy definition of *imago*.[1] Jung, who coined the term, theorized it in greater depth as a "subjective and often very much distorted" effigy of a parent, molded from childhood memories and fantasies and carried into adulthood, where it leads "a shadowy but nonetheless potent existence in the mind of the patient" – a gothic image that makes me think of the grotesque "character heads" of the eighteenth-century German sculptor, Franz Xaver Messerschmidt, and the singing busts in Disneyland's Haunted Mansion.[2]

There is, indeed, an uncanny power to Jung's *imagoes*, undead death masks scowling down at us reproachfully from some half-forgotten curio shelf in the unconscious. "Even when the parents have long been dead and have lost, or should have lost, all significance, the situation of the patient having perhaps completely changed since then," Jung writes, "they are still somehow present and as important as if they were still alive. The patient's love, admiration, resistance, hatred, and rebelliousness still cling to their effigies, transfigured by affection or distorted by envy, and often bearing little resemblance to the erstwhile reality."[3]

Totems of "the dead religion of psychoanalysis," as Lecter dryly called it, Jung's *imagoes* are true to the word's historical roots.[4] The original *imagoes* were the wax masks of ancestors, cast from life and enshrined, after death, in the homes of the aristocracy in ancient Rome. They served as models of rectitude, reminding upper-class Romans of their hereditary role as public exemplars of personal propriety and civic virtue. Stern, unsleeping judges of what goes on behind closed doors, they were charged – cathected, Freud would say – with psychic energy, so much so that the Romans seemed to view them as half-alive, like those spook-house busts that follow you with their eyes. Pleading his client's case before a jury, Cicero urged the assembled citizens to think not of how the accused would face his family,

---

1 Thomas Harris, *The Silence of the Lambs* (New York: St. Martin's, 1988), p. 149.
2 C.G. Jung, "The Theory of Psychoanalysis," in C.G. Jung, *Collected Works of C.G. Jung, Volume 4: Freud and Psychoanalysis*, ed. and trans. R.F.C. Hull and Gerhard Adler (Princeton, NJ: Princeton University Press, 1961), p. 134.
3 Ibid.
4 Harris, *The Silence of the Lambs*, p. 149.

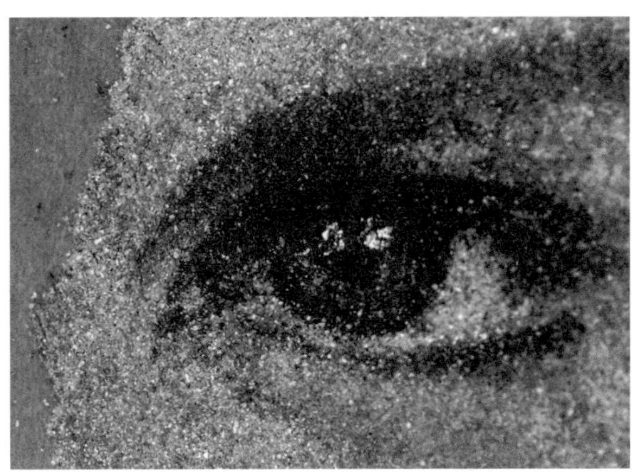

if convicted, but what he would say to the heartbroken mask of his illustrious father.[5] When a family member died, professional actors donned the wax masks for the funeral procession, where the walking dead not only "provided for the audience an instantaneous genealogy of a noble old line," as the classics scholar Shadi Bartsch points out, but "cast an assessing gaze on the successor to the dead" as well.[6]

II. Revenants

Paul Schmid, Heide Hatry's portrait of her father, who died in 1993, is an *imago* for our times – a projection, in the Jungian sense, of the artist's conflicted, sometimes piercingly painful dreams and memories of her father, materialized in ash – cremated remains[7] – on wood covered with beeswax.

In keeping with Hatry's almost pagan relationship to relics, her rendering of a photo of her father, in flecks of burned bone ground into grit, is equally a ritual object, a thing to conjure with. In his essay "The Function of the Unconscious" (1935), Jung talks of "primitive man's" communion with "ancestral spirits," which for him are nothing more than "broken-off bits of the psyche," "manifestations of unconscious complexes": the mythologized image of the parent "is unconsciously projected, and when the parents die, the projected image goes on working as though it were a spirit existing on its own. The primitive then speaks of parental spirits who return by night (*revenants*), while the modern man calls it a father or a mother complex."[8]

Hatry isn't some postmodern primitive, but she *was* haunted – by her father's untimely death, and by the suicide of her friend Stefan, the subject of her portrait of the same name. And she was raised in an atmosphere of fervent religiosity, on an isolated farm in southwestern Germany, where she communed with the unseen – Jesus, by any other name. Her family were Pietists, members of a reform movement within Lutheranism that arose in the seventeenth century, advocating a more passionate, personal faith over the dry doctrinal emphasis of the official church. "I was a dedicated Pietist," she says. "I was talking to Jesus every day – not only in the morning and in the evening, when I prayed for about an hour each time, but also during the day. He was my invisible friend."[9]

---

5 Shadi Bartsch, *The Mirror of the Self: Sexuality, Self-knowledge, and the Gaze in the Early Roman Empire* (Chicago: University of Chicago Press, 2014), pp. 124-125.
6 Ibid., p. 124.
7 Not her father's, which weren't available to her, but a suitable substitute – the cremains of animals, obtained from an animal crematorium.
8 C.G. Jung, "The Function of the Unconscious," in C.G. Jung, *Collected Works of C.G. Jung, Volume 7: Two Essays on Analytical Psychology*, ed. and trans. R.F.C. Hull and Gerhard Adler, rev. Bollingen Series XX (Princeton, NJ: Princeton University Press, 1966), p. 186.
9 All unattributed quotes are taken from the author's interview with the artist, conducted in Hatry's New York apartment on July 27, 2016.

Slogging away at her mind-glazing chores, she "told him everything; it was like having a psychologist who was listening to everything I had to say. I even had the feeling that he was talking back."

When Stefan took his own life in 2008, however, God was silent; Hatry, who had lost her religion long before, was marooned on her berg of grief. His death opened a wound in her mind that was only half-healed. "Suddenly, this whole pain with my father's death came back. It was insane. I thought, 'I'm not surviving this.'"

III. Memories

Paul Schmid raised pigs for slaughter. Pigs are a constant presence in Hatry's childhood memories, snuffling, jostling, squealing, shitting, dying. A "very intelligent man," her father took care to build the pig stable downwind, but every now and then the wind changed, blanketing the farm in the acrid, ammoniac reek of pig manure, a gagging, eye-watering mix of "spoiled meat, spoiled eggs," and the swampy, rotten stink of excrement. "When I had to go inside the stable, the smell was so *thick* that I felt physically unable to walk into it."

Packed, into concrete cells, the pigs were miserable creatures. Bred for lean meat, they were susceptible to heart attacks. A company picked up the pigs that had died, then "made food for livestock out of these dead animals." Following the industry logic that gave us mad cow disease, the feed they manufactured was high in dead pigs. There was a symmetry to the thing; George Grosz would have loved it.

There was an even more fearful symmetry to the prisonlike stables, the comings and goings of the trucks that took the animals to slaughter, the transformation of living things into mere "material," although Hatry was too young to notice the historical parallels. No one had ever told her that *Judenschwein* ("Jewish swine") was the Nazi's preferred epithet. For that matter, she'd never even *heard* of the Holocaust until she learned about it in school, incredibly, a sickening jolt that left her with a sense of collective guilt she's never shaken off.

Some of her recollections make her childhood sound like a cross between *Charlotte's Web*, as drawn by George Grosz, and *White Ribbon* (2009), Michael Haneke's gothic tale of an ingrown, morbidly religious village in rural Germany. Lunch at her grandparents' sometimes struck a David Lynchian note. "I didn't want to gnaw the skin off the pig ears (because I hated that the hair got stuck between my teeth) and I cried when I had to gnaw the meat off a whole rabbit head," recalls Hatry. Her grandfather, who'd been a prisoner-of-war in Bordeaux during the Second World War, admonished her to clean her plate. He and the other starving POWs had been forced to bury a pig that had died of god knows what causes, he recalled. After dark, they exhumed it and ate it. "I imagined it full of maggots and blown up [from decomposition]," she says. "How could you possibly complain after hearing something like that?" She is, needless to say, a vegetarian.

One of the reasons she left home, at fifteen, was because she

> couldn't stand to hear the crying pigs in the morning when they were picked up for the slaughterhouse. It sounds very much like human weeping – like a baby in pain, totally piercing. It was so loud that I woke up every morning the pigs were taken away, and then I couldn't fall asleep; I was crying, because it was contagious, like when you come across some teenagers who can't stop laughing and you have to laugh, too, even though you have no idea what they're laughing about.

IV. REGRETS

All of which makes Hatry's childhood sound like a PETA video with a voiceover by Werner Herzog. Life on the Schmid family farm was hard, but it wasn't without its charms. There was her mother's love of flowers, and her father was "quite creative," too, in his own way. A rural *bricoleur*, "he used everything in a way you wouldn't use it." Collecting junk with his tractor, he'd "build something out of it, part of a barn or whatever." He would've appreciated her creative misuse of butcher-shop sweepings in *Heads and Tales* (2009) – grotesque, queasy-funny headshots of female faces fashioned from untreated pigskin, with "fresh pig eyes" and lips made of raw meat.[10] (Imagine a *Vogue* photo shoot, styled by Ed Gein.) "I think he would have found it hilarious, what I did with pig parts," she says. She learned to draw sitting on his lap, watching him sketch animals.

As with Stefan, circumstances conspired against her seeing her father's body. Most of us would regret being robbed of that ritual encounter and the closure we're told it will bring, but for Hatry, with her belief in the occult power of the palpable, the loss was devastating. "It was horrible; that I couldn't say good-bye was one of the most tragic things in my life. I had several things that bothered me very much. First, that I hadn't spoken a single word in our language, *Schwäbisch* (Swabian),[11] with him after I had moved out. He so wished I'd talk to him in *Schwäbisch*, but I wouldn't do it. I *hated* it! I found it so vulgar, all the sounds. I regret this *so* much. Have you read Philip Roth's *The Dying Animal*? I cried so hard when I read the scene where she's lying in his arms, dying of breast cancer, and he asks, 'Do you regret anything?' and she regrets that she didn't speak Spanish to her father. I totally understood. What I found so shocking was that that was a regret she would have on her deathbed; it would follow her."

---

10 Heide Hatry, "Creating Life," artist's statement about *Heads and Tales*, 2009, archived on Hatry's website, http://www.heidehatry.com/art_statementHT.html.

11 An Alemannic dialect spoken in Swabia, a region in southwestern Germany covering a good part of the state of Baden-Württemberg, Swabian is all but incomprehensible to speakers of standard German, or *Hochdeutsch*.

V. Séance

Hatry anguished over things said and left unsaid; sins of commission, sins of omission. And then it came to her – an *imago* for an image culture; a talisman for solo séances; a relic for the religion of loss. "I suddenly had the idea of what I had to do," she writes, in her artist's statement for *Icons in Ash*: "Create portraits of them using their own ashes."[12]

Portraits of the dead made *of* the dead, Hatry's *Icons* are cathected with psychic voltage. They owe their cathartic effect, she thinks, to

> the strange sensation that although the person of the deceased has been dispersed, disintegrated, returned to an elemental state, the almost magical rearrangement of her or his *Ur*-components in a likeness suggests a vague sense that death has not actually conquered . . . They're still gone, but the part of them that remains in me is energized by the reminder of who they were. And the charged material of their ash remains certainly focuses that reminder.[13]

It's a sentiment that would make perfect sense to any Roman aristocrat, in daily dialogue with the *imagoes* in his atrium.

Even her likenesses of her father and her friend – fashioned, unlike the other portraits in the series, from animal cremains since their ashes weren't available – are powerful mediums, channeling their subjects. Assembling their images from specks of bone implanted one by one in warm wax, on the point of a scalpel ("all these tiny, tiny pieces, dust to dust, ashes to ashes"), she wept as she worked. "And then something incredible happened," she says, first with Stefan's portrait, then with her father's. She wanted so desperately for the bone dust to be theirs that, through a kind of transubstantiation, it *was*.

> When I was imagining that these were Stefan's ashes, I started talking to him. I explained what I thought was wrong with him, then I yelled at him, 'Why didn't you *tell* me something was wrong?!' And after a short time, I was okay. I thought at the beginning it would never have been possible to get over this, but after I had made the portrait, I felt so consoled by it. And because of my intense imagination, I felt like he *was* there.

She imagines, too, that he, and her father, are *still* there, "still somehow present and as important as if they were still alive" (Jung). "I feel close to these people, connected; my memories have an objective basis that I felt had collapsed before I made the likenesses," she says. "My relationship hasn't just stopped, but all of the unresolved or difficult-to-abandon aspects of it persist in the daily (or at any rate regular) communion their presence engenders."[14] Her *imagoes* re-member the dead.

---

12 Heide Hatry, "Background Info," e-mail to the author, January 29, 2016.
13 Ibid.
14 Ibid.

VI. MIND OVER MATTER

Atheist to the bone, I can't help but raise a skeptical eyebrow when Hatry starts talking about her horror at the American practice of scattering ashes, a ritual whose consignment of the Dear Departed to the winds strikes her as unconscionable, a blithe obliteration. To a materialist, I point out, the person in question ceased to exist the instant his or her brain activity flatlined; anything else is magical thinking. The belief that who we are – the soul, if you're inclined to such beliefs; the self, if you're not – is somehow separable (yet, oddly, inseparable) from the three-pound hunk of gray matter in our skulls is, to materialist philosophers of mind like Daniel Dennett, no more than a consoling fiction.

Hatry mulls it over. Perhaps this sense of an ineffable presence in her portraits *is* "all happening in our minds," she allows. Then again, she contends, her ability to imagine that the glittering specks of gray, black, and white really *are* her father's ashes, or Stefan's, "is only possible if you *have* an artifact, which allows you to let your mind go to work."[15] She draws an analogy to the splinters of the True Cross and bits of saints' bones in reliquaries all over Europe; does it matter if they're what they're alleged to be, as long as they kindle the imagination?

She's right, of course. Her *Icons* bring back the dead, if not from the heaven she dreamed of in her Pietist childhood, at least from the afterlife of our memories, dreams, reflections – where, of course, they never died.

"The power of the dead is that we think they see us all the time," writes Don DeLillo, in his novel *White Noise* (1985). "The dead have a presence. Is there a level of energy composed solely of the dead? They are also in the ground, of course, asleep and crumbling. Perhaps we are what they dream."[16]

---

15 Heide Hatry, e-mail to the author, July 28, 2016.
16 Don Delillo, *White Noise* (New York: Penguin Books, 1999), 97.

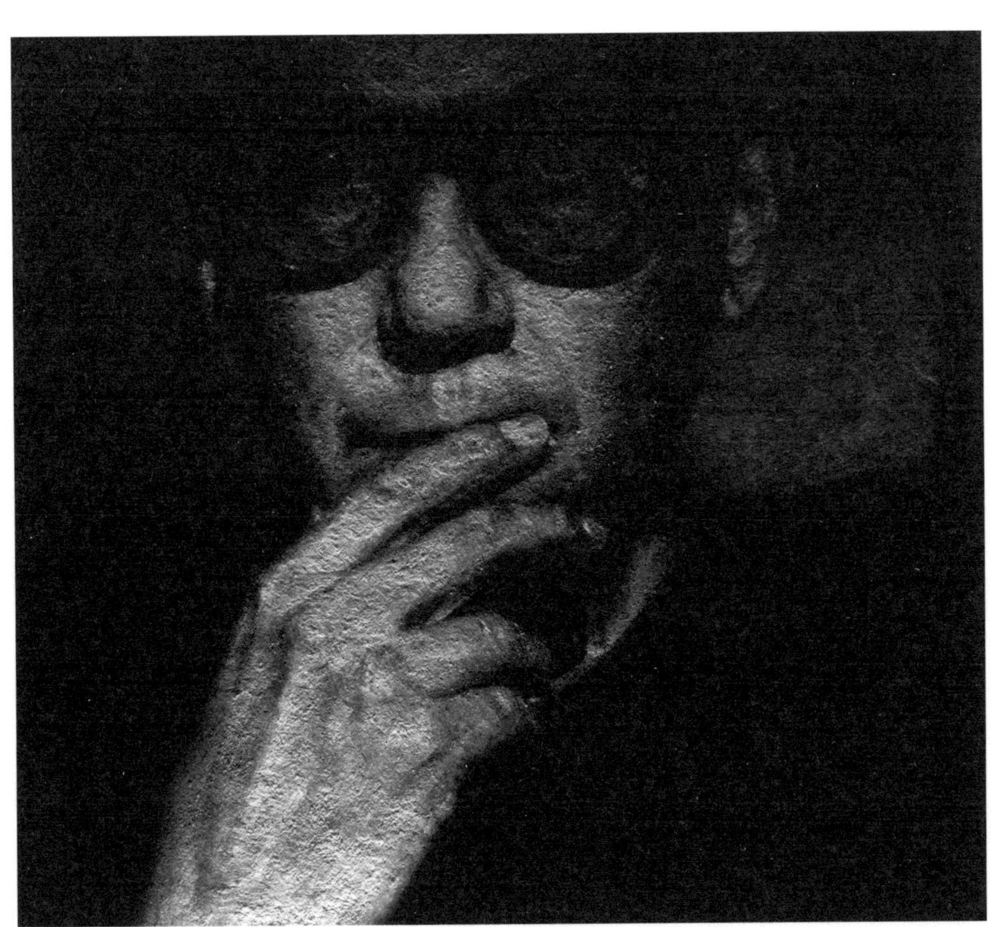

Notes on Lazarus

Rick Moody

What do we know about Lazarus? In the Eastern Church, Lazarus of Bethany, who lived on thirty years after his resurrection by Jesus Christ, was said in later years never to have smiled – presumably owing to things he saw in the underworld. And: the insistence in the biblical account on Lazarus smelling horrible is satisfying. In literature descriptions of scent make a passage more indelible. There should be more biblical smells.

"Jesus wept," it is well known, is the shortest verse in the Bible (John 11:35). This sentence describes Jesus' confrontation with the death of Lazarus of Bethany. There is reasonable consistency, among the many English translations, on this passage, although I have found the much inferior "Jesus cried."[1] The awesome strength of the passage is in its brevity. The brevity articulates the grief.

There are thirty-two modern cases (that is, cases in the twenty-first century) of people whose hearts spontaneously restarted after they had been pronounced dead. A significant number of these deaths are owing to drug overdose. The technical name for a heart restarting without assistance is "auto-resuscitation." It's also called: Lazarus syndrome.

Why is it that Jesus feels such waves of grief at Lazarus' death, when he knows that resurrecting Lazarus is possible? Is it simply because he feels the loss that his sisters Mary and Martha of Bethany feel? Is the sibling relationship such as to suggest the enormity of death as no other does?

Maybe Jesus weeps so over Lazarus' tomb because he knows what is commenced as a result. According to John 12, the Jews of Jerusalem plotted to kill Lazarus a second time immediately after his resurrection.

The "grave clothes" of Lazarus are bandages covering both face and body, at the time he climbs up and out of the tomb. He is effectively mummified. Covering the face removes what's most human about Lazarus. His body is evacuated of its spirit in the tomb. When Jesus wants to reveal what is human about the resurrected Lazarus, he first has to have the grave clothes removed, meaning, first, unwinding the covering on the face of Lazarus.

1 Here's a good list of translations of John 11:35: https://www.biblegateway.com/verse/en/John%2011:35. The International Standard Version gives "Jesus burst into tears."

Why Lazarus? Why Lazarus more so than any other deceased candidate who might have been proposed among those in the Jewish community? Lazarus is selected for his excellent abilities to serve in a heroic capacity. Jesus must have felt as much. That Lazarus had an honest face. Perfect for the moment of unveiling.

Then in John 12, Jesus goes back to Bethany, to check up on Lazarus, and they have a meal together. Oh to have been a bystander! Did Jesus ask him about the four days in the underworld? Weather? Politics? That year's agricultural yield? "But Lazarus was one of them that sat at the table with him."[2] The scene goes on to discuss the issue of poverty: "For the poor always ye have with you."[3] Lazarus is scarcely mentioned at the table and yet always present.

Lazarus is not resurrected for all eternity, as Jesus promises the believers after Judgment Day. Lazarus gets his human death sentence commuted temporarily. His is the kind of miracle that we all long for and are suspicious of. A revival tent miracle. (After my sister's death, I remember any number of movies wherein dead characters came back. I watched these films, mostly glossy and dim, with envy.) I heard a sermon about Lazarus recently: *Unfortunately I must disappoint those of you who, because of this story, are hoping for the resurrection of your own relatives.*

The question, for me, is what did Lazarus feel? The eternal repose, the sense of traveling down and into oblivion, must be reassuring in a way. I think of oblivion as potentially satisfying. Imagine Lazarus of Bethany living at the edge of the Roman empire, good friends with some itinerant Jew, some wandering mendicant, whom everyone wanted to kill. A verifiable rabble-rouser, afoul of the authorities. Dying, for Lazarus, may have been a relief from constant political adversity and physical threats of the Romans. And then having to be raised up from that eternal repose, to face, again, the contemporary horror?

Let's catalog some resurrections. There is, e.g., Terry Callier's song "Lazarus Man" where we find Lazarus with a fever to recount his journey, with utmost urgency ("Since he bid me to rise/ I ain't been to sleep!"),[4] and it does so while employing the story of Lazarus allegorically. Callier, an African-American folk singer from Chicago who made a number of recordings in the 70s, completely dropped out of the music business, only to be rediscovered by British deejays (and Beth Orton) in the 90s.

Callier's Lazarus is also, at least when Callier himself performs the song, African-American, and it's interesting to think of the narrative re-purposed to describe the struggles of the disenfranchised (as the Jews themselves would have been in Lazarus' own time). Callier's

---

2 Ibid., KJ, John 12:2.
3 Ibid., John 12:8.
4 Terry Callier, *TimePeace*, Audio CD (Talkin' Loud Classics, 1998).

two chords, here, are modal like Miles Davis and John Coltrane ("Lazarus Man" feels closely related to Coltrane's "India"), so it's also to situate Lazarus in the heroic liberation of jazz, the kind of music they play at New Orleans funerals: elegiac, tragicomic, mnemonic, celebratory.

Callier's Lazarus seems to have something in common with the outlandish Western tradition in which Lazarus (and his sisters Mary and Martha) are put out to sea by hostile Jews, to drift all the way to Provence, where Lazarus becomes bishop of Marseille, after which he is put to death during the persecutions associated with the reign of Domitian. In this tradition, his head was preserved and venerated.

The Marseille narrative, which gets taken up and embellished by French writers of the medieval period, is Gnostic in the way it ties up loose ends (the Mary in the Lazarus story is Mary Magdalene, even though there's no evidence for this; and: Lazarus is a thief, like Barabbas, who was crucified next to Jesus of Nazareth), and in this way it indicates the Lazarus story is one of those pieces of the New Testament that is so powerful that people want to claim it, to manipulate the particulars, to sew up the loose ends, to dream further dreams. Additionally, in the Eastern Orthodox tradition, Lazarus became a bishop in Cyprus. He may or may not have been appointed to the post by the Virgin Mary herself. So it is said.

Henri Cole's poem "Hens" also deals with a Lazarus: "I can't resist picking up little Lazarus,/ an orange-and-white pullet I adore. 'Yes, yes, everything will be/ okay,' I say to her glaring mongrel face."[5] Cole's very considerable gift is for a richness of metaphor in which human struggle, human longing, constantly appear recast into things observed in nature, and in the hen named Lazarus we feel both Lazarus' raising anew, in tragicomic form, a figure of sport, an entrée, or a layer of eggs. As in Cole's work elsewhere, the metaphorical layering is so dense that Lazarus' incarnations shimmer multiply before us at first, some of these layers are very funny.

At least until Cole's Petrarchan turn in the sixth line of this luminous sonnet-like form, when again Lazarus, bereft of smile, comes face to face with the particulars of suffering and non-being: "Poor Lazarus –/ last spring an intruder murdered her sisters and left her/ garroted in the coop."[6] The dread never far off, a muscular, unflinching, exceedingly sober gaze at the facts of the world: "There's a way the wounded/ light up a dark rectangular space. Suffering becomes/ the universal theme."[7] Maybe, in this incarnation of Lazarus, his story tells a precisely human truth: that there is *eternal recurrence* to earthly suffering.

---

5 Henri Cole, "Hens," *The Atlantic* (October 2009), http://www.theatlantic.com/magazine/archive/2009/10/hens/307670/.
6 Ibid.
7 Ibid.

The site of Lazarus' tomb is contested. Like many places in and around the Holy City – contested for thousands of years. There is a tomb, now underneath a mosque, the al-Uzair, which the Muslims sealed off. So it was until the Franciscans cut a different entrance into the tomb. None can say for certain if it's the *actual* tomb of Lazarus or not, but there have been churches in the area since the fourth century. It is more an exemplary tomb, a place plausible, and – because plausible – spooky. The tomb, originally, was connected to Lazarus' house.

In "Dig, Lazarus, Dig!!!,"[8] Nick Cave (and his Bad Seeds) reduce Lazarus (nicknamed Larry in the verses) to a rock-and-roll drug adept, a hallucinating drug addict, a sort of fin-de-siècle decadent trying to achieve satori (I'm using a Beat terminology) through deformation of the senses, and this, in the chorus – "Dig yourself, Lazarus, dig yourself back in that hole" – indicates the coming-awake of Lazarus, in which Lazarus, realizing the enormity of his resurrection, tries to return to the underworld.

I sort of hate this song. It's as if Nick Cave is the Susan Sontag of contemporary music: a popularizer of other more trenchant avant-gardes. The secret weapon of The Bad Seeds, in my view, was Blixa Bargeld, a founding member of the ensemble, and lead guitarist, and former member of Einstürzende Neubauten, whose inability was his mastery, and who gave The Bad Seeds a genuinely unpredictable element. The sheering away of Bargeld (and Mick Harvey) made the band sort of a pop band, the way I see it, and Cave tried to resist this transition into more palatable material by making the Grinderman album (a sort of garage rock side project), and then *Dig, Lazarus, Dig!!!*, somewhat in imitation of the Grinderman sound. It's a fake punk rock album, and the song "Dig, Lazarus, Dig!!!" is obviously influenced by New York punk. When Cave, on "Lazarus," doesn't sound like Mark E. Smith of The Fall, he sounds a bit like Richard Hell (of The Voidoids), and the lyrics allude to New York (and San Francisco), and you know he means the drugs and chaos, the energy, the *Todestrieb* of punk.

It would all seem like self-mythologizing and lyrical excess of the kind that makes for great performance, but does not withstand close lyrical scrutiny, were it not for two brushes with *trauma*. One of these things is Cave's own remarks about the Lazarus of Bethany: "Ever since I can remember hearing the Lazarus story, when I was a kid, you know, back in church, I was disturbed and worried by it. Traumatized, actually. We are all, of course, in awe of the greatest of Christ's miracles – raising a man from the dead – but I couldn't help but wonder how Lazarus *felt* about it. As a child it gave me the creeps, to be honest."[9] *Traumatizing* is such a great word for the Lazarus story, and the "actually" that comes after it here gives "actually" a force that it doesn't ordinary have. It's true, as with the Annunciation, in which Mary must confront the angel, Lazarus *is* truly traumatizing, and

---

8 Mute Records, 2008.
9 https://en.wikipedia.org/wiki/Dig,_Lazarus,_Dig!!! (italics mine).

this is *actually* the case. The slacker punk of Cave's song is the closest he can get to the traumatic not-dead quality of Lazarus, the nearness of Lazarus, the recognition of *daily life* in the Lazarus story: anymore and he might be scared to death.

In this way, it becomes clear why there are three exclamation points in the title of Cave's song, as opposed to the one that would clearly do the job reliably: they are Trinitarian.

The other trauma is the loss of Cave's son, Arthur. His son, as is well known now, fell to his death in Brighton, England, in 2015, and on *Skeleton Tree,* his recent album of compositions mostly written before Arthur's passing, but recorded after, you can feel the haunting of Arthur everywhere. In "Jesus Alone," the first track on *Skeleton Key,* it's as if you feel the Jesus of Nazareth who weeps over Lazarus' grave. Jesus wept. Jesus wept. Jesus began to cry. Jesus started crying. Jesus wept. And Jesus wept. Jesus cried. Jesus wept. And at this Jesus wept. Jesus burst into tears. Jesus wept. Jesus wept. Jesus wept. "With my voice I am calling you"[10] is the refrain of "Jesus Alone," and it's both Cave trying to call to Arthur across the trauma of loss, and it's Jesus alone, without the comfort of the divine, aggrieved by the loss of Lazarus, by what he knows, or in the knowledge of what comes next, when, after the dinner with the resurrected Lazarus of Bethany, he must enter the city of Jerusalem and proceed, well, to Golgotha.

"Evidently, this was needed,"[11] Franz Wright says of Lazarus, in a sort of a free translation of an uncollected piece by Rilke, "The Raising of Lazarus," perhaps a rehabilitation of a fragment of Rilke, a fragment that could not be completed to anyone's satisfaction, because looking accurately upon Lazarus is to be traumatized into silence, to know what Lazarus knew is to be traumatized. The antecedent of "this" in "Evidently, this was needed" is purposefully vague. The passivity of the sentence is exactly the kind of German abstraction that one associates with Rilke, and the use of "evidently" is funny and sly, because in Wright's blood-curdling rendering of Rilke's Lazarus, it's all about *proof,* all evidentiary.

Maybe Lazarus suffered from the extremely rare Cotard's syndrome, in which he believed he was dead already. One can imagine, in the pre-modern era, when sanitation and medicine were not what they are now, that death was so often at hand, so imminent, that one came to believe one already had the condition. And maybe Jesus of Nazareth did what he did (as when he cast out the demons, in Matthew 8:28, by transferring them into a herd of swine) to try to commute psychic suffering. Maybe Jesus abbreviates the preoccupation with death.

---

10 Nick Cave and The Bad Seeds, *Skeleton Key,* Audio CD (Mute Records, 2016).
11 Franz Wright, "The Raising of Lazarus," Poetry Foundation (October 2015), https://www.poetryfoundation.org/poetrymagazine/poems/detail/58345.

Evidently, what is needed is a transit across a dialectical pairing, a Hegelian opposition, viz., life and death, a way to render the longing of the one for the other, and: I wrote these lines after spending time by the deathbed of a loved one, an ebbing out of life, and what I found in the five days before and the two days after was not a dialectical pairing, a Hegelian opposition, but rather an incremental transit, in which self is pitted, mottled, interstitial, but breath continues, and then, after breath, a hovering of presence in the absence, as if the other who was no longer there was there again, and as I write these lines I can feel her. Her self was a fragment of self cast about into available repositories, a death and not-death in language, a dissemination of fragments, a broadcasting of residuary self, a hovering into this draft.

David Bowie's "Lazarus," from *Black Star*, his last album, combines different strata of meaning about Lazarus, and fuses them together. The song is stately and slow-moving, it is a development of incremental change, with fragments of melody on sax and guitar emerging out of a dirge of bass and drums. The first verse is narrated by a Lazarus-like figure from heaven and indicates some of the contradictions of a heavenly repose ("Look up here, I'm in heaven/ I've got scars that can't be seen").[12] But the second verse seems to frame "up here" more as a place of isolation, perhaps the latitude of fame, and of danger ("I'm so high it makes my brain whirl"), which in the significantly unsettling video for the song, is the space of the clinic, the space of illness, the place of physical destitution, like Lazarus' grave.

Then the song rises up into some sort of chorus/bridge, which only occurs once (for such a rhythmically straightforward song it is structurally rather odd and fragmentary). It is of the kind, in the Bowie catalog, that invites biographical speculation. It's never clear whether this song is *actually* autobiographical, or just has the veneer. What does "Then I used up all my money/ I was looking for your ass"[13] mean? The easiest interpretation of Bowie's "Lazarus" would be that it articulates Bowie's feelings after his onstage heart attack of 2004. He did brush up against mortality. But the video for "Lazarus," with its hospital imagery, seems more to describe the mortality of Bowie's later battle with cancer. It transcends illness by celebrating illness.

You could also argue that the song has a much deeper purpose. You could argue that its purpose is to describe Lazarus, the guy who died and who was raised from the dead, in all his complexity, in his death and non-death, with all the mixed emotions, the awe and confusion and dread and trauma, that attend upon the Lazarus story. The "Lazarus" video is rich with irony, and the "I'll be free" out-chorus of the song seems especially ironic, and meant to convey the dread of its opposite. Freedom and non-being being both identical and inimical.

---

12 David Bowie, *Blackstar*, Audio CD (ISO Records, 2016).
13 Ibid.

In Bowie's portrayal of Lazarus, he's the character who occasions irony, as if irony is a thing that is best understood by those who have experienced death, as if irony is the inevitable style of those who have been to the other side, those who have come back to tell of it, like Virgil and Dante. (I'm betting Tiresias understood irony, too, which would mean that irony is also a thing you understand if you have been both a woman and a man.)

Jesus of Nazareth is supposed to have descended into Hell, or to have *harrowed* Hell, during the period between the Crucifixion and the Resurrection, weeks after Lazarus was raised, but there's almost no real scriptural support for the trip. There are sermons about it from the second century, and there are epistles that mention it or allude to it, during the period of the early church, but no real scriptural support. Why did he have to do it? Because all *humans* have to do it, experience death and the afterlife, and irony and trauma, death and not-death, and Jesus of Nazareth was one of us.

Did Jesus know what Lazarus knew? Did Lazarus tell him about it at their dinner? And what does Lazarus tell us about death, in the end? If he could talk, what would he say? That death is not the end, that life is not the end, that life is in the oneiric realm, full of deaths and endings that are commuted into beginnings, and that the feelings one has about all of this are of woe, and trauma, and humility? About what Lazarus knew, one weeps.

Or: Lazarus didn't smile, and got decapitated for this and other crimes, for the traces of his story, for the retelling of his story, for being a bystander to Christ's ministry, and in his story again and again he is reborn to retell.

Death: An Eco-Centric Interpretation
Linda Weintraub

Sap – fluid part of a plant
   Sap – fluid essential for life and associated with vigor
      Sap(ient) – wise
         Sap(iens) – relating to humans

Sap – to drain or deprive of the fluid part of a plant
   Sap – to subvert by eroding the substratum
      Sap – to weaken, exhaust, or undermine
         Sap(iens) – relating to humans

Sap(ling) – youth or a young tree
   Sap – foolish, gullible
      Sap(py) – lacking in good sense, silly
         Sap(iens) – relating to humans

Sap(r) – dead or decaying organic matter
   Sap(ro) – rotten
      Sap(ro) – putrefaction
         Sap(iens) – relating to humans

Interrogating Disease Ecologically

Predators devour their prey from the outside. Disease organisms nibble at their victims from the inside. To the grizzly bear (predator) and the spirochete (disease organism), your body is just food. This ongoing ecological dinner party is rosy from the perspective of the imbiber, and dismal from the perspective of the consumed. Humans are quite skilled at satisfying their appetites by killing plants and animals without becoming meals for other organisms. Still, they are vulnerable to disease.

As opposed to symbiosis, in which the microbes that inhabit our bodies function to maintain your health, disease is a competitive interaction between you and microorganisms. As long as your organism's immune system is intact, there is peaceful coexistence between disease producers and disease receivers. The symptoms of disease don't occur until the disease arms race is no longer balanced and victory either accrues to the attackers or the attacked.

To ecologists, disease is a fundamental ecological mechanism. Even diseases that are not lethal can reduce populations by debilitating an organism so that it is less sexually successful. This also makes them more susceptible to other diseases, to predators, and to environmental stress. Ecologically, health is defined as resistance to a threat. Illness is evidence of an unsuccessful response. As a result, disease is a test of fitness. By eliminating compromised organisms, it tunes the genetic vigor of the species. In this sense, disease is a tool of evolution.

INTERROGATING DEATH ECOLOGICALLY

When death occurs, an organism ceases to consume food, water, and air. But this does not mean it ceases to impact its environment. Once the organism is no longer able to organize its chemistries, the energy bonds and the molecules of the corpse are dismantled. Death releases the molecules that comprised the organism's physical substance. Through decomposition, the materials are sorted and then liberated to resume the processes that they were engaged in prior to being temporarily recruited to form a living being. The final act of every living organism involves returning its storehouse of essential ingredients to the environment, where it becomes available for utilization by other organisms.

This process seems grizzly, but it is efficient. When someone's heart stops pumping blood, tissues and cells are deprived of oxygen and begin to die. Some die within minutes. Others persist up to twenty-four hours after death. However, the millions of microorganisms in the body's intestines don't die with the person. These organisms break down the dead cells, starting in the intestines and then raiding other parts of the body. At the same time, dead cells are discharging enzymes that cannibalize themselves, decomposing tissues are releasing green lung fluids that trickle out the mouth and nostrils, and tissues are emitting gases that blister the skin and swell the abdomen. After death, there is always a mess. Decaying organic matter isn't pretty and it smells foul. But the ecosystem provides a clean-up crew. The turkey vulture, the blow fly, the carrion beetle, the maggot, and some kinds of fungi are ecological "sanitation" workers. They savor the mess, feed upon it with relish, and recycle it through their digestive tracts.

Few humans take comfort in this cycle. We tend to believe that death is the terminus of life on Earth. The last breath is where biographies are said to end. A void exists where a relative, or friend, or pet once lived. Ecological perspectives, however, introduce the alternative view that our bodies are personal collections of impersonal physical matter. They consist of components on loan from the ecosystem. Because each occurrence of death replenishes the ecosystem, environmentalists can be sanguine about it.

Even group deaths that occur within a given habitat do not automatically concern environmentalists. Alarm is not warranted when the reduction in the population of one species frees resources that allow another species to thrive. When this occurs, resources have not been wasted and the abundance of total organisms within the habitat may not have diminished. This group death would not constitute an unequivocal end point.

When, however, a group death applies to all the members of a species in all of its habitats, and it ceases to contribute to the pulse of life on the planet, it is pronounced "extinct." Extinctions constitute evolutionary and ecological end points. Fossil records indicate that the earliest extinctions once occurred at the plodding rate of between 0.02 to 0.002 per year. Current extinction rates have now accelerated to approximate 0.27 per year.

Ecologically, it is death's relationship to diversity that stirs alarm. Ecology texts often refer to diversity as "richness," indicating that species are enriched by genetic diversity, habitats are enriched by species diversity, while species are also enriched by habitat diversity. Each diminishment of diversity, therefore, impoverishes an ecosystem. Environmentalists recognize that maintaining biodiversity is like filling a safe deposit box with as many different currencies as possible. Each contributes to our security against a fluctuating ecological futures market.

In sum, while death assures the health of an ecosystem, ecologically, it is diminishment of diversity that is cause for bereavement and preventive action.

Interrogating Your Attitudes Toward Disease and Death

Is it ethical to intentionally introduce disease for the purpose of strengthening the organism (i.e., inoculations)?

If you are a gardener, would you rejoice or mourn the extinction of slugs?

Are you selfish if you withhold the molecules of your body from the food chain after death through cremation, embalming, mummification, or cryogenics?

Conventional ways of dying include drowning, starving, burning, suffocating, poisoning, freezing, injury, and disease. Humans have amended this list by adding death by – for example – industrial pollution, consumerist lifestyles, and atomic fall-out. Are all causes of deaths equal?

Should breast implants, artificial joints, pace-makers, and prostheses that do not degrade biologically be banned as environmental blights because they are not recyclable once their owners become corpses?

Should the government set up a federal agency to ensure the quality of corpses by outlawing drugs, growth hormones, preservatives, pesticides, asbestos, and other toxins that accumulate in the body's cells?

Should the government provide free burial to those willing to be buried in depleted soils?

Should graveside rituals, eulogies, sacraments, and obituaries become celebrations of the dead person's ego-abandoning act of generosity to the ecosystem?

What are the environmental effects of applying technical means to extend life spans?

Do species become extinct because they are obsolete?

Can efforts to prevent death be excessive, as when Keiko, the killer whale that starred in the movie *Free Willy* beached himself in Norway? The Humane Society of the United States, committed to returning the whale to the wild and "freedom," spent seven years and more than $20 million. He died before he could be released.

Examine your relationship to dead animals by responding to the following questions:

> Do you enjoy carnivorous meals?
> Do you wear leather?
> Have you buried a pet?
> Have you killed an insect or a rodent?
> Do you collect road kill?
> Have you dissected an animal?
> Do you hunt or fish?
> Do you disinfect your toilet?

If your pet dies, are you more likely to cremate the carcass, eat it, taxidermy it, entomb it, expose it to the elements, feed it to other animals, preserve it in formaldehyde, or preserve the parts?

Can death be spiritually replenishing for the survivors, as well as physically replenishing for the ecosystem?

POSTSCRIPT

The foregoing text represents the victor in a contest that was waged in my mind between competing contributions to this volume. Its rival has remained such a tantalizing alternative that I have drafted a few paragraphs to acknowledge its claim to your attention. Simply put, it locates Hatry's project in two cultural contexts that are equally prescient. One involves

'Neo Materialism', a discourse that has assumed a dominating position in twenty-first-century philosophy, cultural theory, feminism, social studies, science studies, and theology. The avalanche of words reflecting the creative contributions of Neo Materialists from each of these disciplines convey the urgency of replacing the dismissive attitudes imbedded in current norms of producing and discarding materials. Neo Materialists are seeking ways to reverse the reliance on digitized, data-driven, abstracted, mediated, and simulated experiences that currently drive contemporary culture by paying tribute to the actual substances that occupy planet Earth. The other context is occupied by a growing legion of artists actualizing Neo Materialist mandates. This emerging artistic niche honors matter, materiality, and the processes of materialization. The art examples that follow provide compelling examples of the specific approach to Neo Materialism. These art works confirm the timeliness of Hatry's project.

The artist China Adams had her entire body x-rayed. She then offered her bones for sale while she is young and healthy. Collectors must wait for her to die before they claim the bone they purchased. She did it to test the 'futures market' – peoples' assessments of her eventual worth as an artist.

Marc Quinn sculpted his bust. His medium is his own frozen blood – nine liters extracted over a period of five months. In another work of art, he created a portrait of John E. Sulston, who won the Nobel Prize for sequencing the human genome. The work is created with bacteria containing Sulston's DNA. Quinn placed it in agar jelly so that the bacteria would replicate. This artwork literally perpetuates Sulston's life.

Jae Rhim Lee enables the deceased to live on, materially and ecologically. By creating an infinity mushroom and an infinity burial suit, the artwork not only decomposes the body; it removes the toxins that have accumulated in the body due to ingesting pharmaceuticals and food additives and environmental blight. In this manner Lee ensures that the corpse's molecules will augment the fertility of the soil and enhance botanical vitality.

Wenda Gu created "alchemical ink" using powdered Chinese hair for his monumental ink paintings. Gu considers this genetic ink to be an art object. In China, powdered human hair is traditionally used as a medical treatment for anxiety. While traditional ink fabrication uses charcoal powder for black pigment, Gu created ink that utilizes the original Chinese prescription of powdered human hair. Gu explains: "The human hair-made ink is now given a conceptual function to cure cultural anxiety."

Justin Crowe mixes cremated human ashes into a glaze which he uses to coat bowls, vases, candle holders, coffee cups, urns, and other ceramic items. In one art project, Crowe used the mixed ashes of more than 200 people to create a dinnerware collection called *Nourish*. He comments: "Integrating someone's ashes into ceramics is a way of infusing their memory into everyday life."

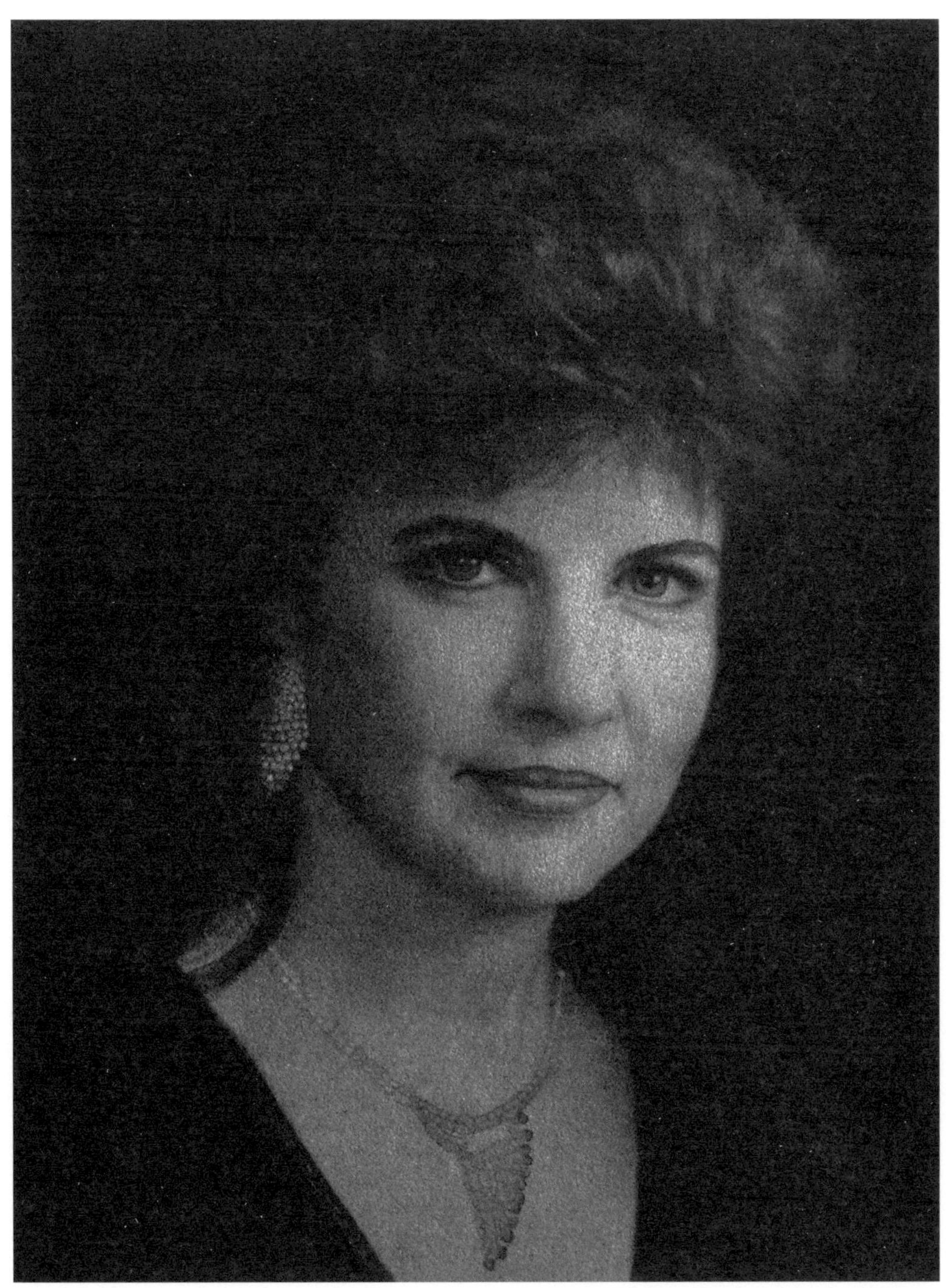

The Pornography of Death, the Fading of Grief
Naief Yehya

The Unbearable Truth of the Dead

Pornography is, in essence, any kind of representation that is considered unacceptable by those who have the power to suppress speech in society. Pornography is not a thing but rather a policy, an act of censorship imposed on certain depictions considered transgressive. It's not about what is depicted but about what is considered beyond the borders of acceptability. Nevertheless, when we think about pornography, the first images that come to mind are those of naked bodies, explicit sexual acts, and the display of bodily functions. Pornography is about obscenity – showing what should be ob-scene or off-scene – breaking taboos, and doing so by not only provoking but also exciting the viewer with the spectacle of the forbidden. The formula of pornography includes things taken out of context, and the fine-tuning of two elements – arousal and shame.

The obsession with hiding sexual matters became prevalent during Victorian times and has been an essential part of Western culture ever since. Until the nineteenth century, death was a perfectly acceptable fact of life, but it gradually transformed into an unmentionable subject, something to be kept away from children and polite conversation. From a time in which it was common to have public executions, corpses rotting in the streets, and wakes with an open coffin, we shifted into an era in which the facts of death are hidden from the public gaze, disguised, and even denied. In an age of total exposure through the Internet flood of images, we can now see images of pretty much anything, but very often, in a compulsive and misguided effort of modesty, the veil of censorship covers the images of death. We are not allowed to see the bullet-ridden bodies of children massacred at a school or the crushed victims of American bombs in the Middle East or indeed, almost any corpse that might be unpalatable. We have sanitized the horrors of our time by pixelating the gore, blurring the faces of the deceased, and suppressing the depictions of carnage in most media. We have relegated those images to feature films where special effects can be hyper-realistic and non-threatening. Corpses have become exploited subjects in a thrilling form of entertainment.

Grief and Ritual

Death rituals are performance and communion; their main objective is to show respect, unite friends and family in sorrow, and begin a healing process. Every culture has created its own ceremonies to deal with bereavement according to their beliefs. The secular West however, hasn't found satisfactory rituals and seems to believe that the best way to mourn is not to mourn at all, because it's a time-consuming, unpleasant, and uncivil self-indulgence. We tend to treat grief much as we do lust – as an embarrassing weakness of character. We can assume that grief never really goes away. It would be difficult to believe that a single event is capable of healing and bringing closure. C.S. Lewis wrote: "Sorrow turns out to be not a state but a process. It needs not a map but a history..."[1] In a time of compulsive individualism and information overload, we have apparently lost the skills to express and accept grief. Information on the death of celebrities and the news of thousands of people killed in war, terrorist attacks, and disasters flows in the social networks along with jokes, frivolous comments, announcements of birthdays, promotions, and cute cat videos. We have embraced life as a sequence of chaotic and undifferentiated (but almost always censored) postings in our timelines, which leads to a severe devaluation of empathy.

Sex and Death

There has been a shift in taboos over the last 200 years in which sexual images have become more and more abundant and tolerated while the images of death have turned toxic and scandalous. This has created a de facto pornography of death, one that rewards the viewer with a stimulating frisson and an adrenaline hit at the very sight of blood and guts. In a time of near-infinite wars and catastrophes – both man-made and natural – ugly visions of death, dying, tortured, and decomposed bodies have been transformed into objects of enticement and seduction. Dozens of "porntubes" and similar Internet sites offer hard-core pornography, images of sadomasochism and all possible varieties of extreme fetishes, side by side with videos of actual murders, brutal accidents, torture, and general carnage. We can argue that this is not new. Since ancient times, people from diverse corners of the world have been obsessed with the ghoulish and the grotesque. Artists have represented, sometimes in great detail, hellish visions of pain, dismemberment, and terror. Historically, these images induce strange and contradictory feelings of fear, alarm, repugnance, excitation, and a certain amount of relief by placing the viewer as a witness, across an abyss of suffering. By showing horrific scenes, as something that happens to someone else, in a sort of distant reflection of oneself, a sacrificial projection transforms pain and death into something to be observed and even enjoyed.

La muerte

I was born and raised in Mexico, where death rituals are famously extravagant. El Día de los muertos, is the most common cliché evoked every time someone wants to portray an irreverent celebration of the departed. This tradition carries distorted reflections of the legacy of pre-Hispanic rituals and also incorporates an assortment of Christian elements. The fascination with the image of death has been explored by a number of Mexican artists – José Guadalupe Posadas, José Clemente Orozco, Diego Rivera, Frida Kahlo, Martha Pacheco,

---

1 C.S. Lewis, *A Grief Observed* (San Francisco: Harper Collins, 1996), p. 56.

and Teresa Margolles among others. The imagery of this celebration is also observed in the popular cult of *La Santa Muerte*, a deity in the image of the classic Grim Reaper, which is rapidly gaining followers in Mexico and other parts of the world. But the colorful altars, the sugar and chocolate skulls, the *cempasúchitl* flowers, and all the imaginative *ofrendas* or offerings to the dead, could not have prepared us for the horrendous torture and executions videos posted by narco cartels in the twenty-first century. In these videos, we witness men and women being interrogated, tortured, mutilated, and decapitated in grotesque efforts to intimidate the police, the army, and rival gangs. One of the most atrocious videos available on the Web shows three men and two women, alleged members of the Zetas, being hacked into pieces with axes and machetes by masked members of the Cartel del Golfo, and then thrown into smoking barrels to be dissolved into what is called *pozole*, an ironic reference to the original Aztec pozole soup, which they used to prepare with corn and possibly human flesh. Pozole is still eaten on special occasions but, needless to say, with pork meat. Some of these videos even have *narco-corridos* as background music to make clear their intention to entertain and excite the viewer. This type of macabre material has found its natural channel of circulation on the Web, where it's shared, preserved, and reproduced with minimal risk of being traced or censored. These materials, as well as jihadi execution videos, comprise the contemporary vanguard of the pornography of death.

Vanished Students, Vanished Certainties

On September 26, 2014, forty-three students from a rural school in Ayotzinapa, Guerrero, were abducted by the police, possibly with the collaboration of the army, and were then presumably handed over to a local narco gang. It is believed that the criminals tortured them and afterward cremated their bodies. Even in a country that has made several international headlines over the last decade because of its terrifying levels of violence and human rights abuses, this case is particularly horrifying. The incinerated remains of the majority of the students have yet to be found, and the families of the disappeared are still struggling to get some answers. The few ashes that have been recovered have become a contentious issue. Investigators have even suggested that the government may have planted evidence in an effort to close the case. The disappearance of the students brings to mind Heide Hatry's *Icons in Ash*, a series of portraits constructed with funerary ashes that appear to float on a base of beeswax. These images can be seen as relics, objects that might not bring closure to the bereaved but may offer some kind of material certainty, and some physical connection with the departed. For the parents of the forty-three students, the absence of proof of their children's death makes their loss all the more heartbreaking. Perhaps being presented with as much as a fistful of ashes might make their loss slightly more bearable. It's probably a natural need to try and keep the dead alive, to keep them close in some strange and vague way. In our unwillingness to confront the reality of death and the needs of the mourner, our culture begat a pornography of death, a cruel, sad, and dehumanizing expression of cynicism and callousness that characterizes the peculiar and sometimes sinister techno culture of our times.

How Much Death Can Life Bear?

Franz Josef Wetz

Media vita in morte sumus: "In the midst of life we are in death." So intones a Gregorian chant from the Middle Ages, to which Rainer Maria Rilke seems to allude with the words: "Der Tod ist groß./ Wir sind die Seinen/ lachenden Munds./ Wenn wir uns mitten im Leben meinen,/ wagt er zu weinen/ mitten in uns."[1] Although it is common knowledge that we ourselves and our next of kin will one day die, still most appear to be taken by surprise when their number, or that of their loved ones, actually comes up. None of them, it seems, had seriously reckoned with it. To die "sometime," however, means never to die. The uncertainty of our hour of death cradles us in its illusion – meanwhile, anything can befall anyone at any moment. So long as we are alive, we have been "saved" by life for the time being. Everyone knows this, yet most contrive to ignore it. Almost everybody hopes for a postponement, a stay of execution: *not yet*! Knowing the hour of our death with certainty – recorded on a birth certificate, in a passport or on a wristwatch – would be unbearable. But, just because we do not know, we feel ourselves to be in the perpetual vicinity of death. The gravely ill fall irrevocably into this vicinity as soon as they are confronted with bad news. Suddenly life is departing, as they knew it would. All at once, they find themselves just shy of ashes.

Nobody is easily consoled that s/he has to die, and almost all the arguments that claim the opposite range from bad to ridiculous. Biologically, death and dying are, to be sure, a part of the natural cycle; theologically, they have been the springboard to a better world. However, dying and death have lost none of their sting through scientific education, rational palliatives, and religious castles in the air. If one clings to earthly life, one isn't likely to be much comforted by the rosy prospect of heaven beyond the grave. And we do not have to love life inordinately to feel the stark horrors of dying and death. Philosophical counsel does particularly little to help us bear uncomplainingly and with equanimity our inevitable lot, since nobody can stem the incessant flux of things to which we must thus submit. Although death and dying may in themselves be natural and inevitable, for most they represent a catastrophe of the highest order – an existential car-crash, a written-off vehicle. Who among us dies willingly? No one lightly ticks off his life. And, therefore,

---

1 Rainer Maria Rilke, "Schlußstück," in *Gesammelte Gedichte* (Frankfurt am Main: Insel, 1962), p. 233. "Death is vast./ We are his/ laughing mouths./ When we think ourselves in the midst of life,/ he dares to cry/ in the midst of us." Translated by Heide Hatry.

almost everyone hopes to be overtaken by death in their sleep, so as not to have to even be present for it. Yet, however much we mortals cling to life, no one escapes death in the end, and all that is left is a corpse – which, of course, raises the question of how we might or ought to deal with it.

What is a Corpse?

The concept of the dead body is deeply ambiguous. In the first place, we understand by it the cadaver; that is, the corruptible residue of a human being, which is normally buried, burnt, or made available for medical transplantation or clinical anatomy. Apart from the skull and skeleton, the dead body is the most impressive evidence of human transitoriness. On the other hand, the concept of the dead person also relates to the deceased, whose last will regarding their estate and funeral arrangements is normally respected and followed. A *corpse* is laid to rest, while *the dead* are remembered; the former is a lifeless object in the visible world; the latter, by contrast, are a lively subject of memory.

This clear and unequivocal distinction blurs at the sight of a dead body. Here the viewer is confronted with something highly ambivalent: s/he sees something familiar and alien, human and not-human, an organism and a thing. Certainly, a corpse is less than a person, but it is still evidently more than a brute object. Hence the abuse of a corpse also counts neither as damage to property nor bodily harm, but rather as something in-between. Nowadays, in this part of the world, the corpse is even imbued with a certain claim to respect, because it is the decomposable *residuum* of a former person, which simply means *the corpse belongs to the deceased*. According to prevailing opinion, the corpse retains a special value as an object, since it was once a subject. In the corpse, the deceased remains, as it were, present in absence. It still bears for a short time the traits of the dead person, although it is from the outset something wholly other than a human being. However, this ambiguity of the dead body is by no means stable. For, even though the body disintegrates through decay or incineration, and despite its radical decomposition in earth or ashes, the objective character of the human remains persists, though their subjective quality dissipates. Earth to earth, dust to dust!

Shift in Funeral Culture

Today, more than thirty types of funeral are observed, all of which qualify as compatible with the claim to respect of the dead body. Apart from the conventional earth burial in a coffin and the cremation service with the urn at the cemetery, there is also the option of having one's ashes interred in a biodegradable urn in a forest burial ground or *Ruheforst* (peace forest). In addition, a few grams can be shot into space in a small capsule or strewn over an alpine meadow, a woodland area, or on high mountains from the Matterhorn to

Mount Everest. Besides this, air funerals from a balloon, burials at sea or the scattering of ashes in football stadia for fans, players and officials anywhere from Great Britain to Spain are also on offer.

These few quaint examples already make clear that the contemporary right to self-determination extends not only as far as death, but even beyond the grave. More and more people are taking the opportunity to stage-manage their own funerals through the choice of a dedicated occasion with a specific ritual agenda. This diversity mirrors not only modern individualism, which seems to extend the space for decision and action by the autonomous individual into the realm of the post-mortal, but also the popular decline of bonds to religion and church. Particularly in urban areas, ecclesiastical funeral services are increasingly being abandoned in favor of individually curated memorial celebrations, the design of which the dead themselves may already have prepared in their lifetimes. The myriad forms of burial rites reflect the supersession of old clerical funeral rituals by new "patchwork" mourning ceremonies.

Now, however, not all the ways of handling dead bodies aim at their inhumation. In some cases, remarkable as it might sound, it is a matter of their conservation. These include, for example, "diamondization," in which a diamond is produced from the ashes accruing from cremation that can be worn by the next of kin as keepsake jewelry from the deceased. Likewise, family members and friends are now offered glittering amulets as ornamental pieces, in which locks of hair or a few grams of ashes of the departed can be embedded. Something similar holds for the "ash portraits" of Heide Hatry, in which, using the person's actual ashes, the face of the deceased is recreated. On the other hand, matters are conducted quite differently with the "plastinates" of Gunther von Hagens, the creator of the world-renowned, anatomical touring exhibition *Body Worlds*, in which the visitor encounters aesthetically conceived anatomical specimens.

The Elucidation of Life and the Accomplishment of Mourning

Hatry and the anatomist von Hagens are connected by their work on dead bodies. At the same time, there are major differences. While the plastinates remain anonymous, Hatry maps out the individual face in her ash icons. While the plastinates are shown only in exhibitions and handed over to medical or scientific organizations, Hatry entrusts her ash portraits to the next of kin of the deceased. Furthermore, von Hagens' body donors have in their own lifetimes consented to their plastination, whereas, in her artistic work with cremation ashes, Hatry has, up to now, worked only with the consent of the relatives of the deceased. The most important difference, however, lies in their objectives. That of von Hagens concerns scientific education; whereas Hatry's concerns artistic consolation. Otherwise expressed, von Hagens aims in his works at a better understanding of life; while Hatry, by contrast, intends a better mastery of grief.

1) *Body Worlds* simultaneously offers the viewer extraordinary factual information and unusual sensations that leave visitors demonstrably emotionally disturbed and ruminative. As much as what is at stake for the exhibition organizers concerns the transmission of anatomical knowledge, at the same time they intend through the exhibition to render an important contribution to the intensification of conscious life – since, in addition, they want to enhance the sense of health itself, highlight the thresholds and capacities of the body, and ultimately excite engagement with the question of the significance of the human being.

Body Worlds is fundamentally a celebration of life. Indeed, the exhibition moves in the border zone between death and life by bringing into view the interiors of the body in authentic specimens, as is characteristic of anatomy. But, just because of this, the exhibition calls attention to the wonder of life. In *Body Worlds*, life celebrates itself. The human body, which Renaissance philosophers described and honored as the "temple of the soul," here impresses itself as an attraction. The exhibition's goal is to enthuse people for life.

In concrete terms, the exhibition shows the visitor both the graceful design of the body as well as its fragility. In so doing, it becomes clear that the body's vulnerable frailty is actually the venerable price of its complexity. Without its perishability and its finitude, mortal life would be impossible. For this reason, the exhibition demonstrates at the same time the "greatness and misery" of human existence. From the Church Fathers to modern times, via the theologians of the Renaissance, the simultaneous sublimity and nullity of the human being has periodically been highlighted. On the one hand, the human being is deemed a great marvel; on the other, ephemeral dust.

Furthermore, the exhibition calls attention to the uniqueness and specificity of the human being by bringing out the exquisitely structured bodies against the background of our mortal transience. By such means it teaches the viewer astonishment in their own existence, for which wonder there remains little room in everyday life. The exhibition teaches one to look anew upon one's own life as something exceptional. It celebrates life as a present, a gift and, by association, a task. Most of the time, in the hustle and bustle of our quotidian modernity, the distinctiveness of life is incuriously overlooked. By contrast, in the exhibition, quickly gathered reflections start to spread. What is most inconspicuous and self-evident – existence itself – becomes what is most remarkable and strange.

Ultimately, the exhibition innervates the question of the value and significance of the human being. Where do we come from? Where are we headed? What is the meaning of my earthly existence? The amazement at one's own life itself stirs up ultimate questions. Gratitude turns into astonishment. However, the exhibition remains ideologically neutral. It does not answer the ultimate questions. *Body Worlds* is interpretively open to different images of human being.

2) Were Hatry's ash portraits formed from the mortal remains of saints, they would have to be classified as relics, in which, according to the medieval worldview, the venerated departed is moreover really present. Relics offer believers palpable consolation, help and support. The artistically manufactured ash portraits assume a similar function for the grieving, for whom they are able to perform sound service during their "work of mourning." Both the sudden and the expected death of a human being often leaves friends and family stunned and powerless in the face of its irreversibility. Afflicted and overcome – or, indeed, desperate – they are frequently at a loss before this painful, as well as terminal, event. The loss of a once close person is nothing but intellectually and emotionally difficult to bear and to process. All at once, a longstanding conversation partner is hushed, whose silence henceforth will always be the same. Mourning holds the bereaved captive for an unspecified time, such that the question soon acquires an urgency: How will an emotional equilibrium be re-established?

According to Sigmund Freud, mourning is an emotional malaise in which interest in the outer world and the ability to cope with life dwindle. The work of mourning, which can develop into a difficult and protracted process, consists, according to Freud, in the gradual detachment from the beloved person against one's own inner resistances. For this reason, it is frequently burdensome, if not agonizing. The death of a human being challenges the bereaved emotionally and mentally in equal measure. However, the loss must be affectively and cognitively overcome, if one's inner balance and capacity for action are to be restored. According to Freud, the painful work of mourning is concluded when all expectations bound up with the lost love object are finally given up, and the libidinal bonds to the deceased are eventually dissolved.

In this arduous process, Hatry's ash portraits are able to undertake an essential task. Commonly, during grief work, the mourner regularly calls the deceased back into remembrance: in order, on the one hand, to ascertain their proximity; on the other, however, to envision their displacement. The dead person really is no longer there. In this way, it gradually becomes ever clearer that the departed is, in fact, irretrievably gone. The ash portraits are able to take over precisely this double function: they both confront mourners with the missing person in the form of their portrait; while the ash out of which they have been artistically shaped allows their death to be reflected. The ash portrait creates a fictional encounter with the deceased, which can help the mourner to cope with the implacable event, as many experience a strong need to speak with the dead person for a while longer, to sense them somehow, to establish and sustain emotional contact with them. This unaccomplishable need is understandable; after all, the dead leave behind them a vacancy. Often, the communciation is abruptly broken off. For this reason, the bereaved commonly turn to photographs, which they place around themselves in order to step into an imagined dialogue with the one who has been silenced. In peculiarly intensive ways, such a communication is possible with the ash portraits, which emerge from the human remains of the dead person. Since such dialogues are now not real but imaginary – because the ash portrait is of course silent, even though the person portrayed is being spoken with – this corresponds with what is for all practical purposes a mental and emotional separation from the deceased, until the final farewell or leave-taking is one day fully accomplished.

Two purposes emerge: one is the service performed by the ash portraits for the private accomplishment of grief; another is their anonymous presentation in an exhibition for a wider public. In such an exhibition, the ash portraits symbolize, in the manner of Hans Holbein's *Dance of Death* (1526) or Brueghel the Elder's *Triumph of Death* (1562) – two *topoi* of Western cultural history that in literature and painting have been subject to many variations – the well-known words of warning: *respice finem* or *memento mori* ("remember you are mortal!"). The medieval legend of the "Three Living and the Three Dead" also belongs to this context, as depicted in numerous paintings. The story concerns three young boys on a hunt who encounter three skeletons. The latter turn to the living with the admonition: "What you are, so we were; what we are, so you will be." Death has always been personified in such allegorical representations as the Grim Reaper, a skeleton or a horseman, or reified as extinguished candles, withered flowers or the hourglass as a symbol of time trickling away. The ash portraits of Hatry move along this line of tradition. The form, the face, stands for life; the underlying material, the ash, for death, which resides in all life as its disquieting sting.

Detached from the millennia-old question as to whether death signifies an absolute end or the transition into another reality, the ash portraits, like the old allegories previously noted, may call the attention of interested persons to their own mortality, the better to recognize the distinctiveness and uniqueness of our own lives, and perhaps also effect important corrections to our previous life course in order to use our expiring lifetimes meaningfully, or simply not take everything so dourly.

Herein lies a great sympathy between the aims of Hatry and von Hagens. Both ash portraits and plastinates are the result of creative work on human remains. Bluntly stated, this circumstance inevitably throws up a range of ethical questions, especially since the artist Hatry and the anatomist von Hagens are German.

Working on Dead People

Only skilful workmanship and imaginative creativity enable on the one hand the technically demanding as well as aesthetically appealing plastination of the body's interiors for anatomical education, and on the other hand the artistic creation of ash portraits in order to console or create symbols of *vanitas*. Both plastination and ash portraiture require human remains: in the one case, the ashes of dead people; in the other, body donors, into which deep cuts are inserted in order to make visible the surfaces of hidden structures through artistic distortion. Plastinates portray creatively worked-on external views from the body's interiors. But is it even permissible for human remains to be transformed into exhibits of artistic and anatomical art and presented openly in public? Does such action still lie within the protected domain of artistic and scientific freedom? Does it not contravene human dignity to make biological human material, through free creative composition and aesthetic deformation, into a mere exhibit? Against the backdrop of National Socialism, should not Germans in particular show greater sensitivity and renounce such work? These questions both Hatry and von Hagens must acknowledge. In the past, von Hagens has repeatedly been blamed for not merely striving for anatomical education and the transmission of knowledge, but also operating as an artist, insofar as whole body plastinates could be seen as artworks.

EXPLOITATION OF THE HUMAN AS CONTEMPT FOR THE HUMAN

What may be done with corpses? It is well known that under National Socialism book bindings and lampshades were produced from the prepared skin of slaughtered Jews, as soap was also fashioned from their treated body fat. Further, dental gold was broken off the corpses, in order to use it subsequently for SS dental treatment or transfer it to the Reichsbank. Moreover, the hair of the camp prisoners was a sought-after raw material, which was gathered, dried and sold to make rope, felt or carpet by the hundredweight. Last but not least, the ashes of the cremated bodies of the victims were used in some instances as filler in road-building or for thermal insulation in construction, as well as fertilizer in the camps' own farmyards. In short, dead bodies were processed as commodities and industrially exploited; the human transformed into the not-human.

Since the time of National Socialism, all industrial processing of corpses as commodities and their economic use has become intolerable; both would now be judged as aggressive acts of contempt for the human. However, such an assessment is not self-evident. Around three centuries ago, for example, it was not held to be degrading or disrespectful in France to obtain effective remedies from corpses; neither are rosary beads made from vertabrae uncommon in European history. However, with such comparisons, the cultural characteristics of the particular era must be factored in. Since National Socialism, the production of utility objects from human remains has in any case become unacceptable, since at the time such humiliating instrumentalizations also and especially served to deny humanity to the human being concerned, even after death, in symbolic ways. The painful memory here is still all too vivid. While the plastinated corpses of von Hagens and the ash icons of Hatry have nothing to do with all this, because they present what is human as human, the question persists as to whether it should be permissible to work dead people into consoling or educative artworks.

Every day living people are turning themselves into artworks: this extends from street performers to ballet dancers; from actors to opera singers; from film stars to pop stars (as well as the action- and life-performances of the modernist avant-garde, the creative happenings of cultural modernity). Here, the work merges with the corporeal performance: every tiny gesture; every mimetic reaction; every bodily movement is art. The artwork has thus turned into an art event, the presentation of the artwork essentially depending upon human agency. To give just one contemporary example, the American photographer Spencer Tunick often arranges naked people "in piles" in artistic poses, which he subsequently shoots. People with a marked predilection for tattoos also like to look upon their bodies as artworks. The same goes for bodybuilders with their keenly contoured "formed flesh." They understand themselves less as athletes than sculptors and sculptures, in one and the same person. It sounds so strange: bodybuilding, dance and pantomime are all attempts to transform one's own body and personal life into an artwork. The most significant example in art is probably Orlan.

However, there are only a few examples of the transformation of dead bodies into artworks. Under the title *Self*, the contemporary English artist Marc Quinn models his head at regular intervals out of his own frozen blood, in order to document the mutations in his physiognomy. Yet up to now there have hardly been any artworks that use authentic body parts. Admittedly, this could have arisen not only for ethical reasons, but also especially on technical grounds; for artists have, as a rule, major problems with the procurement and preservation of body parts. The few artistic specimens originate predominantly from anatomists like Honoré Fragonard or Frederik Ruysch, who have enjoyed easy access to dead bodies and the knowledge of conservation.

Since there is no problem of decomposition with skulls and bones, numerous artworks or quasi-artistic creations exist all over the world, however. Impressive examples include, for example, the *Schädelkult* (skull cult) exhibition or the famous Hallstatt Charnel House in Austria, where around six hundred beautifully painted skulls can be marvelled at. What is more, in Rome and elsewhere in Europe, many places may be visited with candlesticks, chandeliers and other objects fashioned from human bones. However, up to now, one seeks in vain for such artworks made from human ashes as Hatry produces. Nevertheless, the question arises: Why should human ashes and dead human bodies not be transformed into consoling and anatomical artworks respectively?

The Ethical Problem

According to the so-called object formula, it is ethically objectionable to make the human being – a subject with their own value – into a bare object or to use them as means to an end. It is thereby *not* prohibited, that is to say, to use a human being as a thing or a tool, which would certainly be wholly unrealistic, because human beings constantly serve as objects or means to ends for each other: the taxi driver for the passenger; or the saleswoman for the customer. The object formula prohibits, however, the human being from becoming a *bare* object or *bare* medium. To address the question of whether Hatry's project *Icons in Ash* or von Hagen's *Body Worlds* are ethically admissible, the object formula is of the utmost importance.

At first glance, the answer seems certain: both are ethically objectionable, insofar as they use the dead person as artwork and exhibition piece and thus at the same time as a means to an end. However, appearances are deceptive, since the object formula does not lend itself to being transferred to human remains in any event. That is to say, this formula justly prohibits the alienation of human subjects or living people as mere objects or things; only human remains are no longer subjects or people. As the corruptible residue of a human being, a corpse possesses overriding object quality. This much even the representatives of religious views must acknowledge – otherwise they would not allow the extraction of tissues and organs for purposes of transplantation, nor the surrender of a corpse for academic anatomy, and not even assent to its cremation or decomposition under the earth. Yet we hold all this to be permissible, just because we no longer look upon the corpse, viewed in isolation, as a subject, but as an object. Hence it makes no sense to think the human remains would be desecrated as objects by their artful presentation for the purpose of grief work and education, or by the eyes of viewers.

Of course, they are here also being used as a means to an end. But that is also true for anatomical dissection, which instrumentalizes the cadaver as a medium for training and research, as well as for the forensic autopsy, which uses the corpse as a means for the establishment of the truth, for organ transplantation, in which the dead body of the one is used to save the life of another, and for the presentation of skulls and bones in memorials, as for example in Cambodia or Rwanda, where human remains are inserted as a means of warning of terrible crimes. All this, therefore, is only ethically justified because it is certain that a corpse is no longer a person.

However human remains may be used as objects, this should never be only as a means to an end, because they were indeed once a subject and therefore to them, as already laid out, a certain claim of respect already applies. As the corruptible residue of former persons they thus may also not be used for arbitrary purposes. The view is unanimous that one may not produce from corpses functional objects like keys or coat stands. In such a case, one would be changing the human into the not-human. In artistic or anatomical design, respect for what is typically human may not be lost. The artistic estrangement of human remains may only go so far; the dead material in the work cannot be wholly dehumanized. It is, indeed, impossible to say with certainty how the claim of a dead person for due respect can be fulfilled and the moral sensibility of the citizen in a pluralistic society be best held in mind. However, it can be easily recognized that dead human material is not thereby more respected because one gives it over to the earth for decomposition, to the crematorium for burning, to anatomy for instruction, to medical transplantation for the saving of life, or to forensic medicine for crime education, than when one, with the consent of the concerned parties or relatives, makes it available for lay anatomy or ash art. Of course, the last will of the deceased here must always take precedence as long as, by its enactment, public order is not compromised, nor public health endangered. Beyond this, the purposes pursued in respect of the treatment of the corpse must be able to be regarded as ethically justified. Anatomical education, health promotion, accomplishment of mourning, and the *memento mori* surely fulfill this demand adequately.

The recognition that the viewers of *Icons in Ash* and *Body Worlds* almost invariably display great solemnity, fascinated curiosity, and reflective involvement attests to the ethical admissibility of both cultural events. In any event, it seems that the works and their ambience create an atmosphere that apparently invites a gripped reverence. The emergence of such experiences never depends on the exhibits alone, but also quite considerably on the design of the spaces. But what allows us to tell whether an exhibition offers exhibits a worthy stage? In the end, the behaviour of visitors decides this. The setting of an artistic or anatomical presentation is adequate when an exhibition succeeds in evoking strong, intensive, and memorable perceptions, thought processes, and associations in the viewer. The gravity with which people encounter the ash portraits and plastinates is not due to the fact that they are receiving something terrible to behold to which they may not be equal. How one views the exhibits essentially depends upon the eyes with which one sees them. The sobriety with which people engage with the ash portraits and plastinates derives much more from how they are here confronted with the marvel of life, its complexity and fragility, and with the question of its accomplishment in bereavement. Finitude adjusts everything.

This text was translated from the German by Dr. Simon A. Thomas.

Stones and Ashes
Siri Hustvedt

I keep one of my father's passports on a shelf above my writing desk. He died on February 2, 2004. He was cremated and then buried in the small cemetery of the rural church in Minnesota he attended as a boy. It is a short walk from there to my grandparents' small farmhouse, which now stands empty, its white paint scarred with gray. The immense maple tree, the grape arbor, the peony and lilac bushes, the pear and apple trees are still vigorous. They are no longer tended by anyone, but the bushes and trees bloom, and the fruit comes back every year.

We visit the grave. We plant flowers.

What are we visiting?

No human culture discards its dead without ceremony. To leave the dead without rites is personal and collective ignominy. It seems that even the Neanderthals buried their dead.

Although it was long thought that mourning was an exclusively human trait, research suggests that other primates, elephants, and some birds grieve for their fellow creatures; that cultural practices handed down from one generation to the next are not ours alone.

The variety of human customs that attend death is stupefying. The Vikings placed the corpse in a long boat, set it on fire, and pushed it out to sea. The Zulus burn the dead person's property because they fear the presence of the spirit in those things. Pierre Clastres, the French anthropologist, who in 1963-64 wrote an account of the two years he spent with an isolated people in Paraguay, *Chronicle of the Guayaki Indians*, reported that members of the community were vague and unforthcoming when he inquired about their death rituals. One person would say one thing, another something else. It made no sense to him. Not long before Clastres left the tribe, an old woman (who had not been told that the outsider was to remain ignorant) informed him that the Guayaki eat their dead. The consumption of corpses was intended to break the connection of spirit to body, and thereby free or banish the spirit so it could do no harm to the living.

Human beings grieve, fear, and worship the dead.

In a village in northern Thailand in 1975, I frightened the children who thought I was a spirit. They had never seen a person so tall, white, and blonde. They ran away from me shouting "pii, pii," the Thai word for ghost.

The people of many cultures mark out space for the dead: burial grounds, stones, totem poles, urns, mausoleums, tombs cut directly into the rock face of cliffs, tombs suspended from mountain sides, and coffins elevated on stilts yards above the earth.

Lewis Mumford wrote, in *The City in History*, "The city of the dead antedates the city of the living."[1] He argued that people wanted to live close to the burial places of their ancestors, to whom they were drawn with mingled feelings of worship and dread, and that is how the city was born: necropolis before metropolis.

But there is also the literal preservation of the dead: embalming, mummification, various forms of holding on to the corpse. In the Museo Chileno de Arte Precolombino in Santiago, Chile, one of the curators explained to me that a long-vanished tribe in what is now a part of Chile were a hunting-gathering people; but they engaged in elaborate rituals and embalming practices. This came as a great surprise to anthropologists because they did not expect such sophistication from hunter-gatherers. Their afterlife was given far more attention than their before-life.

The Aboriginal people in northern Australia preserve and paint the bones of the dead. A people in Africa wear the bones of the dead while they mourn. The English of the Victorian period were partial to jewelry made from the hair of a dear, dead person. In part because burial space is limited and graves must be turned over in sixty years, increasing numbers of South Koreans are converting the ashes of their loved ones into colorful strings of beads that can be displayed at home.

My grandmother used to hear my grandfather moving around the farmhouse after he died. Once she saw him lift his hat from the hook on the back of the kitchen door. It is not uncommon for people to hallucinate the dead in their grief, but the phenomenon is poorly studied, perhaps because scientists resist the idea of ghosts. These specters mostly bring comfort to people in mourning. They are vivid reincarnations of a lost beloved, waking dreams of intense wishes. One woman I read about saw her deceased cat roaming contently in the rooms they once shared.

Few of us are free of the feeling that death, that most ordinary of all ordinary facts about our existence, is also unutterably strange. When the person is no longer there, we try to preserve what was in what is – with signs and tokens. People die around me; but when

---

1 Lewis Mumford, *The City in History: Its Origins, Its Transformations, and Its Prospects* (New York: Harcourt, Brace & World, 1961), p. 7.

I cared for the dead person, the loss is of me, not outside of me. "It is the dead, not the living, who make the longest demands," Antigone says to her sister Ismene, in the play by Sophocles, "We die forever." The tragic heroine refuses to let her brother go without tending to his body, without giving him the funeral rites he deserves. She defies the legal decree that has forbidden it, even though she knows it means her own death.

It is true that we are forever dying. It is also true that we cannot treat the bodies of our dead as if they were no different from the trash we routinely take out to the curb. We must symbolize the loss and care for the remains in one way or another. How we do that depends on our culture, but cultural practices evolve and change.

I will be burned and then buried in Greenwood Cemetery in Brooklyn on top of or underneath my husband, depending on which one of us dies first. When we found the spot in that huge necropolis, I felt happy. How odd that feeling was. I do not want to die. I am always worrying that I will die before I have written what I still hope to write, and yet I am pleased with the burial plot, pleased to think of it verdant in spring and summer, rouged in fall, and desolate or white in winter, despite the fact that I, snuffed of all consciousness, will not enjoy the shifting seasons anymore. (Do we hallucinate our own ghosts?)

I love the Tom Waits song with its insistent refrain, "We're all gonna be just dirt in the ground." I sing along, I dance, I laugh. I am not sure why.

I am glad that the ground where my father's ashes are buried is marked with his name. My mother is ninety-three. She has asked me to bury half of her ashes beside my father and to take the other half to her native Norway. She wants me to scatter them on the graves of her parents in the town of Mandal where she was born and spent her childhood. On the small mountain that rises above those graves is the house my grandfather designed and where my mother lived as a girl. From there one can look straight out to the sea.

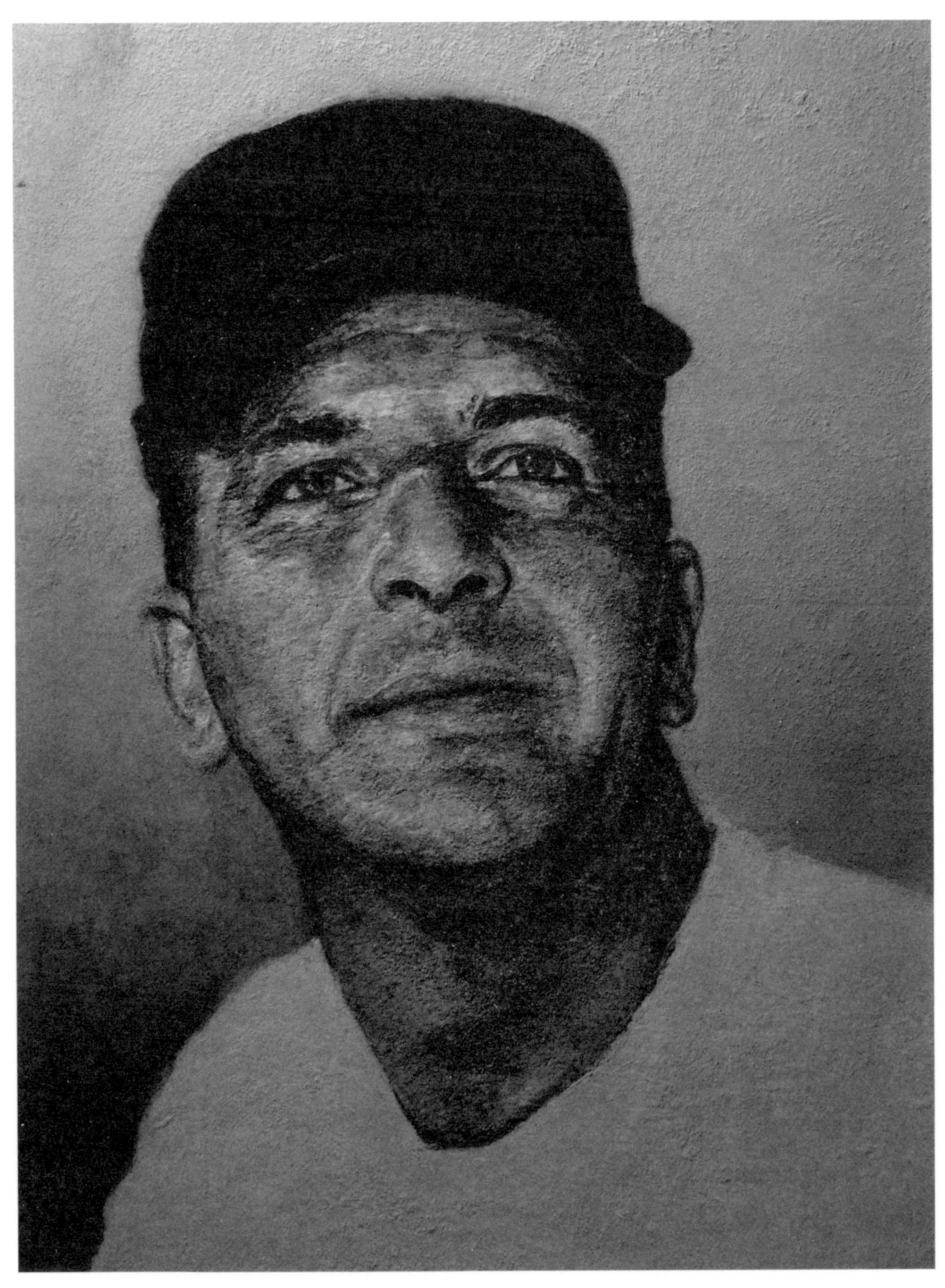

Lydia Millet

My father was a professor and museum curator whose scholarship mostly concerned Meroitic, an ancient language of what's now called Sudan. He worked on deciphering this little-understood language for most of his adult life, though he also did excavations in Egypt, places I never visited with lovely names like Gebel-Adda and Illahun. When he died he left behind an extensive personal library of books on ancient Egypt, to be donated to a southern U.S. university. My task, in the weeks after his death, was to catalog this library so that the university had an inventory.

It was summertime in Toronto, humid and green outside. My father's study was dim and cool and took up much of the basement, a long room with wooden floors and a wooden desk, lined with bookshelves. There was a flat-drawered archival cabinet in the center for the oversized books, and a worn armchair sat in a corner, with a reading lamp and a footstool. There were dusty models of Chinese junks on display, an ornate, golden ceremonial sword, a collection of antique toy soldiers. (The toy soldiers contained lead, making them useless to today's children.) He'd been the son of a diplomat and spoke Mandarin as a child, raised partly by a Chinese nanny while his father was posted to Shanghai and Harbin and Peking, and he treasured many things Chinese, as well as all things ancient Egyptian.

Mostly his realm was constituted of the stuff of trees: wood and paper. There was almost nothing plastic, unless you counted the filters of a few cigarette butts we found stashed behind some of the books. (He'd died of metastatic lung cancer, but apparently continued smoking in secret long after his diagnosis.) It was a place of the past, of bygone centuries. And decaying. Mildew and moths. My father always neglected the physical, himself as well as his things. He ate sparingly, abjured all forms of exercise save walking, and liked his pipe and his whiskey.

My mother had begun the work of cataloging his books during his months of illness, so there was a document set up on her computer; her small study was next to his large one, and I sat there to type, my infant daughter sometimes nearby. I'd bring a book in and open it, enter the details from the title page, replace it on the shelf. Sometimes the books were too large and delicate to be moved easily – huge folios from the nineteenth century full of beautiful illustrations in brilliant color, hand-painted like illuminated manuscripts. These were my favorites, but they couldn't be touched too much. I was afraid to handle them without gloves, and so, for the most part, I did not. Those books I took notes on by hand, then transcribed, since the old computer was not portable.

The catalog was a work of both distraction and devotion. It was curious how well these impulses meshed. My father had been, I think it's fair to say, a denier of the personal and of the self, an admirer of the foreign and other. He denied, among other personal forces and situations, his own impending death; he did not speak of it, as he did not speak of many matters of selfhood. His work had been a labor of love, but he'd seldom spoken of it to us in any detail either. So the books were objects of mystery, highly specialized, obscure and baffling. Many were in French or German or Italian – he could read or speak more than ten languages – and had titles like *The Sarcophagus of Anchnesraneferab, Queen of Ahmes II King of Egypt* and *Versuche zu Zeitbestimmungen für die späte, griechisch-römische Zeit der ägyptischen Geschichte*. All of this represented an esoteric province of his mind, comprehensible only to other scholars in his field.

He had been a private person full and whole, an enclosed world, although he salved the sting of that privacy with his dry, perfectly timed wit and gentle, kindly demeanor. As I recorded the books, mostly ciphers to me, it was this I noticed: a private person may or may not leave a legacy – in my father's case a modest cache of journal articles, a trove of excavated antiquities, some decoded words from ancient times, and a library. Either way they depart a mystery. Only his things remained to speak for him.

There were abundant artifacts in the basement as well as books, because my father was a collector: along with Egyptian antiquities there was a cabinet of antique pocket watches, an array of swords and sword guards, African knives and spears, old guns from the American frontier. A replica of the Rosetta stone, a rusted suit of medieval chain mail, a set of armor from Japan whose black helmet, when we were small, reminded us of Darth Vader. The most valuable pieces went to museums, while the rest went to his family. My ex-husband has some of his weapons still, wrapped away in a closet; myself I have only – besides a few books, of course – a single pocket watch and a few small talismans and sculptures, among them a replica of the Egyptian cat-goddess Bastet.

I liked to have the objects around me while I was cataloging, sometimes get up and touch them or gaze at them. They were more approachable than the arcane texts, possessing a charisma I could more easily recognize. They embodied my father in a language of faces and forms rather than hieroglyphs.

My task was repetitious: there were roughly a thousand books. But I relished it, because doing is not feeling. Doing a task is linear, and with it comes completion, a form of ending that is not death. The end of a task is merely a satisfactory result, the realization of a project that moves us through time. This was a ritual mourning involving no tearing of hair, no rending of garments, no weeping – a quiet and orderly process, as my father's life had been quiet and orderly. Methodical and painstaking, with attention to detail. My memorial task was well suited to him. And to me. There wouldn't be many other rituals, such as, say, religion, in the wake of his dying: he'd been an atheist and a skeptic and helped raise us through that lens. But he'd also been a romantic, and the romantic part I'd clearly inherited, along with his deep love of books.

He'd read to us every night when we were small, or more often told us elaborate tales he made up – sometimes accompanied by his own surprisingly good drawings – and from a young age I followed him down the path of stories till finally I decided to write them for myself. Cataloging the books that had been important to him, but not, frankly, in themselves important to me, was to enter the nexus of us, a place where the form *book*, though not the content of these specific books, was the meeting point.

This was what I recognized as I typed up the titles, the authors, the publication dates: it did not matter that what his archaeological books contained was of little personal interest to me. (Other books he had introduced me to mattered greatly – C.S. Lewis, Edward Eager, Beverley Nichols, P.G. Wodehouse, Philip K. Dick, H.P. Lovecraft, the list was long.) Nor would I fake an interest and suddenly delve into *Assyrian Language: Easy Lessons in the Cuneiform Inscriptions*, as though it contained some hidden key to my father's psyche. What had mattered to my father was learning, while what mattered to me was something else, something like narrative and subjectivity.

But the gesture of recording the books, the knowledge that they would be read by others, satisfied me. They would be everyone's books from now on, his treasures made public, even if the pool of readers remained small – for Egyptologists, though more plentiful now than when he was alive, will never be a mass demographic.

It was enough.

Shortly before his seventieth birthday, in the house where my brother and sister and I had grown up and where he and my mother had lived for more than thirty years, he had died in a cot in a dim room. It was shortly before dusk, while my mother was making dinner. We sat down to try to eat after he died, because my mother asked us to – she didn't want the food to go to waste.

We'd had dinner together every night, the five of us, back when we were younger and lived together in that house. Now we picked disinterestedly at our meal, hardly believing we were doing so, as his body lay on the cot a short distance away. I had a sudden strong conviction that he was still with us. I don't mean I felt the ghost of him hovering or his soul taking flight or any such wishful fantasy; I simply knew his presence in our molecules, the parts of us that were him, bones and skin and DNA. He rushed through us in blood and oxygen. And more: ideas, lodged in our sensibilities. He was dispersed among us, impulses of curiosity and humor and sympathy. He sat at the table as we did, a pulse in the soft pillars of our bodies.

Weegee's and Maciunas' Ashes and Ginsberg's Beard
Jonas Mekas

October 6, 2004

A headline in the *New York Sun* says:
Veronica lake's ashes located… in upstate antique shop.
This reminded me of an anecdote that I cannot restrain myself from telling you.
I think it was 1974. It was a beautiful summer day. Hollis – my wife – and myself we thought it was a perfect day for a picnic in Central Park. So I packed my picnic basket – I was in my Italian period, so it consisted of pepperoni, Italian cheeses, Dapolito's bread, and a bottle of Chianti (it's very good on a hot summer day).
After a couple of hours in the park we decided to pay a surprise visit to our friend Cornell Capa, at ICP (International Center of Photography), just across the street from the park.
Cornell enjoyed the surprise. Especially when we laid out on his office table our picnic supplies.
We had a great time.
I don't remember how the talk turned to Weegee. During the mid-sixties, when I ran Film-Makers' Cinematheque on 41st Street, we became good friends with Weegee and his funny wife, they came very often to see films and hang around.
"You must have some of his work at ICP," I said.
Capa laughed:
"His work? Not only do I have his photographs, I have his ashes. Look."
And he opened his desk drawer. It was a huge old-fashioned office desk with huge drawers. It was full of routine office drawer junk – pencils, rubber bands, pencil sharpeners, old batteries, etc.
"Look, here are Weegee's ashes." And he pointed to a little urn. "I didn't know where to put it, so I stuck it in the drawer…"
He closed the drawer and we continued our picnic.
You may not find this story funny, but that afternoon we all thought that it was very funny.

Now, after telling you this anecdote about Weegee's ashes, I must tell you another story, I must.
It's about the ashes of George Maciunas.
In 1997 the young people of Vilnius were celebrating Fluxus and its creator George Maciunas. Tomas Venclova, a poet who was teaching at Yale University's Slavic Department

was about to visit Vilnius around that time. He decided to bring a present to the Vilnius Fluxus enthusiasts. He decided to bring George himself back to Lithuania by way of his ashes.

But he faced a problem: the ashes of George Maciunas, according to his wishes, were cast into the Atlantic Ocean in Greenwich, Connecticut. Venclova turned to the scientists and posed a question: Suppose I fill up this little flask with the water from the Long Island Sound Bay. What is the probability that some of George's ashes would appear in this flask? Prof. Chikanyan of Yale's Physics Department came to the conclusion that yes, some atoms of George definitely had to be in that flask. As a matter of fact, millions of them.

So Venclova took the flask to Vilnius and, in a special celebration, it was emptied into the Vilnele river that runs through Vilnius, symbolic of George Maciunas' return to Lithuania, his native country.

P.S. December 29, 2009

The other day, as I was sorting out some old papers, my eye stopped on a clipping, a photograph I had cut out from *Vienybe*, issue of May 15, 1983, a Lithuanian weekly paper that used to come out in Brooklyn, now defunct. The caption to the picture read:

> It's five years since the death of George Maciunas, the initiator of the Fluxus movement. His last wish was that his ashes be cast into the Atlantic Ocean. This photograph was taken near the Greenwich, Connecticut lighthouse. In the picture from left to right: Barbara Moore; a writer from *Artforum* magazine; composer Yoshi Wada who during the casting of the ashes into the ocean performed a moving, sad piece; the artist Ay-O; Nijole Salcius; and Nijole Maciunas-Valaitis, George's sister.

O.K., this will be the last footnote on this subject.

Not exactly the same, but similar.

In 1963 Barbara Rubin persuaded Allen Ginsberg to shave off his beard – she did it herself at the Film-Makers' Cooperative when it was still at 414 Park Avenue South. She put the beard in a little box and placed it on the shelf next to the film cans. As years went by everybody forgot about it. But the other day, as I was sorting out my books and stuff, I came upon a little box. I opened it: it was Allen Ginsberg's beard... I closed the box and put it back next to his books.

Remain

Claudia Steinberg

On my father's last day on Earth, the day before his burial, I cut off a lock of his hair and, without a flash, took a final photograph of his bony face in the dark room where he was on display. For one year I looked at the grainy, black-and-white image of his remote, foreign features every day, each time hitting the same rock of incomprehension. Eventually I buried the photograph in a drawer forever. Only once did I ever open the little jewelry box that contained his hair – I know I still have it somewhere. Neither one of these mementos, stolen with trembling hands from that terrifyingly cold space, got me any closer to his presence or his absence.

Heide Hatry's portraits based on photographs of the departed and rendered in their ashes remind me of that last image of my father, its diffuse particles of light and shadow similar to the sandy surface of pulverized bones enriched with coal and painstakingly affixed onto a plane of slightly warmed beeswax: resurrecting a portion of the atomized body back into a glimpse of its former gestalt demands all the patience inherent in the immortal matter of ashes.

But while my ghostly photograph is now interred thousands of miles from my father's grave, Hatry fuses image and relic and transforms her material into the ultimate likeness of the deceased. "How slender a masse will remain upon an open and urging fire of the carnal composition?" muses the seventeenth-century physician Sir Thomas Browne in his book *Urn Burial*.[1] But only a fraction of these shockingly reduced remains are needed to revive that composition in the second dimension, to restore – from the anonymity of dry calcium phosphates and traces of sodium and potassium – a person's individuality, if only of one moment once captured by the camera, as tiny as a grain of sand in the large measure of their life.

Hair, nails, teeth and bones are as important to the shaman's evocations of the soul as the palette of light and darkness is to the painter. There is magic intent in Hatry's renderings of faces – whether of her father, of friends, or of the writer James Purdy – in the grisaille palette of ashes and black pigment. While a photograph only arrests a shadow, her posthumous portraits uniquely share – on the same terrain – illusion and authentic matter. The

---

1 Sir Thomas Browne, *Urn Burial* (New York: New Directions, 2010), p. 59.

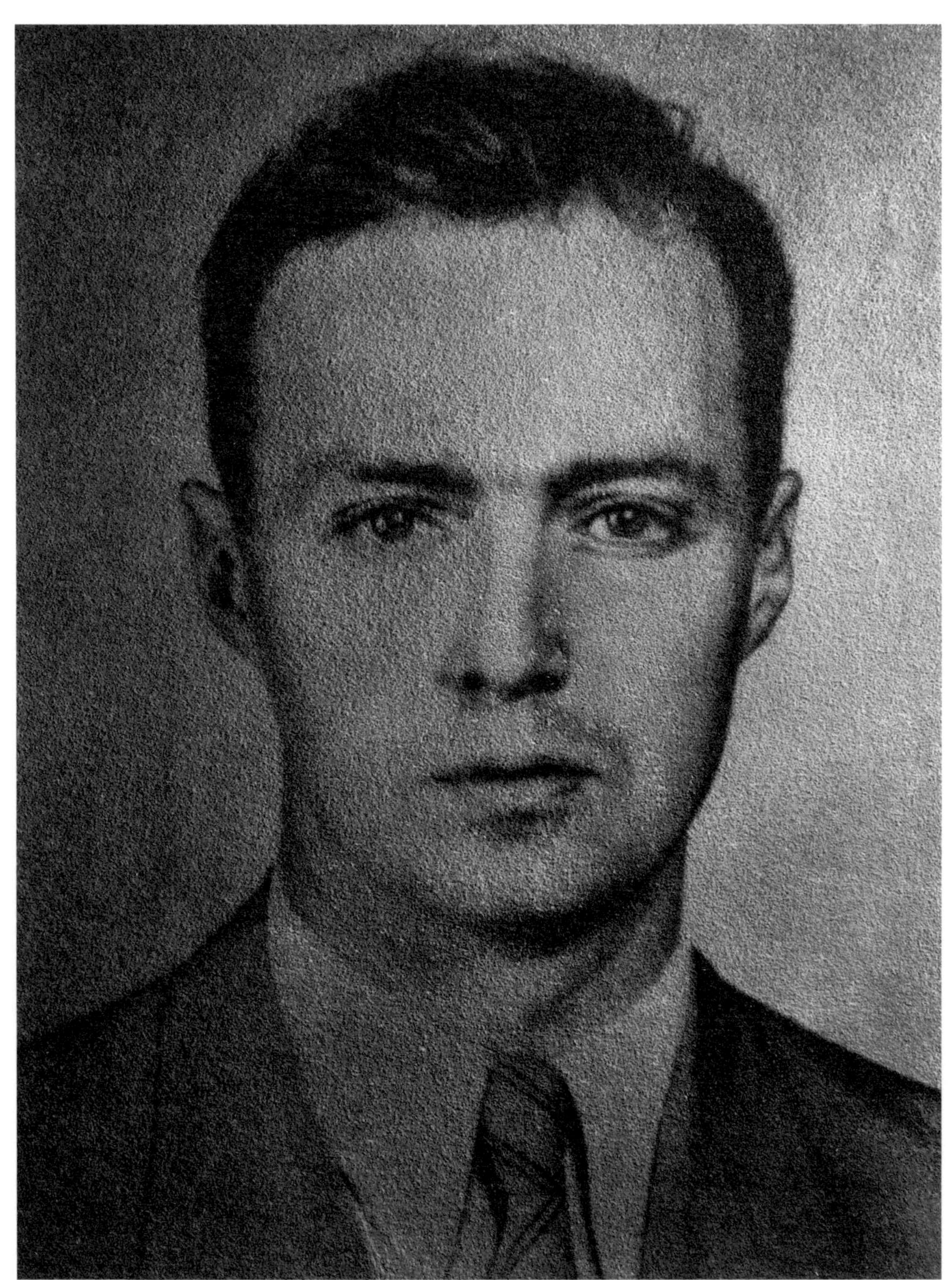

splinter of someone's past and their timeless physical incarnation produce what the writer Mark C. Taylor has called "the metaphysics of presence."[2] Against the tsunami of disposable images, she works with the one, non-interchangeable substance closest to eternity, on the human scale.

Neither ashes nor the dust we are destined to become without the intervention of fire, the fine sand of our ground skeleton nevertheless lends itself to be scattered into the wind or the sea. Elegantly abstract, if cruelly indifferent to our former appearance, cremation is often chosen by those who fear the imprisonment of the grave, the sepulchral cold and dark, or fear the grim spectacle of decay. Ashes are our most durable remains. Again Sir Thomas Browne: "He that hath the ashes of his friend, hath an everlasting treasure."[3] Dry, clean, architectural and "noble," as Philippe Ariès called them *In the Hour of Our Death*, bones are also the designated seat of the soul in many cultures. Though raised Catholic as a child, I rather independently envisioned my soul as a golden bone lodged horizontally in my pelvis, radiating unless stained by sin. But as any visit to an Eastern European cemetery with their enameled photographs of the deceased on the grave stones or to a museum holding coffins with portrait paintings from ancient Egypt will prove, the soul largely resides in the face of a person and in the images thereof.

---

2 Mark C. Taylor, "Sacred Bones," *Cabinet Magazine* 28 (Winter 2007-08), p. 63.
3 Browne, *Urn Burial*, p. 60.

Ashes to Ashes? Not at All

Luisa Valenzuela

Conversing with death is accepting it for what it is: the ineluctable corollary of life, its sacred continuation. So too is giving thanks for the time that it granted our loved ones and for the time it grants us, to linger in this so-called vale of tears that is so often made of smiles, smiling at those who were among us and who, thanks to Heide Hatry's art, have left us the imprint of their faces; face as portrait of the soul, created through the mediation of ashes from something – their perishable body – that used to be and now no longer is.

Western culture refuses, to a great extent, to look death in the eye. It chooses to ignore it, mentioning death only in a hushed voice. But there are magnificent examples of a different gaze, courageous and open. I am thinking of two instances (from semi-lachrymose, at least to non-Capuchins, to celebratory): of the Capuchin crypt in the church of Santa Maria della Concezione dei Cappuccini in Rome, Italy, with its meticulous rococo ornament made from the bones, highly polished centuries ago, of four thousand monks; and of festivities in Mexico associated with the celebration of the Day of the Dead, when cemeteries are abundantly festooned with flowers and invaded by music, dining, and even dancing, and where in private homes altars of the dead, lit with candles and bedecked with the bright orange flowers of the Aztec marigold, reconvene the memories of those who have left forever – yet not forever, because they are alive in the hearts of family and friends grateful for their passage here on Earth.

These are the vibrations that Heide Hatry captures in the affectionate and subtle ministrations of her posthumous portraits in ash. What a beautiful way to offer those who have departed a permanent presence in this world, in a portrait whose likeness is much more than that of a portrait: it is part of their very being – a small measure of immortality here-and-now.

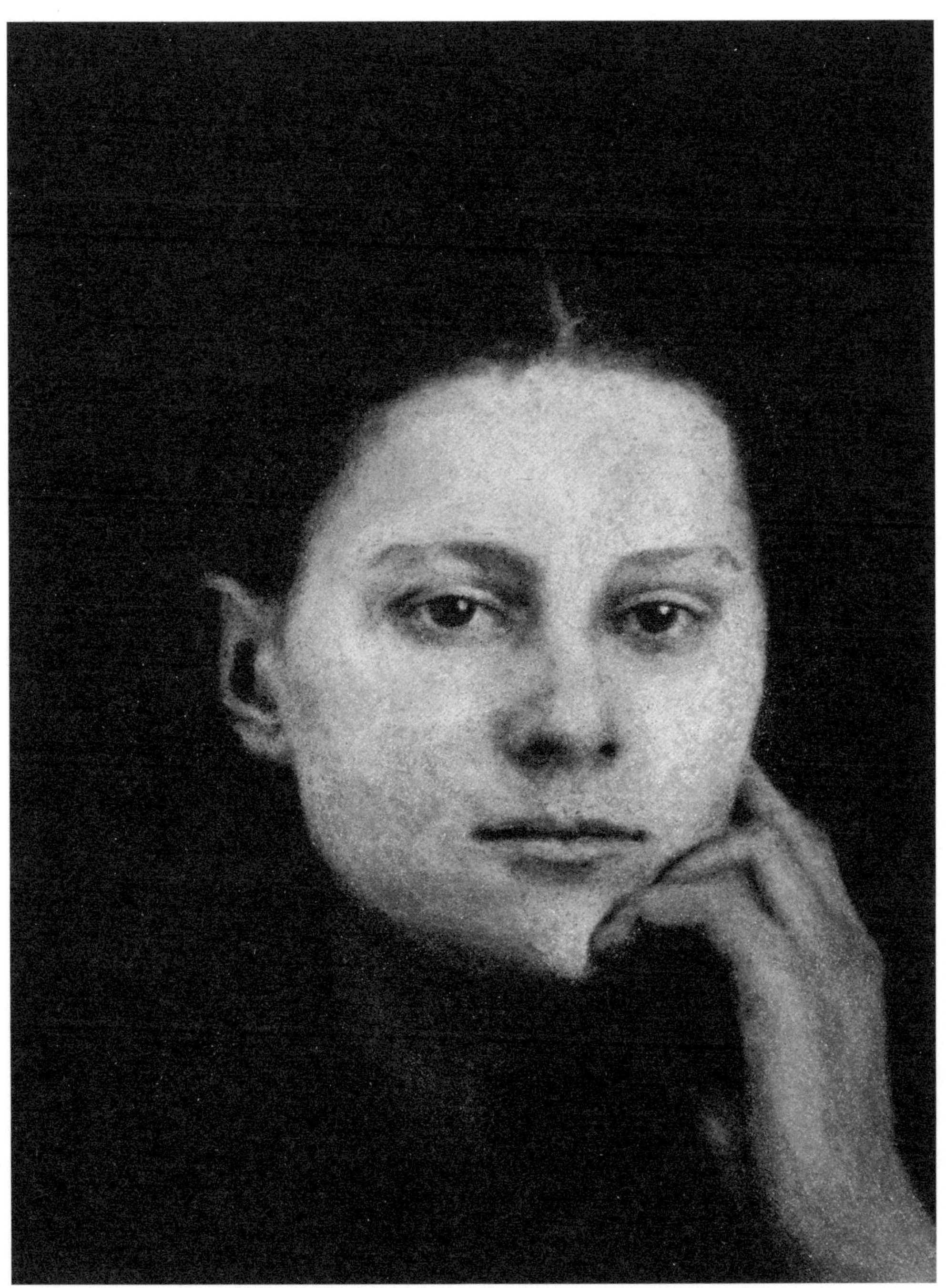

Technique

Unlike the traditional means of memorializing the dead in art, these human ash portraits propose an intimate and direct means of engaging their memory, and their substance, rather than the fairly detached, abstract, heroic, or clinical approaches that have typified modern Western art and funerary practice.

Three different techniques have been used to create slightly different effects:

(a) Loose ash particles from the person depicted (and birch coal and white marble dust) are applied in a painstaking mosaic process into beeswax, bedding the ash gently into the wax.

(b) Ink drawings or air-brush paintings are created directly upon a pure and slightly uneven surface of ashes.

(c) Ink drawings or air-brush paintings are created upon an emulsion of ashes and binder, giving the portrait the feeling and texture of a fresco mural painting.

List of Portraits

Biographies of Authors

Michaël Amy is a writer, lecturer, critic, and art historian with a PhD from New York University's Institute of Fine Arts. Amy is Professor of the History of Art in the College of Imaging Arts & Sciences at Rochester Institute of Technology. He works in the areas of Renaissance, Baroque, modern and contemporary art. He is the author of *One to One: Conversation avec Tony Oursler* (Facteur Humain, 2006), and *Michaël Borremans: Whistling a Happy Tune* (Ludion, 2008), and has published numerous articles, catalog essays, exhibition reviews, and interviews with artists.

Hans Belting, PhD, is an art historian of medieval and early modern European art, as well as contemporary art and theory. From 1970-80, he was Professor of Art History at the University of Heidelberg, and from 1980-93, Professor of Art History at the University of Munich, occupying the chair formerly held by Heinrich Wölfflin and Hans Sedlmayr. In 1993 he left Munich to build a PhD program called Kunstwissenschaft und Medientheorie at the newly founded School for New Media (Hochschule für Gestaltung) at Karlsruhe which cooperates with the Center for Art and Media Technologies (ZKM). His many books include *Likeness and Presence: A History of the Image Before the Era of Art* (1984), *The End of the History of Art* (1987), *The Germans and Their Art: A Troublesome Relationship* (1998), *The Invisible Masterpiece: The Modern Myths of Art* (2001), *An Anthropology of Images: Picture, Medium, Body* (2011), and *Faces: Eine Geschichte des Gesichts* (2013).

Elizabeth A. Burns is the Creative and Operations Director of The Burns Archive. She has coauthored several books, including *Sleeping Beauty II: Grief, Bereavement & the Family, American and European Traditions*, *Geisha: A Photographic History, 1872-1912*, and *Stiffs, Skulls, & Skeletons*. Burns has curated and organized dozens of exhibitions, including those on criminology, spirit photography, early flight, Lewis Hine, African American history, and various medical topics. She has consulted on numerous documentaries, feature films, and television productions. She is the photographic archivist and research consultant to HBO/Cinemax series, *The Knick*, and associate technical advisor to PBS's *Mercy Street*.

Stanley B. Burns, MD, FACS, is an internationally distinguished author, curator, historian, collector, archivist, and consultant. The Burns Archive, his collection of over one million historic photographs, is recognized as the most important private comprehensive collection of early photography. He has authored forty-six books, over 1100 articles, curated over one hundred exhibitions, and consulted on dozens of documentaries and feature films. His 1990 landmark text on postmortem photography *Sleeping Beauty: Memorial Photography in America* ushered in a new era of appreciation of the importance of these images. Each year since then, exhibitions have been created from the Archive, including *Le Dernier Portrait* at the Musée d'Orsay and *Securing the Shadow: Posthumous Portraiture in America* at the American Folk Art Museum.

Mark Dery is a cultural critic. He has been a professor of journalism at NYU, a Chancellor's Distinguished Fellow at UC Irvine, a Hertog author in Columbia University's Hertog Fellowship program, and a Visiting Scholar at the American Academy in Rome. An independent writer and scholar, Dery has lectured extensively throughout the United States and abroad, and has published widely in academic and mass-circulation publications, most notably *The New York Times, Cabinet Magazine, Bookforum, Rolling Stone, The Los Angeles Review of Books*, and *Wired*. Dery's books include *The Pyrotechnic Insanitarium: American Culture on the Brink* and *Escape Velocity: Cyberculture at the End of the Century*. His latest is the University of Minnesota essay collection, *I Must Not Think Bad Thoughts: Drive-by Essays on American Dread, American Dreams*. He is at work on a biography of the author, illustrator, and legendary eccentric Edward Gorey for Little, Brown.

Thyrza Nichols Goodeve is a writer who writes "with" rather than "on" contemporary art and artists. Her interests range across art as a "structure of feeling," human/nonhuman animal ontologies, the aesthetics of wonder, theories and practices of writing, the interview as essay, the history of modernism(s), surrealist methodologies, dystopias and utopias, and the metaphysics of technology. She is currently compiling her collected writings for publication, *No Wound Speaks for Itself: Art, Vulnerability, Writing, Attitude*, cover designed by The Quay Brothers, with a preface by Avital Ronell.

Anthony Haden-Guest is a writer, reporter, cartoonist, and sporadic performer. He was born in Paris, grew up in London, has lived in Rome, San Francisco, and Los Angeles but is long settled in New York. He won a New York Emmy for writing and narrating a program about the coming of Eurotrash to Manhattan. His books include *Bad Dreams, True Colours: The Real Life of the Art World* (Grove Atlantic), and *The Last Party: Studio 54, Disco and the Culture of the Night* (Morrow). His collections of cartoons and rhymes are *The Chronicles of Now* (Allworth) and *In the Mean Time* (Freight & Volume). He publishes on paper and online and his more ambitious current projects include an animated movie, a follow-up book on the art world, and a much-illustrated memoir.

Heide Hatry is a New York based German artist, often described as neo-conceptualist, whose work transforms, transcends, or transgresses the customary relationship of artist to both audience and art. Among her fundamental preoccupations are identity, gender roles, the nature of aesthetic experience and the meaning of beauty, the effects of knowledge upon perception, and the human exploitation of the natural world. She studied and taught art at various schools in Germany while simultaneously conducting an international business as an antiquarian bookseller. She has curated numerous exhibitions, has shown her own work at museums and galleries around the world, has created nearly two hundred artist's books and edited more than two dozen books and art catalogs. *Skin* (2005), *Heads and Tales* (2009), and *Not a Rose* (2012) document both her own art and amount to collaborative conceptual artist's books involving some of the most interesting thinkers and authors in the world.

Eleanor Heartney is a Contributing Editor to *Art in America* and *Artpress* and has written extensively on contemporary art issues for many publications. Her books include *Critical Condition: American Culture at the Crossroads, Postmodernism, Defending Complexity: Art Politics and the New World Order, Postmodern Heretics: The Catholic Imagination in Contemporary Art*, and *Art & Today*. She is a co-author of *After the Revolution: Women Who Transformed Contemporary Art*, and *The Reckoning: Women Artists of the New Millennium*. She received the College Art Association's Frank Jewett Mather Award for distinction in art criticism in 1992 and was honored by the French government as a Chevalier dans l'Ordre des Arts et des Lettres in 2008. Heartney is a past President of AICA-USA, the American section of the International Art Critics Association.

Phoebe Hoban has written about culture and the arts for a variety of publications, including *The New York Times, New York Magazine, The Wall Street Journal, Vogue, Vanity Fair, GQ, Harper's Bazaar, ARTnews*, and *The New York Observer*, among others. Her biography *Basquiat, A Quick Killing in Art* (1998) was a national bestseller and a *New York Times* Notable Book of the Year. Her biography *Alice Neel: The Art of Not Sitting Pretty* (2010) was named one of the Best Books of the Year by *New York Magazine*; one of the Ten Best Books of the Year by *The Village Voice*; one of the Ten Best Biographies of the Year by *Booklist*; and a *Sunday Times* Book Review Editors' Choice. Her most recent book, a biography of Lucian Freud, *Lucian Freud: Eyes Wide Open*, was published in April 2014. She lives in New York City.

Siri Hustvedt was born in Northfield, Minnesota. She has a PhD in English literature from Columbia University and is a lecturer in psychiatry at Weill Medical College of Cornell University. She is the author of a book of poems, *Reading to You*; six novels, *The Blindfold, The Enchantment of Lily Dahl, What I Loved, The Sorrows of an American, The Summer Without Men*, and *The Blazing World*; four collections of essays, *A Plea for Eros, Mysteries of the Rectangle: Essays on Painting, Living, Thinking, Looking*, and *A Woman Looking at Men Looking at Women: Essays on Art, Sex, and the Mind*; as well as a non-fiction work, *The Shaking Woman or A History of My Nerves*. In 2012 she was awarded the Gabarron International Prize for Thought and Humanities. *The Blazing World* was long listed for Man Booker Prize and won the Los Angeles Book Prize for Fiction in 2014. Her work has been translated into over thirty languages. She lives in Brooklyn, New York.

Gavin Keeney is an independent scholar, editor, writer, and critic. His most recent books include: *Dossier Chris Marker: The Suffering Image* (2012), *Not-I/Thou: The Other Subject of Art and Architecture* (2014), and

Knowledge, Spirit, Law: Book 1, Radical Scholarship (2015). He has taught, lectured, and served as visiting critic in architecture schools in the United States, Canada, the United Kingdom, the Czech Republic, Slovenia, Australia, and India, and is the Creative Director of Agence 'X', an artists' and architects' re-representation bureau founded in New York City in October 2007.

Thomas W. Laqueur was born in Istanbul and grew up in southern West Virginia where his father was a pathologist in a hospital belonging to the United Mine Workers. Laqueur studied philosophy, history, and biology at Swarthmore College and modern history at Princeton and Nuffield College, Oxford. He began teaching at UC Berkeley in 1973 and is a passionate graduate and undergraduate teacher. Laqueur's work has been focused on the history of popular religion and literacy; on the history of the body – alive and dead; and on the history of death and memory. He writes regularly for the *London Review of Books* and *The Threepenny Review*, among other journals. He has won the usual fellowships but is most proud of the Mellon Distinguished Humanist Award, the proceeds from which he used as seed money for programs in religion, human rights, and science studies at Berkeley – all of which are now self-sustaining.

Deborah Lutz is the Thruston B. Morton Professor of English at the University of Louisville. Her most recent book, *The Brontë Cabinet: Three Lives in Nine Objects* (W.W. Norton, 2015), was a finalist for the PEN/Weld Award for Biography. Other books include *Relics of Death in Victorian Literature and Culture* (Cambridge University Press, 2015), which was supported by an American Council of Learned Societies Fellowship, *The Dangerous Lover: Gothic Villains, Byronism, and the Nineteenth-Century Seduction Narrative*, and *Pleasure Bound: Victorian Sex Rebels and the New Eroticism*. She is the editor of the Norton Critical Edition of *Jane Eyre*, and her writing has appeared in numerous journals, collections, and newspapers, including *The New York Times, Victorian Literature and Culture, The Oxford History of the Novel in English*, and *Cabinet Magazine*. She has been interviewed by *The New York Times, NPR, Salon, New York Post*, and *The History Channel*, among others.

Jonas Mekas is a Lithuanian born poet and filmmaker, since 1949 residing in New York. He is famous for developing the diaristic form of cinema with films such as *Walden* and *As I Was Moving Ahead Occasionally I Saw Brief Glimpses of Beauty*. He is equally known for the creation of a series of organizations for the promotion of the avant-garde cinema, such as Film-Makers' Cooperative, Film-Makers' Cinematheque and Anthology Film Archives. He was editor of *Film Culture* magazine and during 1958-78 movie critic for *The Village Voice* with a weekly Movie Journal column.

Lydia Millet is the author of eleven books of literary fiction, most recently *Sweet Lamb of Heaven* (2016), which was a finalist for the National Book Award in fiction. Her previous books include *Mermaids in Paradise* (2014), the novel *Magnificence* (2012), about loss and extinction, which was a finalist for the National Book Critics' Circle and *Los Angeles Times* book awards, a story collection called *Love in Infant Monkeys* (2010), a finalist for the Pulitzer Prize; and the novel *My Happy Life* (2002), which won a PEN-USA fiction award. She received a Guggenheim Fellowship in 2012 and lives in the Arizona desert, where she also writes for *The New York Times* and works at the nonprofit Center for Biological Diversity.

Rick Moody is the author of six novels, including the *Ice Storm* and *Hotels of North America*, three collections of stories, a memoir, *The Black Veil*, and a collection of essays, *On Celestial Music*. He has an online music column at *The Rumpus*, and writes the column entitled "Rick Moody, Life Coach," for *LitHub*. He teaches at NYU and at Yale, and lives in Astoria, New York.

Marc Pachter is a cultural historian who takes a particular interest in American/European cultural relations. He is Director Emeritus of the National Portrait Gallery, Smithsonian Institution and launched his interest in biography as a literary form as Editor of *Telling Lives: The Biographer's Art* (New Republic Press). He was called the Smithsonian's "Master Interviewer" when awarded the Institution's Gold Medal. Pachter lives in New York, Bangkok, and Berlin.

Steven Pinker is an experimental psychologist who has done research in visual cognition, psycholinguistics, and social relations. He grew up in Montreal and earned his BA from McGill and his PhD from Harvard. Currently Johnstone Professor of Psychology at Harvard, he has also taught at Stanford and MIT. He has won numerous prizes for his research, his teaching, and his nine books, including *The Language Instinct, How the Mind Works, The Blank Slate, The Better Angels of Our Nature*, and *The Sense of Style*. He is an elected member of the National Academy of Sciences, a two-time Pulitzer Prize finalist, a Humanist of the Year, and one of *Foreign Policy*'s "World's Top 100 Public Intellectuals" and *Time*'s "100 Most Influential People in the World Today." He is Chair of the Usage Panel of the *American Heritage Dictionary*, and writes frequently for *The New York Times, The Guardian*, and other publications.

George Quasha, artist/poet/musician, explores an extra-medium principle in language, paint-drawing, sculpture, video, sound, and performance. Awarded a Guggenheim Fellowship (2006), his video art includes *art is: Speaking Portraits*, recording over a thousand artists/poets/composers in eleven countries (saying what art/music/poetry is). Along with the theory of *principle art*, work is presented in the books *Axial Stones: An Art of Precarious Balance* (foreword by Carter Ratcliff) and *art is (Speaking Portraits)* (2016). His twenty books also include, in poetry, *Glossodelia Attract (preverbs)* (2015), *The Daimon of the Moment (preverbs)* (2015), *Things Done for Themselves (preverbs)* (2015), *Verbal Paradise (preverbs)* (2011), *Ainu Dreams* (1999, with Chie [Hasegawa] Hammons), and *Somapoetics* (1973); and, about art, *An Art of Limina: Gary Hill's Works and Writings* (2009, with Charles Stein; foreword by Lynne Cooke). Recipient of a NEA Fellowship (poetry), he is co-publisher with Susan Quasha at Station Hill of Barrytown.

Wolf Singer studied medicine in Munich and Paris and then specialized in neuroscience. After a postdoc training in the UK and several years of research group leader in Munich he was nominated director at the Max Planck Institute for Brain Research in Frankfurt, Germany. There he founded the Frankfurt Institute for Advanced Studies, became the scientific director of the conference program "Ernst Strüngmann Forum" and in 2009 founded the Ernst Struengmann Institute for Neuroscience in Cooperation with Max Planck Society, where he now pursues his science as Senior Fellow. His research is devoted to the analysis of the neuronal underpinnings of higher cognitive functions and focuses on the functional organization of the cerebral cortex. In addition to his scientific core activities he engages in public discourse on philosophical issues concerning free will, epistemology, and the philosophy of mind. The respective books and essays are mainly written in German.

Claudia Steinberg is a New York based journalist born in Germany. She has been covering a wide range of subjects like art, travel, design, social issues, and fashion for German publications like *Vogue, Die Zeit, Cicero, Kunstzeitung*, and *Frankfurter Allgemeine Zeitung*. She has been the U.S. correspondent for the German architecture and design magazine *Architektur & Wohnen* since 1999 and has also written for the home section of *The New York Times, Surface*, and *Interior Design Magazine*. In 2004 a book of essays on art and food appeared in collaboration with photographer Bärbel Miebach, followed by *The Art of Living*, published by Monacelli Press in 2009. In 2012 she wrote and co-directed a documentary on the New York Waterfront for the French/German television station *Arte*. She is currently working on a collection of oral histories about life in the Rockaways.

Adele Tutter, MD, PhD, is Assistant Clinical Professor of Psychiatry at Columbia University and is on the faculty of the Columbia University Center for Psychoanalytic Training and Research and the New York Psychoanalytic Institute. Her interdisciplinary scholarship, focusing on the relationship between loss and creativity, has earned the Ticho, CORST, and Menninger Prizes of the American Psychoanalytic Association, among other honors. Author of *Dream House: An Intimate Portrait of the Philip Johnson Glass House* (University of Virginia Press), editor of *The Muse: Psychoanalytic Explorations of Creative Inspiration* (Routledge), and co-editor of *Grief and Its Transcendence: Memory, Identity, Creativity* (Routledge), she is currently completing *Mourning and Metamorphosis: Poussin's Ovidian Vision*. She is in private practice in Manhattan.

Luisa Valenzuela was born and currently resides in Buenos Aires, Argentina. She lived in Paris, Barcelona, and spent ten years in Manhattan (1979-89) where she was Writer in Residence at Columbia University and later at NYU's Writing Division. She is a frequent traveler to Mexico where she's published by Fondo de Cultura Económica, amongst other houses. Her work is widely anthologized and translated, chiefly into English: the short story collections *Open Door*, *The Censors*, *Strange Things Happen Here*, *Other Weapons*, and *Symmetries*, and the novels *Clara*, *He Who Searches*, *The Lizard's Tail*, *Black Novel (with Argentines)*, and *Bedside Manners*. Her most recent novels are *El Mañana* (2010), *Cuidado con el tigre* (2011), and *La máscara sarda, el profundo secreto de Perón* (2012). In the United States: *El gato eficaz/ Deathcats* (bilingual, 2010) and *Dark Desires and The Others* (2011). Valenzuela is a foreign honorary member of the American Academy of Arts and Science.

Peter Weibel is Chairman and CEO of ZKM | Center for Art and Media Karlsruhe and professor of media theory at the University of Applied Arts Vienna, is considered a central figure in European media art on account of his various activities as artist, theoretician, and curator at biennales in Venice, Seville, and Moscow. He publishes prolifically in the intersecting fields of art and science.

Linda Weintraub is a curator, educator, artist, and author of several popular books about contemporary art, including *TO LIFE! Eco Art in Pursuit of a Sustainable Planet* (University of California Press). Weintraub's previous books include *In the Making: Creative Options for Contemporary Artists and Art on the Edge* and *Over: Searching for Art's Meaning in Contemporary Society*. Weintraub served as the Director of the Bard College museum where she curated over sixty exhibitions. She was the Henry Luce Professor of Emerging Arts at Oberlin College and is currently on the faculty of the Interdisciplinary Master of Fine Art program at the University of Hartford. Her current book project is *Ecological Materialism: Art-is-an Environmental Health Clinic*. Weintraub received her MFA degree from Rutgers University. She maintains a homestead on an eleven-acre property where she practices permaculture. These principles guide her studio practice, which includes communal art projects entitled *Grandmother Earth: Beyond Death*.

Franz Josef Wetz, PhD, teaches philosophy and ethics at the University of Education in Schwäbisch Gmünd, Germany. His principle research concerns the implications of modern natural science for the human self-conception in its existential, cultural, ethical, and juridical regards. Wetz is the ethical advisor to the famous anatomical exhibition, *Body Worlds*, and a member of the scientific advisory committee of the Giordano Bruno Foundation among other scientific organizations. He is the author of numerous books, including *Kunst der Resignation*, *Illusion Menschenwürde*, *Baustelle Körper*, and *Rebellion der Selbstachtung*. His most recent book is *Exzesse. Wer tanzt, tötet nicht* (2016).

John Wronoski is an antiquarian bookseller and art dealer, founder and proprietor of Lame Duck Books. He has published nearly a hundred rare book and art catalogs, many of them considered definitive in their fields, as well as the art monograph, *Boris Lurie. A Life in the Camps* and the book-length catalog, *The Stamp Act Defiance Placard, First Act of the American Revolution*. He is a specialist in the assessment and sale of literary archives for writers, artists, and scholars, and has worked in that capacity on behalf of numerous prominent figures, including several Nobel laureates. A long time ago he studied philosophy at Swarthmore College under David Lachterman, regarding whom Stanley Rosen said, "He might be the one person I ever met who was smarter than me." Of course that has no bearing at all on the intelligence of the present subject.

Naief Yehya is an industrial engineer, journalist, writer, pornographographer, and cultural critic, who was born in Mexico City and has lived in Brooklyn since 1992. He writes for several publications in Mexico, Spain, and Latin America and has published three novels: *Sanitary Works* (Grijalbo, 1992), *Going Home* (Planeta, 1994), *The Truth About Life on Mars* (Planeta, 1995); two short stories collections: *Tales of Bad Women* (Plaza & Janés, 2002) and *Slices* (Conaculta, 2012); and the essays: *The Transformed Body. Cyborgs and Our Technological Heritage in the Real World and Science Fiction* (Paidós), *War and Propaganda: Mass Media and the Myth of War in the US* (Paidós), *Pornography: Mediated Sex and Moral Panic* (Plaza & Janés, 2004), *Technoculture* (Tusquets, 2009), *Pornography. Sexual and Technological Obsession* (Tusquets, 2012), and *Pornculture* (Tusquets, 2013). Yehya's work deals mainly with the impact of technology, mass media, propaganda, and pornography in culture and society.

Acknowledgments

My deepest thanks belong to Thyrza Nichols Goodeve, Laura Hatry, Christine Isherwood, Hannah Monyer, Margret Schepers, Luisa Valenzuela, Daniel Wechsler, and John Wronoski, who have listened for endless hours as I went on about my enthusiasm, my doubts, my new ideas, my doubts, my surrender, my doubts, my new ideas, my doubts, and my pain. They helped get this project where it is today.

I am also very grateful to my gallerist, Adam Boxer, my publishers, George and Susan Quasha, my editor, Gavin Keeney, the translators Ruth Martin, Simon A. Thomas, and John Wronoski, my legal advisor Gale P. Elston, as well as to all of the contributors to the book, who have written stunning and thoughtful essays, which are essential to an understanding of the depth and texture of the project, and to my daughter, Laura Hatry, without whom I would not have realized any of my books, and who has supported me in every possible way.

And for all of the help, guidance, and inspiration that came in so many different ways, I also want to thank: Elizabeth C. Baker, Isabelle Baumann, Gwendolyn Bellmann, David Bergman, Erica Bernstein, Werner Bofinger in memoriam, Dianne Bowen, David Bowie in memoriam, Lou Boxer, Svetlana Boym in memoriam, Robert Brashear, Kathy Brew, Eli Brown, Juliane Camfield, Cabinet Magazine, Jessie Castilla, Leonard Cohen in memoriam, Paul Craddock, Amy Cunningham, Steven D'Arpa, Taylor Daynes, Gayatri Devi, Mario Diacono, Caitlin Doughty, Richard Edwards, Layla Ferrández Melero, Matt Flowers, Forest Lawn Memorial Park (LA, CA), Peter Frank, Susan Gubar, Caitlin Gramm, Green-Wood Cemetery (NY), Gunther von Hagens, Sherry Hauer, Thomas Hesse, Richard Humann, Siri Hustvedt, Heinz-Norbert Jocks, Robert Flynn Johnson, Darren Julien, Paul Manfred Kästner, Robert Kelly, Gregory Ketant, Nineli Khachikian, Lance Kinz in memoriam, Larry Kleiman, Adam Kluger, Jakob Köllhofer, Paul Kopeikin, Rufus Knight-Webb, Simone Kussatz, Thomas W. Laqueur, Kris Latocha, Jane LeCroy, Tarrah von Lintel, Lucy Lippard, Herbert Lust, Catharine A. MacKinnon, Sinisa Mackovic, Bonnie Marranca, Dennis Martin, Midmarch Art Press, Svetlana Mintcheva, Macu Moran, Brian Morris, Sina Najafi, Francis M. Naumann, Cynthia Navaretta, Linda Norden, Katiana Orluc, Marc Pachter, Amanda Palmer, Katie Peyton, Herbert Pföstl, James Purdy in memoriam, Princeton University Press, Christoph Reuter, Avital Ronell, Maddy Rosenberg, Michelle Ross, Anna Salmone, Nelson Santos, Iris Schieferstein, Andrea Schnabel, Carolee Schneemann, Elmar Seibel, Chris Shultz, Wolf Singer, Peter Soetje, Laurie Staub, Charles Stein, Marie Stein, Claudia Steinberg, Stefan Stux, Aldo Tambellini, Irina Tarsis, Sara Thorson, Sam Truitt, Adele Tutter, John Uecker, Cynthia Ventura, Richard Vine, Len Walker, Monika Walter, Angelina Whalley, Bill Wilson in memoriam, Dusty Wright, Franz Wright in memoriam, Jiannan Wu, and Haolun Xu, Ruonan Yan, Honza Zamojski.

Published by Station Hill of Barrytown, the publishing project of the Institute for Publishing Arts, Inc.,
120 Station Hill Road, Barrytown, New York 12507, a not-for-profit, tax-exempt organization [501(c)(3)].
Online catalog: www.stationhill.org
e-mail: publisher@stationhill.org

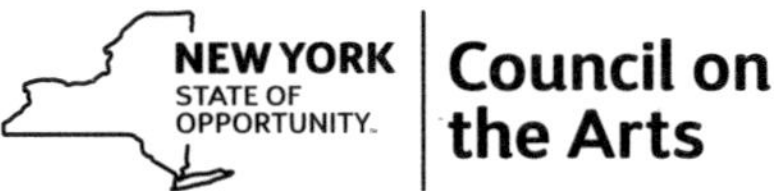

This publication is supported in part by grants from
the New York State Council on the Arts, a state agency.

Text editors: Heide Hatry and Gavin Keeney
Copy editor: Marie Stein
Photo editor and design: Heide Hatry
Layout: Laura Hatry
Typeset in Adobe Garamond Pro
Printed in Poland on Munken Print Cream Paper 150g
Bound in Cialux 1581, screenprinted, embossed, and with printed sandpaper tipin

Cover image: Marie Smith, 2016
All artwork produced and photographed by Heide Hatry, 2008-2016

Library of Congress Cataloging-in-Publication Data
Names: Hatry, Heide. Works. Selections. Title: Icons in Ash / by Heide Hatry.
Description: Barrytown, NY: Station Hill of Barrytown, 2017. | Includes bibliographical references.
Identifiers: LCCN 2016048489 (print) | LCCN 2016049168 (ebook)
ISBN 9781581771619 | ISBN 9781581771633
Subjects: LCSH: Dead–Social aspects. | Portraits–Psychological aspects. | Dead in art.
Hatry, Heide–Themes, motives.
Classification: LCC GT3150 .I29 2017 (print) | LCC GT3150 (ebook) | DDC 393–dc23
LC record available at https://lccn.loc.gov/2016048489